Henry Broadhurst

F. Jenkins Héliog Paris

# HENRY BROADHURST, M.P.

*THE STORY OF HIS LIFE FROM
A STONEMASON'S BENCH TO THE
TREASURY BENCH*

## TOLD BY HIMSELF

WITH AN INTRODUCTION BY
AUGUSTINE BIRRELL, K.C.

London : HUTCHINSON & CO.
Paternoster Row          1901

# INTRODUCTION

WHY Mr. Broadhurst, who has been both a stonemason and an Under-Secretary of State, should pitch upon me, who have never been either, or done him any kind of injury, to write a wholly unnecessary and therefore impertinent Introduction to his sturdy Memoirs, would be beyond my power of guessing, had I not often noticed the absurd timidity of men who have reaped to the full all the advantages of what is called an "imperfect" or "irregular" education when they find themselves engaged in what they conceive to be a literary enterprise. As this timidity is often their only one, we may be thankful for it. Yet it is absurd enough.

Here is Mr. Broadhurst, who stands foursquare to all the winds that blow, who has earned his own living ever since he was twelve years old, who got married at nineteen, who knows all the mysteries of the forge and has wrought in stone, who has faced with ready wit and determined aspect every kind of audience, big, little, and respectable, friendly, false, and furious, in almost every town in Great Britain, who has defended his character from calumnious assaults, frontal, side, and secret, who has drafted reports, framed resolutions, considered amendments, and made play with statistics, who has piloted Bills through all their stages in the House of Commons, who has spoken on innumerable occasions in that difficult Assembly, both from the front benches and the back, above the gangway and below it, who has been greeted with every kind of cheer, not excepting the ironical, who has known both failure and success, what it is to win and what to lose an election, to be in and out of Parliament—and yet when it comes to the making of a little book, this hero of a hundred fights, this tanned veteran, is as shy as a girl at her first dinner party, trembles at the task he has undertaken, and claims the aid of the first literary gentleman he encounters in the lobby.

Hazlitt has written a famous essay " On the Shyness of Scholars "; an essay might be written " On the Shyness of Stonemasons when they commence Author." It is a shyness perhaps not difficult to account for. To a man who has learnt a regular trade, anything outside it seems difficult. To despise the amateur is a sound, healthy note of the skilled hand who has been taught, peradventure with many kicks, both to learn and to mind his own business.

So (after what rebuffs in other quarters I never

cared to inquire), in what he took to be his necessities, Mr. Broadhurst turned to me. It was in vain that I assured him he needed no assistance either in the preparation or revision of his own Memoirs. He persisted that he did, and told me so often that, though he could build a house, or the best parts of one, he could not write a book, and depicted with so much stormy eloquence the pitfalls and gins and snares that beset (so he imagined) his path, that I could not but place my poor services and hackneyed experience at his disposal. I promised to do this, and a promise is a promise when made in the lobby of the House of Commons, even though its performance may make you ridiculous.

Of course, when it came to the point, my stipulated services (save this Introduction) were not really required. When Mr. Broadhurst left off bemoaning his "imperfect" or "irregular" education, and sat himself down to put his Memoirs together, he found himself at no great disadvantage after all, and in a space of time that would have brought no discredit upon the nimblest-witted writer Fleet Street ever bred, produced a manuscript which could hardly have required less correction and revision had it been the work of the most hardened of living biographers.

It is ungrateful to complain, as some may be heard doing, of the multiplication of Memoirs; for of all the books that get themselves written in these bad days, Memoirs are the most likely to contain something worth reading, the least likely to be altogether futile. The place where a man was born, the origins and occupations of his parents, the kind of education he managed to get, his friends and contemporaries, the circumstances in which he first went out into the world, and how he fared there—none of these things can fail to be interesting. It is not *Life* that is dull.

Mr. Broadhurst, for example, tells us in his first paragraph that he was born at Littlemore, near Oxford. What can be more delightfully unexpected than Littlemore? and in 1840! During all Dr. Newman's solemn years of retirement, when such strange visitants, reserved for fates so varied as J. A. Froude and Mark Pattison and the repulsed Manning, came tapping at his door, the village lanes resounded with the merry cries of the future Parliamentary Secretary of the Trades-Union Congress, a body which records a movement certainly no less significant than the one inseparably associated with the name of the great Cardinal of Rome.

The chief significance of this Memoir is derived from the fact that hitherto in England we have had but few politicians who have found their way to the Treasury Bench from a poor man's cottage. There is a considerable sameness in the early histories of even Under-Secretaries of State. They are apt to come from the same places and to display a tedious similarity of characteristic. Sometimes reports reach the outer world of an Eton dinner, where Prime Ministers past, present, and future sit cheek by jowl, Bishops jest agreeably with Field-Marshals, Governors-General of India and Canada exchange confidences of a kind never likely to be published by the indiscreetest of widows, Secretaries of State, old Parliamentary hacks, palm off upon Ambassadors, past-masters in the art of polite inattention, narratives to which the House of Commons has long learnt to turn its deafest ear, and all alike gaze with boyish rapture upon each other's garters, stars, and ribbons. At the given signal they rise in their places, clink their glasses, and cry as one man, " *Floreat Etona !* " How hard they strive to believe that they owe it all to Eton ! It is an affecting scene, even when read about in a copyright report. Gratitude to an ancient foundation of learning, be it school or college, is always pleasing, and for my part I greatly prefer Johnson's filial regard for Pembroke to Gibbon's contempt for Magdalen ; though if it were a question of rational basis, it could hardly be disputed that the historian had more reason for his contempt than the moralist for his affection.

But in the matter of the Eton dinner, those who stand outside in the raw air, blowing down their fingers to keep them warm, would scarcely be doing justice to whatever education they have picked up elsewhere if they did not take occasion to point out that perhaps the majority of these well-decorated guests owe their careers and their pleasant (if they are pleasant) places in the sun, not to their old school, famous as she is, but to the fact that they belong (nor are they to be blamed for doing so) to the classes of society from ranks of which the occupants of such offices and posts as theirs have been of necessity selected.

Mr. Broadhurst has done something to break this monotony. He was not at Eton nor at Christ Church, though his acquaintance with the latter seat of instruction was at one time extensive, peculiar, and lofty (see p. 8). This imparts zest and novelty to the pages of the Memoir.

Mr. Broadhurst's entirely honest account of his early education will hardly excite the approbation of that solemn body the National Union of Teachers, who see all things in the desk and the primer. In the frankness of his aversion to his studies, his aloofness from his masters, his unfeigned delight in bidding them a long farewell at the scandalous age of twelve, his passion, still strong in him, for the open air, and for all such sports and pastimes as are open in " Merry England " to the sons of the cottager, the youthful Broadhurst would have made, had his lot been different, a first-rate public school boy. But, indeed, of Englishmen it may be said generally that they are all woven strangely of the same piece. "Were I not a game-preserver, I *must* have been a poacher," said the old squire, in tones of sorrowful conviction. In most of our Toryism there is a strong dash of the Radical, and most of our Radicals are well-bottomed in Conservatism. The task of our poor teachers is indeed stupendous.

Of the animated and useful part Mr. Broadhurst has played for thirty years in what are called Labour questions, a brief, modest, and somewhat too impersonal account will be found in the following pages. He was fortunate in the hour of his birth, and has been able to see the law as to workmen's combinations, conspiracy, and employers' liability placed upon a firm, just, and, on the whole, rational basis. Seldom has such rapid progress been made so peacefully in matters so dangerously charged and stuffed to the mouth with class prejudice and angry passions. If there are any fine gentlemen left who sneer at the extension of the suffrage and "Beales, M.A.," and are not yet alive to the probable horrors the gift of the vote averted, their attention may be called to the questions they will find considered in this Memoir.

Mr. Broadhurst has most usefully devoted a generous and well-informed page to the position, often hard, always dangerous, of the Labour Member in the House of Commons. Here he has his hand on the very pulse of the machine. In that direction lies the future of representative institutions in England. The path is not yet clearly defined, it cannot be seen climbing the distant hills—obviously it must traverse a difficult and confused tract of country; but that it will lead to a place of honour and safety it were cowardice to doubt; and it is as a forerunner that Mr. Broadhurst will be best remembered, and his Memoir, frank and good-tempered, be longest read.

A. B.

# CONTENTS

# Contents

# A FOREWORD

MANY friends whose opinions on many questions I value have from time to time urged me to commit to writing some experiences of my life. After many appeals to do so I commenced the task, only to abandon it on the ground that the mistaken zeal of friendship had prompted me to an act of folly and presumption. But during the last few years I have received numerous applications from divergent quarters in Great Britain, and from persons outside the United Kingdom, for notices of my career. And these repeated applications have reawakened the idea of giving my life's story as a whole and in fairly consecutive order, rather than in piecemeal articles. It is a risky undertaking, and I must, with others who have gone before me, prepare myself for the consequences of my rashness. Diaries, memoranda, and the like have not been in my line, and I must therefore rely upon a fairly good memory, together with such aid as I can gather from reports and other printed documents concerning matters with which I have been associated in later years. Let me at once assure my readers that I never had a way marked out in my own mind. I have gone from point to point as circumstances seemed to require me. "One step's enough for me," as Cardinal Newman sang. I am not conscious of ever having a goal for my ambition—that is, if I have at any time possessed an ambition. I have never burnt the midnight oil considering my next move. Each succeeding morning I have done the work nearest to hand. On the Saturday in November, 1872, when I had done my last day's work as a stonemason, I should have thought the man beside himself who had then ventured to tell me that it was my farewell to my trade. I left the firm which then employed me, fully intending to obtain employment in some other firm the following week. That is now twenty-eight years back, and I have not yet sought the other firm. Even at this distance of time I constantly dream that I am working at my trade, and the sudden awakening to reality dispels the delusion almost with a shock. I still keep sufficient of my tools to make another start, though I fear I should not be a first-rate hand at it were I to try. Whatever positions I have occupied, I have blundered into them or stumbled upon them without thought or premeditation. With these explanations and apologies to those who may care to read these pages, I commit myself to the tender mercies and indulgence of the public.

# HENRY BROADHURST

## CHAPTER I

*BLACKSMITH'S FORGE AND STONEMASON'S BENCH*

I WAS born in the parish of Littlemore, near the city of Oxford, in the month of April, 1840. My father was a journeyman stonemason with a large family, of which I made the eleventh or twelfth member. Our cottage, which stood some distance from the village, was the largest of a group of three, the two smaller lying at the back after the style of an old-fashioned pigeon-cote. In the dark and dreary months of winter, stoats, weasels, and field-mice abounded in the surrounding fields, and my earliest recollections are full of the keen delight which we children took in the untrammelled life of the fields and orchards and brooks. Chief among our pastimes we reckoned a hedgehog hunt, in which we felt a keener zest because of the reward gained from the sale of its quills. Money was scarce enough to make such considerations of value, for the wages of a journeyman stonemason at that time varied from twenty to twenty-four shillings a week during nine or ten months of the year, while the remainder were spent in enforced idleness. Yet, despite the narrowness and privations of the life, I loved my home and the rough, free existence, spent largely in the open air, working in the garden and tending the pigs.

No life is without its drawbacks, and into mine came the inevitable and irksome restraint of education. I was sent to a private school, and for the fee of sixpence a week I received plenty of teaching combined with plenty of stick. The schoolmaster doubtless possessed an excellent capacity to teach, but my capacity to learn was by no means equally large. We held divergent views in the matter of spelling, and when a controversy arose, I as the weaker naturally went to the wall, and the man with the cane triumphed. Happily, my services were frequently needed at home, and about the age of twelve I finally escaped the taskmaster and was able to apply myself to more congenial pursuits. These pursuits possessed at least the advantage of variety. When I could be spared from the garden and other work at home I was employed on casual jobs—anything that brought recompense was welcome : digging neighbours' gardens, carrying messages, tending pigs on stubble land after harvest—all was grist that came to the mill. Gleaning was a special delight, and the united efforts of our family in the harvest-field would sometimes result in several bushels of wheat, barley, and beans. In the fruit season we used to take the garden produce to market in Oxford, and if

prices proved good our reward took the shape of a
dainty called "short cakes" and a little extra sugar—
then costing eightpence and tenpence a pound. This
meant a little jam for the winter, and for present
enjoyment a fruit pudding or apple dumplings.

My first regular employment was in a blacksmith's
shop. Life in the forge I found full of new delights.
Blowing the bellows, taking the horses home after
shoeing, wielding the heavy hammer while the smith
fashioned the shoe with the smaller one, cutting threads
on bolts and nuts, all interested me hugely. I felt
myself a person of importance. The blacksmith
himself was no inconsiderable person, under the shade
of his spreading sycamore. His opinion on all kinds
of subjects was eagerly sought by all sorts and conditions of people. In the village club he was a person
to be reckoned with; at the village feast, bedecked with
blue and white ribbons interwoven and festooned, he
would proudly bear aloft one of the banners. Big,
brawny, and sober, no one dare take liberties with
him, but all esteemed him highly. My father, as
a chapel-goer, did not believe in the frivolity of village
feasts, and therefore wore no ribbons; nor were clubs
more to his liking. What wonder then that I, a
hero-worshipper like all boys, should set up the blacksmith on my shrine as the ideal man, with his great
frame neatly clothed in black, shoddy coat, and smart
trousers somewhere about six inches too long, and
rolled up over the boots to show the bright yellow
calico lining.

But I was not allowed to worship my hero long. The time came for me, as it had come for my brothers before me, to learn my father's craft. Reluctantly I bade farewell to the forge and the fields, where I had found many friends among the beasts and birds and living things. My work in the forge had lengthened my limbs and hardened my muscles till I was in a physical condition to meet the demands of any employment. I had by this time reached the age of thirteen, and was big, strong, and active beyond my years.

My father's employers gave permission for me to enter the shop as a beginner, and thus opened out the new and broader life of a stonemason. As the youngest employee many duties besides the acquisition of a knowledge of my trade fell to my lot. At eight o'clock in the morning I had to see that hot tea and coffee were ready for thirty or forty men. Then at ten I must start on my tour of "the shop" to see how many pints of beer would be wanted at eleven, and this task had to be repeated at three o'clock. There were plenty of public-houses close at hand, but I must fetch the beer from one nearly a mile away, because the landlord was foreman of the yard—a position invested with large authority. Therefore the duty of fetching the beer meant a long trudge twice a day for me. If a man did not drink beer he was regarded by his fellows as a muff or a "Ranter." Such men were, however, the exceptions. Most of us found it advisable to obtain our Saturday night and Sunday beer at the same house, so that the foreman must have found the custom from the shop a profitable affair. Such circumstances would be hard to find to-day; the trades-unions have changed all that, as well as the once common practice of paying wages in the public-house, which has now been made illegal.

About this time the second cholera epidemic broke out in England. Oxford did not escape the contagion, and our shop, being situated in a poor district by the river-side, became the centre of the plague's ravages. I can vividly recall the scenes of terrible wretchedness that took place round about the wharf where we were at work, as victim after victim was brought out of the houses by the plague authorities, and carried away to the temporary hospital on the outskirts of the town. Strangely enough, these scenes inspired me with no terror, and every day my father and I walked through the midst of the plague-stricken district to the scene of our labour. Amid such conditions I speedily passed through the stage of initiation into the stonemason's craft. My experience of those days convinces me that most lads will learn their father's trade quicker than any other; while a father naturally interests himself more in the advancement of his son than in that of one who is not related to him.

I continued to work in and about Oxford for two or three years, chiefly occupied in repairing and en-larging churches and colleges. I must turn aside here to tell an amusing incident which occurred many years afterwards in connection with the university city. Some time after I had entered Parliament I remember having a conversation with dear old Sir John Mowbray, who represented Oxford from 1868 until his death in 1899. Our talk ran on the university, and on his remarking that I seemed to have a good deal of knowledge about the various colleges, I informed him that I had been at Christ Church. I shall never forget the look of bewildered incredulity that passed over his benevolent countenance, pain mingling with pity at the thought that I was trying to delude him into a belief that I had been a student at " The House." His relief was instantaneous and perceptible when I gently explained that my connection with Christ Church College was confined to the roof, where I had assisted in fixing a number of new chimney-pots.

I conceived a great affection for the old city which I have never lost. Its grey walls and ancient buildings were always a source of delight, and I would gaze with awe and wonderment at the great men in their caps and gowns as they paced the quiet quadrangles and the broad walks of the college gardens.

An incident which occurred during this period strongly impressed my mind with the necessity of some kind of technical instruction. I obtained employment at Wheatley some half-dozen miles from Oxford, where a new church was being built. By this time I had become fairly competent at my work, and greatly liked it. The first task set me was to work a huge block of stone, weighing probably a ton or more, into a base to carry one of the columns of the church. The design was a square tapering to an octagon and finishing with a circle. The square and the circle offered no difficulties, but how to obtain eight equal sides was utterly beyond my comprehension. To add to my distress my work lay at some distance from the men in the shop, and I was under the constant surveillance of a hard-hearted and uncouth foreman. I only realised my difficulty between the breakfast- and dinner-hours, so that I could obtain no assistance from my mates. My perplexity reached the height of distress. I knew the foreman was no friend of my father, and therefore would give me but a short shrift if he found me in such a dilemma. I was also fully alive to the fact that if I took an undue time over the task my wages would suffer at the end of the week. How I prayed for the dinner-hour as the weary hours dragged by ! But all things have an end, and at last my opportunity came. The persuasive power contained in a pint of beer soon induced one of the masons to describe the procedure, which I realised in an instant, with amazement that I had not intuitively discovered the simple process for myself.

While on this point I may digress a moment in order to point out how different was the treatment meted out to a youth in the workyard in those days. Generally the language and manner of the men were coarse and brutal in the extreme. The man was never recognised in the boy, who was regarded as created for the sole purpose of ministering to the fancies of his elders ; any lack of ready obedience brought down upon the victim's head a storm of abuse, not unfrequently accompanied by more substantial admonitions in the shape of kicks and cuffs.

# CHAPTER II

## *"IN JOURNEYINGS OFTEN"*

WITH the completion of the church at Wheatley began what I may call the third phase of my life. As every student of political economy is aware, there is a certain percentage of the industrial life of the nation which must be migratory in character by force of circumstances. Just as when you look into a kaleidoscope, after taking your fill of one pattern you give the instrument a turn, and the pieces of glass fall away into new positions, some scarcely moving, others covering a wide area before they find a fitting resting-place,—so in the sphere of labour the changes and chances of commercial life and the caprices of fashion keep a large army of working men in a state of motion, sometimes over short distances, some- times from the southern counties to the western, or the eastern to the northern. Few men escape this experience ; my turn now arrived, and for five years I was like Cain, a wanderer on the face of the earth.

As I have said, the church at Wheatley was nearing completion, and the discharge of the hands in the mason's yard began. My turn soon came, and I found myself—a hobbledehoy—out of employment. All my endeavours to get work in Oxford and the surrounding district failed. Business was slack, and masons were a drug in the market. So, as it happened in Robinson Crusoe's case, " my head began to be filled with rambling thoughts." I quickly made my decision to seek my fortune farther afield, and from that moment I never again permanently resided under my parents' roof. I started on my venture into this new life one Monday morning with high hopes and a cheerful countenance. The night before my foot had kicked against something in the pathway, and a patient search in the blackness of a pitch-dark night had been rewarded by the discovery of a rough purse full of coppers. I took this treasure-trove for a happy omen ; and, indeed, before the end of the week I had found employment in the town of Buckingham. My life there, and subsequently at Banbury and in Bedfordshire, where I stayed nearly a year, passed uneventfully in the exercise of my trade.

About this period I paid my first visit to the Metropolis, where I found employment for a short time in the firm of George Myers & Son. Like all country-bred lads, I was astounded at the life and movement of London. The teeming masses of humanity rushing in all directions, bent, as it appeared to me, on getting clear of their neighbours, yet never succeeding in shaking off their pursuers, the roar of the streets, the glare of the lamps at night-time, inspired in me a curious mingling of fascination and distaste. The same conditions were reproduced in the workshop.

Above, below, and around me machines throbbed and whirled ceaselessly. The homely surroundings and social interests of country life had no existence here: life seemed a new thing, almost unearthly. I began to long for the sunlight on the quiet fields, the green hedgerows, and the music of the woods. Even the Houses of Parliament, with the great Clock Tower, my chief delight, could not compensate for the absence of the joys of rural life. A month's stay in modern Babylon was quite sufficient for me, and, gasping like a fish out of water, I set my face towards the open country.

After a week's wandering I found employment at a country house near Pangbourne, in Berkshire, a most delightful spot. The beauty of these new surroundings, and their contrast to the close air and grimy streets of London, inspired me with a strong desire to make a long stay here. Unfortunately, the work I was engaged upon was soon completed, and in a short time I found myself back in London. My return route lay through Reading and Windsor, and as I possessed a little money I made the journey by easy stages. In those days railway fares were much higher, and most working men, even though they had the means, regarded travelling by rail as an expensive luxury, only to be indulged in by the lazy and foolish.

On my arrival in London I found that a firm of builders, Lucas Brothers, were in want of masons at Lowestoft, and that they were paying the passage by sea to Great Yarmouth of employees engaged in London. Here was a chance offered which just suited me. I had never seen the sea, much less sailed upon its heaving breast. Accordingly, I found myself aboard a crazy old tub of a steamer pounding heavily down the Thames. Besides ordinary passengers, I found a number of other masons bound on the same errand as myself. In such company the day and night passed rapidly and jovially, and so liberally did I contribute my quota of the entertainment that when the steamer reached Great Yarmouth I had not a halfpenny to bless myself with. My companions were in no better case, so we had perforce to tramp to Lowestoft, though this proved less of a hardship than we expected, as the distance turned out to be only ten miles.

After a stay of a few months I left the coast and found my way to Norwich, little suspecting that my wanderings were to cease for some six years. My employer was a Mr. Lloyd, who had a thriving business in church erection and renovation and also in gravestones. He was a splendid master, and a bit of a character in his way. He insisted upon thorough accuracy and finish in all work done for him, with the natural consequence that in his " shops " was displayed some of the finest mason's work I have ever seen. I well remember my first conversation with him. I had asked him, as is usual in the trade, if he were in want of hands. He asked me what I was, and I replied, " A mason." Turning a keen and searching glance on me, he suddenly rapped out in a grating voice, "Are you a mason, or only a man calling yourself a mason?" Somewhat taken aback, I assured him that I had gained my livelihood as a worker in stone for some years; and after a few moments' consideration he consented to give me a trial. Apparently he found his startling question satisfactorily answered by the manner in which I handled the chisel, for after eight hours' work he readily complied with my request for an advance of half a sovereign (two and a half day's wages), of which I stood in sore need.

In Mr. Lloyd's "shop" I spent some of the happiest days of my life. The wages were only twenty-four shillings a week of sixty hours. If you were late in the morning you forfeited a quarter of a day's pay, not, as is now the case, simply half an hour's or an hour's wages, according to the time lost. On the other hand, there were many compensations. Frequently I have taken a half-holiday without any deduction of wages, and as frequently I gave a few hours' work late at night or early in the morning without putting it down as overtime. It was a give-and-take system, and I am not far wrong in saying that I took a great deal more than I gave, though always with Mr. Lloyd's approval. I remember one autumn being in his yard six weeks without doing a stroke of really profitable work. Twice during that period I gave notice to leave, promising to return when work was found for me, but on neither occasion would my generous employer listen to my request. Fortunately, when matters were beginning to look desperate orders came in, enabling me to make up for the period of inaction.

A particular feature of this firm was the friendly and indeed familiar relations of master and men. Mr. Lloyd was in special request for small repairs and rectifications in churches and country houses, which could only be carried out by a mason. Consequently, we were often obliged to drive a long distance to the scene of our labours. Many a score of miles did I travel with Mr. Lloyd in his little trap on such journeys, taking our lunch together in roadside inns and enjoying our pipes while the pony was baited. Pleasant times were these. Jack was as good as his master, and his master scorned to be better than Jack. Times have changed since then, and manners with them. The struggle for a living wage has put an end to the friendly relations often subsisting between employer and workman, and to-day I fear it would require a long and exhaustive search to discover such conditions of employment as I have described.

During a period of terrible depression in trade—I think it must have been the winter of 1858-9—I left the city of Norwich in search of work on what proved to be a disastrous journey. My time of setting out was not well chosen, but necessity knows no law. I started about the middle of December, only to return after nearly four months' absence, during which I tramped about twelve hundred miles without succeeding in finding a single day's work. I directed my steps in a southerly direction, making Southampton and Portsmouth my goal. My reason for steering in that direction was that I had heard of the construction of the Royal Victoria Hospital at Netley, and that many hundreds of masons had found employment on the works. Unfortunately for me, the same idea had attracted many others out of work by reason of the slackness of trade, and I found the road swarming with men imbued with the hope of finding employment on the Government buildings. Alike in our hopes, we were also destined to be alike in our disappointment. When I arrived, footsore and weary, at Portsmouth, my boots refused to be held together any longer by string, or any other device of the mechanical mind, and utterly collapsed—like the famous "One-hoss Shay." The hard and flinty southern roads had done their work, and through the holes in the leather the stony places had inflicted wounds and sores on my feet. Faint, weary, with spirit broken, I knew not where to turn. Happily, in my hour of need I met some good Samaritans. They were fellow-masons who, tired of the weary search for non-existent work, had enlisted in the Militia Battalion of the Cheshire Regiment, called out for service at Portsmouth to replace the regular battalions decimated in the terrible Crimean War. Tolerably well fed, warmly clothed, and securely housed, these militiamen appeared the picture of prosperity and happiness.

They lent a ready ear to my necessities, and at their suggestion I entered my name on the sick-list of my trades-union, and obtained a week's lodging in its headquarters in that town. My militia friends generously guaranteed to provide me with food during that period. Accordingly, they proposed to their comrades in barracks that they should be allowed to introduce an old chum, fallen on evil times, to the mess, that he might share the bounties provided by the garrison commissariat. Tommy Atkins, true to his traditional character for good fellowship, agreed to the proposal with acclamation. I was at once installed in barracks, and, so far as meals were concerned, became a private in the Cheshire Militia. Discipline, especially in the militia, was much slacker in those days, and I had no difficulty in eluding the notice of the sergeants. For the time being I lived, as it seemed to me, like a lord, while the accumulation of my sick-pay (ten shillings a week) meant the possibility of new boots. With such a contrast as was afforded by my past destitution and misery and my present plenty and comfort, it was little wonder that the service of " the Widow at Windsor " presented an alluring prospect. Moreover, just at this time two of my militia friends were transferred, at their own request, to the Royal Engineers. The bounty received for this transaction was temptingly large. I resolved to don the scarlet tunic, and accordingly presented myself to the recruiting officer. But for some reason or other her Majesty was at the time not anxious to avail herself of my services—I believe my height was below the standard; so I was obliged to content myself with joining in the high jinks which accompanied the spending of the bounty received by my two friends.

Restored in health and spirits, not to mention shoe-leather, by my week's rest, I set out again on the tramp. I was at all times a good pedestrian, and I felt so full of life and vigour that I resolved to walk to Brighton in one day. The distance to be traversed was about fifty miles, and I had no misgivings about my power to accomplish it. But the fates were against me. I started from Portsmouth on a bright, wintry morning, the air keen with frost; but before the lapse of an hour I walked into a storm of rain, which increased as the hours went on, until long before I reached Arundel I had not a dry thread on my body. Dragged down by the weight of my soaking clothes, the water squelching out of my boots at every step, I was only too glad to call a halt for the night at Arundel. I soon had reason to wish myself back in barracks, for the hostelry at which my slender resources permitted me to stay was not distinguished by its comforts, lacking especially a respectable fire to restore warmth to my rain-chilled frame and to dry my clothes. In fact, next morning, when I rose to resume my journey, some of my garments were almost as wet as when I took them off the night before. The rain had ceased in the night, and the damp weather had given place to frost. Welcome as this keen, sparkling air was to a pedestrian, I soon discovered its disadvantages ; for before I had covered two miles of my day's journey every stitch of clothing I was wearing became as stiff as a board. So far as comfort went, I might as well have been arrayed in Greatheart's suit of mail.

Notwithstanding my impeding clothes, I made good progress, and arrived in Brighton at an early hour. A brew of hot tea and a chop sent me to bed in a happy frame of mind, believing my troubles were over, for the frost had every appearance of holding. When morning arrived I found I had reckoned without my host. The frost, gripping my sodden boots, had turned the leather to the consistency of cast iron. With great difficulty I got them on ; but when I came to walk, their unyielding surface chafed my feet sorely, reopening the wounds which had all but healed. Walking under these circumstances keenly tormented me ; but in spite of all I managed to cover the ground between Brighton and Tunbridge Wells in ten hours. The next day I walked into London ; lame and well-nigh exhausted, I thought the long New and Old Kent Roads would never come to an end, while Westminster Bridge appeared to my leaden limbs like a little mountain. I crawled past the Houses of Parliament, little thinking that their corridors and lobbies should one day become as familiar to me as any place on earth, until in Johnson Street, Westminster, I hailed with delight the masons' club-house, where I was entitled to four days' and nights' rest and the sum of one shilling per day.

I remained the prescribed period in London, and then, having been totally unsuccessful in my search for work, I once again set out upon the high-roads, and by devious routes found my way back to Norwich. As I have said above, my tramp had lasted nearly four months, a time of much suffering and considerable privations, and totally unrewarded by any work.

I think my readers would be interested if I turned aside for a moment to describe the conditions under which such a long tramp was possible to a man with scarcely any means. Before I started on this unfortunate journey I had been out of work for a week or two, so that my entire capital amounted to less than ten shillings, and I finished the tour with the sum of sixpence in my pocket. At no time during my progress did I possess more than ten shillings, and on many occasions I was without even a penny. My trades-union had relieving-stations in nearly every town, generally situated in one of the smaller public-houses. Two of the local masons are appointed to act as relieving-officer and bed-inspector. The duty of the latter is to see that the beds are kept clean, in good condition, and well aired, and the accommodation is much better than might be expected. When a mason on tramp enters a town, he finds his way to the relieving-officer and presents his card. On this card is written the applicant's name and last permanent address. In addition he carries a printed ticket bearing the stamp of the last lodge at which the traveller received relief. He was entitled to receive a relief allowance of one shilling for twenty miles and threepence for every additional ten miles traversed since his last receipt of relief money. Thus, if fifty miles have been covered the man receives one-and-ninepence. In addition he is allowed sleeping accommodation for at least one night, and if the town where the station is situated is of considerable size, he is entitled to two or three nights' lodging. Besides a good bed, the proprietor of the official quarters is bound to furnish cutlery, crockery, and kitchen conveniences for each traveller, so that the relief money can all be spent on food. There is also no temptation to spend the small sum received on intoxicating drink, unless its recipient chooses to do so. The system is so perfect that it is a very rare occurrence for an impostor to succeed in cheating the union. Unfortunately, the stations did not exist everywhere, and when they were separated by forty or fifty miles—not a rare occurrence in the southern counties—the traveller's life became a hard one. I have frequently had to provide supper, bed, and breakfast on less than a shilling, so it may be readily imagined that my resting-places were never luxurious hotels. When I look back to those days, and compare my condition and surroundings with the present time, it is like a peep into the Dark Ages. During the whole of that tramp, and over all those hundreds of miles, I do not remember more than one occasion upon which I got a lift on the road. Even an ordinary drayman little cares to pick up for ever so short a distance any person having the appearance which I presented at that period. But this was my last big tramp, and it was the longest lapse from employment that I have ever experienced in my life.

The hardships of these journeys in search of work were sometimes lightened in a less official manner. Members of my trade were always ready to relieve to the best of their power a distressed mason, provided he could prove his *bona fides*. The system worked something after this fashion. A man in search of employment, if a member of the trade society, always carried his card of membership in his pocket. As he went along he gathered the names and places, between town and town, where work was going on. It might be a public institution like an asylum, prison, or workhouse, or it might be a village church or a country mansion. The practice was to make one's way to these on the chance of obtaining work. If, however, no hands were wanted, a friendly gossip would ensue with one or more of the men in the shop. If there was a society man amongst them, he would ask whether you had your "card," and if this was produced it was an established custom for him to endeavour to collect what he could to assist you on your way. If it was nearing night-time, one or other of the masons would, in addition to the collection, offer you accommodation for the night, and send you off in the morning with such addition as his means or his mind might incline him to add to your possessions. Of course, if there was a relieving-station at hand the official lodging-house would be your sleeping-place, except in the frequent instances where you would meet an old shopmate, who would insist upon your sharing his sleeping-quarters and sitting at his more liberally provided board. The probability was that you had previously offered the same hospitality to him or to some intimate friend under similar circumstances, or that you would be called upon to do so at a future time.

In the course of my wanderings I feel in with many men bent on the same search as myself, though belonging to different trades. Sometimes it would be a bricklayer, sometimes a tanner, and sometimes an engineer. If our goal was the same town or village, we would journey together as long as our ways lay in common. Whatever our callings might be, the member of the party who had met any luck seldom failed to publish the fact ; and on several occasions I have either received or provided a homely but welcome meal. The old saying, " The best friends of the poor are the poor," was exemplified in my experience. I have a vivid recollection of reaching a town within fifty miles of London one cold Christmas Eve. I had a shilling to draw and two beds—*i.e.*, two night's lodging—to my credit, besides an extra shilling for Christmas Day. My pockets were entirely innocent of coin, so that I was obliged to exercise great frugality. Accordingly, I hit upon the obvious expedient of taking my Christmas cheer in a lump, combining dinner, tea, and supper in one meal. But the landlady of the inn—

good soul !—would have none of it. Nothing would satisfy her but that I should freely share in the good things of her own table. Many a time have I wished to meet again this kindly hostess who turned my semi-starvation into a feast of fat things.

The larger part of the next two or three years, until I became a permanent resident in the Empire City, I spent in Norwich. The intervals, when slackness of trade drove me forth, were passed entirely in the Eastern Counties, in Beccles, Ipswich, and Colchester. The first employment I obtained after my weary tramp cost me a painful experience. I was employed upon some stone steps worked out of what is called " Rag Portland." This is a rough stone full of little shells with knife-like edges. From long disuse of the chisel my hands had grown so soft and delicate that almost directly I set to work they became a mass of blisters, which quite disabled me for two or three days. With my straitened means a long rest meant starvation ; so I had recourse to drastic treatment. First I dissolved a quantity of salt in warm water, and then, having pierced the blisters with a large needle, I held my hands in the water until the salt had soaked well into the wounds. A constant repetition of this treatment rendered me fit to resume work at the end of two days. After some un-important changes, I obtained employment in the firm of Lucas Brothers, remaining with them until my removal to London.

From the very first I took a great liking for

Norwich, which the lapse of time did not diminish—in fact, I believe that had there been a wider choice of employment I should have settled down for life under the shadow of the cathedral. I found much solace and delight in the surrounding country ; in particular the village of Thorpe appealed to me with ever fresh charms. I have always regarded it as the prettiest village in the country. The charming old church, the red-tiled houses, the green slopes running down to the river's edge, backed by high, wooded land, with Whitlingham in the foreground, all combine to produce a scene of exquisite peacefulness and beauty. Even to-day, after the lapse of forty years, I can never pass the view without renewed admiration.

During this long stay at Norwich the American Civil War was in progress. Amid the strong feeling of sympathy with the Confederates then prevailing in England, I well remember the power and energy with which Mr. Jacob Henry Tillett championed the cause of the Northern States in the columns of *The Norfolk News*. In later years I became personally acquainted with Mr. Tillett, and for a time we sat together in the House of Commons, enjoying frequent talks of old days in Norwich and the Eastern Counties.

A notable feature in the religious life of the city was the sixty minutes' afternoon service in St. Andrew's Hall, conducted by the Rev. Thomas Wheeler. Mr. Wheeler was a natural orator, possessing in a remarkable degree the ability to tell quaint and effective stories to illustrate his subject. I have never met another man possessing such skill in enchaining the attention of an audience of children, a feat not over easy to compass.

At this time I lived every hour of my life; I do not think the wealthiest or most exalted person in the land obtained half the joy from mere existence that I did.

# CHAPTER III

## *EARLY DAYS IN LONDON*

I THINK it was in 1865 that I removed to London. I quickly found work in a firm of sculptors, Farmer & Brindley. They were then engaged on the carving work in the block of Government offices adjoining Downing Street. I do not mean to imply that my engagement with this firm meant that I was in any sense competent to do carving work. My duty was to chisel down the rough blocks of stone as they were fitted in the building until they assumed the roughest outline of the intended decoration. Then the carver took up the work, shaping the stone in accordance with the artistic design until the finishing touches were given. The branch of masonry on which my energies were employed is called in the trade " roughing-out," and was a higher class of work than I had hitherto experienced. Masons engaged on this kind of work received a halfpenny or a penny per hour more than the wages paid for the mechanical labour in the workshop, besides other little advantages of no interest to the public. Spurred by an ambition to improve my prospects, I conceived the idea of myself becoming a carver, and to this intent I bought some cheap books containing sketches of ornamental work in foliage and the like on one page, with a blank sheet opposite for copying. The study interested me greatly, and for some time I persevered in my intention ; but ultimately I grew tired of the work, which involved considerable exposure to the weather, for nearly all the carving had to be done upon the building itself, and not in the workshop.

The last straw, however, which led to my final resolution not to continue in this branch of the trade was my employment on the Houses of Parliament. For a considerable interval I had been working in the "shop" of my old employers, George Meyer & Sons, who were carrying out some decorative work on the Guildhall. Tempted by the superior rate of payment I returned to "roughing-out" under Mr. Herp, who had received the contract for the carving work on the Clock Tower and the new corridor which joined it to the main buildings of the Houses of Parliament. The time of year was November, and the north-east wind blowing up the river made my task a cruel one. At times the bitter blast would numb my hands until it was impossible to hold a chisel. My very bones would be penetrated with its icy edge until I felt as if clothed in a garment of lace. Little wonder that I gladly went back to the mason's shop, where some shelter, at least, was afforded.

From this period till the end of 1872 I was employed by many different firms. My old acquaintance with ecclesiastical stonework was renewed by my engagement with a firm of church decorators in Charlotte Street, Fitzroy Square. They worked both in stained glass and the stonework in church interiors—communion tables and altars, altar rails, fonts, pulpits, and so on. They had business connections with the Continent and also with the United States, but the bulk of their productions was supplied to English customers. This class of work possessed great interest to those engaged in it and demanded considerable skill, though scarcely as much as the uninitiated would imagine. There was also a third department, in which mosaic and incised work was carried on. The partners were young men of exceptional abilities, and but for unfortunate circumstances I am convinced they would have attained the position of one of the leading firms in the world. Subsequently I was employed upon many of the best-known buildings in London, and traces of my workmanship might be found in Westminster Abbey, the Albert Hall, St. Thomas's Hospital, Burlington House, the Guildhall, and the aristocratic residences in Grosvenor Place, Grosvenor Gardens, and Curzon Street, Mayfair, though I am certain that the prolonged and minute search necessary to find such traces would not be rewarded by any startling artistic discovery.

The even tenor of my life was now broken by the first considerable Labour dispute in which I had taken a part. In the spring of 1872 the men engaged in the building trades agitated for a reduction in the working hours and an increase of one penny per hour in their wages. The union officials had given the usual six months' notice to the employers, the period to expire in the month of May; but the employers decided to anticipate a strike, and locked the men out. The result was a month of enforced idleness. I was elected chairman of the lock-out movement in my own trade. Rarely, I suppose, in the history of Labour disputes was a lock-out conducted on a more amicable basis. No breaches of the law occurred, and so quiet was everything that scarcely anyone save those interested in it was aware of its existence.

Ultimately, a conference was agreed upon, consisting of a committee of the Masons' Society (of which I was a member), and an equal number of representatives of the Master Builders' Association. The joint committee was presided over by Mr. Hannen, the brother of the late Lord Hannen; and the chief figures on the employers' side were Mr. Charles Lucas, and Mr. Bird, the secretary of their association. After two meetings the conference drew up the conditions of the resumption of work. They consisted of an immediate advance of a halfpenny per hour, a further advance of the same amount to be conceded in the following year if trade was good, and the reduction of the hours of work from fifty-six and a half to fifty-two and a half per week for nine months in the year, and to forty-seven for the remaining three months. One signal advantage gained was that work should cease at noon on Saturdays. Under the system then in force work was continued on Saturdays till one o'clock, an hour after the usual dinner-hour. A serious consequence of this custom was that the men frequently celebrated the end of the week's work with a glass of beer, and, imbibing it on an empty stomach an hour after their usual meal-time, rapidly became intoxicated. Nothing succeeds like success, and the practical capitulation of the masters on the men's terms induced many employers who had hitherto refused to recognise the Masons' Society to change their policy; some firms even going so far as to instruct their foremen to give the preference in taking on new hands to members of the society.

This was my last experience of direct responsibility for the conduct of a trade dispute, not greatly to my sorrow, for during the progress of the lock-out and the conference I conducted all the negotiations on behalf of the masons. I had to attend all the meetings, speaking on occasion several times during the day, and always confronted with the dread of doing or saying anything that might increase the differences of the contending parties. It was rarely before midnight that I reached home, worn-out with worry and fatigue; and for fulfilling this important office I received only a shilling a day more than those who took no active part in the proceedings beyond drawing their strike-pay. How little the superior critic of the Labour world knows of the circumstances under which those who are sometimes called " unscrupulous agitators " gain for their fellows a fair reward for their labours ! I do not mean to imply that I was the only prominent representative of the men affected by this lock-out. On the contrary, the leaders of the allied trades—the brick-layers, carpenters, etc.—were entitled to quite as much credit for the successful ending of the dispute and the furthering of the cause of Labour. But I have not alluded specifically to them because I desire to confine myself strictly to those affairs in which I had a personal interest.

It must not be supposed that my failure to proceed far with the free-hand drawing studies, which would have qualified me for the higher branches of my trade, arose from laziness. The fact is that I was becoming more and more immersed in trades-union interests, and this course gradually led me into the political arena. Soon after my settlement in London I became attached to a political organisation called a " Working Men's Association," and I also joined the Reform League. The labour of organising in connection with the trades-union and the political delegations in which I was interested were peculiarly congenial to my temperament and aspirations ; but of course they left me no spare time for study. Those were stirring times in both spheres of activity—vast processions, great demonstrations organised by the united trade and political associations ; and only those in the inner circle can realise what self-sacrifice and arduous labour working men who took an interest in the advancement of their class were called upon to endure, and all, be it remembered, without monetary reward. The sole incentives were ardent convictions and a deep sense of patriotism. I think I was present on all the great demonstrations of this time, generally in the character of a delegate of my trades-union. I remember particularly the long march from the Mall, past Marlborough House, to the great field at Fulham, through drenching rain and seas of mud on a bleak wintry day, when the men of London met to demand that extension of the franchise which was eventually conceded in the Reform Act of 1867. Equally vivid is my recollection of the vast procession through the West End of London to the Agricultural Hall at Islington. I took part, too, in the memorable occasion of the pulling down of the Hyde Park railings.

Concerning this great demonstration, which was forbidden to enter Hyde Park at the whim of the Tory Government, I must enter into rather more detail, because, although my personal experiences of this eventful day were not particularly striking, the whole business contains an element of dramatic interest, and marks an epoch in that struggle for liberty and free speech which reactionary rulers have vainly endeavoured to crush. The affair arose out of the rejection of the Franchise Bill. The Reform League determined to hold a gigantic mass meeting in Hyde Park to protest against the Government's action.    Due notice of this intention was given to the police, when, like a bolt from the blue, the Home Secretary, Mr. Spencer Walpole, blankly refused permission for the meeting to be held in the Park. A considerable discussion in the newspapers followed ; great indignation was everywhere expressed against this obscurantist and tyrannical action, and the leaders of the League determined to pursue their intention, despite the official prohibition.    Accordingly, on the day fixed—May, 1866—two processions were formed and marched to the Park.    The first was led by Mr. Beales, the President of the Reform League, and it is interesting to recall that two of his companions were Professor Thorold Rogers (who represented the Oxford Reform League) and Mr. G. J. Holyoake. This procession started at six o'clock in the morning from the offices of the League in Adelphi Terrace, and proceeded by way of Regent Street to Hyde Park Corner.    At Oxford Circus its numbers were swelled by a large contingent from the Holborn Branch, who were preceded by a brass band and a large tricolour of red, green, and blue.    Amid the jeers, the laughter, and the cheers of the spectators who lined the streets in large numbers and filled every window on the route, the immense procession moved forward towards the gates of the Park.    So vast were the numbers that when the leading carriage was traversing Bond Street the rear rank had not left Holborn.    Meanwhile, tremendous preparations had been made to bar the way of this great multitude into the Park.    Before the Hyde Park Corner gates, the Marble Arch gates, and in the immediate vicinity, over sixteen hundred constables, mounted and on foot, were stationed.

The scene about Hyde Park Corner when the carriages of the Reform Leaguers reached the spot was extraordinary. Barricades of omnibuses were on every side; the carriages of the wealthy blocked the way; and right across the entrance to the Park was drawn a double line of mounted constables. Behind them stood a crescent-shaped line of foot-police. The leading carriage of the demonstration was driven up to where the police were stationed, and its occupants descended and, surrounded by the Holborn contingent, walked up to the gates. Their progress was checked by an inspector of police, who informed Mr. Beales that he could not enter the Park, by order of the Commissioners. Some little scuffles between police and demonstrators took place here and there, and then Mr. Beales and his comrades remounted their carriage and proceeded to Trafalgar Square, where they addressed a huge meeting from the base of Nelson's Monument.

It had been arranged that the members of the Clerkenwell Branch of the League should assemble on the Green and march to the Marble Arch, and there join forces with the other branches. A procession of several thousands followed the band, and before Oxford Street was reached the union with other demonstrators had swelled their numbers to at least fifteen thousand. Banners of all hues fluttered in the air, the men tramped steadily to the music of the bands, and the whole scene, except for the absence of glittering arms and uniforms, resembled the orderly progress of a disciplined army rather than a hastily arranged procession of civilians. From one of the banners the portrait of Gladstone smiled his approval on the crowded ranks ; beneath it ran the appropriate motto, "Gladstone and Liberty : An Honest Man's the Noblest Work of God." A companion banner bore the effigy of John Bright, with the inscription, " John Bright : Manhood Suffrage."

Nearing the Marble Arch soon after seven, all kinds of rumours concerning the police and the other demonstration met them. Some said the gates had been thrown open by the police, others asserted that the police had been overcome and the gates forced by the crowd. But when the head of the procession reached the Marble Arch they were confronted by firmly closed gates and a strong cordon of constables before them. Some part of the procession passed on in the direction of the Bayswater Road, but the greater number turned down Park Lane with the intention of trying the Hyde Park Corner entrance.

It was just at this moment that my own experiences of the demonstration began. I was working for Farmer & Brindley at the time on the Foreign Office in Downing Street, then in the course of construction. Anxious to take some part in the projected gathering in Hyde Park, I hurried home to Pimlico as soon as my work was done, and reached Hyde Park Corner at seven. Great masses of workmen were hastening to the same spot from Westminster and Lambeth, and so formed a large body of reinforcements. Finding the police in possession of the gates, we edged round into Park Lane. Here a scene of indescribable confusion and tumult prevailed. The narrowness of the thoroughfare, the pressure of the demonstrators from the Marble Arch, increased by the sympathisers and onlookers from Hyde Park Corner, turned the Lane into a huge, swaying, shouting mob. Luckily, I fell in with a squad of my own shop-mates, and keeping well together we managed to protect ourselves from injury. A curious incident occurred just as we left Piccadilly. A hansom cab drove past, whose two occupants were accompanied by a big, black retriever dog. Either from love of sport or incited by its master, this dog suddenly leaped from the cab and made a dash at us. One of our number, a brawny, North Country mason, met the attack with a blow of his fist, which caught the brute just under the jaw, and, as Bret Harte puts it, " the subsequent proceedings interested him no more." If the men in the cab had not hastily bidden their driver to put on full speed ahead they would have shared the fate of their dog, for the feeling of exasperation had risen higher and higher till the crowd was in just the mood which, if provoked too rudely, leads to desperate deeds and revolutions.

The vast crowd surged this way and that, endeavouring

to find an outlet ; every instant seemed to threaten wholesale suffocation unless the pressure were relaxed. Suddenly the iron railings bent and cracked, either from the exertion of intentional force by some active spirits or else from the unpremeditated and irresistible movement of the crowd. The barriers down, a vast body of men poured through the breaches, many injuries were received, and the police, hearing of the occurrence, came tumbling up from the main gates and charged the struggling mass with drawn truncheons. They might as well have charged the Falls of Niagara. Mrs. Partington confronting the Atlantic with her broom was not a more ludicrous picture. They belaboured the front ranks with their batons, but were swept aside like flies before the waiter's napkin. The cries of distress, the angry shouts, the hoarse voices of the constables, and the tramping of thousands of feet filled the air with a confused din utterly beyond description. I did not see any actual personal violence done, but I could hear the angry noises which denote rough work in my immediate vicinity. One man was carried out on a stretcher, his head a mass of wounds from the truncheon of a constable ; six persons received severe injuries, and were taken to St. Mary's Hospital ; and for many weeks after this eventful day I used to see the constables about King Street Police Station with their arms in slings and their heads in bandages.

Soon after the crowd entered the Park a meeting was convened, and resolutions denouncing the action of the Tory Government were passed. Of this I saw and heard nothing, for my attention was centred on a more exciting subject. Finding themselves overpowered, the police sent for assistance, and presently, above the heads of the crowd, I could discern the plumes of the Horse Guards Blue and the dark bearskins of the Foot Guards. Two companies of the latter and two troops of the cavalry, under Colonel Lane-Fox, composed this force. The soldiers received quite an ovation from the people in the Park. Cries of "Three cheers for the Guards—the people's Guards!" were raised and warmly taken up. There must have been quite two hundred thousand demonstrators in the Park, and the spectacle as the Household troops advanced, followed by the Grenadiers with fixed bayonets, was a striking one. Amid loud and prolonged cheers the soldiers marched and wheeled and marched again ; but the crowd seemed quite confident that there would be no firing and no resort to cold steel. The commanding officer possessed more discretion than the Home Secretary, otherwise Peterloo might have been re-enacted on a hundredfold larger scale. But after watching the soldiers for a short time the crowd gradually and without uproar dispersed, and the Park was left in quiet. For myself, I had gone home some time before without having sustained any more serious injury than a bruised arm and a sore spot or two on my feet, where the enthusiasm of the crowd had got the better of me.

Those were years of extraordinary exertion, making heavy demands upon one's physical strength. During the whole of this period I scarcely ever lost a single hour's work in the morning, though I seldom retired to bed before midnight, and was always up again at 4.30 a.m. Nearly all my work as a delegate was entirely gratuitous ; occasionally, indeed, I received a shilling a day when engaged on behalf of my trades-union, but this sum never sufficed to remunerate me for my out-of-pocket expenses, such as cost of travelling and similar outlay. The scanty leisure which my employment left me was divided between the affairs of my trades-union and the Reform Movement. Thus I gradually became deeply engrossed in political and Labour questions. It was difficult to distinguish between the two, for those were the days when men began to concentrate the political power of the trades-unions, and to bring it to bear upon Parliament to secure reforms in the laws relating to Labour and trade combination. This absorption in what I may call, for want of a better term, public life at length grew so great as to demand all my energies. In September, 1872, I was appointed delegate of the Stonemasons' Society to the Trades-Union Congress, and at the Congress I was elected a member of the Parliamentary Committee. A month later my employment on the Curzon Street works came to an end, and from that time I bade a final adieu to the stonemason's bench.

My appointment as delegate and my election to the Parliamentary Committee were a recognition of activity in my own Union. After the passing of the

Franchise Act of 1867 I had largely devoted my energies to committee work in the Stonemasons' Society. My personal experiences had taught me the necessity of many changes in the Union rules. It is part of our constitutional practice that the rules should be open to revision every three years; and accordingly, at the due time, I brought forward several proposals. In the face of much opposition I succeeded in carrying a resolution that this revision of rules should be conducted by a committee of delegates from every district, elected for this purpose. I next proposed the establishment of a Superannuation Fund, by which a small pension was to be granted to men who had been members of the Union for a minimum number of years on condition, not of the attainment of a certain age, but of certified inability longer to pursue the trade of mason. The amount of this pension was decided by the number of years during which the recipient had been a member of the Union. After a struggle extending over several years this proposal was also added to the statute-book of the Union. I then turned my attention to the question of allowances to the unemployed. My experience of the tramping system led me to the conclusion that the search for employment on foot from county to county, often continued over a long period, was liable to develop in men of weak character permanent demoralisation, and to instil a distaste of settled life. While not desirous of putting hindrances in the way of a man's leaving his home to find fresh employment elsewhere, I was convinced that he ought not to be compelled to go on the tramp in order to make himself eligible for relief. I therefore advocated a system of small weekly allowances for a limited period to men out of employment, payable in the town where the applicant resided. Although this reform was not immediately carried out, its eventual success was well assured; and I believe the scheme has worked out without substantial injury to or fraud upon the funds of the Union.

But I was not satisfied with these changes. In those days the Central Lodge, which formed the executive government of the Union, was not permitted to remain in one town for a longer period than three years. As the members of the lodge were perforce local masons, this rule meant that, with the exception of the secretaries, every third year saw a new executive called into existence. Such a system could not but be highly detrimental to the interests of the Union, as I succeeded in proving to the majority of the members. After some discussion we resolved that the headquarters of the Union should be permanently fixed in London, an innovation which has proved highly beneficial. For a time I occupied the position of Chairman of the Central Committee. The chairman, it must be understood, had no emoluments attached to his position beyond those received as a member of the Central Committee—*viz.*, one shilling for each meeting attended. This sum, in an era when plentiful tramcars and cheap omnibus rides were unknown, frequently fell short of the expenditure necessary to reach the place of meeting. During my chairmanship, after frequent failures, I succeeded in inducing the Central Committee to exercise executive powers. I was moved to do this by the conviction that with a firmer control from the central body many strikes in various parts of the country might be prevented, while others would be considerably shortened. Employers and their representatives were then, and I have no doubt are still, too apt to treat their own workmen with very little consideration, often displaying an unreasonable repugnance to talk over what the men consider to be grievances. This failure to observe the minor courtesies of life is equally shared by the men, so far as my observation goes. I reasoned that if an outside body, exempt from local prejudices, could intervene and act as a go-between, interviewing masters and men, the causes of dispute might frequently be adjusted without having recourse to the extreme measure of a strike. In course of time I impressed my conviction on the committee, and it was agreed to add this executive function to its duties.

The first occasion on which this new departure came into operation was in connection with a strike at the Avonmouth Docks. The Central Committee received a telegram announcing the sudden cessation of work by a large number of masons, and requesting, in the name of an improvised strike committee, the immediate dispatch of a sum of money wherewith to pay a strike allowance. The cost to the Mason's Society would have amounted to nearly £100 a week during the continuance of the strike, and the payment of the first week's allowance would have intensified the difficulty of a settlement. The General Secretary in London immediately summoned a special meeting of the Central Committee, which promptly appointed two of its members to investigate the case and report upon it to the committee. I was one of those chosen for this mission. Early next morning we proceeded to the scene of action, and at once summoned a meeting of the men and heard their complaints. Accompanied by a delegation of the masons we next proceeded to the docks; a brief conference with the contractor and the chief engineer followed, ending in the adjustment of the differences and the resumption of work the following morning.

My next experience of conciliation work was less satisfactory. Curiously enough, the scene of operations was in the same district, but on the other side of Bristol. A strike had been proceeding for six weeks when I, with other members of the Central Committee, went down to try to bring the dispute to a close. When we arrived in the neighbourhood we found among the men a widespread spirit of antagonism to our mission. To such an extent did this spirit exist that threats of violence if we dared to visit the works were freely indulged in. On the principle that threatened men live long, we paid little heed to these menaces and proceeded with our task. But the stubbornness of the men baffled all our efforts at conciliation. Had their persistency been exercised in a better cause it would have been magnificent ; under the circumstances it was merely fatuous. On the other hand, the employer displayed an unusually reasonable spirit, readily expressing his willingness to submit the whole question to arbitration. He even went so far as to agree that our Central Committee should act as the court of arbitrators, offering to pay a handsome subscription to the Bristol Hospital if we found him in the wrong, on condition that if the judgment went against the men they should subscribe a donation to the same institution. But nothing would induce the men to submit to arbitration. At a mass meeting of the men we warned them that our report to the Central Committee might lead to the cessation of their strike pay, but all to no effect. The threats of violence were not executed, but the strike went on. On receipt of our report the committee gave them a week's notice to close the strike, and at the expiration of the limit cut off supplies, with the result that soon after the men came to terms with their employer.

In the third case which I shall chronicle our presence was equally unpleasing to the men, but terminated with a happier result. Like the preceding one, this strike, which took place in a town in the north of England, had lasted six weeks when the Central Committee intervened. I, with another member, was again appointed to institute an inquiry into the causes of the dispute. The General Secretary telegraphed to the men on strike to arrange a meeting in readiness to receive us, and he also asked the employer to be within reach in case we wanted to see him. When we arrived we found the men assembled, but their attitude was anything but reassuring. Before the meeting had proceeded far we were threatened with expulsion from the room. Both of us, however, had had plenty of experience of the value of such threats at similar gatherings, so they had little effect on us. We persevered in our mission, with the result that, having arrived on Saturday afternoon at four o'clock, we made such headway in establishing a line of communication between contractor and workmen that on the following Tuesday work was resumed. A fortnight later these very men who had received us with strong opposition sent a vote of thanks to the Central Committee, acknowledging the great services rendered by us, and expressing regret that our visit had not been made at an earlier period of the dispute.

During this period of my life I became greatly interested in a co-operative experiment. After the quieting down of the political agitation for reform in 1867 Mr. Alfred Walton, a retired clerk of the works in the building trade and a stonemason by training, gave a series of addresses to the building trades and operatives of London in favour of Co-operative Building Societies. The theory was a sound one and the object most desirable. After prolonged effort and the expenditure of much labour a start was made to put Mr. Walton's theory into practice. A company was formed, a board of directors appointed, and business premises taken in the Euston Road. The directorate consisted of representatives of various branches of building trades, and I was a member of the board. Several of my colleagues were men of exceptional ability and large experience, both as experts in estimates and in quantity taking. We began by tendering for small contracts, but met with little success. The premises we had hired were the property of the Aerated Bread Company, and fortunately this company was able to supply us with a considerable amount of repairing work in their various premises in London. Had we been content to confine ourselves to this class of work, which soon became sufficient to make it profitable, until we had established the concern on a firm basis, I believe the company might have grown into a permanent institution. Unfortunately, the sin by which the angels fell wrought our ruin. We succeeded in obtaining a contract for more ambitious work in the shape of the erection of a mission-hall and schools in St. John's Wood. Paradoxical as it may sound, this success proved a disaster. For some time the enthusiasm of our shareholders had been gradually evaporating. To carry out building operations capital is an absolute necessity, but more capital the shareholders apparently had no intention of supplying. Having obtained the contract, we called a meeting of shareholders for the purpose of appealing to them to pay up arrears. Very few attended beyond the directors ; but the contract had already been signed, and we were compelled to proceed. We had recourse to all the expedients we could think of, except borrowing money at a high rate of interest. Each of the directors, in addition to paying up the full value of his shares, advanced money from time to time according to his means to meet the company's expenses. A serious source of inconvenience and loss was the fact that merchants would not extend to us the same credit which they granted to private building firms.

Our theory was to employ the shareholders as far as possible on the company's work. The managing director, who lived on the premises in Euston Road, was a workman of superior education, with a high ideal of the future of Labour ; but I had more than once harboured a suspicion that his practice fell far short of his preaching, and doubted his industry and close application to his duties. All the directors were men who had to work from ten to twelve hours a day at their trade, so that it was impossible for them to take an active part in the direction and management of the building operations in St. John's Wood, which were of necessity left to the entire control of the managing director. None of the directors except the manager received any fee for his services. Most of us lived at least two or three miles from Euston Road, and the directors' meetings usually kept us from home till midnight, while we were obliged to be up next morning at a very early hour. Under these circumstances it will be recognised how impossible it was for the board to exercise personal oversight on the works. But a time came when some of the directors felt that the works were not progressing as rapidly as might reasonably be expected, and suspicion arose that the fault lay at the door of the managing director. So strongly was I impressed with this view of the matter that out of my working time, which of course meant a considerable loss to me, I determined to pay a surprise visit to the works. I left my home at 4.15 one morning, and arrived at the works before 6. I immediately secreted myself in a favourable position, where I could not be observed, but from which I could see all that passed. Six o'clock was the time for commencing work ; but when a neighbouring clock chimed the hour, out of thirty men engaged on the building operations less than half were ready to begin. Some arrived ten minutes late, others were twenty minutes behind time ; while the managing director, who should have been there without fail to blow the whistle at six o'clock, turned up half an hour late. His consternation at my sudden appearance is not easily imagined. I will pass over the scene that followed ; suffice it to say that I had discovered one big leak in our good ship, and hastened to lay my discovery before a special meeting of the board. Unhappily, my exposure came too late ; for when the building was at length completed we were reduced to bankruptcy, and the company on which we had set such sanguine hopes was wound up. For my part,

I lost not only my share capital and the money I had advanced at various times to meet pressing calls, but three years of hard work at the sacrifice of much individual comfort.

Such was my first and last personal experience of productive co-operation, and in truth it was a desperate venture. All the influence of the trades interested in building was dead against us; obstacles real and artificial barred our way at every turn. Yet I am convinced that had the remnant of that board of directors joined together to carry on the business as a private venture, there was amongst them sufficient ability, energy, and experience to have made the undertaking a success in the long run.

I think this is a favourable opportunity to digress a little from the high-road of my narrative in order to dwell upon the wide contrast between the present condition of the working class and that which existed in the early fifties, conditions which I clearly remember in my own experience. The great strides made in every point of life—working-hours, wages, education, quality of food and clothing—amount to little short of a revolution. To take the question of food, in my early boyhood my mother has often given me a shilling to purchase a four-pound loaf, and the change out of the shilling only amounted to twopence and occasionally a penny. Its quality was equivalent to loaves baked of the flour doled out to persons in receipt of outdoor relief, coarse enough to turn the stomachs of even the poorest.

Sugar was a luxury indulged in only on rare occasions ; farm labourers and other poorly paid workers frequently flavoured their cup of tea with a pinch of salt. Fresh meat was then a rare event on the table of the ordinary labourer. In clothing we fared no better ; our garments were coarse and uncomfortable. Portions of the workaday dress of a stonemason were composed of materials not found now even in the cheapest slop-shops ; yet these poor garments were frequently used for Sunday wear before they descended to workshop service.

The status of Labour has advanced with equal strides, for where now the employee may meet his employer on equal terms at the Arbitration or Conciliation Board, in my early years Labour had practically no rights and no recognition. The natural outcome of this neglected condition was degraded habits, brawling, and drunkenness ; for however widespread and deplorable the insobriety of the working class may still be, there is no comparison with the drinking habits of fifty years ago. As I have said in an earlier chapter, it was quite a common occurrence for the foreman of the works to be a licensed victualler also. As in the majority of cases the foreman acted as paymaster, it is not a matter of surprise that wages were paid over the bar of his public-house. We can scarcely be surprised that the men who received their pay thus readily believed the best way to propitiate the foreman and retain their employment was to spend freely on his liquors. Work did not cease then as it does now at midday on Saturday ; usually the time of leaving was very little earlier than on the other days of the week. This fact combined with the custom described above mostly resulted in the wage-earner's arriving home in a state of intoxication, before the housewife could manage to obtain any of his hard-earned money for the satisfaction of the domestic needs. Sometimes, indeed, an energetic wife would meet her husband outside the works ; but even then she had to accompany him to the public-house where the wages were handed over. Consequently, she too would have her glass, often with the gravest results to her sobriety and good name. When I look back upon the revolting sights witnessed in my boyhood, wherein both men and women took part, some of the worst of the cases happening almost under the garden wall of a bishop's palace, I look upon the present condition of my fellows with a lively sense of thankfulness. To maintain that the world is not moving upwards, notwithstanding temporary checks and drawbacks, is to ignore demonstrated facts.

This optimistic view must not be taken as indicating any lack of knowledge of or sympathy with the lamentable condition of the seething masses of poverty-stricken and neglected beings still to be found in our great centres of industry, and forming a constant menace to our common well-being. But practical Socialism has made vastly greater progress in this country than anywhere else in the world ; and in all probability Great Britain will continue to lead in the van. I believe it to be the duty of every civilised nation to regard all her citizens as a father looks after the children of his household, giving all, as far as possible, equal opportunities for betterment, and providing for an old age of peace and freedom from anxiety. The present system of treating all applicants for relief alike, differentiating in no way between the meritorious and the incurably idle, borders on criminal neglect. To the latter class the Poor Laws have no terrors or shame ; to the deserving they are cruel almost to death. I am far from believing that the wealthy desire that the poor shall pass their declining years herded together in barrack life. But if only they could be induced to share for a few days the lot of their poor brethren they would, I am sure, willingly make sacrifices to provide a more acceptable refuge for the wounded in the great battle of competition.

Another respect in which the amelioration of the lot of the working classes is conspicuous is in the means of transit. Upon this subject I must confine my comparisons to the metropolitan area. Though the tremendous growth of London has outpaced the capacities of the railways, still, those who remember the condition of affairs as recently as forty years ago have seen a wonderful improvement. When I first came to live permanently in London there was no Underground Railway, while bus fares were fifty and sometimes seventy per cent. higher than at present. The great system of tramways, binding the north, south, and east with the centre of the metropolis, and affording the working classes a cheap and comfortable mode of transit, was utterly unknown.

During the years I lived in Pimlico I worked for some time on a new police-station in Worship Street, which meant a walk of at least one and a quarter hours. As this was on paving-stones which soon tire the feet, I had to allow an additional ten to fifteen minutes for a rest before beginning work. Thus I was compelled to leave my house at 4.30 a.m. At night it was possible to obtain a bus ride part of the way, but the charges were quite beyond the means of a workman.

One of the greatest dangers to the health of the worker who has a long distance to walk to his work is the risk of getting wet in the early hours of the morning without an opportunity of changing his clothes until work is ended and home regained at night. Many times in my mason's life I have begun my day of ten or twelve hours in soaking garments, shivering with damp and misery. The Underground Railway has changed all that; and though I am not unmindful of the constant complaints made by workers against the London railway companies—often with much justice—still, I feel certain these complaints would be robbed of much of their bitterness had those who make them the experience of the tribulations we endured in my early London days.

The first section of the Underground Railway was not opened till 1863. In 1870 the line from Blackfriars to South Kensington was constructed. In 1871 it was extended to the Mansion House, and in 1875 to Bishopsgate Street. The circle was not completed till 1884. Innumerable extensions have been and are still being made in this mode of transit. To-day a working man can travel fifteen miles on the Metropolitan and District Railways for twopence, nineteen miles for fourpence, and twenty-eight miles for sixpence. In 1897 the two underground railways issued something like ten millions of cheap tickets, representing a total of twenty million passengers. These tremendous figures are, of course, exclusive of the working class passengers carried by the suburban trains of the great aboveground companies, which, roughly speaking, carry an additional twelve or thirteen millions at cheap rates in the twelve months.

Taking all means of transit into consideration, I am inclined to believe that the worker of to-day has secured an additional hour a day for himself as compared with the worker of 1870—a most substantial advantage, without reckoning the saving in pocket and the better preservation of his health.

Of all the larger railway companies which feed London the Great Eastern Railway is the most conspicuous in its relation to the working classes, not only because of the immense numbers—enough to make up a respectably sized provincial town—it daily brings into and carries away from London, but because it was the pioneer in the matter of issuing cheap tickets. Cheap tickets were first issued to workpeople on this line in 1871, but only in a very restricted fashion. To-day a workman can buy a packet of six return tickets for sixpence on Saturday or Monday for the ensuing week. In 1896 more than five and a half millions of these cheap tickets were issued, as compared with 902,556 in 1874. The same railway now issues another grade of cheap tickets for the use of clerks, shopmen, and warehousemen. These tickets cost half the ordinary return fare with a minimum of fourpence, and are available immediately after the departure of the last workmen's trains, arriving at the London termini not later than 8 a.m. In 1890 1,855,460 persons availed themselves of this concession ; in 1896 the number increased to 3,964,517— a marvellous increment !

As regards present-day problems I am entirely in favour of the municipalisation of tramways, and rejoice in the County Council's acquirement of this form of transit. If it were found practicable, I would equally support the State ownership of railways. At any rate, I consider that serious inquiry might be made into the possibility of the purchase by the State of the Metropolitan and District Railways. This suggestion cannot be termed extreme, and its comparatively limited responsibility is not calculated to alarm the apprehensions and excite the strenuous opposition of those averse to State ownership. Indeed, I conceive it to be one of the essentials for solving the vitally important question of over-crowding than that the State and the municipal authorities should join hands in controlling the transport of the vast army of workers who find employment in the heart of the Empire City.

# CHAPTER IV

## *MY POLITICAL CAREER BEGINS*

MY entry into the arena of political strife was gradual, but I think I may fairly reckon the year 1872 as the real starting-point in my political career. I have already said that in November of that year I finally ceased to work at my trade. As it happened to be winter-time, I did not hurry myself to obtain a fresh engagement, but preferred to take a week or two's rest in the cold, dark days of a London November. But his Satanic Majesty did not find a client in me; my holiday was spent in change of occupation rather than in idleness.

The success which had attended the movement for higher wages and shorter hours in the building trade had given an impetus to the Labour cause generally, more especially in the metropolitan district. Among the various branches of the industrial army encouraged to place their affairs on a better footing were the gas-stokers of the South of London Gas Works. They were agitating for a reduction of their working hours, and I was approached by one of their number, a man named Webster, for advice in the task of organising their forces; indeed, the stokers repeatedly invited me to place myself at the head of their movement. But this I refused to do, insisting that they would be better served by a man of their own craft who knew the ins and outs of the business, and who would thus be better qualified to understand their desires and give effect to them. At the same time, I assured their representatives that I should be glad at any critical moment to give them advice, should they apply for it. The movement made rapid progress for a time, but the men became excited, and showed signs of taking the bit between their teeth. Perceiving their state of mind, I repeatedly warned them against extreme measures, especially against anything in the nature of a strike, for their Union was almost destitute of funds and entirely lacking in experience of Labour disputes. Unfortunately, some of the wilder spirits managed to secure control of the organisation and at once rushed to extremes. The consequence was a partial strike, followed by a prosecution ; the strike completely collapsed in a few days, and what under abler guidance and more cautious procedure might have grown into a strong and permanent association, fell entirely to pieces.

Before Christmastide had fairly arrived the extraordinary number of five hundred summonses were issued against the gas-workers. The charge preferred was one of breach of contract under the Masters and Servants Act of 1866. But eventually they were indicted under the Conspiracy Laws, which rendered them liable to two years' imprisonment with hard labour.    The case came up for hearing at the Old Bailey before Mr. Justice Brett, afterwards Lord Esher.    The Gas Companies were represented by the present Lord Chancellor, then Mr. Hardinge Giffard, Q.C. ; but the men had neither the knowledge nor the means to draw up a defence for themselves. In their extremity they appealed to me, and although I protested that as they had disregarded my warnings I had washed my hands of the whole business, I could not turn a deaf ear to their entreaties and abandon them to their fate.    Besides, I saw clearly that the undisputed victory of a powerful corporation like the Gas Companies could not fail to have an extremely hurtful effect on the cause of industrial progress.    Accordingly, I hastily consulted a number of the members of the Parliamentary Committee of the Trades-Union Congress, and in the course of a few days a special Defence Committee was formed and funds were collected.    By this means we were able to retain the services of a well-known firm of solicitors, Messrs. Shaen and Roscoe, who in turn instructed Mr. Straight and Mr. Montague Williams to conduct the case for the defence.    After a long trial five of the defendants were sentenced to twelve months' imprisonment. This sentence instantaneously evoked a loud and widespread outcry against its injustice, and a movement quickly followed for the repeal of the iniquitous Masters and Servants Act and the abolition of the jurisdiction of the Conspiracy Laws over trade disputes. Concurrently with this agitation strenuous efforts were made, with the valuable aid of the London Trades Council, to raise money to pay the costs of the defence of the strikers and to maintain their families while they were in prison.

I well remember the Christmas of 1872. I had been ordered by the Defence Committee to visit the families of the imprisoned men and to report on their necessities. Some lived on the south side and some on the north of the Thames, so that I had not completed my task before night fell. I was then groping my way about West Ham and Barking Creek, and as the night was exceptionally dark I found great difficulty in steering straight in the badly lit and straggling district. At one point I discovered my way entirely barred by a high wall. Ignorant of my whereabouts, I climbed up some railings to reconnoitre, only to find that the railings had been freshly tarred, and my garments clung lovingly to them. With difficulty I managed at length to detach myself without leaving behind any essential portion of my clothes. I was in the midst of congratulating myself on this escape when my foot slipped and I found myself sprawling headlong in a pool of liquid mud. My appearance when I reached home late that night was enough to terrify the stoutest heart; plastered from head to foot with mud, my clothes torn and smeared with tar, I felt readier to turn scarecrow than enter a decent house.

The combined forces denouncing these outrageous sentences now represented so large an industrial army that we felt strong enough to bring pressure to bear upon the Government for a mitigation of the sentences. A petition was accordingly drawn up and presented to the Home Secretary, Mr. Henry Bruce, afterwards the first Lord Aberdare. By dint of strenuous agitation the Government was at length induced to release the prisoners at the end of four months. In the meantime the committee had provided for the prisoners' families and kept up their payments to the benevolent societies to which they belonged. I may here mention that twenty-two years later, during the sitting of the Royal Commission on the Aged Poor, over which Lord Aberdare presided, I happened to come across a letter received from him during the agitation of which I have been speaking. I was surprised to find, on reminding him of the matter, that he remembered every detail of the case as if it had occurred only the year before.

The law that persecutions ultimately end in a great accession of strength to the persecuted was not falsified in this business. The prosecution and imprisonment of the gas-stokers rendered a great service to the Labour cause by awakening the public conscience to the iniquity and injustice of these old laws. Mr. William Harcourt and Mr. Henry James in a debate in the House of Commons raised the whole question of the amendment of the criminal law, the Masters and Servants Act, and the law of conspiracy. The Parliamentary Committee of the Trades-Unions hastened to seize the opportunity, and by means of floods of literature and frequent public meetings and demonstrations in the industrial centres of the midland and northern counties assiduously educated public opinion. The success of this propaganda was witnessed at the General Election of 1874, when most of the candidates, on appealing to their constituencies, were compelled to promise support to the demand for the repeal of the obnoxious Acts. The result was the passing of two new Acts in 1875— the Workmen and Employers' Act and the Protection of Property Act. Much of the credit of these Acts is due to two of the most able Parliamentary lawyers of the day, Sir William Harcourt and Sir Henry James.

At the end of this agitation in 1873 I was appointed Secretary to the Labour Representation League. This body was established to promote the return of working men representatives to Parliament and to assist candidates favourable to the Labour cause. One of the first electoral contests in which I was officially concerned was on my own behalf. The League possessed an active and enthusiastic band of supporters in Greenwich, who were burning to try their strength at the London School Board Election of 1873, and insisted on running me as a candidate. So great was their eagerness that my name was entered before I had given my assent. However, I threw myself into the contest, and addressed meetings in all parts of the division, which, if my memory does not play me false, then stretched from Woolwich almost to the Crystal Palace. We had very little electioneering machinery to speak of, and not more than half a dozen helpers—all of them working men, who could ill afford to give time from their employment to aid us; but we managed to make a right good fight. Altogether, I do not think the contest cost more than thirty pounds, exclusive of small sums spent in travelling and other petty-cash expenditure. We had some splendid meetings, and I polled something like six thousand votes, failing to secure a seat on the Board by only a few hundred votes. It was a fortunate thing for me that I did not succeed, for it would have been impossible to have given the necessary time to the educational requirements of so vast, and in some parts so densely populated a district of the metropolis.

In connection with this contest an amusing incident occurred which may be worth the telling. I was on my way from Cannon Street to address a large open-air meeting at Woolwich in support of my candidature. In the same compartment sat a well-dressed man, who, after a few general remarks, introduced the subject of the School Board Election. He informed me that he understood the working man candidate was making considerable headway and, although a stranger to the district, had earned the good opinion of a large number of voters. He went on to ask me what I had heard of the candidate and whether I knew him. When I had answered the latter question in the affirmative, he wanted to know my opinion of him. Preserving a grave demeanour,

I assured my questioner that I had known the candidate for the greater part of his life, and though I had formed no extravagant opinion of his ability or fitness for this responsible position, I thought it a very proper thing for such a man to be on the School Board, and that the constituency would be doing the right thing to elect him. I added that I personally would do all in my power to secure his return, and I advised my friend to go to the open square in Woolwich where the candidate was to address a meeting, and where he would have an excellent opportunity of judging the man's suitability for himself. We parted at Woolwich Station; and as soon as my turn came to speak I spotted my man in the crowd, and was highly amused to see his bewildered expression as recognition of the speaker gradually dawned upon him. I believe he became an enthusiastic supporter of my candidature, and my failure at the poll was certainly not due to his abstention. For twenty-three years I made no further attempt to gain a seat on any School Board; but at the end of that time I became a candidate for the Cromer School Board and was elected without opposition.

The Labour Representation League, though not immediately successful in realising its aim, still, effected a good purpose by attracting public attention to the question of the rights of Labour to representation, as well as by inspiring the minds of working men with high and laudable aspirations. There had, of course, been attempts to return working men to Parliament before the formation of the League, but the General Election of 1874 was the first occasion on which such efforts were attended with success. Two Labour representatives were elected, Mr. Thomas Burt for Morpeth, and Mr. Alexander Macdonald for Stafford. With the former election the Labour Representation League had no direct connection. But in the Stafford contest the League was not only responsible for the introduction of Mr. Macdonald to the constituency, but also played a prominent part in securing his success at the poll. As Secretary of the League I was in direct communication with working men in many of the English and Welsh boroughs, and the Committee of the Stafford branch of the League asked me to go down to Stafford to submit to the local executive the names of several working men from whom a candidate should be elected. I was strongly urged to allow my own name to be included in the list; but this I refused to do.

Ultimately Mr. Macdonald was chosen, and threw himself into the contest with great vigour, receiving all through the struggle the constant support of the League. When he was at length returned triumphantly, public opinion outside the county assigned his success to the action of miners, he at that time being at the head of the National Union of Coal-miners, whereas, of course, there was not a miner in the borough. It was entirely an affair of working men of all trades, supported by a number of sturdy Liberals not of the working classes, but who saw in the contest a good prospect of winning a seat for the Liberal party.

The Stafford contest did not by any means engage the undivided attention of the League during that General Election. On the contrary, I was busily occupied in furthering the causes of other candidates in various parts of the country. Suddenly, at the eleventh hour, I found myself involved in an election on my own account. The constituency which had the honour to be the scene of my first attempt to enter Parliament was the ancient borough of High Wycombe, and my opponent was Colonel Carrington, who had held the seat in the Liberal interest since 1868. The attempt was foredoomed to failure, for I only arrived in the town about twenty-four hours before the time fixed for the poll. As a matter of fact, when I received the invitation I was electioneering three hundred miles from London, and the idea of contesting High Wycombe had never entered my mind. Nevertheless, I could not have had a more pleasant introduction to Parliamentary contests. The Wycombe people were a warm-hearted and open-handed community, they took the keenest interest in the election, and my active supporters were by no means confined to the wage-earning class; in reviewing the incident I am strongly inclined to believe that if I had had a week's notice of my candidature I should have captured the seat, notwithstanding the great and well-deserved influence of the Carringtons.

I have been engaged in many contests in many parts

of this country, but I never took part in a more thoroughly good-humoured one than that at High Wycombe; my opponent treated me with the utmost courtesy, which I was willing enough to reciprocate. The enthusiasm of the electors found an artistic vent in a profusion of ribbons, rosettes, and posies, and on the day of the election they adorned me with so many of these party emblems that I bore the appearance rather of a prize ox at Smithfield Show than an ardent politician. Our side canvassed every dwelling in the constituency, no slight task in so short a time; and we held some capital meetings in the Sunday schools belonging to Nonconformist places of worship; in some cases we even obtained the use of the chapel itself. A few months after my unsuccessful attempt I paid a second visit to High Wycombe, when, greatly to my surprise and gratification, the people presented me with a purse of twenty sovereigns, an illuminated address, and many other little tokens of sincere friendship  Even to this day I never travel on the Great Western line through Wycombe without recalling with a sense of pleasure how I set out on my forlorn hope from Maidenhead on a raw and foggy morning in the winter of 1874.

# CHAPTER V

## ON THE THRESHOLD OF PARLIAMENT

IN October of the next year the Trades-Union Congress, which met in Glasgow, elected me as their Parliamentary Secretary, a post I retained until ill-health compelled my resignation in September, 1890, after an unbroken membership of the Executive Committee for eighteen years. This new appointment did not interfere with my duties as Secretary of the Labour Representation League, which I continued to discharge until its dissolution. From that time I devoted my energies to the work of the Congress, though continuing to take an active part in political movements. There was much to occupy the attention of the leaders of Labour in those days. Continuous watchfulness was imperative to guard the administration of the Labour legislation of 1875. Each year revealed new wants and new opportunities ; each year increased the demands on our time and energies, as the records of the Congress will reveal.

My own duties were largely concerned with the dissemination of literature, preparing reports, recording the work which the Executive Committee had accomplished each year, and pointing out the objects yet to be attained. In addition, we endeavoured to extend our sphere of influence by holding public meetings in most of the great provincial towns. One of the first objects on which our efforts were centred was the passing of Mr. Plimsoll's Merchants' Shipping Bill, which became an Act in 1876. In its support we organised one of the largest deputations ever brought together in London, composed of delegates from all the trades-unions in Great Britain.

It was in 1876 that I first tried my hand at legislation. I drew up a Bill for the abolition of the property qualification attaching to membership of local governing authorities. My object was, of course, to enable working men to become members of town councils, vestries, and similiar bodies. Few people remember that at the time of which I speak legislation existed which effectually debarred wage-earners from these bodies. The qualification was dependent upon the number of wards constituting a town. In small towns it was a £15 assessment or £500 deposit in the bank, but in the case of towns with large populations the amount of the qualification was doubled. I entrusted this measure to Mr. Mundella, who introduced it in 1876, and two years later it was added to the Statute Book. As a result the only qualification necessary for election to local authorities at the present moment is that of being a ratepayer. So far as legal disqualifications are concerned, there is nothing to prevent the poorest ratepayer in the country becoming the chief magistrate of his town.

The next question to be tackled was that of the liability of employers to compensate their workpeople for injuries sustained in their employment. In 1876 Mr. Macdonald, to whose election to represent Stafford I have already alluded, introduced a measure dealing with this subject which the Executive Committee had drawn up. It was entitled the Compensation for Injuries Bill, and was read a second time, with the result that the Government appointed a Select Committee to deal with the whole question. By a curious concidence the witness who gave the strongest support to the workmen's demands was the very man—Mr. Justice Brett—who four years earlier had sentenced the poor gas-stokers to twelve months' imprisonment. Notwithstanding the unanswerable arguments of this learned judge in support of our case, we were unsuccessful in obtaining any legislation during the life of that Parliament, though the work done both inside and outside the House of Commons proved of the utmost value in educating public opinion on this important subject.

Two other questions occupied the attention of the Executive Committee during this year. The first concerned the lamentable loss of life and destruction of property arising from boiler explosions, due either to neglect or to the employment of unqualified men. We brought the matter before the House of Commons, and drafted a Bill, which in later years it was my privilege to introduce for the first time to Parliament. The other subject was the emendation of the Trades-

Unions Act of 1870, which experience had shown to require improvement in some important particulars. We induced the Government to bring in a short measure (which became law the same session) enabling unions to hold real property and removing other irritating little obstacles to the growth of the movement. These legislative triumphs were followed in 1877 and 1878 by the introduction of the Consolidating Act dealing with factory and workshop laws by the Home Secretary, Sir Richard Cross. By carefully framed amendments the Committee secured several important improvements in the Bill, which was a great advance on previous legislation, especially in the matter of reducing the hours of labour of women and children.

Before leaving this somewhat tedious but necessary account of the legislative labours of the Executive Committee, I must devote a little space to a very important and direct outcome of the Committee's action—*viz.*, the proposed codification of the criminal law of Great Britain.

The harsh treatment accorded by the law to the representatives of the Labour cause for so many years had plainly opened their eyes to the uncertainties as well as the severities of our criminal law, and under the advice and with the assistance of men like Mr. Frederic Harrison and Mr. Henry Crompton, the leaders of the trades-unions resolved to utilise the political power and influence behind them in endeavouring to obtain a clear and intelligible statement of the criminal law of the country and to purge the Statute Book of some of its antiquated and obsolete criminal enactments. Such a codification would, it was thought, remove some of the pitfalls and uncertainties from which the working man had suffered in the past in his endeavours to raise his condition to a higher level in the body politic. The subject was fully debated in every trade in the kingdom; innumerable resolutions in favour of the proposal were passed; and pamphlets advocating this legal reform were issued in large numbers by the Committee. Turning to more practical methods of attaining this object, the Committee at length approached Sir James FitzJames Stephen, the greatest living authority on the criminal law, and a strong sympathiser with the cause of legal reform. After several interviews and a good deal of correspondence, Sir James consented to the Committee's request that he would deliver a lecture on this important topic under the auspices of the Parliamentary Committee of the Trades-Union Congress. The lecture, which took place at the Society of Arts under the presidency of the Right Honourable Lord Coleridge in the enforced absence of Lord Chief Justice Cockburn, proved a great success, attracting much public attention, and giving cohesion to our labours and direction to our efforts. Arrangements had been made for a full report of the proceedings, and in returning a corrected proof of this report which I had sent him, Sir James wrote the following letter :—

"My dear Sir,—

"I return the copy of the lecture with the alteration of a few words. On looking over the report of what passed on that occasion I have been pleasantly reminded of what was a memorable meeting to me. I hope it may be of service to the public. I doubt whether any other class of persons in England would have shown half the interest in the subject which was shown by the members of the trades-unions. I can only say that if it is ever in my power to show particularly how deeply I am sensible of their kindness, it will give me pleasure to do so.

"Believe me,

"Ever faithfully yours,

(*Signed*) "J. F. Stephen.

"H. Broadhurst, Esq."

Shortly after this Lord Cairns, then Lord Chancellor, invited Sir James Stephen to draft a Criminal Code ; the draft Code was duly drawn up, and submitted to a Commission of legal experts at the instance of the Government. After passing safely through this ordeal, the Code was introduced to Parliament in the shape of a Bill. But there the matter ended so far as any further progress is concerned. In 1883 Sir James published in three volumes his "History of the Criminal Law of England," which, I believe, is considered by those capable of forming an opinion the most valuable publication on the subject ever compiled. In February of that year I was gratified to receive from him a copy of the work with the following inscription on the title-page : "Henry Broadhurst,

Esq., M.P. With the Author's kind regards and grateful recollections."

From this it will be gathered that for some years previous to 1883 I had been in frequent communication, both by letter and by personal interviews, with this distinguished lawyer. The recollection of my first interview with him I retained very vividly for many a long day. Not that he showed me the slightest lack of civility. On the contrary, he was most considerate and courteous; but his great stature and his hard, penetrating look filled me with awe till I felt like a pigmy in the presence of a giant. But this not altogether unnatural feeling soon wore off, giving place to a warm regard and admiration during our somewhat lengthened acquaintance, which I believe I might truthfully say ripened into friendship.

Another eminent man with whom I became acquainted at this time was Professor Toynbee. I first met him at the Trades-Union Congress of 1877, which he attended entirely unknown to those present. He asked my permission to occupy a seat where he might closely follow the proceedings. I saw him on many subsequent occasions, continuing to meet him at intervals until his death in 1883. I especially remember hearing him deliver two lectures in the Cambridge Hall, Newman Street, Oxford Street, in the course of which he criticised Henry George's book on Land Nationalisation with great zest and freedom. But the second of the lectures made too great demands upon his enfeebled frame, and I fancy he never fully rallied from the physical exhaustion its delivery entailed. He put into these lectures a vast amount of intense feeling, both passion and pathos, and his strength was inadequate to the immense mental strain to which it was subjected. I never met a man more absolutely in earnest, a soul so full of its theme. His intensity resembled the spirit which actuated the Hebrew prophets rather than the Laodicean attitude characteristic of the modern reformer.

The reform of the criminal law was by no means a solitary example of the way in which the efforts of the Parliamentary Committee were exerted, not merely for the working classes, but on behalf of the community at large. In fact, we fulfilled the functions of the Radical wing of the Liberal Party. Reform of the Jury Laws, amendment of the Summary Jurisdiction Act, reduction and restriction of legal costs and payments to the Clerks of the Peace, modifications of the Shipping and Patent Laws were all planks in our platform, which, affecting the working man chiefly, undoubtedly touched much wider interests. This phase of our work procured for us the co-operation of many men entirely unassociated with the Labour cause, who manifested a keen interest in the wider aspects of our work. Some even went so far in their appreciation as to offer liberal contributions to our funds. One of these distinguished admirers was the late Lord Bramwell, who, to say the least of it, was no thick-and-thin supporter of the combination of Labour against Capital. Yet he called on me one day to express his personal thanks to the Committee for our labours in the public interest, and handed me a cheque for £10 as a mark of his appreciation of what had already been accomplished, and as an earnest of his faith in the Committee's capacity to secure many of the objects on which we had set our minds. But to all such well-wishers I had but one reply—that while fully conscious of the high compliment paid to the Committee by the offer of money from men of such eminence, the Committee had made it an invariable rule to accept no contributions from other sources than the trades-unions. During the fifteen years of my secretaryship that rule was never broken, and I believe I am justified in saying that neither before nor since that period has money been accepted from the general public by the Committee in aid of its propaganda. This must not be taken to mean that our wealth was so abundant that we could afford to regard lightly any offers of financial help from the outside. On the contrary, the Committee had difficulty in obtaining sufficient contributions from the trades-unions to carry on its work at all, and the infrequence of our meetings was dictated by the meagreness of funds to meet the travelling expenses of the members of the Committee. In those days the holding of a committee meeting involved considerable expenditure. One or two members travelled from the West of England, others from Scotland, and not a few from the northern and midland counties of England. Their railway fares and the regulation allowance of twelve shillings and sixpence a day—not too liberal an allowance, considering the expensive nature of London lodgings—made a serious drain upon our exchequer. A meeting of the full Committee seldom cost less than forty pounds.

The next popular agitation in which I was interested had no direct connection with the cause of Labour. Between 1875 and 1880 occurred the devilish atrocities of the Unspeakable Turk in Bulgaria, and a voice was heard in the land calling for vengeance upon the murdering and ravishing crew let loose by the black-hearted tyrant at Constantinople. I became associated with the Eastern Question Association, of which the Duke of Westminster was President, but Mr. Gladstone supplied the motive power. I was present at the first gathering of a few people interested in the subject, out of which the association grew. Among these few were Mr. George Howard, the present Earl of Carlisle, and William Morris. I devoted all my spare time to the furtherance of the movement. I organised a Workmen's Committee to the Association and personally conducted its operations. On one occasion I succeeded in obtaining in less than a week some fifteen thousand signatures to a petition condemning the Bulgarian Atrocities, and urging the Government to take immediate action against the Turk, the signatories consisting almost wholly of office-bearers of the various branches of the trades-unions in the United Kingdom. This petition was conveyed to the House of Commons on top of a four-wheeled cab, and presented to Parliament by Mr. John Bright. To complete the task of preparing this petition I was compelled to employ relays of men night and day for nearly a week. A continuous stream of postmen staggering under sacks filled with letters containing signatures flowed into my offices. The whole affair was a remarkable illustration of what can be accomplished in a week by a well-organised body. Mr. James Rowlands, for some time Parliamentary representative for Finsbury, was my chief assistant in this great effort.

The first proceeding of the Eastern Question Association was to convene a national conference in St. James's Hall. The delegates were drawn from the accredited representatives of Liberal Associations and the Nonconformist Churches, as well as many distinguished individuals belonging to all denominations and all grades of Society. It is difficult to give any adequate idea of the excited state of the popular mind in London at that time, though the regrettable occurrences at Exeter Hall in March, 1900, and the uproar which followed upon the news of the relief of Ladysmith, may enable my readers faintly to realise the condition of affairs. Jingoism had grown rampant under the glamour of the Beaconsfield Government; the Great Macdermott was trumpeting the Jingo hymn, "We've got the ships, we've got the men, we've got the money, too!" nightly from the music-hall stage; and everywhere the fashionable club-lounger and the man in the street were possessed by the demon of brutality and openly glorified the Turkish Empire in their frenzied hatred of the Russian. In the midst of this uproar the Eastern Question Association resolved to hold their first public meeting in Exeter Hall. I had by this time attained some reputation as an organiser, and so the arrangements for this gathering were to a large degree entrusted to me. With the aid of a number of well-known and experienced working men I consented to organise this assembly, whose voice was to condemn the Eastern policy of the Government, and support Mr. Gladstone's efforts on behalf of the Balkan States.

It was a great undertaking, demanding much careful planning, but we spared no pains to make the gathering a thorough success. Admission was by ticket only, and these tickets were distributed among the political and trades-union associations of the metropolis. We had a large staff of stewards present at the entrances and in the hall itself, supported by a numerous body of police to regulate admission. It was arranged that the doors should be opened an hour before the time fixed for the commencement of the meeting. How to entertain the huge crowd during this interval was a problem that beset us, and we solved it by providing some music. One of my former mates at the mason's bench was organist at a West End place of worship, and I knew that his choir was composed entirely of working men and women. Having secured the consent of the proprietors of Exeter Hall to use the organ, I induced my friend and his choir to lend us their services. I then proposed to William

Morris that he should write an inspiriting song to be rendered as a prelude to the Chairman's address. The following is a copy of Morris's verses, which were sung to the air of " The hardy Norsemen's home of yore " :—

### WAKE, LONDON LADS!

#### BY WILLIAM MORRIS

Wake, London lads! wake, bold and free!
    Arise, and fall to work,
Lest England's glory come to be
    Bond-servant to the Turk!
Think of your sires! how oft and oft
    On freedom's field they bled,
When Cromwell's hand was raised aloft,
    And kings and scoundrels fled.

From out the dusk, from out the dark,
    Of old our fathers came,
Till lovely freedom's glimmering spark
    Broke forth a glorious flame:
And shall we now praise freedom's dearth
    And rob the years to come,
And quench upon a brother's hearth
    The fires we lit at home?

O happy England, if thine hand
    Should forge anew the chain,
The fetters of a tortured land,
    How were thy glory vain!
Our starving men, our women's tears,
    The graves of those we love,
Should buy us curses for all years,
    A weight we might not move.

Yea, through the fog of unjust war
    What thief on us might steal,
To rob us of the gifts of yore,
    The hope of England's weal?
The toilsome years have built and earned,
    Great men in hope have died;
Shall all the lesson be unlearned,
    The treasure scattered wide?

What! shall we crouch beneath the load,
    And call the labour sweet,
And, dumb and blind, go down the road
    Where shame abides our feet?
Wake, London lads! the hour draws nigh,
    The bright sun brings the day;
Cast off the shame, cast off the lie,
    And cast the Turk away!

A copy of this song was handed to every person entering the hall, and the Rev. G. M. Murphy, a Nonconformist minister of much note in South London, read it out verse by verse in the old Methodist fashion, after which the choir sang it twice to accustom the audience to the time and tune. The effect when the burning words were thundered forth by the vast assembly was electrifying. I believe this was the first occasion on which music and singing were introduced to while away the time of waiting at a political meeting; since then the practice has grown rapidly into favour, until it has now become practically universal.

A trusty band of sympathisers had been drawn up at the two entrances of the hall. They were all acquainted with the features of the leaders of the Jingo mob, and their experience of the London rough gave them an almost intuitive knowledge of the kind of individuals who would seek admission for the purpose of making a disturbance. Notwithstanding these precautions, many Jingo sympathisers managed to get in; but their efforts to interrupt the proceedings proved abortive in face of the overwhelming mass of sympathy with the objects of the meeting. I took my turn at one of the doors in order to see what was going on, and I marked one powerful young fellow, who I felt certain was bent on mischief, making a rush for the hall. Seizing him by the collar, I threw him to the floor, and a policeman—over six foot four, one of the finest specimens of humanity I have ever seen—caught him up by the extremities and carried him bodily out into the street. This action had a striking effect on the mob outside, and no further attempts at disturbance occurred. The result of the meeting was a great success in the way of enheartening the association and its supporters, and all who were present agreed that it marked a new epoch in the public attitude towards the Eastern Question.

A second venture in the same direction, however, proved abortive. It was proposed to hold a mass meeting in the Agricultural Hall, at which Mr. Gladstone was to be present and make a speech. After a considerable amount of time and money had been spent on the preparations and the most elaborate precautions against interruption and attack from the outside had been arranged, Mr. Gladstone was induced by his friends, who were alarmed at the uproar created by the announcement of the meeting, to advise the Workmen's Committee to abandon the idea. Widespread and acute disappointment was felt by the working classes all over London ; but our chagrin was lessened by the receipt of the following letter from Mr. Gladstone explaining his reasons for withdrawing his promise to speak :—

"73, HARLEY STREET,
"*February* 20*th*, 1878.

"DEAR SIR,—

"I have to acknowledge the receipt of the Resolution passed yesterday at a Meeting of the Workmen's Neutrality Committee ; and I cannot feel any surprise that you and your coadjutors, promoters of the Meeting at the Agricultural Hall, should, after the passing of such a Resolution by a body so trustworthy, have resolved to proceed no further with the plan at the present moment.

"In your end and aim, which, as I understand them, were to support the Government in all measures taken in the interest of peace and of freedom, I have received ample evidence that the great mass of the working men of this country are firmly united with you. Nor can I think that your preliminary labours have been thrown away, when I learn that they have supplied you with proof of the anxiety, not of thousands only, but of tens of thousands, without reference to domestic politics, to testify this feeling by their presence and attention at a calm and orderly assemblage.

"As to the means you had chosen, the question is a nice one, what amount of urgency in the actual state of public affairs is such as to justify you exposing masses of the people to the possible inconveniences which, in Meetings on a vast scale, it is often practicable for a few handfuls of persons, opposed to sober discussion, to bring about. The courage with which, upon a new change of circumstances, you have taken upon yourselves the responsibility of this choice appears to me to increase, and not to diminish, your claims to the confidence of the great bodies of working men on whose behalf you act.

      " I remain, dear Sir,

          " With sincere respect,

             " Faithfully yours,

                " W. E. GLADSTONE.

" MR. H. BROADHURST."

About the same time a large meeting of representative working men was summoned to consider the advisability of holding a demonstration in Hyde Park in support of Mr. Gladstone's position. Unfortunately, a division of opinion on the question of the day on which the demonstration should be held occurred, and, if I remember rightly, Mr. Bradlaugh threw all the weight of his great influence into the scale for holding it on a Sunday, with the result that when a vote was taken Sunday was decided upon by a majority of one. I immediately withdrew from the proceedings, for I felt certain that the trades-unions would not turn out on a Sunday, whereas if a working-day, especially Saturday, had been fixed upon, I knew there was every chance in favour of unanimous co-operation. Sunday meetings for trade or political purposes were then almost unknown in London. My misgivings were confirmed by the event, for the demonstration resulted in a fiasco, partly due to faulty organisation. Great confusion ensued, and Mr. Bradlaugh and others were personally assaulted.

As my readers will notice from the address on his letter, Mr. Gladstone was at this time living in Harley Street. The rampant Jingoism of London subjected him to every form of brutal and vulgar insult, and indeed for him, as for many other prominent opponents of the Turk, it was almost unsafe to go out unattended. In the provinces, however, quite another state of affairs obtained, and the tide of public opinion was over-whelmingly on Mr. Gladstone's side. One of the most enthusiastic and brilliant gatherings ever held in Birmingham assembled in Bingley Hall to support his policy. His arrival in the midland city resembled the return of a great and victorious warrior. It required all the skill of the renowned police force of Birmingham to maintain order in the streets among the thousands of people, almost delirious with excitement, who lined every street through which Mr. Gladstone passed to and from the meeting—in fact, I believe in all the main thoroughfares strong barriers were erected to keep back the admiring crowds. I shall never forget the scene in the hall itself. Three speeches delivered that night indelibly impressed themselves on my memory—the speeches of Mr. Gladstone, the late Dr. Dale, and Mr. (now Sir) Henry H. Fowler. I think I am right in saying that this was the first occasion on which Mr. Gladstone met the Methodist lawyer who was so soon after to become closely associated with him in the House of Commons.

The soul of the country was stirred to its very depths by the marvellous eloquence, the touching pathos, and the burning passion of the great Liberal leader's speeches. I shall not be guilty of exaggeration if I say that the Nonconformists of Great Britain to a man, ay, and a woman, had ranged themselves on his side. They looked upon him as the deliverer of nations, the inspired leader of peoples, as a giant of unsurpassed strength wrestling with and conquering the powers of injustice and oppression. His country was the world; mankind of every colour and creed were his brothers. Not once in many centuries does a nation possess a son who commands such universal and almost inexhaustible admiration as was lavished upon William Ewart Gladstone in those days. I have often felt that at this period many a man would have esteemed it an honour and counted it a happy martyrdom to die for the great Chieftain. In those days I saw much of Mr. Gladstone, frequently having to call at his house. Sometimes he would visit me at my offices at Charing Cross; and from that time until his retirement from the political arena no man gave me a firmer grip of the hand, a heartier greeting, or more encouraging words, than our beloved leader on every occasion when I came in contact with him. I took part in nearly every public event connected with the Eastern Question and the Bulgarian Atrocities, and this brought me into close contact with a class of people whom I otherwise should never have met.

Before I leave this account of my pre-Parliamentary days I must refer to one other event connected with trades-unionism, an event disastrous in many ways to men and to employers. It happened in this way. The masons employed on the new Law Courts asked for an increase of wages amounting to a penny an hour. The contractor responded by offering a halfpenny an hour by way of compromise. But this the men refused, and a prolonged strike resulted. There was nothing at all remarkable about that; but a new move was made by the employers, who, for the first time in the history of Labour in this country, took carefully planned and effective measures to import foreign labour on a large scale. France, Germany, and Italy were ransacked by the Employers' Association for masons, and men were even imported from New York. This procedure introduced a new feeling of bitterness into the eternal struggle between Capital and Labour. The difficulty of reasoning with the Italians and Germans, owing to linguistic differences, rendered picketing practically useless; with the French no trouble was experienced, for the all-sufficient reason that, so far as I remember, not a single Frenchman crossed the Channel to oppose us. But a large number of Italians and Germans, particularly the former, were brought over under the auspices of the Employers' Association. The only way to open up communications with these foreigners was to organise an efficient band of interpreters; and this, with our limited resources, proved by no means an easy task. We had to secure reliable men in sympathy with the cause of Labour, and having obtained them, one of the Committee had always to be on the spot to see that our desires were duly carried out, and that the interpreters were not " got at " by the employers.

The first batch of Germans came from North Prussia ; to meet these men and to get between them and the employers' agents without bringing ourselves within the meshes of the law demanded considerable skill, some daring readiness of resource, and above all a free expenditure of money. The Germans took kindly to the liberal supply of food, drink, and tobacco gratuitously provided by our Committee ; but I must do them the justice of saying that I never remember seeing one of them intoxicated. We entertained them as royally as our circumstances admitted, and they enjoyed our companionship, what was lacking in knowledge of the two languages being supplied by signs and tokens of good fellowship. We gave them the best views of London obtainable by drives through the streets and trips on the river ; we showed them all the sights by day, and the nights we passed in conviviality and the singing of our respective national songs, which seemed to be enjoyed with a zest in proportion to our inability to understand each other's language. When subsequently we " rounded up " our flock (to use a shepherd's metaphor) and carried them in triumph down the river for reshipment home, we had the satisfaction of feeling that at last we were relieved of one of the greatest burdens ever imposed upon us in strike or lock-out. The fraternal farewells were prolonged and hearty, and an onlooker might well have fancied he was witnessing the parting of beloved comrades-in-arms, rather than the farewells of men, strangers alike by nationality and tongue. We were greatly struck by the smartness and superior intelligence manifested by a number of the Teutons hailing from Berlin ; and it required no extraordinary acumen to see that if these men had stayed we should have found in them formidable competitors. Fortunately for us, these very men were the most willing, not to say anxious, to yield to our wishes and to return to their native land when they discovered the false pretences under which they had been lured to London.

The Italians were men of a very different type, by no means as intelligent or possessing the same physique, and we found them difficult to get hold of. In fact, our attempts to intercept them mostly fell through ; the greater number reached the works and continued in employment until the end of the dispute. But the most difficult of all to deal with were the New York men, though I do not think they were American-born. They were about the keenest men at a bargain I have ever come across. Their inexhaustible wants amazed us ; try as we would we could never satisfy them ; and after squeezing our organisation like a sponge, they deserted to the enemy and started work !

Of course these endeavours to wean the foreigners from the employers entailed an enormous cost on the Masons' Society. The provision of food and lodging for the immigrants, the expenditure on sight-seeing to keep them in good humour, added to the burden of supporting our own members out of work, had a devastating effect upon the financial resources of the Union. Resort was had to a general levy, with the usual chilling effect upon the weak and less enthusiastic members. During a part of the time those members of the Union who were in employment in London paid a shilling a day in addition to the usual contribution, and this brought their weekly payments to a total of seven shillings—a severe strain on the loyalty of the men. In addition, those members who had saved any money advanced it or some part of it (as the case might be) to the central office. By this means, coupled with the credit obtained from the licensed houses to which our lodges and relieving-stations were attached, we were able to discharge all our pressing liabilities, and none of the sick or infirm suffered any considerable inconvenience by reason of deferred payments. In those days it was a common practice in times of stress for the landlord of the public-house at which the branch of the Union was located, to allow payments due to him to stand over till it was convenient to discharge the account. He would even advance money out of his own pocket to the Union without charging interest, and without using the influence thus obtained to induce the men to drink more than their custom.

This was the last Labour struggle with which I was personally associated. At the time I was not working at my trade, and I took no part in the executive work of directing the strike. Indeed, I had been opposed to the policy which led up to it, being convinced that with a little more caution and discernment this disastrous struggle, like many of the wars history records, might have been avoided. But the majority decided otherwise : an open rupture with the employers followed ; and when that had occurred I felt it my duty to assist in strengthening a position undesirable in itself. But I only entered the arena when specially invited to do so by the Strike Committee. There was one occasion during the dispute when it might have been settled by arbitration. Mr. George Godwin, the editor of *The Builder*, offered his services through me as arbitrator or intermediary to bring the contending parties to a settlement. The offer was communicated to a specially convened meeting of delegates, but unfortunately was rejected by them. Two months later they deeply regretted their mistake ; but it was too late : the contest was fought out to the bitter end, to the loss of both sides and to the disorganisation of the masons and their Society. One consequence of this dispute and the importation of foreign labour was the revival of the question of an international committee representing the workers of all European countries and the United States. Although even now this matter has not advanced far, certain steps were taken which brought this desirable goal nearer in view.

# CHAPTER VI

## *WITHIN THE PRECINCTS*

DURING the period when the Eastern Question occupied men's minds to the detriment of all other questions, the subject of Labour representation in Parliament was not entirely forgotten. Although the League specially formed to promote the cause had practically ceased to exist, the seed sown by it was taking root. The Parliamentary borough of Stoke-upon-Trent had twice been contested in the interest of Labour without success. In 1878, in view of the approaching General Election, the Liberal and Labour Party of the borough met, and after consultation invited Mr. William Woodall, a local manufacturer, and myself to contest the constituency against the two sitting members, both Conservatives—Mr. Robert Heath, who owned large coal and iron works in the neighbourhood, and was very popular, and Dr. Kenealy, the defender of the Tichborne Claimant. From this time until the election I was naturally a frequent visitor to the Potteries towns included in borough of Stoke. I addressed many public meetings during the two years of my candidature, though none of them, curiously enough, were exclusively trades-union gatherings. I found the work-people of these towns the most intelligent and broadminded of any industrial communities I had hitherto met. Their one desire was that I should succeed, and to secure success they wisely recognised the necessity of obtaining the support of all classes. They were consequently content that I, though primarily a representative of Labour interests, should fight the election on general political principles. I had, when first approached on the subject, refused to listen to the proposal, feeling that my time was fully occupied by my duties as Secretary of the Parliamentary Committee, and the prospect of contesting a constituency consisting of some half a dozen towns, each of sufficient importance to possess its own local governing authorities, and representing large commercial interests, looked too serious to gain an easy consent from me. Besides, I considered my slender income totally inadequate to meet the demands of a House of Commons life. But the combined pressure of Liberal and Labour Parties in the constituency was too strong for me; my own feelings were overruled, and I accepted the invitation.

When the dissolution came at last, I became painfully alive to the difficult project to which I was pledged. With my colleague, Mr. Woodall, I at once embarked on a series of meetings which in about six weeks had totalled up for each of us between sixty and seventy separate gatherings. The chief towns were Tunstall, Longport, Burslem, Hanley,

Stoke, Fenton, and Longton, with districts like Etruria, Cobridge, and others thrown in. I found in my new occupation all the elements of excitement. We seldom finished our last meeting before midnight, and occasionally it was nearer one o'clock than twelve before I could end my day's round of oratory and sit down to dinner. As the next day's work began at 7.45 a.m. with a round of the polling-stations, my margin of sleep was narrow. But it was a fine contest: the whole borough seemed one continuous mass-meeting; and our gatherings were all enlivened by vocal and instrumental music. We had the advantage of an extremely popular townsman as the Chairman of one Election Committee, Mr. John Wash Peake; but this influence was counteracted by the local influence of Mr. Robert Heath, who employed a great body of men, and was a native of the district, retaining many characteristics of his earlier and less prosperous years. He had sat for the borough since 1874, and his ample means enabled him to bring into play to an almost unlimited extent all the legitimate machinery of electioneering. In those days it was legal to use hired vehicles to bring voters to the poll, which closed at four in the afternoon, and not at eight o'clock, as it now does.

When the eventful day arrived streams of conveyances of every shape and form filled the streets flaunting Mr. Heath's colours; while, unless my memory plays me false, neither my colleague nor myself had a single vehicle at our disposal except that in which we drove through the different towns.

During the contest Dr. Kenealy had practically dropped out of sight. Certainly no notice was taken of his candidature, and no reference was made to him from our platforms. The Heath interest was directed mainly against myself as a stranger and a Labour candidate, and for a time I thought myself doomed to failure. However, the result proved that the enthusiasm manifested at our meetings, and the demonstrations of popular favour in the streets, were genuine expressions of the feelings which animated the voters, for both Liberal candidates were returned with a combined majority of over ten thousand votes.

The wild scene of the election will never be effaced from my memory. Every factory and workshop was closed. The streets were lined with enthusiastic crowds from early morning till late night. A procession of Pottery girls, dressed in their best and decorated with the Liberal colours, paraded the streets, encouraging the voters to support the Liberal cause, and doing much to stimulate the energy of those over-confident people who are often the cause of the loss of an election. On the day after the poll the two Members were called upon to drive through the whole length of the Potteries district. In many cases work had not been resumed, and the whole country-side seemed to have given itself up to the celebration of the great victory. In Longton market-place enthusiastic supporters seized me and carried me round and round the square shoulder high, to the no small risk of my limbs, my niece watching the procession with mingled amusement and terror from a coign of vantage near the Town Hall. It is not too much to say that on this occasion the wives of the voters and the working girls engaged in the Potteries showed a power and influence over the fortunes of the election which I have never since witnessed in the same degree, either in my own contests or in the great number of elections in which I have taken part all over Great Britain.

As an example of this influence let me mention an incident that occurred in the midst of the campaign preceding the election. My colleague, Mr. Woodall, had previously taken an active part in School Board work in Burslem. The Tories fastened upon this fact to make a determined attack upon the policy of popular education. They endeavoured to incite the worst passions of the working classes against him by accusing him of causing unnecessary and extravagant expenditure to the ratepayers. These efforts were mainly concentrated on Longport, whose walls were plastered with posters making these accusations in the biggest type obtainable. Speaking at a large midday meeting in the town, I took up the cudgels on Mr. Woodall's behalf, claiming that if there was one thing more than another that entitled him to their suffrages it was this very fact that he had insisted upon the best class of instruction being imparted by the most competent teachers to their boys and girls. I enlarged on the value of education, pointing out that no class of society held a monopoly

of brains, and that the children of the poorest among
them, if they had equal opportunities with the rich,
would be as receptive as the boys and girls of the
wealthiest in the land. Immediately in front of me
sat an exceptionally robust and well-built woman,
clasping to her bared breast an infant, who appeared
to be only a few months old, but showed plain signs
of having inherited the splendid physique of his mother.
These two I took as illustrations of my argument,
and immediately mother and child became the cynosure
of every eye. I referred in complimentary terms to
the fine proportions of the pair, asking my critics
whether that child, given the same opportunities of
training, would not equal in intellectual attainments
any child born of wealthy parents. If means and
opportunities were provided to develop his faculties,
I maintained that for aught we knew the infant might
in the future be a great soldier, sailor, poet, or statesman.
As I proceeded in this impassioned strain I saw the
mother clasping her child tighter and tighter to her
bosom, and when the meeting was over she came up
and gave me a slap on the shoulder that nearly sent
me sprawling on my face, assuring me with an emphatic
adjective not now commonly used in polite society
that if her man didn't vote straight for Woodall and
Broadhurst she would give him the handsomest licking
he had ever had in his life. This declaration, delivered
in the loudest of tones, secured a far more enthusiastic
ovation than my eloquence had aroused. My experience of her influence exhibited in the touch upon

my shoulder convinced me that in the whole of the constituency we should not find a sturdier supporter than " her man."

During the contest I put up at a commercial hotel, the freehold property of the landlord who presided over its hospitable board. Curiously enough, it was the rendezvous of the leading Conservatives who were working in Mr. Heath's favour; yet I have never been treated better or enjoyed greater privacy than during my four weeks' residence at this house. I became fast friends with mine host, and since his death his widow has remained a friend of my family circle, though she has never abated one jot or tittle of her sturdy adhesion to the Conservative Party.

The contest over, I hastened back to my secretarial duties and devoted myself assiduously for a couple of weeks to making up for lost time. The House of Commons was no strange place to me; to many of the members I had been personally known for several years. I had constantly led deputations to the leading politicians on both sides of the House, and on many occasions friendly consultations had taken place between prominent Front Bench men and myself as the representative of the trades-unions. With the officials in and about the precincts I was also pretty intimately acquainted, as in my position of Secretary to the Parliamentary Committee I had enjoyed the *entrée* of the Lobby from 1873. Consequently, in many instances I needed no formal introduction to the members of the House; on the contrary, I was enabled to perform that pleasing duty to my colleague, who was making his first entry, and whose knowledge of his fellow-members was extremely limited.

The result of the General Election was an unmistakable justification of the foreign policy advocated by Mr. Gladstone while in Opposition, and a material strengthening of the work of the Eastern Question Association. The theatrical character of Lord Beaconsfield's return from Berlin and other incidents of the Jingo campaign quickly faded from memory; Liberalism was in the ascendant, and Mr. Gladstone sat for the second time on the Treasury Bench as Prime Minister of Great Britain and Ireland.

During the preceding five or six years I had thought my work sufficiently heavy and exhausting, and had imagined that it would be next to impossible to add to my undertakings and engagements. This proved to be a singular delusion, for in the years that followed my entry to the House my labours may be said to have been doubled and my opportunities for rest proportionately lessened. Nothing but my iron constitution and enthusiasm for the work could have sustained me in this trying period.

I found myself face to face with an entirely new situation, imposing new responsibilities and requiring larger means. During my married life, which commenced at nineteen years of age, I had always practised a fair measure of frugality; but a seat in Parliament and a salary of £150, out of which I had to pay for any clerical assistance I required, seemed utterly incongruous. But the situation had to be met, and I met it by maintaining the same habits at home and abroad as before my election, with the exception of such changes as were unavoidable when Parliament was sitting. In the matter of dress I followed the same line of conduct. For years past all my clothes had been made at home by my wife, and for several years of my Parliamentary life my wife remained my only tailor—a circumstance which I fancy is unique in the history of the English Parliament. But with all these economies my financial position was far from comfortable.

Having gained the right to sit in the House, with Mr. Macdonald and Mr. Burt as my Labour colleagues, I felt, as Secretary of the Parliamentary Committee, I ought to take advantage of the new Parliament and the presence of the Liberal Party on the Speaker's right hand to do something definite and substantial at an early stage on behalf of the workers of the United Kingdom. The result of the pressure I was able to apply was that the Government decided to bring in a Bill dealing with employers' liability to compensate workmen for injuries received in their service. The Bill was put into the charge of the President of the Local Government Board, Mr. Dodson, afterwards Lord Monk Bretton, and it was down for the second reading in the month of June. On the night preceding the debate I was summoned to Oxford to what proved to be the death-bed of my mother, and I did not reach home again until the early hours of the next morning. I was engaged all the day with some trades-union deputations; and thus it was under circumstances of great depression and physical exhaustion that I rose to make my maiden speech before the Mother of Parliaments—an ordeal that must be endured before its hateful nature can be fully realised. Some there are who can undergo this searching trial without flinching, but not many. As I rose from my seat a strange feeling of isolation crept over me, and when I had uttered the words " Mr. Speaker," I felt as if the floor were opening to swallow me, and I almost wished my feeling would come true. But after a few minutes I overcame my nervousness and let myself go as freely as if I were addressing a gathering of labourers or artisans. I spoke for about forty minutes, and immediately I sat down Mr. Gladstone came to me, and with hearty congratulations and a warm shake of the hand bade me welcome to the House. His example was followed by Sir John Holker, the late Attorney-General in Disraeli's Ministry, and by some other members. I experienced a vast feeling of relief at having made my bow to that critical assembly. Physically and mentally, it was the most unfortunate night of the whole year that I could have been called upon to make my maiden effort; but circumstances dictated the occasion, and I had to meet it as best I could. From that moment my fear of the House was dispelled, and when occasion arose I seldom hesitated to impose myself on its attention.

Although the Employers' Liability Bill was in the care

of Mr. Dodson, and owed much to his able assistance in the various stages of its progress through Parliament, yet the technical part of the work fell entirely to the share of Sir Henry James, the Attorney-General, and Sir Farrer Herschell, the Solicitor-General. The Committee stage of the Bill was fought with great persistency by some of the large employers, assisted by able legal members of the House. Despite the strenuous opposition the Bill became law in January, 1881. This was a great triumph for the trades-unions, which for fourteen years had persistently agitated for the recognition of the principle, and had undergone the searching ordeal of the Select Committee of 1876-7. We were not fully satisfied with the Act, which possessed some glaring defects, as we had not failed to point out during its passage through Parliament. For example, it did not put an end to the doctrine of "Common Employment," which, even after twenty years more of ceaseless effort, still flourishes to a certain extent. At the same time, we fully recognised that it established a number of great and broad principles upon which a further superstructure could be erected in subsequent years.

I did not feel disposed to rest content with this legislative triumph, but turned my attention to a fruitful cause of dissatisfaction among my constituents. At that time all Quarter Sessions business relating to the townships of the Potteries had to be transacted at the county town of Stafford, nearly twenty miles distant. When the facts of the case had been brought before me, I approached the Home Secretary with the request that Hanley, the central town of the Potteries district, might be constituted a Quarter Sessions town. This concession obtained, I further urged that Mr. Brinley, who belonged to an old family in the neighbourhood and practised on that circuit, should be appointed the first Recorder. In this I was also successful; and the first meeting of the Quarter Sessions was inaugurated with much ceremony. I took great pleasure in my success in this direction, which entirely disproved the theory that a Labour representative could be of no service to the general and commercial interests of his constituency, and would confine his attention to voicing the desires of the working classes only.

During that Parliament many enactments affecting the Labour cause were successfully carried. The first was the Merchant Seamen's Payment of Wages Act, which abolished the penalty of imprisonment for breach of contract in the case of seamen, and substituted for the old system of Advance Notes, which it made illegal instruments, a system of Allotment Notes, enabling sailors to make remittances to their relatives and to open accounts at the Post Office Savings Bank; shipowners were also compelled to pay all wages within two days of a ship's arrival in port. Another beneficial section made the granting of licences to seamen's lodging-houses conditional on the character of the landlord. A second Act also related to the mercantile marine, and promoted the safety of the sailor by some stringent regulations concerning the transport of grain cargoes, which must now be carried in bags or longitudinal bulkheads.

To give a rough notion of the multifarious character of the work of the Parliamentary Committee of the Trades-Unions, I will enumerate a few of the matters which it fell to my lot as secretary at this time to deal with.

Public attention was called to the blood-poisoning in the wool-sorting trade, and the Government was induced to make inquiries.

Complaints reached the Committee that the contents of some books in use in National Schools were prejudicial to the cause of trade combination, so an interview was arranged with Archbishop Tait, then Primate of England, with the result that the offending books were withdrawn from circulation. Although the deputation which waited upon his Grace the Archbishop at Lambeth Palace on this occasion was composed of men who were far from being noted for their Anglican proclivities, yet Archbishop Tait received them with the remarkable graciousness for which he was justly celebrated. No deputation could have received a warmer welcome, obtained a more patient hearing, or experienced a readier desire to meet its request. The correspondence between his Grace and myself which led up to the interview was a fitting prelude to so pleasurable an interchange of courtesies and so satisfactory a result.

Our attention had often been called to the

frequency of fatal accidents caused by entrusting steam-engines and boilers to unqualified and ill-paid men. Accordingly, the Committee introduced a Bill requiring those in charge of such machinery to hold certificates of competency in all cases where they had been employed on such work for less than two years. Although several Bills dealing with boiler explosions have since been passed, the root question—*viz.*, the competency of the men in charge—has not yet been settled by the legislature. Probably the Workmen's Compensation Act of 1897 will induce many employers to exercise greater caution in the selection of men for this important work.

A subject entirely different in character which took up much of the Committee's time was the "oversizing" of cotton goods in Lancashire. It was alleged that this practice was bringing British goods into great disrepute in the Eastern markets, and that the humidity of the weaving-sheds necessary to incorporate the foreign substance into the cotton goods inflicted serious and often permanent injury to the health of the workers. After innumerable memorials, public meetings, resolutions, and deputations to the Government, the Home Office was induced to send a medical officer from the Local Government Board, together with an experienced factory inspector, to inquire into the matter, with the result that the complaints of the workers were admitted to be substantially correct. A committee of experts was appointed to investigate the whole subject; but a sudden change of Government prevented immediate legislation, and seven or eight years elapsed before effect could be given to the reforms we suggested.

In 1883 Mr. Chamberlain, as President of the Board of Trade, introduced a Bill relating to deep sea fishing. Among other regulations it contained a clause requiring skippers engaged in the deep sea fisheries to hold a Board of Trade certificate, and also to keep a log of accidents and loss of life at sea, as well as a record of punishments, payment of wages, and other matters pertaining to the interests of the man before the mast. Another beneficial clause provided that Board of Trade officers should act at each port *in loco parentis* for boys without parents or proper guardians who wished to become apprentices on fishing-boats. The Parliamentary Committee exerted all its influence to back up this measure affecting a large class of workers, and it became law. I did my utmost to secure the insertion of a clause making it compulsory for a first mate to hold a certificate; but in this I failed, although this useful addition to the law was legalised some years later.

The reform of the Patent Laws and the laws relating to imprisonment for debt had long commanded the attention of the Committee. Both questions were taken up by Mr. Chamberlain, and Bills were brought in to deal with them in the session of 1883. This was the first session in which a Grand Committee of the House of Commons on Trade and Law was constituted. I was appointed a member of this Committee. Close application and unflagging attention to the business in hand were absolutely essential to follow these two measures intelligently ; and when it is remembered that in those days the House frequently sat till three or even four o'clock in the morning, it will be understood that my first experience of Grand Committee work was sufficiently trying.   Eventually, by distributing the aggregate cost of taking out a patent over a number of years, the Patent Laws were rendered much less prejudicial to the needy inventor ; while in the matter of the Bankruptcy Law I was enabled to carry an amendment by which, in the case of the bankruptcy of an employer, a working man became entitled to the same compensation as a clerk—*viz.*, four months' wages. The same amending measure raised the value of household goods, tools, etc., exempt from seizure for debt from £10 to £20.   I also took a share in passing a Bill introduced by Mr. Samuel Morley to prohibit the payment of wages in public-houses.   It fell to my lot to pilot this measure in its later stages through the House.

# CHAPTER VII

## A CHAPTER OF REFORMS

NOT long after these events I was called upon to play the *rôle*, sufficiently common in these days, of Special Commissioner. This was not in the capacity of a journalist, but in the interests and at the direction of the Parliamentary Committee. For seven years incessant complaints had reached the Committee from the " Black Country " concerning the condition of the men and women employed in the nail-, nut-, bolt-, and chain-making industries. After careful investigation of the whole question and frequent consultations with representatives of these trades, the Committee decided to draw up a Bill prohibiting the employment in the forges of girls under fourteen years of age. This Bill secured the first place on a Wednesday afternoon in May, 1883 ; and that I might be strengthened in my advocacy of the measure by first-hand information, I was instructed to make a personal investigation. In this work I was accompanied by a workman, the acting-secretary of a local trades-union, and also by a journalist, whom at my suggestion the editor of *The Daily News* deputed to write up the subject. Great care was necessary to keep the news of our visit from leaking out in advance, because it was notorious that the hired children in the little smithies mysteriously and rapidly disappeared whenever it was rumoured that an inspector or an inquisitive stranger was approaching.

We started on our tour of inspection from Birmingham early in the morning, and by this means were able to cover a large part of the district before any warning of our presence could be communicated to the workshops. What we saw amply justified the proposals contained in the Committee's Bill. In many cases we found children of both sexes and of ages ranging from tender years to fifteen or sixteen, scantily clothed and badly fed, working together in one tiny smithy about the size of an ordinary cottage wash-house. They were barely instructed in the first elements of education; while the pittance they earned bore not the remotest proportion to the sacrifice thus offered at the altar of cheap goods.

I visited one poor little wisp of a mother between six and seven on a raw February night. She was making what seemed to me an endless chain, for as fast as she had finished one piece of work, another confronted her. I was almost amazed that she did not use the last embers of her vitality to put an end to an existence as hopeless and confined as that of any convict condemned to life imprisonment at Portland. Yet all her week of ceaseless labour brought her was seven shillings, from which must be deducted cost of firing, charge for use of tools, and a weekly payment to the woman who took care of her last baby during the working-hours. These deductions left a remuneration of no more than three shillings and sixpence for six days' strenuous labour of a character only fitted for muscular men.

Elsewhere I found a bevy of girls engaged on making spikes some eight inches long out of bar-iron nearly an inch in diameter. The proprietor of this shop scowled savagely when I entered, and to my civil inquiry whether he did not think this rather heavy work for young girls, gruffly answered with a negative emphasised by an oath. Now, to cut bar-iron of this thickness into lengths requires the expenditure of considerable force. In the first place, one has to up-set it sufficiently to form a head, and then to hammer the other end to a point. For this purpose the girls were required not only to wield a heavy hammer with one hand whilst manipulating the tongs in the other, but also to employ the right foot on a treadle, which set in motion an instrument called an " Oliver." This machine consisted of a treadle-lever which actuated a heavy hammer in addition to the one wielded by the right hand ; in other words, the " Oliver " supplied the place of a second right hand, the only difference between it and the human " striker " being that it required no wages. In my opinion, this duplication of physical force would have entailed too great a strain on a sturdy man, let alone a young girl of fourteen. The employer asseverated that the work was perfectly easy, and that I was deceived by appearances, ending in an invitation to try for myself. Laying my pipe on a bench and doffing my coat, I seized the tongs, gripped the bar-iron, blew the bellows, and heated the metal. Then carrying the red-hot bar to the anvil, I wielded the hammer with all my force until I had formed the point of the bolt, avoiding the use of the "Oliver," which needed long practice to manipulate properly. When I had finished the bolt I threw it into a corner, exclaiming : "There you are! I have done what you wanted, and I should not like to stand ten hours a day at the work even with the aid of the 'Oliver.'" The man stared in disappointed amazement, and could only mutter, "Ay, maister, thee's done that work afore to-dee !"

What the cunning rascal expected to see, and what would have inevitably happened to an unpractised person, was this. To the onlooker it appears a simple matter to take a piece of iron out of the forge, lay it on the anvil, and hammer it into shape. But, as a matter of fact, if the iron is not kept exactly level upon the anvil in the place where the hammer strikes it, nothing will prevent its flying out of the grip of the tongs, and probably inflicting a serious wound upon the striker's face. But the reader will remember that I had worked for a considerable time in a blacksmith's shop during my youth; so the old instinct came back at a moment's notice, and I recalled without effort the one essential precaution, and thus was able to finish the job without injury and without gratifying the genial proprietor's desire.

Before the date of the second reading of the Bill, which I was appointed to move, I provided myself with a miniature model of this " Oliver," fashioned of wood. By holding it in my left hand and manipulating the lever with the fingers of my right hand I could demonstrate the principles on which the machine worked. When the day arrived I carried this model into the House of Commons before the Speaker had taken the chair, and placed it beneath the seat I intended to speak from. During my speech, when I arrived at the point where I was protesting in the strongest terms against the use of the " Oliver " by women, and especially by young girls, I produced the model from beneath the bench and exhibited its working to the amused and startled House, carefully explaining to the Speaker that the machine was perfectly harmless and would not on any account " go off," an assurance not unnecessary in those days of dynamite explosions and Fenian conspiracies.

This, I believe, was the first occasion on which the Mother of Parliaments had received an object-lesson. Among many other journalistic comments, Mr. Punch took the opportunity of dealing divertingly with the matter. I venture to reproduce the comments from the diary of " Toby, M.P. " (*Punch*, May 19th, 1883).

" *Wednesday.*—' I knew what would happen, when I let Playfair bring in those pots of Oleo-Margarine,' the Speaker said this evening, as Lady Brand gave us a cup of tea. ' "They're only little ones," Playfair urged. "Yes," I said; "that's true enough. If they were the size of a sponge-bath, of course you wouldn't bring them in." But I weakly yielded; and now here's Broadhurst brought in a nail-making machine, which he calls an Oliver, and works away to illustrate the motion for the second reading of a Bill to amend the Workshops Act.'

"'Couldn't you have got Winn to have given him a Rowland for his Oliver?' I said, seeing the Speaker was really distressed.

"'No,' he answered sadly; 'I Winn-a do. The thing must be met by an Order of the House. It'll grow till place becomes sort of workshop, and we'll have to build a shed on the site of the old Law Courts to keep the materials for illustrating speeches. We shall have Labouchere next bringing in a cobbler's stall and showing how they make boots in Northampton, whilst he pleads the right of the constituency to have two representatives.'

"House a little startled when Broadhurst first produced his machinery. Thought it might have something to do with explosions. But only made nails. Most interesting process. You put a piece of iron-piping in at one end, turn a handle, and ten-penny nails flow in abundance from other end.

"'Dear me,' said Bobby Spencer, who over the ring-fence of his collar watched process with childish delight. (Subsequently, in cloak-room, tried his hand with machine and made a few nails for private circulation only). ' Really charming ; but should have thought it would have brought down the price of nails. Tenpence apiece seems a good deal, don't you know.'

" Thing sure to spread. Daresay, in moving Agricultural Holdings Bill to-morrow night, Dodson will have a collection of spades, mowing machines, steam-ploughs, and a few drain-pipes. Interesting in its way. Makes House a sort of superior Polytechnic ; but likely to become inconvenient as custom grows. Speaker's quite right. He ought to have put down his foot on Playfair's pots.

" *Business done.*—Miscellaneous. Threw out Broad-hurst's Bill, Oliver and all, by swinging majority."

One of the chief factors in procuring this defeat was the action of the Women's Rights people. My main object was to prevent by legislation the employment of girls under fourteen in these workshops. As their parents could not afford to support them until that age, the girls would be sent out as domestic servants, or in some other capacity less degrading and more profitable than bolt-making. But the fine ladies who desired political enfranchisement were up in arms on behalf of the rights of women to become bond-slaves before they reached maturity. So for a time these people succeeded in binding the chains of their unsexed sisters still tighter ; but it affords me some measure of consolation to remember that more than ten years afterwards the representatives of the bolt-makers came to the Parliamentary Committee appealing for assistance in the amelioration of the lot of the women employees, and that when asked by me what would be the most effective manner of remedying their lot, they unanimously declared that no proposal submitted to them would accomplish their object so successfully as the Bill I had introduced in 1883.

In the same session Sir Henry James brought forward his Corrupt and Illegal Practices Bill, and when the House went into Committee upon it I moved an instruction that the official expenses of the Returning Officer should be charged to the local rates and not to the candidates. I divided the House, but was beaten by a two to one majority. This result was due to Mr. Gladstone, who pointed out that the insertion of such a clause would be highly inconvenient ; but he went on to promise that if I introduced a separate Bill embodying such a clause he would give it his support, and he believed it would receive a large measure of favour in the House. Acting on this hint, I subsequently introduced a Bill on these lines, but the luck of the ballot was against it, and I could not secure an evening for its consideration. Later on, at his request, I handed over the charge of the measure to Mr. Sydney Buxton, who hitherto has met no better fortune than I did.

At this time my work began to tell severely upon me. My duties both in the office of the Parliamentary Committee and in the House itself increased in magnitude almost daily. The office was a place of call for many foreign students of the economic and political conditions of Great Britain, Americans being the most frequent visitors. This demanded the expenditure of much time, the one thing I could least afford to spare, and I was confronted with the impossibility of keeping the routine work of the office up to date. Accordingly, I hired a clerk from a neighbouring establishment. He was a pensioner from a Government office, possessing great ability, a thorough knowledge of French, and was, in fact, a scholar and gentleman. Unfortunately, he had one fault which nullified all his good qualities—he was too fond of the bottle ! Many a time did I supply the miserable creature with clothes and food, but as often the former rapidly disappeared to the nearest pawnshop to supply the wherewithal of drink. At last he was overcome by a forgetfulness of the rights of property, a lapse from the paths of rectitude which placed me in a most difficult position. I gave him notice to leave; but his earnest pleading and his oath of reformation broke down my determination, and I allowed him to remain. But a repetition of the fault finally severed our association.

By great good fortune I had introduced to me a young man who remained with me until his deeply lamented death in 1893. For the first time in my life I experienced the benefit of having an assistant in whom I could repose absolute confidence, and on whose work I could rely. He was a strange young man, utterly unlike the average youth. Possessing considerably more means than I did, he was unaffected by the meagre salary I could afford to pay. His one object in life was to serve me to the best of his ability, and I can truthfully say that no man ever received more thorough devotion than he displayed to me. When he first came to me he had had no experience of office work and was extremely retiring and shy. He had, however, learnt shorthand, and soon became the fastest and most accurate stenographer I have ever dictated to. He could also readily read and write in the French language, and after a time, though in a less degree, in German. His attachment to me became so great that soon he filled the place of a devoted son rather than a hired secretary. Not only was his assistance a great relief to myself, but it was a decided advantage to the trades-unions of the country. My salary had been advanced to £150 in 1881, and ultimately to £200, but out of this I had to pay for such office help as I required, so that to obtain the services of one so qualified as Mr. Maxwell in return for a merely nominal remuneration was an extraordinary piece of good fortune. His knowledge of French was particularly useful, and saved the Committee and myself much time and money. It often happened that callers at the office had but a scanty knowledge of English, but nearly all could speak French. Hence Mr. Maxwell's presence made communication easy.

While we were making more or less headway in Parliament with the measures I have mentioned, the cause of Labour was not at a standstill in the great world outside St. Stephen's. The highly successful meetings of an International Trades-Union Congress held in Paris in October, 1883, gave ample evidence of the healthy state of the movement. Delegates from Unions in France, Italy, Spain, and Germany were present, and the British trades were fairly represented. The Parliamentary Committee sent Mr. Bailey, its Chairman, Mr. Burnett, its Treasurer, and myself; and other British delegates were present. The Standing Orders regulating the procedure of this gathering were, generally speaking, modelled upon those of the British Trades Congresses.

It fell to my lot to conduct most of the correspondence between the English delegates and our French hosts, and I took care to stipulate that as far as possible Sunday meetings should be avoided. There was, it is true, a reception held on Sunday night; but attendance was optional, and some of us never went near it. Several evenings were devoted to large public meetings in the industrial quarters of Paris, and on every occasion these were crowded with an enthusiastic audience. Unfortunately, their success was somewhat marred by the interruptions of the extreme wing of the Labour Party in the city, whose leaders were chiefly of Italian birth and imbued with Anarchist ideals. Scenes of the utmost confusion frequently occurred, the frenzied shouts and utter indifference to the calls of the Chair being a revelation to the phlegmatic British workman.

Some of these scenes were highly amusing. I remember in particular one Italian who presented himself at two successive meetings, and mounting the platform, tore open his shirt and vest. Pointing to the wounds on his breast received in fighting the battles of Liberty, he declaimed at the top of his voice against capitalists and *bourgeoisie* alike. This performance, though highly dramatic, was unwelcome to the greater part of the audience, who had assembled to hear about the progress of Labour in different parts of the world.

The only delegate who was master of two languages was an Italian workman who spoke French moderately well. The speeches of the rest had to be translated, which in some cases was an advantage, but in others the contrary. This made the proceedings slow, and the frequent interruptions often prevented the full number of speeches being delivered. Nevertheless, our ignorance of French in no way prejudiced our audiences against us, as the hearty receptions we met with proved; and with wonderful intuition, due, no doubt, to the quickness of the Gallic mind, the people managed to cheer again and again at precisely the right points.

After hearing nothing but French for eight or nine hours daily for nearly a fortnight one could not help picking up many words, and on the occasion of my speaking at a public meeting in the Belleville Arrondissement—formerly Gambetta's constituency—I ventured my first two words in French before the public. The chairman of the meeting had been a working engineer, had become a member of the Paris Municipal Council, and had played a prominent part in the Commune. When the Commune was suppressed by M. Thiers' Government the engineer escaped to London, where he spent several years in English workshops. He consequently spoke English well, and delivered a most elaborate oration, introducing me as a stonemason who had become a member of that most aristocratic Assembly, the Parliament of England. He then assured his audience that I could not speak a word of French, but promised that my speech should be translated by a gentleman present for the purpose. When I began with a few words of French evidently well enough pronounced to reach their understanding, the whole meeting rose in a body and cheered tumultuously, till I was obliged to beg the chairman to inform the audience that my vocabulary was exhausted, an announcement that elicited as loud a cheer as my French introduction. Before the meeting was half-way through the Italian element made its presence felt, and the scuffling and noise which ensued turned what might have been a successful meeting into a bear-garden. From the platform it looked as though murder was being committed ; but when the combatants were at length separated, and I was expecting to see a whole heap of corpses, to my surprise not a swollen face or a spot of blood was to be seen.

I shall always look back with pleasure upon this visit to the French capital, because it gave me an opportunity of making the acquaintance of the late Mr. George Morland Crawford, the Paris correspondent of *The Daily News*, and his distinguished wife. Through their kindness I met several Frenchmen of note. I was especially delighted to obtain an introduction to M. Clémenceau, who was present at a breakfast party at Mr. Crawford's house. I was greatly impressed with M. Clémenceau's strength of character, and it was a keen pleasure to renew the acquaintanceship a few years later in London.

Altogether, we regarded this Congress as the most successful effort hitherto made to bring about an international trades-unionism. But, for my part, I always despaired of any absolute unity between the workers of Europe being brought about by the agency of federated associations like the British Trades-Union Congress. I felt assured that a more practical mode of procedure would be for the trades of each country whose products competed with each other in the world's markets to enter into friendly relations, and, if possible, to regulate some of the conditions under which such competition was conducted. Later on this idea was partially adopted by the textile trades of Northern France and England, and it was still further developed by the conference of English, French, German, and Belgian miners—a gathering which has become an annual affair, I believe to the benefit of all concerned.

The Congress attracted attention throughout Europe, and the Press of most countries published leading articles dealing with our proceedings. Especially was this the case in this country, where nearly every paper, dailies and weeklies alike, devoted much space to the subject.

# CHAPTER VIII

## *THE PROGRESS OF LABOUR QUESTIONS*

THE year 1884 was full of activity in the world of politics so far as the trades-unions and the industrial world generally were concerned. First and foremost stood the demand for assimilation of the county to the borough franchise. Mr. Gladstone's Government had enjoyed three years of power, which had been employed to good advantage for the welfare of the people. But already the political watchman could see signs of the coming sunset; and warned by these tokens, the representatives of Labour felt that no time must be lost if the desired extension of the franchise was to become anything beyond a dream. Conservative workmen joined with their Liberal fellows in the desire to see equality in relation to the ballot-box between town and country. Thus in the ranks of the labouring classes there reigned practical unanimity on this question. It was desired to make this state of affairs known to Mr. Gladstone, and to assure him that whatever constitutional steps his Government might see fit to take in the coming session, he could rely on the undivided support of the people.

At the behest of the Trades-Union Congress a national deputation, representing every class of male worker from all parts of Great Britain, was organised. It was the largest, the most representative, and the most successful thing of the kind I have ever been responsible for.

The Committee found no difficulty whatever in obtaining a sufficiently numerous deputation; the trouble was to regulate the number of those desiring to be present and to keep it within manageable bounds. Then there was the verification of each delegate's credentials, and the task of keeping them informed of the arrangements. Another arduous duty was the selection of speakers by the Committee; it was essential to keep the numbers down, and yet every interest had to be represented. Altogether the deputation numbered two hundred and forty, and the aggregate cost of the proceedings (each association represented bearing its quota of expenses) amounted to £500. We were received by Mr. Gladstone in the large Council-room of the Foreign Office, and everything went like clockwork. The speeches were short, sharp, and to the point; the whole proceedings occupied less than an hour. It was a memorable day's work, and its influence reached all political circles.

This deputation was followed in the summer by the striking Franchise Demonstration in Hyde Park. Thousands of agricultural labourers marched through the streets of London to the Park, where speakers addressed them from seven platforms. Over one of these I had the honour of presiding. The procession assembled on the Embankment between Blackfriars and Westminster Bridge, whence it proceeded by St. Stephen's, Parliament Street, and Whitehall, to Hyde Park. As we passed along Whitehall I remember seeing Lord Carrington and a party of friends standing at an open window in his house; he greeted the procession with enthusiastic cheers, and waved his hand in token of encouragement. Among those at the window was the Prince of Wales, apparently deeply interested in the demonstration and pleased at its imposing appearance. His Royal Highness also waved his hand in recognition of someone known to him in the procession. So far as I am aware this is the only occasion on which a member of the Royal Family has practically taken part in a great political movement among the people. So enormous was the length of the procession that the rear did not enter the Park until some time after the formal proceedings had ended. For precision of movement, orderliness, and effective display it was, in my opinion, by far the finest demonstration of our time.

The Tory Party was enraged beyond measure; and Lord Randolph Churchill, in a speech at Edinburgh, was driven to suggesting that the movement had no strength or feeling behind it because it was unaccompanied by any outburst of popular passion! He apparently wished his audience to believe that if the

people had been in earnest in their demands, the railings of Hyde Park would have been levelled, as they
had been twenty years earlier. I have no hesitation
in saying that had the policy of Lord Derby's Government in 1866 been followed by the Liberal Administration of 1884, popular rights would have been asserted
in a similar unhesitating manner. But in place of
obstruction and resistance the Home Office and the
police authorities offered every facility for the successful carrying out of the proceedings, and no damage
was done to even the smallest shrub or flower in the
Park.

I remember that a day or two after the demonstration
Mr. Lowther rose in the House to ask Mr. Shaw
Lefevre, the First Commissioner of Works, whether it
was true that persons had been employed at the
instance of the Government to remove some of the
fencing in Hyde Park which would have obstructed
the progress of the procession on the occasion of the
demonstration ; and further, whether this work was
done at the public expense. I immediately jumped
up and inquired of the Commissioner, before he
replied to the first question, whether it was true
that many Government employees were employed
all the year round for the purpose of keeping
in order a riding-track called Rotten Row for the
pleasure of a particular class of persons in the
metropolis. This suggested to Mr. Furniss the
humorous sketch which is reproduced here, and in
which I am depicted riding a great war-horse bare-

backed, with a dumpy hat on my head and a short "cutty" in my mouth.

However, the Tory Party, recognising the weight of the movement, soon came to terms with the Government, and a Franchise Bill was passed. This was followed by an Act extending the hours of polling from four to eight o'clock at night, and by a redistribution of seats. Thus the General Election of

MR. BROADHURST IN ROTTEN ROW.
(*From Punch, by kind permission of the Proprietors and Mr. Harry Furniss*).

1885 was fought under conditions which placed new and wide political power in the hands of the working classes. To many minds, even among prominent statesmen, this large extension of popular rights seemed to presage the introduction of continuous Liberal rule and the total demolition of the Tory Party. How such prophecies, confident enough at the time, have been falsified by the course of events, is patent to all.

But I must retrace my steps a little to refer to a

debate which closely affected a most important class of workers, and in which I took the keenest interest. In May, 1884, Mr. Chamberlain introduced a Bill providing greater security of life and property at sea. In a memorable speech of nearly four hours' duration he formulated one of the gravest indictments ever uttered against practices then in vogue in the mercantile marine. Many a ship, it was fearlessly asserted, would prove more profitable to her owner at the bottom of the sea than if she arrived safely in port. It was alleged that many a man had grown rich by the deaths of his under-paid victims who manned his rotten "coffin ships." The shipping interest in the House and out of it furiously opposed the measure, and fought it tooth and nail. Of course, the shipping trade contained then, as it does now, many of the noblest and best of men. But it was undoubtedly true that others were steeped in the foulest crime, and, like the ghastly monsters of the deep sea, battened on the corpses of the poor sailormen. The Opposition, however, succeeded in blocking the Bill in its second reading stage, and it was referred to the Royal Commission, whose report is lost in oblivion. Yet if the country had grasped the significance of a quarter of the terrible facts contained in Mr. Chamberlain's long speech, and had not been rendered apathetic by the continual reports of terrible shipping disasters which the newspapers contain, the conscience of the nation would have demanded the immediate passing of this beneficent measure.

About this time I was kept busily engaged by a great increase in the correspondence department of the Parliamentary Committee's work. Communications, mostly in the shape of requests for information and guidance, poured in from workers in the United States, Canada, the Australasian Colonies, and, to a more limited extent, from European countries, notably France, Germany, Denmark, and Italy. Copies of Acts of Parliament affecting Labour, draft Bills, and reports of the Standing Orders of the Trades-Union Congress were constantly despatched to various parts of the English-speaking world. Much of the success achieved by the organisation of Labour outside this country, especially among our own kith and kin, is due to the lead given by British working men, the encouragement they gave, and the hope they inspired.

In the meantime our propaganda outside St. Stephen's was being actively spread. The labours of the Parliamentary Committee were continually being brought under the notice of the workers in all parts of the country. Conventions of delegates representing various industries were frequently summoned at some central town, and I was generally invited to address them on the importance of work in Parliament, ending, of course, with an appeal for increased aid to carry on our labours. In many cases large public meetings were assembled for the same purpose. These efforts were not confined to England, for we soon found that the Scottish workman had a keen appreciation of the benefits to be derived from exercising pressure on the House of Commons. At Greenock, Glasgow, Aberdeen, Dundee, and Edinburgh, I attended very successful trade meetings convened for this purpose.

I think it was in the winter of 1881-2 that a rather comic incident occurred. On my way from Glasgow to Aberdeen I encountered so severe a snowstorm that I was compelled to stop from Saturday night to Monday morning at Perth. Among my unfortunate fellow-passengers who took refuge from the storm in the same hotel was a Scottish minister on his way from Edinburgh to some remote country kirk, where he was to preach his trial sermon as a candidate for the ministry of that kirk. I vividly remember the reserve manifested at first by my clerical friend, and how it thawed under the genial influence of a hot supper. Seeing in me an obscure person of no importance, he proceeded in no measured terms to abuse Mr. Gladstone for some action he had taken in previous years relating to Church patronage in North Britain. By a progress of reasoning which baffled my wits to follow he explained that but for Mr. Gladstone's wickedness he could have been in possession of a living without having to undergo the abominable competitive process of trial sermons. As he continued to dwell upon the unwelcome prospect before him in the morning, and the examination to be undergone at the hands of the congregation, his description of the Grand Old Man's character grew still more violent and vituperative.

As became a humble layman, I sat silent for a

long time in the presence of this youthful instructor of mankind, until my patience was exhausted, when I gently informed him that in a week's time I was engaged to deliver a political address in the city of Edinburgh, and that I should feel it my duty to inform the audience of the kind of language indulged in by one of their theological students, adding that I was an ardent admirer and supporter of the great statesman. When he heard that I was also personally acquainted with Mr. Gladstone his dismay knew no bounds, and with an almost startling suddenness he stuttered out his recantation. He implored me to take no further notice of his language, whose strength he attributed largely to the adverse circumstances of the night and the prospective difficulties of the morrow. So earnest were his pleadings and so profuse his apologies that I at length suffered myself to be prevailed upon to give my word of honour not to repeat the incident to a Scottish audience, and this is the first occasion in which the story has been made public.

Next morning I was overwhelmed by a thousand civilities; he anticipated my slightest wish, and the intervals between looking after my comfort he devoted to hearty confessions of penitence and reiterated expressions of devotion to Mr. Gladstone and the Liberal Party. He was still engaged in this manner when I pursued my journey to Aberdeen, where, in spite of the severe weather, I found as large and enthusiastic audience as heart could desire.

From Aberdeen I proceeded to Dundee to keep an

engagement with the Trades of the town. It was still snowing hard and blowing lustily, but a fine gathering managed to assemble in one of the public halls. At half-past ten I crossed the River Tay in company with Sir John Leng to his hospitable mansion at Newport, and seldom have I more earnestly yearned for the end of a journey than I did that night. It was a pitch-dark night with blinding snow and an intense cold, while a strong east wind was sweeping over the two miles of river we had to traverse. So black was the night that it was impossible to see the land, and our only guide to the landing-stage was the sound of a large bell on the pier-end. Such occasions as this give a zest to a cosy room, a roaring fire, and other creature comforts, for which the homes of North Britain are so deservedly celebrated.

Altogether, I was not sorry, after filling my engagements at Edinburgh and Glasgow, to turn my face Londonwards; though my recollections of the Scottish people were of the most grateful character, and I bore with me substantial tokens of their kindness and hospitality in shape of a handsome meerschaum pipe, the inevitable stone jar of Scotch whiskey, sundry tins of tobacco, and many complimentary Addresses presented by the Trades of the great city of the Clyde.

By the beginning of 1885 the Parliament of 1880 had spent its best powers, and in June vested interests once again proved their power by overturning the Government on the question of the increased taxation of beer. A Conservative Government was formed, and Parliament dissolved, while a General Election was fixed for the following November. Despite the downfall of the Liberal Government, important progress was made in Labour affairs, notably in the matter of inspectors of mines, whose number the Parliamentary Committee had exacted a promise from the Government to increase, and who were reinforced by seven new inspectors. Attention was also called to the irregularity of permitting an agent of the Employers' Liability Assurance Association to act as coroner in the case of an inquest of a labourer killed during his employment. Although the Lord Chancellor had no control over the appointments of deputy-coroners, he gave expression to his opinion of the undesirability of such a proceeding, and thus prevented the recurrence of what might easily have become a public scandal.

But a still more important question with far-reaching results occupied the attention of the Parliamentary Committee in 1885. Complaints concerning the administration of the Employers and Workmen's Act of 1875 had frequently reached us from the northern and midland counties. It was alleged that summonses for breach of contract against employees, disputes as to wages, measurements or weights of work done, were heard before magistrates who were in most cases themselves employers of labour; and although any magistrate personally interested in a particular case as an employer would withdraw while the case was being heard, still, the other magistrates were probably either engaged in the same branch of industry or a kindred one, or else were neighbours and friends of the interested magistrate. Under these conditions the workmen averred it was impossible to repose confidence in the impartiality of Benches thus constituted. At one meeting of the Committee, I remember, in 1884, Mr. Alfred Bailey, of Preston, a member of the Committee, a stalwart trades-unionist, and one of the most loyal, courageous, and devoted friends the Labour Movement ever possessed, exclaimed in his downright Lancashire fashion that the only way to the root of the difficulty was that Labour should have a representation on the Bench as well as Capital.

I perceived the value of the suggestion, but recognised the enormous difficulties to be overcome before it could be carried out. Still, I resolved to use all my powers to further this object, and privately set the proposal in motion in Government circles. Sir George Trevelyan happened to be Chancellor of the Duchy of Lancaster, and in that capacity had the power—if I could persuade him to exercise it—to create borough magistrates within the confines of the duchy from whatever class he thought proper. He was greatly startled by the daring of the suggestion, but as I pressed it with all my power, the preliminary shock gave place to a practical consideration of the matter. I felt that the outer crust had been penetrated, and rallied to my support Sir William Harcourt, Sir Henry James, and Sir Farrer Herschell.

In the report presented to the Trades-Union

Congress which met at Southport in 1885, the Committee had the satisfaction of announcing that, in consequence of these representations, Mr. Slatter, Secretary of the Manchester Typographers' Association, Mr. Birtwistle, Secretary of the Cotton-Weavers' Association of Accrington, and Mr. Fielding, Secretary of the Cotton-Spinners' Union, Bolton, had been placed upon the Commission of Peace in their respective boroughs. Thus one of the most remarkable departures from the custom and habit of centuries was consummated; public opinion readily grew accustomed to it, and the revolution that many excellent persons had anticipated never broke out. Since that time large numbers of workmen have been appointed Justices of the Peace in various parts of Great Britain. Speaking at a public meeting in Edinburgh a few years later Sir George Trevelyan alluded to this daring innovation in terms highly complimentary to myself, declaring that he looked back upon his action in this matter with the greatest satisfaction and pride.

But this was not the first nor solitary inroad upon the preserves of the privileged classes. I have already referred to the appointment of seven new inspectors of mines. In connection with the whole subject of Government inspectors the trades-unions had for many years claimed that their duties would be more effectively discharged if there was added to the staff a number of practical workers from the ranks of Labour. Resolutions were passed to this effect and deputations organised, with the result that in 1881 Sir William Harcourt offered me the appointment of an assistant inspector.    While fully appreciating the great honour paid to Labour by this offer, after full consideration I declined the appointment for myself, but submitted the name of Mr. J. D. Prior, then Secretary of the Amalgamated Carpenters' and Joiners' Association.    He was accordingly offered and accepted the post ; and other appointments of a similar character speedily followed.    Mr. J. W. Davis, Secretary of the Birmingham Brass-workers' Union, Mr. W. Paterson, Secretary of the Scotch Union of Carpenters and Joiners, Mr. Sedgwick, a member of the Boot and Shoe Riveters' and Finishers' Union at Leicester, and Mr. Birtwistle, junior, as well as one of the working man justices, who has since become a full inspector—all these names, with the exception of the last, were submitted by me to the Home Secretary as vacancies occurred, and all, I believe, performed their new duties with great satisfaction to their superiors.

At the time of committing these reminiscences to writing, I have just returned from a visit to Mr. J. D. Prior, whose work in the Factory Department is admitted on all sides never to have been surpassed in efficiency and good judgment, a quality particularly necessary in this kind of work in order to avoid administrative friction.    My friend Mr. Paterson, after serving a year or two in this capacity, obtained the appointment of Chief of the Glasgow Fire Brigade, a post which he still holds and in which he has met with remarkable success. The City Council have recognised his efforts in a manner highly complimentary and profitable to him. I refer to these facts with pride as evidence that when the Parliamentary Committee had the responsibility of recommending men to responsible positions, they have selected those best calculated to carry out satisfactorily the work of the departments to which they have been appointed, and to reflect credit upon the class to which they belong.

At a later date another appointment of a similar nature was offered to me by the Government. This was during the sitting of the Royal Commission on the Housing of the People, when a measure for the regulation of the conditions of life on canal boats had become law. I had taken considerable interest in the Bill, though the credit of its introduction belongs to the late Mr. George Smith, of Coalville, and I was offered the post of inspector under the Act with a salary of £600 a year and travelling expenses. The offer was a tempting one—an ample salary, a secure position for life, and pleasant work; but after the gravest consideration I declined it. I was deeply immersed in public work at the time of both a political and an industrial nature, and had in charge several important Labour questions in the House of Commons. It seemed to me I had no right to sacrifice these things to my private advantage and personal welfare. Many a time since I have considered my refusal a most unwise step, and as year is added to year I am disposed to ratify that conclusion.

In the latter part of the session of 1885 the first successful attempt was made to gain a fair chance for fair contractors to compete for Government contracts. The department attacked was that of printing. The annual expenditure on printing amounts to vast sums annually, and only firms chiefly unsatisfactory to the worker had been successful in obtaining parts of this work. I brought the subject under the notice of the Treasury, and after some prolonged negotiations, arrangements were made which admitted the best-wages paying house to compete for a portion of the work. This was the origin of the fair wages movement in Government contracts, and it gave widespread satisfaction to the trade in London.

During 1880 considerable agitation had arisen among the fitters engaged in Government dockyards. The Fitters' Union alleged that much of the work done on warships by shipwrights was of such a nature as belonged naturally to the fitters, and was inefficiently carried out when committed to the hands of the shipwrights. This was asserted in particular of the bulkheads and water-tight compartments. I had been constantly referred to on this subject by the fitters, and had submitted several questions to the Admiralty concerning the complaints; ultimately I gave notice of a motion for the purpose of drawing the attention of the House to the matter. At that time Sir George Trevelyan was Secretary to the Admiralty. Before making a speech on this subject I determined to acquire some technical knowledge and with my own eyes examine the work, and accordingly I went down to Chatham Dockyard, accompanied by Mr. Burnett, the Secretary of the Engineers' Association, who was able to coach me in the intricate parts of the work. My own mechanical knowledge was sufficient to assure me of the danger of buckled plates and the necessity of absolute accuracy of building and fitting in the case of water-tight doors, whose value entirely depended upon their capacity to fulfil their functions at a moment's notice. After inspecting two or three ironclads from stoke-hole to upper works I acquired sufficient information for my purpose ; and when my motion came up the Government at once accepted my proposals and promised immediate investigation and reform. Sir George Trevelyan, who possesses an excellent wit, propounded to an admiring circle of Members the following conundrum : What is the difference between Broadhurst and Darwin? Answer : While Darwin was in favour of the survival of the fittest, Broadhurst advocated the supremacy of the fitter !

Sir George has always had a great reputation for happy quotations. I remember a striking example of this faculty which occurred a few years later than the incident I have just mentioned. He was dining with some friends in the House while the late member for East Edinburgh, Dr. Wallace, was speaking. A brother member entering the dining-room was surprised to find Sir George Trevelyan when his eloquent countryman was on his feet, and inquired how it was that he, a Scotchman, was not in his seat. "Ah," replied Sir George, "you see we're Scots wha hae fra' Wallace fled!"

# CHAPTER IX

## *MY VISIT TO SANDRINGHAM*

SOON after I entered Parliament a conversation with the late Mr. J. Beale, the champion of popular local government in the metropolis, directed my mind to the question of the iniquitous system of building leases. My interest in the subject was increased by my own experiences both as tenant and recently owner, especially as my wrath had been raised by a notice from my ground landlord. I determined to take action in Parliament to draw attention to the grievances from which leaseholders suffered. The member for Hereford, Mr. R. T. Reid, now Sir Robert Reid, undertook to prepare a Bill on the subject and consented to his name being attached to it. In 1882 I succeeded in getting an afternoon debate on the subject in the House. *

When the Bill was first circulated I could not have reckoned on half a dozen votes in the House, but

* Some friends of mine living in a district where the life leasehold system (to which I will refer later) prevailed, had presented me with some striking photographs of cottages in various stages of dilapidation and utterly unfit for human habitation. These photographs I brought into the House, and during my speech submitted them to the Speaker and to Members of the House—the first occurrence of the kind, I believe, in the history of that Assembly.

so rapid was the progress made by the measure in popular favour that in the division on the second reading I found III supporters in my lobby. Of course I was overwhelmingly defeated; but a big question had been ventilated, and a variety of issues springing from this attempt to redress the leaseholder's grievances was brought before the public in consequence of my Bill. The first outcome was the formation of a Leasehold Enfranchisement Association, with branches all over the country, and the public was soon put in full possession of the facts of the case by the pen of Mr. Howard Evans, a journalist on the staff of the *Echo*. Other issues raised by the debate on my Bill included the taxation of ground-rents, and the unjust and sacrilegious effect of the leasehold system on Nonconformist places of worship in cases where no freehold sites were available.

My Bill found particular favour in places like London, Grimsby, Liverpool, Huddersfield, North and South Wales, and parts of Worcestershire, Devonshire, and Cornwall, and communications from the last three counties revealed to me a system of leasehold of whose existence till then I was totally ignorant, and which appeared to me peculiarly iniquitous. It was known as the "three life" system, and under it you purchased a site to be held during the lifetime of three persons nominated by the purchaser. At any time you could be called upon to prove the existence of any or all of the three lives. On the death of one, and in some cases two, you were allowed, on the payment of a further sum, to nominate another life to fill the vacancy. When the last of the persons thus nominated died, the land and all you had placed upon it reverted to the original owner. The people heartily disliked this " three lives " system, particularly in Devonshire and Cornwall, and when I visited the West of England to explain my Bill and rouse a feeling of hopefulness in the West country, I was right royally received. A great gathering was held at Camborne, the miners' Division of Cornwall, men coming from long distances to attend it. The agitation spread rapidly and soon began to make its influence felt. A large landowner in the neighbourhood of Devonport headed a conciliation movement by offering land plots for a definite period instead of the uncertain tenure dependent on three persons' lives. Others speedily followed his example, and in a number of instances estates were offered in freehold plots in parts of the country where previously the " three lives " system had reigned supreme. Thus lasting and beneficial reform was obtained without the aid of legislation by the wholesome pressure of public opinion. At the same time the evil monster Monopoly still lives ; he is only less aggressive than he formerly was.*

* In July, 1900, I attended a meeting of the Liberal delegates from all parts of that Division, held in Camborne to support the candidature of the present Member, Mr. W. S. Caine. I was then thanked by all I met for the work done for them eighteen years before, and was told there was scarcely such a thing known as new leases on the three lives tenure.

In order to enlighten the mind of the " man in the street " upon this question Mr. Reid collaborated with me in bringing out a small hand-book as an aid to its study. It formed one of the " Imperial Parliament " series edited by Mr. Sydney Buxton, M.P., and published by Swan Sonnenschein. The case for reform was stated by Mr. Reid with wonderful lucidity and its legal bearings indicated with excellent clearness. Whether there was ever any sale for the volume I do not know; at any rate, I have never received any profits from its sale, so I can scarcely look back upon this literary venture with any personal self-congratulation.

Some years later, while on a visit to Dorsetshire, I was informed of a particularly scandalous instance of the injustice of the leasehold tenure. A little community of Nonconformists had built a chapel on an estate near the place in which I was staying. When the lease expired the landowner, who had only recently succeeded to the estate, refused to renew it on any terms whatever. These poor people were compelled to find some other place to worship God in, and their little sanctuary, erected and maintained with so much sacrifice and love, was turned into a workshop for the estate carpenter. By a strange and tragic coincidence the first work done in the dismantled sanctuary was the making of a coffin for the landowner, who died almost immediately after evicting the Dissenters.

In other instances I was informed of the abominable

extortion of grasping landlords who, on the expiration of a lease, would impose heavy fines for its renewal, knowing well that the Nonconformists would sacrifice a great deal to retain their chapel, for unless the lease was renewed they would be unable to obtain another site in the neighbourhood.   These cases, together with an incident to be related further on, led me to introduce a Bill giving to Nonconformist communities under certain conditions power to acquire compulsorily, sites for chapels.

Mainly owing to the splendid work done by Mr. George R. Sims in the columns of *The Daily News*, the question of the housing of the poor was occupying public attention in a large degree when I entered Parliament.   Railway extensions were being carried on apace, the displacement of large populations of the labouring classes was constantly occurring, and though much had been done to provide accommodation for the houseless in some parts of London, the inevitable distress and overcrowding had made the subject a burning question.   Naturally my own experience gave me a keen interest in the matter, for I knew how largely the question of rent bulks in the domestic economy of the working classes.   The rent problem, notwithstanding all the efforts of the philanthropists, still awaits a satisfactory solution.   A man who earns thirty shillings a week has to pay about a fifth in rent.   His travelling expenses to and from his work will usually amount to another shilling, so there he is with seven shillings a week the first and inexorable charges on his income, leaving only twenty-three shillings to meet all the requirements of his family— food, clothes, medicine, coal, club, amusements, charity, and contributions to his place of worship. Add to this the period of non-employment during which rent must be paid just the same, and it will be admitted that the question of rent in the large urban centres is one of the gravest and most difficult problems the social reformer has to face.

I frequently put questions to the Government on the subject, and ultimately asked them to appoint a Royal Commission to investigate the whole question. Before my request could be granted the matter was taken out of my hands by Lord Salisbury, who placed a motion in the Orders in the House of Lords for the appointment of a Commission. The Government at once accepted the motion, and proceeded to form a Commission under the presidency of the Prince of Wales. Sir Charles Dilke was appointed Chairman, and among the members were the Marquis of Salisbury, Cardinal Manning, Lord Carrington, Lord Brownlow, Mr. Goschen, Mr. Samuel Morley, the Bishop of Bedford, Mr. Torrens, Mr. Godwin, Sir Richard Cross, and Mr. E. E. Stanley. I was also invited, and accepted a seat on the Commission. At the end of its sittings I succeeded in obtaining the signatures of a majority of the Commission to a resolution condemning the leasehold system. I also put in a memorandum of my own, suggesting a mode for the cheap and easy transfer of small properties through the agency of

"MR BROADHURST AND SOME OF HIS CONSTITUENTS."
(*By kind permission of the proprietors of "Black and White."*)

municipal authorities.   This idea would have provided
facilities for the exchange of small estates at a nominal
cost, with perfect security to the title of the holding
by means of a registration office.

It was while serving as a member of this Commission
that I had the honour of being presented to the Prince

of Wales, and from that day till now I have received
at his Royal Highness's hands unvarying kindness
and consideration. The Prince invited the whole of
the Commissioners down to Sandringham—in the first
place, I presume, as an act of hospitality, but secondly
that the Commissioners might inspect for themselves
the cottages on the Sandringham estate. From
various reasons I was unable to accompany them ; his
Royal Highness was good enough to accept my
apology, and wrote me a very pleasing letter to say so.
The letter, which is written in the Prince's own hand,
is so characteristic of his kindliness of heart and
thoughtful consideration that I make no apology for
quoting it in full :—

"SANDRINGHAM, *November 8th*, 1884.

" DEAR MR. BROADHURST,—

"Many thanks for your very kind letter. Both
the Princess and myself are so very sorry that you are
unable to pay us a visit here next week, but we perfectly
understand and appreciate the reason.

"Believe me, truly yours,

"ALBERT EDWARD."

A little later I received a further proof of his
Royal Highness's goodwill. Hearing that I made it
a rule not to dine out, and that I did not possess a
dress-coat, the Prince of Wales renewed his invitation
in a form which I could not refuse without being
guilty of unpardonable boorishness. He assured me
that arrangements would be made during my stay at

Sandringham to meet my wishes and insisted upon booking dates there and then.

I will not pretend that I accepted this offer of Royal hospitality with anything but the greatest delight. I spent three days at Sandringham with the Prince and Princess, and I can honestly say that I was never entertained more to my liking and never felt more at home when paying a visit than I did on this occasion. I arrived at Sandringham on Friday night and remained until the following Monday evening. On my arrival his Royal Highness personally conducted me to my rooms, made a careful inspection to see that all was right, stoked the fires, and then, after satisfying himself that all my wants were provided for, withdrew and left me for the night. In order to meet the difficulties in the matter of dress, dinner was served to me in my own rooms each night.

During the visit we walked and talked, and inspected nearly every feature of the estate, including the stables, the kennels, and the dairy farm, all of which strongly appealed to one who, like myself, was country bred. The Princess herself, with characteristic graciousness, showed me over her beautiful dairy. But what pleased me most was a visit we paid to several cottages on the estate. The Prince took an evident pride in the beauty and comfort of the homes of his people, and I was particularly struck by the scrupulous courtesy of his Royal Highness in obtaining permission from the housewife before crossing the threshold.　To the dwellers in cities this may seem an observance demanded by the most elementary politeness, but those who, like myself, have lived in a country cottage know by experience how often this elementary rule is more honoured in the breach than the observance.　In too many cases people march into the houses of the poor without a by-your-leave or the least apology for an ill-mannered intrusion on the privacy of the home.　Again, I was pleased to find that the villagers we met on the road, though perfectly respectful, showed no sign of servility or obsequiousness in their manner of greeting the members of the Royal Family.

After a long walk round the farms, across some fields and back to the village by the roadway, the Prince took me into what is called the village club. The club is in other words the village public-house, the difference being that it is not conducted for profit.　A high standard of conduct marks the administration of the establishment, and a similar behaviour is required from those visiting it.　To prevent drunkenness a limited quantity of refreshment only is allowed to any one person in one day. The Prince invited me to partake of the refreshment of the house, and I was quite ready to comply.　We had, I think, a glass of ale each and sat down in the clubroom, where we found several farm labourers enjoying their half-pints and their pipes.　No excitement, no disturbance, no uncomfortable feeling, was evinced by those present.　No condescension or patronage was displayed by the Prince towards his neighbours and friends. The beer was very good and of a homely and acceptable flavour. Strong and plain but clean chairs and tables formed the furniture of the apartment. I remarked to the Prince that the chairs looked as though they were of the best build and strongest specimens of High Wycombe produce.

"Yes," he said, "they are firm seats ; many a politician wishes his was as safe."

Among other objects of interest I remember the Prince pointing out with pride a valuable present given to him by the people of Norfolk on the occasion of his wedding. I assured him that I clearly recollected both the occasion and the present, for I was then a working mason in the city of Norwich, and I had to lose a day's work, which, unfortunately, meant for me the loss of a day's wages. "But," said the Prince, "you are none the worse now, Mr. Broadhurst?" To which I answered that I was still four shillings out of pocket, the day's wages of a mason in Norwich at that time.

On Saturday night, before retiring, his Royal Highness consulted me about my wishes for Sunday morning. I told the Prince that I was not a member of the Established Church, but a Dissenter, and that I hoped to find a Methodist place of worship in the neighbourhood. He himself did not know of one, but assisted me by all means in his power to discover the whereabouts of the nearest chapel, which turned out to be several miles from Sandringham in the direction of the coast. Thither I wended my way on Sunday morning, but found there was no service, only a Sunday school being held. I listened to the teaching a while and then returned to Sandringham. In the afternoon the Prince inquired how I had fared in the morning, and I took the opportunity to suggest that a chapel nearer the centre of the estate would be a great boon to such of the villagers as were Nonconformists. I reminded his Royal Highness that some of the stoutest patriots and most loyal citizens were to be found among hereditary Nonconformists, and that the Throne had no more valuable and trustworthy subjects than the great majority of Dissenters. The Prince took my remarks in very good part and thanked me for my words, especially as being spoken in the presence of his two sons. I must add that during my stay I had several conversations with the late Duke of Clarence and the present Duke of York, and found in both a total absence of affectation or haughtiness. I left Sandringham with a feeling of one who had spent a week-end with an old chum of his own rank in society rather than one who had been entertained by the Heir-Apparent and his Princess.

This visit, and the memory of the chapel in a back lane some miles away from the people, finally settled my determination to attempt some legislative remedy for this grievous disability under which Nonconformists were labouring. Accordingly I wrote an article which appeared in the first number of *The*

*Methodist Times*, a marked copy of which I sent to the Prince of Wales, who acknowledged it in kindly words. I followed this up with a Bill which I introduced in the next session. On the debate on the second reading Sir William Harcourt supported the Bill on behalf of the Government with all his power, but the Opposition talked it out.

The next occasion on which I was brought into contact with the Heir-Apparent was on the formation of the Council of the Imperial Institute. Soon after the sittings of the Royal Commission on the Housing of the Poor had closed, I received an invitation to attend a preliminary gathering to consider the proposal to erect a building which should represent the resources and the industries of the British Empire. I was chosen a member of the Council and of the Building Committee, and served on both bodies until the completion of the enterprise and its opening by the Queen in 1893. The Prince of Wales was Chairman of the Council, and the meetings were usually held at Marlborough House. When the plans and designs for the building were submitted for approval, I discovered that it was intended to use terra cotta dressings instead of stone. Against this proposal I made a determined stand. I used every means in my power to alter this arrangement, and I believe it was mainly due to the Prince's sympathy and support that stone dressings were eventually adopted. During the progress of the building operations I found that a portion of the best part of the stonework had been sublet to a Derbyshire firm of quarry-masters. I at once brought the matter under the notice of the Building Committee. When invited to explain, the contractor asserted that London masons could not work that class of stone. I replied that this was absurd, and backed up my opinion by offering to show my capacity to work it, although many years had elapsed since I had last practised my craft. In the end the contractor had to give way, and the work was executed in London, to the great delight of the London masons, to the satisfaction of the architect, and to the advantage of all concerned—except, perhaps, the contractor.

In 1892 I served on the Royal Commission on the Condition of the Aged Poor. Lord Aberdare presided at the Enquiry, and the Prince of Wales was also a member and a constant attendant, and displayed a most keen interest in the Enquiry. In the winter of 1893 his Royal Highness had a few days' shooting within four miles of my Cromer home. During his visit he was good enough to send a message that, owing to unavoidable circumstances, he regretted he was unable to keep his intention of paying me a visit and taking a cup of tea in my cottage. He requested me, if I could conveniently do so, to meet him at the station on the morning of his departure. This I did, and I was greatly struck by the keenness with which he discussed some confidential proposals relating to the Draft Report of the Aged Poor Commission. To my wife, whom he had not met before, his

Royal Highness was exceedingly kind, expressing to her the pleasure he had derived from his acquaintance with her husband.

Another pleasing incident connected with the Prince occurred in 1889 when I founded the Cromer Golf Club. His Royal Highness, in response to my invitation, consented to act as patron and gave the first prize, a handsome silver bowl.

When an address was presented to the Prince by the Committee of Workmen who had conducted the Industrial Exhibition at the Agricultural Hall, I accompanied the Presentation Committee to Sandringham The ceremony was exceedingly simple and pleasing, both to the givers and the Royal recipient. Business engagements compelled me to leave Sandringham earlier than the Committee, and when I arrived at the station I found that his Royal Highness was going to Ely by the same train. Directly he knew of my presence in the station he sent for me and insisted on my joining him in his saloon carriage, and I had a very pleasurable journey indeed.

In thus recording my meetings with the Prince of Wales I should like to make it understood that I have no purpose to serve. Many paragraphs have at times appeared in various publications respecting alleged, and in some instances partially true, incidents in the course of meetings between his Royal Highness and myself—hence this reference to them. In order to apologise for these references—if apology is needed—it should be mentioned that the two Royal Commissions here referred to are, as far as I know, the only ones on which one so near the throne has served. I only desire to make known to those whom it may interest how, in all his intercourse with me, his Royal Highness showed the greatest kindness and consideration without the slightest trace of patronage or condescension. I have not usually given what are called " Royal Votes " in the House of Commons, and no favour was due to me in that respect. But I have at all times experienced from his hands such treatment as might be looked for from a high-minded and well-bred English gentleman.

Mr. Joseph Arch was a member of the Royal Commission on the Condition of the Aged Poor. Sandringham is in the centre of the division for which Mr. Arch then sat in Parliament. There was no member of the Commission with whom the Prince seemed to enjoy a chat or a joke more than with the representative of the agricultural labourers. I had some part in Mr. Arch's first and last contest in North-west Norfolk, and I think I may truly say that no estate in that constituency offered less opposition to his candidature than Sandringham did.

# CHAPTER X

## *THE 1885 CAMPAIGN*

THE Trades-Union Congress of 1885 held in
Southport was looked forward to with considerable interest. The near approach of a General
Election in which some millions of workers would
exercise the franchise for the first time heightened
the expectation of the trades-unionists in everything
pertaining to political life. It was generally anticipated
that the result of the elections would be a large
increase in the number of Labour representatives in the
Imperial Parliament. A Conservative Ministry had
been formed in June, but the remainder of the session
was almost entirely occupied with the routine business
of winding up affairs preparatory to the national contest.
One notable step, however, marked the existence of
this interim Government. This was the appointment
of a Royal Commission to inquire into the condition
of trade. For some years preceding a persistent
agitation had been carried on in the country and
kept alive by a small number of men who claimed
to be suffering from lack of employment in the sugar
trade, caused, as they alleged, by the competition

of Continental rivals who were aided by bounties from their Governments. This faction had constantly and violently attacked the Trades Congress, its Committee, and more particularly its Secretary. Attempts had several times been made to foist upon the Trades Congress bogus delegates representing this faction. But one of the Standing Orders of the Congress enjoined that all expenses of delegates attending the Congress should be borne by *bonâ fide* workmen's associations, and it required little subtlety to perceive that the funds for these so-called delegates of the sugar-workers might come from non-Labour sources.

For many years I had been the subject of bitter and unjustifiable abuse. Misrepresentations and calumnies were showered upon my head. Resolutions reflecting on my private character, which were alleged to have been passed at meetings of workpeople in clubrooms and other places, constantly appeared in a certain class of newspaper, but investigation always revealed the fact that these meetings were known only to small and interested cliques. At the Trades Congress held in London in 1881 some of these men had been forcibly ejected from the hall, and another had been obliged to withdraw by the order of the chairman. The centres of this disaffection were London and Clyde district. There existed more than a vague suspicion that behind these men and the sugar-refiners in whose interests they were agitating stood the Tory Party; and this suspicion was strengthened by the careful manner in which many of the Conservative leaders avoided committing themselves to any opposition to a Protective system; in so much that it was generally believed that if they possessed a majority and the Government side of the House they would not hesitate to impose countervailing duties on imported sugar. Only those who were behind the scenes in political life at the time can realise how potent and various were the weapons wielded on behalf of the Fair Trade Movement. The advocates of countervailing duties on sugar received considerable sympathy from Protectionists in other industries, with the result that the Conservative Government appointed a Royal Commission to inquire into the whole question of Fair Trade. But they were careful to pack this Commission with tried henchmen, including only one representative of Labour, Mr. Birtwistle, who was well known as a trusty supporter of the Conservative Party. I raised the question in the House of Commons, pointing out the one-sided composition of the Commission, and claiming that on such a question Labour should be adequately represented. As a result Lord Iddesleigh, the Chairman, invited me to join the Commission, an invitation that I refused point blank, feeling that its acceptance after I had raised the question would place me in an invidious position. Eventually Mr. Drummond, a London compositor, was appointed a member of the Commission, but as he, like Mr. Birtwistle, belonged to the Ministerial Party, this appointment did not remove the objections to the composition of the Commission. It will be in the memory of many that after sitting for a year or two and gathering, doubtless, much useful information concerning the advantages of Free Trade, the Commission utterly failed to gain sufficient evidence to state a case for Protection, and its recommendations practically amounted to the advice to manufacturers to make the best of the existing conditions and rely on their own efforts, unsupported by bounties, to overcome commercial depression and re-establish the reign of prosperity. But the Conservative Party have apparently never forgiven my attack on this Commission and my refusal to act as a pawn upon it, and so deep-seated is this feeling that from that day to this no seat upon a Royal Commission appointed by a Conservative Government has been offered to me, though on one occasion at least Parliamentary usage entitled me to an invitation. I will cite two conspicuous instances of this survival of blind passion and prejudice.

In 1890 the German Emperor made proposals to the Governments of Europe to join in an International Conference on Labour Questions in Berlin. I felt that possibly much good, and certainly no harm, might accrue to the cause of Labour from such a Conference of the Powers, and I exerted all my influence to assist the matter. The proposal was not altogether original, for some years before, when Lord Granville held the post of Secretary for Foreign Affairs, overtures had been made to the same end which emanated, if not from the Swiss Government itself, at least, from some influential citizens of the Alpine Republic. The suggestion came to me through the foreign correspondence on Labour questions which passed the Parliamentary Committee, and I immediately wrote to Lord Granville asking if any proposals of the kind had reached the British Foreign Office, and if so, whether there was any possibility of such a Conference being held. Nothing, however, came of it ; but when I saw the proposal revived by a personage so energetic and influential as the German Emperor, I hoped for a more successful outcome. My interest in the matter was not so much personal as official. The longer hours of labour and lower scale of wages on the Continent operated unfairly against our countrymen in times of fierce competition. On the other hand, in several European countries the educational facilities for the people were certainly superior to English institutions. If these subjects were intelligently discussed, I was hopeful that considerable improvement in the conditions of the life of the labouring classes might result, and indirectly, that it might facilitate International Trades-Unionism. For these reasons I threw myself vigorously into the matter, exerted pressure on the Government to give favourable consideration to the proposal, and had several interviews with the Under-Secretary for Foreign Affairs, urging him to advise that British delegates be sent to Berlin. In the end the Government accepted the proposal, and I at once set to work to draw up a list of intelligent workmen representing the great industries most frequently in contact with Germany in neutral markets who would be fitted by their knowledge and business capacity to serve as delegates. The selection of the British representatives rested mainly with the Board of Trade, and I had interviews with the President of the Board of Trade on the subject of the *personnel* of the delegation. But out of the dozen names submitted by me only two—Mr. Burt, M.P., and Mr. Birtwistle—were chosen. Mr. Burnett, the Labour Correspondent of the Board of Trade, could, it was submitted, represent the iron trades, and in any case he would attend in his official capacity. Thus there were practically only two Labour representatives, the other members being drawn from the official and capitalist classes, a wise selection being Sir W. Houldsworth, M.P., and Sir John Gorst, M.P. As a matter of fact, I could not have attended the Conference had I been invited, for two reasons. My health was in too feeble a state to permit my undertaking the work ; and in the second place I had made up my mind to resign my secretaryship to the Parliamentary Committee at the end of that year, and was anxious to devote all my strength to the task of handing over the office to my successor without complications or arrears of work. Still, the fact remains that after practically forcing the Government to accept the proposal, taking infinite pains over the subject, and readily laying my knowledge and experience at their service, I was not even offered a place upon the Commission.

To take another flagrant example. In 1885 I introduced a Bill for the abolition of the tied-house system, and in the following year, at my instigation, a Royal Commission was appointed to inquire into this and kindred questions arising out of the liquor trade. I may say in passing that I reintroduced the Bill again after the General Election in July, 1895, and found that the interest in the measure was so keen and widespread that I was overwhelmed with correspondence from all parts of the country. Again, at the General Election of July, 1895, the Bill created considerable interest. Many candidates applied for information respecting the details of the Bill, and in a large number of constituencies the question exercised considerable influence. Some of the Liberal Members who survived the storm assured me that they owed their success to the support they gave to my proposals in regard to tied-houses more than to any other cause. I believe I am justified in saying that I was the first Member of the House of Commons to raise the question in a practical form. This by the way, but I am anxious to explain the prejudice excited against me. When, as I have said, a Royal Commission was appointed to deal with the question at my instigation, my claims to a seat were passed over in silence.

But to return to my doings in 1885. From the close of the Southport Congress to the closing of the polling-booth in the last English constituency in the following November, I experienced the most severe period of prolonged and sustained exertion in speaking and travelling in the whole of my public career. On leaving Southport on September 14th, I proceeded to Chester, where I had promised to address a political meeting. It was here that quite unexpectedly occurred one of the happiest memories of my life. At Chester I met Lord Rosebery on his way to visit his chief at Hawarden. On the following day my Chester hostess arranged to drive my wife and myself over to Hawarden Castle, that we might have a look at the Liberal leader's famous residence. In Hawarden Park we met Lord Rosebery, who informed us that it was the desire of Mr. and Mrs. Gladstone that my wife and I should lunch at Hawarden Castle. Thus for the first and last time I had the honour of being entertained by the Grand Old Man at his country seat and of seeing him in all his glory amid his beloved books. Dressed in tweeds of old times well worn, trousers a little short and slightly frayed at the bottom, he presented a totally different appearance to his House of Commons costume. It was only on his approaching me that I noticed his clothes, which on an ordinary man would have been thought untidy. After the commencement of his conversation one did not see his covering, one only saw and heard his mind. To a greater degree than any other person I ever met he could, and did, adapt his talk and his subjects to the person he was addressing. What an attainment ! A very pleasant and instructive time I spent, for Mr. Gladstone played the host to perfection, pointing out all the views of interest in the park and the village, not omitting the fine old church. I remember just before we went into lunch Mrs. Gladstone whispered in my ear that I must on no account lead her husband into a political conversation, as he was suffering from hoarseness consequent on a severe cold. I faithfully observed her injunction; but to her dismay and the entertainment of his guests directly we sat down Mr. Gladstone launched into a conversation, or rather a monologue, and despite all his wife's appeals he talked unceasingly until the close of the meal. I returned to Chester that evening loaded with flowers gathered by Mrs. Gladstone, and full of delightful memories of the visit.

At this time of my life I believe I could have worked from one week's end to another without an hour's sleep and no rest but the refreshment of a cold bath and change of garments; but my stamina was pretty severely tested by the next few weeks of 1885. In the early part of October I attended the annual gatherings of the National Liberal Federation at Bradford, and addressed several of the public meetings. Thence I proceeded direct to Scotland to fulfil a series of political engagements, the first of which was at Dumbarton, where Mr. R. T. Reid, Q.C., was contesting the division against the sitting Member, Sir Archibald Orr Ewing. I changed trains at Glasgow and took a local train to Helensburgh, on the Clyde. The house where I was to stay was situated at the head of Loch Long, about sixteen miles from the station. I left Bradford at nine o'clock in the morning and only arrived at my destination about midnight. Those who know this part of Scotland will remember that the line to Helensburgh for some distance runs close to the riverside. During the afternoon a strong gale sprang up from the west, and when we reached Clydeside the tide was running up strongly before the wind, and in the more exposed parts beat against the train and even invaded the carriages. By the time we arrived at Helensburgh both wind and rain had rather increased than moderated, and the conveyance which was to take us to our destination at the head of Loch Long and had left there in fine weather earlier in the day was a pair-horse phaeton— not the most suitable vehicle for a night of driving rain and blustering wind. My niece, who accompanied me, the coachman, and I held a council of war as to whether we should proceed or stay at Helensburgh all night. A station official expressed the opinion that the weather showed signs of moderating, and this hopeful view, coupled with the coachman's pleading that our non-arrival would cause grave anxiety, decided me to make the attempt. Selecting such garments as would offer the most resistance to cold and wet from our luggage and hastily donning them, we took our seats in the carriage, my niece being so effectually swathed in wraps that she had to be lifted bodily into the phaeton by a railway porter. Like the railway, the road runs for the most part alongside the water, in many parts only a thin wooden rail separating the path from the black waters of the loch. At one point in our journey where the darkness seemed more than usually intense the horses strayed from the road and seemed to plunge into loose ground or water. It was only by exerting his utmost strength and skill that the coachman averted a serious accident and succeeded in bringing us back to the highway.

The downpour of rain somewhat lessened in volume, but the gale continued to rage in an awe-inspiring manner. To communicate with the driver who sat immediately in front of me I had to put my mouth close to his ear and bawl my loudest. Presently we left the lochside and climbed a hill with apparently nothing to guide us but the uncertain flicker from the carriage lamps. By care, and the remarkable keenness of vision displayed by the coachman, we surmounted the rise and returned again to the lochside and the thin white rail which acted as a guide. But our difficulties were not yet over, for suddenly we drove into the midst of a herd of cattle which had come down from the hills for shelter. Startled by the carriage lamps they bolted in front of the horses, and for a long distance persisted in running ahead of us, so that we could not pass them. Then at intervals we came upon foaming and swollen streams thundering down from the heights above to the loch ; these had a terrifying effect, at any rate on me, though the horses appeared to pay no heed to them. At last we got clear of the cattle, the road improved, and presently, to my great relief, a whistle from the coachman announced that we had reached the lodge gates. I never remember feeling so grateful for the shelter and rest of a warm bed as I did that night. In order to save my niece from undue anxiety I had so adjusted her wraps as practically to blindfold her, and all through the night drive I had congratulated myself on the manœuvre. But when recounting the incident next morning at the breakfast-table she shattered my delusion completely by saying that, suspicious of some object in being thus blindfolded, she had managed to remove the wrap, and had thus been able to realise very vividly what might have happened had we been in the hands of a less skilful driver.

After a day's rest Mr. Reid and I started on his campaign. Although a Scotsman, he was practically a stranger to the Dumbartonshire division, while his opponent, who had sat for the constituency for many years, was a large employer and well known in the district. Electioneering in those mountainous regions, where railways are few and far between, is hard work, and it was necessary for Mr. Reid to visit as many of the villages as possible. For example, we had arranged to address a meeting in the Vale of Leven at seven o'clock on Saturday night. To reach the place we had to leave Mr. Reid's house at two in the afternoon and travel by road, rail, and water. When the meeting was over at ten, a drive of some twenty miles confronted us. As was not unusual, the night turned out dark and stormy, and as the road lay for a long distance by the side of Loch Lomond I had an opportunity of repeating the experiences of the night of my arrival. On this occasion we did not reach home till one o'clock on Sunday morning, when we were quite ready for a well-earned dinner. Nothing would have induced me to stay so long in the midst of so much rain and wind, which deprived mountain and loch alike of their charm, and left nothing to view but a damp grey mist, but for my love of the work and my deep and everlasting regard for one of the noblest and most courageous of men then in the field in the interest of progress. These journeys were not the longest undertaken during my ten days' stay.

From Dumbartonshire I crossed to East Lothian to take part in the contest which Mr. Haldane was waging against Lord Elcho in Haddingtonshire. Communication between the places of meeting proved to be much easier in the Lothians than in Dumbartonshire. The gatherings addressed were admirable in every respect, and before I left I had the satisfaction of knowing that Mr. Haldane was making a great fight of it, that he had every prospect of defeating the young laird. And he did defeat him, and has since held the seat against all comers. Previous to my arrival on the spot the Conservative candidate had referred to me on several occasions, and these references were carefully collected and placed in my hands. I was thus enabled to give a local flavour to my addresses, which but for this would have been entirely lacking, for I had no former acquaintance with the district to fall back upon. But on neither side was language of an abusive or offensive nature used, and when less than twelve months later I met Lord Elcho's father, the Earl of Wemyss, on the Lough Ness golf links, he greeted me with great cordiality and many congratulations on my attempts to learn the royal and ancient game. Next morning he sent a mounted messenger to the cottage where I was staying with an invitation to lunch at Gosford House. Unfortunately I was just on the point of leaving Gullane and was thus compelled to refuse the kindly invitation of one for whom I had conceived a strong personal liking when he sat in the House of Commons as Lord Elcho. Curiously enough, after his defeat in Haddingtonshire Lord Elcho failed for some time to find another seat, but eventually returned to the House of Commons for the borough of Ipswich, which he represented until his voluntary retirement in 1895.

Some years after the Haddingtonshire contest I was playing in the Parliamentary Golf Tournament. My opponent was Mr. Baird, M.P., one of the Glasgow representatives. According to the handicap I had to give him points, and at one time he was five up. By playing for all I was worth I managed to get even, and at the seventeenth hole I had one to my credit. A considerable number of members who had finished their round doubled back to witness the end of our match, and among them was Lord Elcho. By some mischance I was interrupted in my swing at the last tee-shot, and instead of driving the ball squarely I merely topped it, sending it into a furze-bush, greatly to the delight of the North British section of the audience. In the excitement of the moment my opponent followed my example and lodged his ball in the same bush. Putting forth a strenuous effort, I managed to play into the open, but Mr. Baird, attempting the same stroke, was less fortunate, and left his ball in a rather worse position than before. He was not much comforted by Lord Elcho exclaiming, " Play carefully, Baird, or Broadhurst will beat you as he beat me in East Lothian." It was a true prophecy, for with the next stroke I landed my ball within two yards of the hole and won by two up.

But to return to my electioneering campaign. After leaving Scotland I proceeded to Nottingham to assist Colonel Seely and the other Liberal candidates, and then the time arrived to think of my own political interests. The combined Parliamentary boroughs of Stoke-upon-Trent had been separated into two constituencies by the Redistribution Bill of 1884. For various reasons—the nature of which I cannot well go into at this time—I was led to decide not to contest the Pottery borough again. Looking back upon that decision I cannot but regard it as one of the greatest political blunders of my life. I believe now that I exaggerated the difficulty, which appeared so great in prospection, consequent upon contesting the seat single-handed, and inducements in another direction helped me into this fresh political error. However that may be, at that time my resignation seemed a wise step, and, having intimated this to the local Liberal Association, I hastily involved myself in pledges to another constituency in order that I might not be over-persuaded to reconsider my decision, as, indeed, I was heartily and universally pressed to do by the leading Liberals of North Staffordshire. Upon the publication of my letter of resignation, within less than a month I received invitations to stand for some ten or twelve different constituencies in various parts of the country. After due consideration I consented to stand as the Liberal Labour candidate for the Bordesley division of Birmingham. My electioneering tours in Scotland and elsewhere had left me no time for canvassing my new constituency, and when I arrived there, worn and weary with much travelling and speechmaking, the polling was only a few days off. My opponent was a well-known and wealthy brewer of the district who owned a large number of licensed houses in the division. He had expended much time and trouble in nursing the constituency, and had also the advantage of the aid of an able and popular wife and family. Possessing ample means, he was from the wirepuller's point of view, an eminently strong candidate. On the other hand, I found myself in a constituency of which I was totally ignorant, and a complete stranger to the vast majority of the voters.

Before I had been forty-eight hours in the division I devoutly wished I had never seen the place. I was weary and disheartened by my recent campaign, and I found myself quartered in a private lodging-house, with all the discomforts associated with such shelters for the poor in purse. My first meeting was discouraging, and I found my new surroundings well-nigh intolerable. But it was too late to think of retiring from the contest, and there was nothing to do but to face the situation with the best grace possible. Gradually affairs assumed a better complexion; my second meeting was attended with evident success, and from that time the local Liberals supported me most loyally.

It was thought by many of my friends and supporters that the fact of the Conservative candidate being a brewer would rally to my side all sections of the Temperance Party. But even at that time experience had taught me not to place implicit reliance upon such assurances, and my anticipations were subsequently realised. The more cautious of my supporters admitted that my opponent had a big start and that I had much leeway to make up, but they all agreed that by hard work I should yet bear away the palm. The two main points of his political faith were Beer and Fair Trade, and so I was not surprised to hear of the presence in the division of many of my old antagonists—champions of the countervailing duty on sugar and advocates of the so-called Fair Trade. These men professed to represent the London and other trades, and announced that they bore a mandate from the workers to expose and denounce me. Utterly unfounded allegations of disloyalty to the Labour cause, whose falsity had been exposed and denounced time after time by responsible authorities of the trades-unions, were hashed up again and served to the Bordesley electors as a savoury dish, in the hope that time and opportunity to expose the slanders would fail me. But never was a man more heartily supported by members of trades-unions and working men who took a leading part in political life than I was on that occasion. Baffled by the unanimity on my behalf and out-manœuvred at every point, these dispensers of stale abuse soon found Birmingham too warm for them, and the efforts of my persecutors, so far from injuring my chances, vastly increased them.

After ten days of unceasing effort I felt I had made some headway. Unfortunately, I soon found myself confronted by a more formidable foe than the pseudo working men. In one corner of the division there happened to be a ccnsiderable Irish population, and to my dismay the Irish headquarters sent down to Birmingham Mr. T. P. O'Connor, whose ready speech and marvellous energy proved an awkward factor in the contest. Except for the presence of John Bright at one of my meetings, I had to depend entirely on my own efforts and the help of local speakers. On the other hand, my opponent was greatly aided by speakers from the surrounding divisions, and although a brewer, I was assured that he possessed the tremendous advantage of the support of the Church of England Temperance Society, the Anglican visitors, and the charity distributors. Notwithstanding all these forces on his side, I was enabled to administer to him a handsome beating, gaining the seat by some twelve hundred votes.

During this short but hard contest I found time to visit some of the other divisions of Birmingham and speak in support of the Liberal candidates. I also paid a flying visit to Norwich, where Mr. J. J. Colman and Mr. R. S. Wright (now Mr. Justice Wright of the King's Bench) were standing. We had a magnificent meeting, but Mr. Wright failed to secure the second seat. Owing to various allegations, a petition was brought against the successful Conservative candidate, who was compelled to vacate the seat.

The next night I attended a meeting at Yarmouth in support of Captain Norton. I have had varied experiences of hostile demonstrations in the way of stones and chair-legs, but that meeting will long remain in my memory by reason of the profusion of rotten eggs and bags of flour. Once at a Disestablishment meeting in Lancashire the speakers—of whom I was one—were pursued by a fierce crowd of male and female defenders of the Church, who were only to be dispersed by the efforts of the local firemen with the engine throwing water on the people at full pressure. But on this occasion the shower of eggs and flour was absolutely without break. Curiously enough, this malodorous mixture was not aimed indiscriminately at the platform, but only at certain of the speakers who were obnoxious to the audience. Personally I was thankful to find that I had not incurred the ill favour of the wielders of these powerful arguments ; but some of my friends presented a very sorry appearance.

On my return to Birmingham I received an urgent request to proceed to Bury in order to give one night's service to Sir Henry James (now Lord James of Hereford). The great assistance he had rendered to trades-unionism in the early seventies had been well-nigh forgotten by the younger generation, and at this time he was not personally known to the Lancashire workers. Party loyalty as well as trades-union gratitude compelled me to respond to the call ; but in order to get up my case, as the lawyers say, on behalf of Sir Henry, I had to wire and despatch letters in all directions to trades-union officials for reference papers, for my books of reference were all in London and no one there to send them to me. The conditions of the meeting were that it should be confined practically to trades-unionists, and none but trades-union officials were to take part in it, from the Chairman downwards. When I arrived at Bury I found before me a mass meeting of *bonâ fide* working men. By the aid of the Parliamentary Committee's documents I had no difficulty in proving up to the hilt that Sir Henry James's advocacy of, and devotion to, the cause of Labour from the time of his entry into Parliament had been unbroken and unwavering; and by his position as a distinguished lawyer he had been able to render such services to the working classes as entitled him to their undivided support at the poll. On the following day I returned to Birmingham, and shortly after received several assurances from Bury that the meeting had done much good to the Liberal cause; and more than once Sir Henry James has protested that that gathering of trades-unionists secured his return to Parliament as the representative of Bury.

Only once more did I leave Bordesley before the day of poll, and that was to speak for Mr. Cobb, the Liberal candidate for Rugby division. As a special train was provided for my return journey, I was back in time for a meeting of my own the same night.

The scene in Bordesley on the night of the poll was one of extraordinary excitement. Thousands of people filled the streets and squares in the neighbourhood of the Town Hall and the Liberal Club, while the rain poured pitilessly down through an atmosphere of indescribable mugginess. For me the day was one of incessant movement, driving backwards and forwards from committee-room to polling-booth, and it was nine o'clock at night before I could sit down to my first meal since breakfast. Towards midnight I wended my way, accompanied by Mr.

and Mrs. Schnadhorst, to the Liberal Club, where we awaited the declaration of the poll. So confident of success were the supporters of Mr. Showell that up to a late hour at night large sums of money at long odds were offered backing Mr. Showell's chances of victory. I shall never forget the scene beneath the Liberal Club windows when the figures were announced. It is but rarely in a lifetime that one hears such shouts from a great and excited throng as reached my ears that night. I was dragged from an inner room where I had sought refuge from the tumult and compelled to return thanks to the seething multitude below. These were the days when Birmingham was the Mecca of Liberals. It was the shrine of the advanced guard of Radicalism. Nothing could equal its devotion to great ideals. Liberalism was a religion to Birmingham people. Had one then predicted what has since happened, the reply would have been, like the Israelite of old, " If I forget Thee, O Jerusalem, let my right hand forget her cunning."

Domestically I never had a more uncomfortable three weeks than during that contest. Even with the aid of my wife to make the best of our poor surroundings and to give an appearance of comfort and order, it was with the greatest difficulty that I could remain in the place. Mr. Maxwell, my faithful assistant, was ever present, and without him I could not have continued my contest. The one oasis in my desert was the ever-open door of Mr. Schnadhorst's house, and the kindly hospitality shown by his beloved wife. It was a true place of refuge from the storms and discomfort and the jarring discords of political strife.

Although I had met Dr. Dale on previous occasions I had never really come into close acquaintanceship with him till this time. The first occasion on which I had heard him preach was at the Sunday morning service at Carr Lane Chapel. I had the pleasure of spending the evening of that day at his house, and, strange as it may appear, I never seemed to realise his greatness so much as I did over our mutual pipes and friendly chat. The smallest things he said were inspiring and elevating, and an hour in his company increased one's admiration for his character and his deep and broad sympathy for all around him. The more one knew of him the greater became one's reverence for him. He was gentle and strong, humble and elevated in the highest degree. I can call him to mind at will, and then I hear his words as though still present in the flesh.

Throughout the contest I was ably represented by my agent, Mr. W. Allard, whose accuracy, industry, and coolheadedness contributed largely to the victory; and I have ever felt grateful to him for, and shall continue to remember, his rare devotion to my cause. This testimony to his worth is now of no value to him, as all these qualities are well known in whatever part of the country, and they are many, he has been called upon to act as election agent, and especially is he appreciated and valued as the Secretary to the Home Counties Liberal Association in Parliament Street.

No sooner was my own seat secure than the call of duty summoned me to the aid of other candidates almost without a moment's respite. After a flying visit to Chester, which Sir Walter Foster was contesting, I proceeded to Crewe, where the Liberal candidate was the late Mr. George Latham. Considerable excitement had been aroused among the employees of the Crewe works by a circular referring to the election issued by the railway authorities. This document had been interpreted as a hint to the men to favour the Conservative candidate, and feeling ran high on the subject in the Liberal camp. I accordingly made it my chief aim to inspire the workers to use their suffrages as became free and independent citizens. I threw my whole soul into the struggle, and scored a strong point by telling of my memorable adventures when I was passing through Portsmouth on a long tramp in the winter of 1858–9, and was taken in and hospitably entertained by the Cheshire Militiamen, as I have already related. I spoke with deep gratitude of the tender way in which these citizen soldiers had nursed and ministered to me in my hour of need. The recital of that story produced a deep impression on that Cheshire audience. Late the same night I was comparing notes with Mr. Latham on the day's work and mentioned the effect which this reminiscence had made upon my meeting. What was my surprise to learn that at the very time I was receiving the hospitality of the men's mess, Mr. Latham himself was staying in the same barracks as the guest of one of the officers.

A visit to West Staffordshire in support of Mr. Bass's candidature, which next occupied my attention, was memorable for a misadventure of the kind to which political speakers in county divisions are occasionally liable. I accompanied the candidate and his wife to Ednesford, eight or ten miles from Stafford, where we were staying. It was a dark night, with a thick heavy mist, and much of the low lands surrounding Stafford were flooded. During the progress of the meeting the coachman had been informed of a short cut for the return journey. Soon after leaving the village a violent concussion informed us that something had gone wrong. Alighting from the vehicle we discovered ourselves in a narrow lane surrounded by submerged pastures, and on a road the roughness of which threatened to demolish the carriage. The driver was ordered to take us back to the high road, but the lane was too narrow to allow a turning movement, and so we had to push on. Presently another halt was called: the ground had become soft and marshy; the wheels of the carriage and the legs of the horses sank into it so deeply that we were once more compelled to alight. Our efforts to throw some light on the path in front of the horses were frustrated by the immobility of the carriage lamps, which refused to leave their sockets. Nothing was left but for us to turn out and find assistance. So we set off, guided to some extent by a wood on our left. Presently we plunged into a pool of water. Happily we pulled up when only knee deep. After a long hail through the mossy bog we were in the last stages of despair, when luckily we espied a light twinkling through a clearing in the wood. One of our number was despatched to this haven of refuge, and, evading a threatening house dog, he obtained enough information to enable us to quit the inhospitable marsh and by traversing a by-road to regain the highway. Altogether our coachman's short cut cost us about two extra hours, besides the discomfort of being wet to the knee.

After another meeting or two in the Midlands, I at length received an intimation that my electioneering tasks were finished, and I was enabled once again to enjoy the peace and comforts of my own hearth, which never appeared more grateful than after these political wanderings.

At this time I was living at Brixton Hill. Since 1880 I had been a member of the Reform Club, having been elected by the Political Committee in recognition of services rendered to the Liberal Party ; this membership I still retain. But mine was far too busy a life to afford much time to avail myself of the comforts of club life, and indeed my inclination turned rather towards physical exercise than lounging in a club smoking-room. I have always been a good walker, both for speed and distance I have held a fair record, and I had made a practice of walking home from the House of Commons except on rare occasions, when I caught the four o'clock morning train from Victoria Station. In the early eighties late sittings were the rule, and all the last trains and buses had disappeared long before the House would rise. My road was mostly uphill, and generally took an hour for the journey. It may be imagined that such a practice after a hard day's work of sixteen to twenty hours' duration required considerable stamina to maintain. But the sturdiness of my constitution enabled me to keep up the habit regularly until 1888, and even after that time I walked the whole distance at frequent intervals. Those who are ignorant of outdoor life in London in the early hours of the morning would be astonished at the freshness and balmy nature of the air at five o'clock, especially during the summer-time. Between Kennington Gate and Brixton Hill I have many times inhaled with zest the scented air from the fields beyond the rim of Greater London. I seldom carried an umbrella, and for the first six years took no extra precaution against cold except for a light summer overcoat. Only twice was I overtaken by a storm : once it was a snow blizzard and the other occasion was a thunderstorm. Nor did I ever experience any interference from roughs or thieves, even in the darkest and most lonely parts of that long walk. Once or twice I expected an assault and prepared myself to resist, but nothing came of it, and it might have been mere fancy, the result of physical exhaustion, with its inevitable consequence of nervousness. I have read somewhere that coastguardsmen possess the faculty of sleeping on their beats. I know nothing of that, but I am certain I must have been asleep one morning on my way home ; for as I passed Brixton Church I was startled out of my senses by what appeared to my bewildered ears a discharge of artillery. On investigation it turned out to be the clock striking three. When at home I rarely ever failed to spend at least half the Saturday in long walks in the surrounding country ; and this practice I maintained until my golfing days began. From that time nothing but dire necessity prevented me from spending my Saturdays on the links. I have no doubt this love of outdoor exercise materially assisted in keeping me in a sound state of health for so many years.

But to return to the General Election of 1885. Being much occupied in trades-union work at my office, I used the Reform Club much more frequently than had hitherto been my custom. As may be easily imagined, the club was at this time the centre of great political activity. Mr. Labouchere was busily pursuing his policy of endeavouring to influence the Liberal leaders and rank and file to use the large majority they had gained at the polls in favour of Home Rule in Ireland. I do not propose to enter into the negotiations and intrigues which heralded the first Home Rule Bill. This volume is intended to be merely a series of personal reminiscences and not a political history. I only refer to the matter to mention a remark I heard one day in the central hall of the Reform Club. The speaker was an ex-Cabinet Minister who subsequently sat on the Front Bench in the two following Liberal ministries. He had been strongly condemning the policy of adopting Home Rule as a Liberal measure, and wound up with the exclamation, " If this policy is persisted in, it will wreck the Liberal Party ! " How literally that prophecy has been verified is public knowledge. My own opinions on large questions of policy were, I confess, never sought for by the chiefs of the party ; but personally I was in favour of Home Rule, though my judgment would have led to support procedure by resolution rather than by a Bill. However that may be, our leader decided to take the line of Home Rule, and personal opinion gave way to party loyalty, and the great body of Liberal Members manfully supported Mr. Gladstone in his great crusade, which was destined to end so disastrously for him and his cause.

# CHAPTER XI

## I REACH THE TREASURY BENCH

THE new year came, and when Parliament met the Tory Government was immediately defeated on a motion of want of confidence. The procedure was a mere formality, as they were in a great minority, and ministers sat in their seats calmly awaiting the inevitable division. To my astonishment the change of government brought about a momentous change in my life. One busy day, when I was closely engaged in pressing business in my office, a messenger brought me a letter in Mr. Gladstone's well-known handwriting. Hastily tearing open the envelope, I found the following communication :—

"SECRET.]        21, CARLTON HOUSE TERRACE, S.W.
"*February 5th*, 1886.

"DEAR MR. BROADHURST,—

"I have very great pleasure in proposing to you that you should accept office as Under-Secretary of State in the Home Department. Alike on private and on public grounds I trust it may be agreeable to you to accept this appointment, which should remain strictly secret until your name shall have been before Her Majesty.

> "I remain, with much regard,
> "Sincerely yours,
> "W. E. GLADSTONE."

It was not without great hesitation and serious misgivings as to my qualifications for the office that I accepted this flattering proposal. As is the custom, I called immediately upon Mr. Gladstone at his residence in Carlton House Terrace to acquaint him with my decision. He gave me a hearty welcome, and in subsequent conversation he referred to the dark days of Liberalism from 1876 to 1878, and assured me that he had never forgotten my labours and my devotion to the cause of Liberty during those exciting times, when all the worst passions of mankind seemed to pervade the metropolis. He went on to impart to me the fact that he had then determined, when a favourable moment arrived, to recognise my services to the Eastern Question Association in some adequate fashion. Then he inquired what was my answer to his proposal. I at once replied that if it was his wish that I should join the Administration, it should be in some less prominent position than the post he had selected. But on this point Mr. Gladstone would admit no discussion; he brought the conversation to a close by playfully informing me that he would answer for me himself, and that I must prepare at once to enter upon the duties of the office.

I can honestly declare that I left Mr. Gladstone's

house without any of those feelings of exhilaration and pleasing excitement which the gift of office is generally supposed to awaken in the breast of the politician. Like a drowning man, I lived my life over again in the next half-hour. The lowly beginning of my career, its labours at the forge and the stonemason's shop, the privations, the wanderings, and my varying fortunes, stood out in my mind's eye as clearly as so many living pictures. Especially did my memory recall the months I had spent working on the very Government buildings which I was about to enter as a Minister of the Crown. Then, returning to the present, I realised as I had never done before the irretrievable loss which the lack of education in my early days involved. Visions of humiliation arising from the duties of my new office and my meagre capacity and endowments rose before me with startling vividness. The next twenty-four hours were passed in a tormenting alternation of desire and reluctance : of desire to grapple with and overcome the difficulties of the position by sheer force of will, as I had done on many occasions in the past ; and of reluctance to leave my seat below the gangway, where I had fought for the cause of Labour untrammelled by official limitations and the discipline associated with office. I firmly believe that had not Mr. Gladstone shown such a determined intention to attach me to his Ministry, I should have left him that day with a grateful acknowledgment of his kindness, but an unmistakable refusal to accept his offer.

As soon as the appointment was officially announced in the newspapers, congratulations poured in on me from all parts of the country and from all classes of the community. None of these gave me keener pleasure than a letter from an old stonemason, written in a shaky and almost indecipherable hand. I remember him, when I was a boy, as a pleasant, cheery, well-fed man, surrounded by considerable comfort for one in his position, and the thought of his kind remembrance and congratulations greatly cheered me. Many were the letters I received which bore strong evidence in orthography and phrasing that the writers, like myself, were born before the era of Board Schools. A few days later, in the lobby of the House, I received personal and cordial congratulations on my appointment from the Prince of Wales.

This appointment, of course, obliged me to relinquish the post of Secretary to the Parliamentary Committee of the Trades-Union Congress, and my place was taken by Mr. George Shipton.

Scarcely had the change of Government been effected than the Unemployed agitation in the metropolis began to assume grave proportions, culminating in the serious outbreak known as the Trafalgar Square Riots. The police arrangements were ineffectual to suppress disorder, and several shops were sacked by the large criminal element in the crowd. As a result the Chief Commissioner of the Metropolitan Police resigned, and Sir Charles Warren received the appointment. These events naturally threw a large amount of work upon the Home Office, as well as a heavy burden of responsibility, by no means a pleasant initiation for me into official life. But as the days rolled by, I was greatly cheered to find that the experience I had gained in many directions in my old post of Parliamentary Secretary, with its frequent contact with nearly every Government department, stood me now in good stead. The position of an Under-Secretary of State in the House of Commons whose chief is in the same House involves little Parliamentary work, and in the department itself, if one is so minded, the routine duties can be reduced to a minimum. It not infrequently happens that the chief takes upon himself substantially the whole of the public duties of the department, leaving his subordinate with very light work, involving little or no responsibility. But this was not the case with my chief, Mr. Childers. Never did master take more pains in fulfilling the duty imposed upon him by indentures towards his apprentice than Mr. Childers took with me. He not only carefully instructed me in the duties of the office, but gave me many opportunities to act on my own responsibility. A certain class of work was definitely allotted to me, and I was informed that on me would rest the responsibility for its efficient discharge. On several occasions departmental matters, some of them of considerable public importance, were left entirely in my hands to investigate and decide upon. I remember distinctly in one case of an alleged excess of punishment by imprisonment by some county magistrate, I went carefully into the matter, and decided to reduce the sentence, and the men were immediately liberated. In another case, a Bill which had been for several years in the hands of successive Ministers, and which had reference to police matters of the metropolis, was handed over to me, both for consideration as to what (if any) changes should be made in it and to introduce it in Parliament, and if possible to get it passed into law. It involved a loan of something like a quarter of a million of money, and gave to the London police authorities powers of compulsory purchase of freehold in cases where new police-stations were required or existing ones were held on lease. I prepared an elaborate speech, full of convincing arguments, for the second reading stage; but, unfortunately, when my turn came the hour was so advanced that I saw my only hope was to follow the Yorkshire farmer's advice to his lawyer, "Stow the cackle an' get to th' 'osses"—in other words, to throw my speech overboard and simply move that the Bill be read. Thus, in the small hours of the morning, I passed a Bill containing the principle of leasehold enfranchisement, and so far as I am aware not a single Member recognised the central principle of the measure, which to me, the author of the Leasehold Enfranchisement Bill, was naturally a matter of considerable interest.

Mr. Childers had prepared a Bill to extend the Miners' Regulation Act. For this purpose several consultations were held at the Home Office with the officials of that department.  At these consultations I was always present and took part in the discussions. In many cases Mr. Childers accepted suggestions from me designed to safeguard the interests and lives of the miners, and I was present at the final meeting for determining the scope of the Bill.  Domestic affliction prevented my chief from moving the second reading of this measure on the appointed day, and it fell to my lot to discharge that important duty.  But Parliamentary vicissitudes ordered otherwise ; the Bill was not reached that night in time to proceed with it.  No progress was made with it that session, and when the Tories came into office again later in the summer they found a well-matured Bill to amend the Miners' Act ready to hand.

Many people failed to recognise in Mr. Childers a brilliant statesman ; yet it cannot be denied that he was an exceedingly able administrator and a most conscientious and painstaking Minister.  His largeness of heart and kindness of disposition, his patience with the shortcomings and failures of his subordinates, were remarkable.  Mrs. Childers, whom I frequently had the privilege of meeting, was a meet companion to her distinguished husband.  A woman of keen intelligence and wide experience and endowed with many high qualities, she always exhibited a spirit of encouragement and hopefulness ; to me she was a true and sincere friend.

The flow of congratulations and approving comments on my appointment was not altogether unbroken.  I remember one noble lord courteously suggesting that now Mr. Broadhurst had been made Under-Secretary of State for Home Affairs, it would be an appropriate sequel to appoint Charles Peace, the notorious murderer and burglar, Chief Commissioner of Police. This induced some enterprising newspaper man to investigate the family history of the author of this elegant witticism, with a somewhat inconvenient result for the noble lord. In another case the then Parliamentary representative of the Kennington Division, becoming anxious for the fair fame of the Home Office, addressed a question to the Home Secretary as to whether he had seen a report in newspapers that the present Under-Secretary for Home Affairs had been under the surveillance of the police during the lock-out in the building trades in 1872. The nature of the reply to this vulgar personal attack, supplemented by a word or two of advice from myself, effectually put a stop to any further inquiries from this inquisitive young man ; and shortly afterwards this prop of the Constitution was lost in the oblivion of those for whom their constituents have no longer any use.

Early in the session, as soon as the Irish policy of the Government became known, it was evident to most of us that our tenure of office would be brief. Seeds of disruption were widely scattered, and discontent and restlessness were manifest even in the Cabinet itself.

It is extremely difficult for anyone outside the inner circle of a Ministry to form exact opinions on the causes which produced certain results, but I think I am not far wrong in claiming that if there had been a little less independence on one side and a greater capacity for conciliating the divergent interests on the other, as well as a more effective Intelligence Department, the disastrous split in the Liberal Party might never have occurred. For some years previous I had been on pretty intimate terms, politically speaking, with the chief figures in our party. I had been favoured with many interviews of a highly confidential nature, and from knowledge which thus came into my possession I was able fairly to understand the attitude of the various component parts of the Cabinet. Even up to the last week before the fatal division on the second reading of the Home Rule Bill I felt there was some chance of securing the neutrality, if not the support, of John Bright. A very short time before the second reading I had the pleasure of dining at the same table with Mr. Bright, I was the only person present who was not a member of his family, and I was greatly impressed by his evident reluctance to tear himself from the most cherished political associates of his lifetime. This belief I took care to communicate to the proper quarter, but perhaps I was mistaken, or perhaps the efforts put forth to realise my hopes were not sufficiently sincere, or were not made at all.

The shadow of the coming disruption was painfully evident for weeks before the event. Strained relations began to make themselves apparent in outward demeanour. Close friends of the past exhibited a coldness to each other. Nor was this apparent to our own side only. Our opponents, quick to seize their advantage and skilled in political manœuvring, employed all the arts of social life to capture the waverers. The effect of such influence was found in unexpected quarters. The great London mansions were continuously ablaze with brilliant entertainments designed to attract the rank and file of the party. On the other hand, no adequate measures for counteracting these insidious temptations were taken by the Liberals. With other members I undertook the task of attending to some of the waverers. It was a strange experience, this political wet-nursing, and one not likely to recur in our time. Personally, I never wavered for a moment in what I considered my duty—loyalty to the great leader of the Liberal Party. But the personal animus which was imported into the affair both amazed and pained me, and the inevitable snapping of bonds of friendship and amity gave me much disquietude. After a personal acquaintance with Mr. Chamberlain extending over many years, ripening as years went on into what I believe was a mutual confidence in each other, I felt the wrench of separation more than I can describe. I had a great personal liking for the man. To those with whom he is on good terms, he is most fascinating—no airs or high and mightiness. He stands truly by his friends and never leaves them at the critical moment. In this description I am, of course, speaking of his private conduct to those in the circle of his supporters; what he is as an opponent all the world knows. Many of his high qualities commanded my unbounded admiration. In the days when he was the subject of taunts and gibes from the Tories, and when the more timid and Whiggish section of the Liberal Party openly showed their distrust of him, my attachment grew deeper and stronger, so that the separation which perforce ensued at the Liberal Unionist secession affected me in a very special manner.

To the best of my knowledge and belief, in the composition of the Cabinet there were many cross currents at work, and a considerable volume of dissatisfaction. There were influences most strongly mistrustful of Mr. Chamberlain. These influences counted for keeping him from the higher offices in the State; and however strong a Prime Minister may be, he must at times bend to the winds that blow about him. I believe these influences were wholly aristocratic. These people did not like the Birmingham man, and they intended to show their mistrust of him. If I am correct in my conjecture, and I think I am not entirely wide of the mark, it will be seen that a fertile soil already existed for seeds of disruption should the winds of party strife blow them that way. It is another illustration of the old adage that "adversity makes strange bedfellows." The irony of events brought some of those who did not love Mr. Chamberlain to his feet to lead them in the rebellion against their political kith and kin.

The fatal day at length arrived, and with it the division in the House of Commons, which was the outward and visible sign of the cleavage of the Liberal Party. Those of us who took part in the memorable scene will, I imagine, never forget the poignant sensations it evoked as long as memory lasts. The strength of the two sections had been accurately gauged by the Whips, and those of us who had been most active in canvassing the party and endeavouring to bring back the strayed sheep knew only too well that our doom was sealed, and that the magnificent majority of Liberals returned by the constituencies was about to be scattered like autumn leaves before the gale. The moment was intensely exciting. I have many times thought that the greatest artist of the day could not have found a subject more impressive or dramatic than was presented when Mr. Gladstone walked to the desk where the division clerks were ticking off the names of members as they passed through the lobbies. With a marvellous firmness of step, and his mobile features set in an extraordinary expression of gravity and fixed determination, the statesman whom all England had learned to call the Grand Old Man might have been an early Christian martyr marching to his doom. From a point of vantage I was enabled to see him full in the face as he approached, and to me at least the sight was sublime—the look of fixed, almost agonised resolve of a great leader to sacrifice his proud position at the head of a great and powerful party to satisfy the claims of justice and to bestow the blessings of peace and prosperity upon a sorely vexed country.

As everyone knows, this fatal division was followed by an appeal to the country, and once again the United Kingdom was thrown into the turmoil of a General Election, which was fought with extraordinary vehemence and bitterness. For reasons with which I need not trouble the reader I had resolved not to stand again for the Bordesley division, and I had to decide on another constituency. Colonel Seely, the Liberal member for West Nottingham, had voted against the Government on the Home Rule Bill, and it was resolved to contest his seat in the Home Rule interest. At the invitation of the local Liberals, strongly backed by the party officials at headquarters, I consented to make an effort to capture the Colonel's seat. So down I went to Nottingham, and in fourteen days I found myself member for the division. All things considered, it was probably the most eventful contest of that General Election.

I have already referred to the visit I paid to Nottingham in the autumn of 1885 to support the three Liberal candidates, who succeeded in carrying the three seats of the borough. Colonel Seely's success on that occasion was not in the least surprising to those who knew the circumstances. He was a large colliery proprietor, an active and liberal-minded man in local affairs, and possessed the advantage of a hardworking and talented family to support his candidature. All things combined to constitute him an ideal and irresistible candidate, and in 1885 he won the seat by a majority, roundly speaking, of two thousand five hundred. For me, a comparative stranger without local connections or influence, a "carpet-bagger" pure and simple, to attempt to capture this seat within ten months of Colonel Seely's triumphant return seemed the height of madness. But the die was cast; my consent had been given; and before I had time for reflection I found myself in the midst of a hotly contested fight. As at Bordesley I received no outside help for my platform work, and again I found time to assist my colleagues in the other two divisions. The struggle was herculean, and I was almost overwhelmed in the mass of correspondence that reached me from all parts of the kingdom making inquiries as to the record and fitness of various candidates. Added to this was my Home Office work, which demanded my attention for a portion of each day, so that I had but little leisure for rest or time for thought during the two weeks the contest lasted. A good friend lent me his house during the election—a welcome assistance from an economical point of view, but marred by the fact that the establishment was in the hands of painters, the evidence of whose industry was not as music in my ears at six o'clock in the morning, when my previous working day had only ceased at midnight.

But at last the polling day arrived and put an end to all this excitement; and I had the proud satisfaction of hearing that Colonel Seely's vast majority had been wiped out, and that the seat was mine by a majority of eight hundred or so. I had made arrangements to leave Nottingham that same night, successful or unsuccessful, and when the figures were brought to me at midnight I was just on the point of catching the mail train to London. By 8.30 the next morning I had recorded my vote at the Brixton polling-station, and was again on my way to the ancient city of Chester to help my good friend Sir Walter Foster. On his polling day I took part in some meetings in a county division, and got back to Chester at one o'clock next morning to find my friend's seat captured by the enemy. A journey to Nottingham followed, whence I proceeded after a short delay to Mansfield, where a set of brakes awaited for a tour of the Mansfield division in company with the Liberal candidate, Mr. Foljambe, and a splendid electioneering party. At two in the afternoon we set out for the big mining villages, and as we made our way along I was honoured by the presentation of some half a dozen addresses from the miners of the district. Each address, of course, involved a short speech of acknowledgment over and above the speeches at a similar number of public meetings, all in the open air.

At one of the largest gatherings, where a row of lofty trees at our backs spread out leafy branches like an emerald sounding-board, we encountered the Conservative candidate, and I well remember with what dignity and confidence he marched to the outskirts of the crowd while I was addressing it. A local politician at my side informed me of his identity, and I lost no time in welcoming him to the meeting and inviting him to a seat in our brake, accompanied by the promise of an opportunity to address the gathering. An avenue was rapidly opened up in the crowd, and by gentle pressure our opponent was induced to accept the invitation. Erect and defiant, he took his stand on the improvised platform ; but his self-satisfaction soon disappeared, for I could not resist the temptation of gently chaffing him on his martial appearance, and of assuring him that the people, despite the respect in which they held him, had determined to secure the return of his Liberal rival. This little incident greatly tickled the crowd and secured us a splendid ovation.

So we journeyed on through the division from meeting to meeting, till at last we reached Mansfield again and found a large concourse waiting to give us a hearty " welcome home." More speechifying was inevitable, and it was nearly midnight before I sat down to the first meal I had an opportunity of taking since an early breakfast in Chester that morning.

To the ordinary methodical citizen, whose habits work with clock-like regularity, these prolonged periods of excitement and hard work without regular meals may appear almost incredible ; but those who have gone through an electioneering campaign know too well how impossible it is to avoid such experiences. But though in the excitement of the moment one scarcely notices the lack of sustenance, yet in the end Dame Nature exacts a very thorough retribution for the neglect of her claims, as I have found out in latter years.

From Mansfield I proceeded to Nottingham, and after conferring with my chief supporters and agent on matters arising out of my late contest, I left for Derbyshire, where I attended a series of meetings in support of Mr. Jacoby. Next day I addressed several gatherings in the Loughborough division of Leicestershire, and then went north to the Buckrose division to support Mr. W. A. McArthur, now member for St. Austell.

As all the borough elections were now over, and only a few county divisions remained unpolled, I felt that I might rest on my oars, and so returned to London. Here I found the people at headquarters appalled by the terrible extent of the Liberal losses. There was no disguising the fact that the country was in for a period, long or short, of Conservative supremacy. Few Liberals realised how cohesive would prove the elements of Toryism and Dissenting Liberalism which went to make up the Unionist Party. A few, indeed, were clearer-sighted, and amongst them I must number Mr. Chamberlain. I very well remember the last occasion on which the present Colonial Secretary spoke to me before the fatal division on the Home Rule Bill. It was one of the many conversations we held together on the question which way the representatives of Labour would vote, and particularly as to my own course. With great earnestness Mr. Chamberlain assured me that I was about to take part in a division which would effectually wreck the prospects of the Liberal Party for many a long year. But this emphatic warning in no way shook my resolution to stand by Mr. Gladstone and the Home Rule cause. In the new House of Commons Mr. Burt and myself no longer stood alone as representatives of the working classes ; the General Election added no less than nine Labour members, and all proved themselves sound on the question.

The shock to the party system administered by the defection of men like Chamberlain and John Bright among politicians, and Dr. Dale and Mr. Spurgeon in the ranks of Nonconformity, was terrible. Taking the division of West Nottingham, my own constituency, as a sample, I could hardly believe the evidence of my own eyes when I saw the windows of nearly every public-house decorated with printed appeals from John Bright and Charles Haddon Spurgeon to vote against Mr. Gladstone and his followers. The world seemed to have turned upside down, until we almost began to suspect ourselves bereft of our reason.

I left the Home Department, I must confess, with deep and sincere regret. I do not mean regret for the emoluments or the status which the position carries with it—that did not trouble me ; but after six months' close application to my duties I felt I had surmounted many of the initial difficulties of the position. Besides, I had formed many pleasant friendships among the permanent officials of the department. It was like being compelled to withdraw from a contest on the eve of assured victory. I had found the work extremely heavy at first (though the amount and character of the work performed by the Under-Secretary largely depend on his own willingness or unwillingness to undertake them), but my duties had daily become more interesting and varied, and I grew to like more and more of them.

One curious experience that befell me during my short term of office was the discovery that I was entitled, in virtue of my position, to half a carcass of a buck from Windsor, or in lieu thereof one or two guineas—I forget the exact equivalent. I chose the half-buck, and in due course it arrived at the Home Office, whence I had to transport it to my home. It proved rather an alarming addition to my small larder ; but it enabled me to fill a *rôle* which I have found the most grateful in life—that of the dispenser of favours. I was able to distribute among my friends joints of royal venison.

Official life brings with it many opportunities of social entertainments ; but the gaieties of Society, with a big S, never appealed to me. I had no ambition to shine as a diner-out, and few and far between were the occasions on which I dined at private houses. When I first entered the House of Commons in 1880 I was constantly receiving invitations to the usual functions connected with Parliamentary life, including many dinner parties. But my financial circumstances did not permit of my sharing in these entertainments. In the course of twelve months my unwillingness to accept them became pretty widely known, and I found considerable relief in being comparatively free from the frequent embarrassment of having to explain the reason why I could not "go into Society," as the phrase runs.

When I came into office I was assured on all hands that these reservations would have to be abandoned, and that, to begin with, I should have to be presented at Court, a ceremony involving the purchase of an elaborate and costly uniform, as Under-Secretary of State. The mere idea of having to appear at Buckingham Palace in such a garb was altogether too fearful to contemplate. Not that I would be understood to object to such ceremonies as a matter of principle. Variety and picturesqueness in dress I have always admired, in the case of either man or woman ; indeed, I have an affectionate eye for well-harmonised colours and adornment in clothing. But for me, scarcely emerged from a life of vicissitudes and hardships, to don the gold-laced coat and the velvet breeches, the silk stockings and silver-buckled shoes, the cocked hat and dress-sword, appeared such a travesty, that I could not fail to look supremely ridiculous, if not to the outside world, at least to my own eyes.

At length the crucial moment arrived : Mr. Childers appeared in my room to consult my convenience, whether I would prefer the first or the second Levée of the season for my presentation. I lacked the courage to say at once that I did not intend to go at all; but I assured my chief that as the lesser of two evils I should prefer the second Levée, though the third would suit me infinitely better. He would listen to no excuses, and assured me that it was a serious and important part of his Constitutional duties to present me, and that I must be ready to accompany him when the time came. Recognising that further concealment was useless, I made a clean breast of my feelings, and of the horror with which I contemplated the idea of presentation in a Court dress. I did not consider it polite to press the matter any further on this occasion, for I perceived that my statement had considerably shocked the susceptibilities of Mr. Childers. But I set to work immediately to devise some means of obtaining a dispensation from the ceremony.

My first step was to consult one or two friends as to how far I should be justified in refusing to conform to these official usages. One of those whose advice I sought was Mr. Chamberlain, and he strongly encouraged me to persevere in taking relief from attendance at Court. In the course of a few days I communicated to Mr. Childers my fixed resolve to gain a dispensation from attendance at the Levée. He assured me that such a course was impossible, and begged me to save time and further anxiety by giving the necessary orders to a Court tailor.

But I was not to be deterred from my purpose, and after consulting other influential people, I composed a letter setting forth my position, and pleading that I had on one or two occasions received from T.R.H. the Prince and Princess of Wales indulgence to absent myself from functions involving similar difficulties to that which I was now endeavouring to overcome. I further pointed out that the Speakers of the House of Commons had absolved me from attendance at his dinners and levées, adding that under these circumstances I felt sure I should not appeal in vain for Her Majesty's consent to dispense with my presence at the Levée. I have reason to believe that this appeal ultimately came under the personal notice of the Queen, and that Her Majesty was graciously pleased to grant me the dispensation I sought. Thus when I laid down the responsibilities of office I left the Ministerial Bench with the distinction of being the only occupant of such a position who had not been presented at Court or taken part in any of the formal functions, such as the banquet given by the Home Secretary on the anniversary of the Queen's Birthday, the Speaker's receptions, and the like. Up to the present moment I have continued to sit in Parliament, to win elections, and generally discharge my duties to my fellow-men without the aid of either Court dress or evening dress.

It is not to be supposed, however, that my objection to donning these garments arises from any deep and noble principle as a representative of Labour. On the contrary, some of my colleagues in Parliament, as well as several prominent Labour leaders outside the House, observe this usage of Society, and, I must confess, their appearance when thus arrayed is no way inferior to that of their wealthier fellows. I do not think that any Labour member has ever donned a Windsor uniform ; and if my supposition be correct, it naturally follows that none have been able to pay their respects to Mr. Speaker at any of his receptions when Court dress is obligatory. After the General Election of 1886 a departure was made in the order of the Speaker's entertainments. The self-exclusion of eleven members (the number of the Labour representatives in the new Parliament) was felt by Mr. Peel to be highly undesirable. So the accomplished and tactful wife of the Speaker thoughtfully gave us occasional invitations to afternoon tea ; and this concession was subsequently improved upon by the Speaker's giving a morning-dress dinner. I believe this occurred on the Derby Day of 1886, and some thirty members, as well as some distinguished men not members of the House, assembled. The whole of the Labour members were invited, and almost all attended what proved to be an extremely enjoyable evening. I remember having for my right-hand neighbour the late Lord Justice Bowen, who, as everybody knows, was a most accomplished and intellectual man. After discussing many subjects, we turned to the topic of long sentences.

Now it happened that I had acquired some knowledge on this subject, for during the year 1880, on the invitation of the Home Secretary, Sir William Harcourt, Mr. Burt and I had accepted the honorary appointment of Visitors to the Penal Settlements. Our visits were paid at any time we chose, and no notice was given of our coming. If we so desired we were permitted to hold private and uninterrupted interviews with the convicts, so that any complaints might be made freely without fear of subsequent punishment. After twelve months' experience of this work I suffered so much physical and mental distress after each visit that I could no longer continue to act as Visitor. I sent in my resignation, and other Labour representatives were subsequently appointed to the post. The experience gained in these visits led me to the conclusion that long sentences were not effective for the purposes of reformation. Accordingly, I took the opportunity of expressing these opinions to Lord Bowen, and discussed with him the possibility of ascertaining by scientific investigation at which period the repressive effect of imprisonment ceased and the hardening process began. He was keenly interested in the subject, and made many inquiries concerning the details of life in these establishments. I was astounded to find that a judge who had condemned men to long periods of penal servitude, and in all probability would do so again, had never seen the inside of a convict prison, and was largely unacquainted with the mode of life in these establishments. In the end he gave me a promise that he would take the earliest opportunity to inspect one of Her Majesty's prisons.

This dinner, so far as I am aware, was the first and the last of its kind given by Speaker Peel, and I have not heard of the present Speaker making any experiment of a like nature. There may have been good reasons why this innovation never crystallised into a custom ; but I cannot help thinking it unfortunate that so excellent a method of bringing Labour representatives into contact with men distinguished in the spheres of literature, law, art, and science has been suffered to drop out of Parliamentary life.

There was one fashionable function which I attended for years in succession. This was the Garden Party at Marlborough House. As a spectacle it is always worth seeing, for in addition to all the leaders of the political, literary, artistic, and ecclesiastical worlds in this country, many foreign notabilities attend. The chief event, so far as I was able to observe, was the entrance of Her Majesty to the garden from Marlborough House and her progress to the Royal tent, into which none but the privileged few, and they only by invitation, were suffered to penetrate. On one occasion when I was present the Shah of Persia and his little son were the centre of attraction ; at other times it was the Emperor and Empress of Germany, the King and Queen of Denmark, and the Czar of Russia with members of his family. The brilliance of the dresses, the beauty of the garden, and the pleasing strains of the band, made this function a most acceptable diversion in the commonplace round of a workaday world. I was always accompanied at these functions by my niece, for my wife resolutely and steadfastly refused to take part in the frivolities of fashionable people.

# CHAPTER XII

## *IN TROUBLED WATERS*

AS I was now out of office and a free man, the Operative Stonemasons' Society elected me to represent them at the Trades-Union Congress in September, 1886, and by an almost unanimous vote I was re-elected Secretary of the Parliamentary Committee. The resumption of my old work brought me back at once to my former habits of life and spheres of operation. From this period till the close of my connection with the Parliamentary Committee in 1890, when protracted ill-health compelled me to resign my office, I was intimately associated with all the Labour questions which arose in the House of Commons.

The most prominent of these at that time was the Amendment of the Employers' Liability Act of 1880. Mr. Matthews, the Home Secretary, had introduced a Bill on the subject which in no way met the demands of the Congress. During the debate on the second reading the shortcomings of the measure were pointed out to the introducer by deputations, interviews, and other means. But the Government persisted in attempting to force it through the House by sheer weight of numbers.

The Bill was eventually referred to the Grand Committee on Trade, and at the desire of the Parliamentary Committee of the Congress I exerted every effort to induce the Government to amend the objectionable clauses. But I was baffled at every point by a stubborn refusal to make any of the desired changes ; so when the Bill was reported to the House in the autumn session, I moved its rejection. A debate followed, lasting the whole of the night, and the report stage was passed by a majority of fifty.

The main incident of the discussion was a violent attack upon me by Mr. Bradlaugh, who supported the Government. Furthermore, one of the leaders of the Liberal Party severely reprimanded me for venturing to move the rejection of the Bill, on the ground that the debate could only prove abortive and that the Bill was certain to be carried by an overwhelming majority. But the Government majority proved to be anything but overwhelming, and the impression made by the attack on their measure was so great that they withdrew the Bill, and I had the satisfaction of having wrecked the worst drawn-up and most contentious measure ever introduced into Parliament on that question. Moreover, the Government made no second attempt in their remaining four years of office to reintroduce the Bill.

During this time I was under the great disadvantage of being in ill-health, and my medical adviser, Sir Walter Foster, had ordered me to leave London and take a prolonged rest ; but I could not tear myself away from the scene of action until the end of the fight and the rout of the enemy. Had this measure become law, the Bill of 1893-4 could not have been introduced. Although the latter did not reach the Statute Book, yet its chief features created such an impression upon the House that when in 1897 the Conservatives introduced another Bill dealing with the subject, they were careful rather to follow the more liberal line of the 1894 Bill, and not to frame it upon the lines of their abortive Bill of 1880.

In the same year (1888) I was successful in preventing the passing of a Seamen's Pension Bill, which would, in the opinion of most seamen, have injuriously affected their freedom and well-being. It would have bound them hand and foot to the service, and created a servitude of a hateful nature, with insufficient security for alternative benefits.

Two years later I was again interested in shipping matters, this time introducing a Bill with the object of fixing a definite position for the load-line on merchant ships. In the preceding Act (1876) the position was left uncertain, and so far as the law was concerned the load-line might be fixed on the funnel without transgressing the statute. Being unable myself to remain in the House during the later hours of the night, I obtained the assistance of Mr. George Howell to look after the measure in my absence. By dint of amicable consultations with shipowners and the President of the Board of Trade, we were enabled to make such terms as allowed the Bill to be passed that session. Lord Herschell steered it through the House of Lords, and I had the satisfaction of seeing it become law, and of knowing that I had rendered a useful service to that most deserving but sadly neglected class, the merchant seamen of Great Britain.

This was not the first occasion on which Lord Herschell had rendered me valuable service. In the preceding session of Parliament I had introduced a Bill to amend the law of Distraints, and by the aid of Lord Herschell, who piloted it through the Lords, I succeeded in getting the Bill through both Houses. This Act provided that a workman's implements to the value of £5 should be free from distraint for rent ; another clause prevented a landlord who had seized a tenant's goods in lieu of rent from selling them within fifteen days from the date of seizure, instead of five days as in the old statute. This afforded the tenant a better chance of obtaining assistance to save his home being broken up. Other clauses provided for the registration of bailiffs, with the object of preventing acts of illegality so often perpetrated against the defenceless poor. Those who have lived among the poor and seen the grievous wrongs inflicted by the old system of distraint for rent will readily understand the value of this latter clause. The harshness of the old law and the brutality with which it was often carried out were brought home to me by the facts accumulated by Judge Chalmers, of the Birmingham County Court. Any measure calculated to enlarge the power of County Court judges and to raise their status, and thus attract to this field a higher class of barristers, always had my deepest sympathy. The County Court is essentially the tribunal of the poor and friendless ; and in order that those least able to help themselves should have the best chance of securing every protection that the law affords, it is of the first importance that men of high capacity and alertness of perception should be induced to accept County Court judgeships.

When the Trades-Union Congress assembled in Dundee towards the end of 1889, there was little substantial progress to report, for the session had been a barren one. The only striking feature in my report referred to the consent provisionally given by the Government to send representatives to the Labour Convention proposed by the German Government ; with this topic I have dealt elsewhere. But however barren my report was, it cannot be said that the proceedings of the Congress lacked vivacity and excitement. In order that my readers may fully understand the position of affairs at that time, I must retrace my steps and recall the course of events in the political world immediately succeeding the General Election of 1886. After their crushing defeat at the polls the Liberal Party, guided by that greatest of organisers, Mr. Schnadhorst, set energetically to work to regain the ground they had lost in the country. The result was the establishment of the finest organisation in the history of the party.

During the six years of power enjoyed by the Tory

Party an unprecedented number of bye-elections occurred, and in nearly every one I took some part. In certain of these contests I was the principal speaker on the Liberal side, and as a rule I addressed the first meeting of the contest and the final meeting on the eve of the poll, and not infrequently remained in the constituency until the result was declared, when it was considered that my presence on the polling day would assist the candidate. This line cf action infuriated that section of Labour leaders who have since adopted the title of the Independent Labour Party, and at each succeeding Congress I had to face a bitter attack from them. Every effort was exhausted to discredit me in the eyes of the working classes. My simplest words and actions were misconstrued and placed in a false light. Their one aim was to prove that I had been a traitor to the cause which I represented. My enemies had vastly improved upon the crude methods adopted by the champions of the Countervailing Sugar Duties. Fertility of resource and an extraordinary versatility marked every stage of this campaign against me.

These qualities, allied to an utter disregard for the real truth, formed a power which might well have overwhelmed and crushed a stronger man than I. A newspaper called *The Labour Elector* was especially conspicuous for its undisguised and venomous attacks. Paragraphs criticising my action appeared in nearly every column, and the homes of trades-union officials and other workmen interested in political and Labour affairs were flooded with copies of this journal.

As a result I received hundreds of letters, written in good faith by men by no means hostile to me, inquiring if I had seen certain paragraphs enclosed reflecting upon my public life, and whether, if the accusations were untrue, I intended to write a reply to these charges in the next issue of the paper. The reader can easily imagine that the multiplication of such communications entailed a tremendous amount of labour in replies, without taking into account their effect upon one's mind.

Of the straightforward frontal attacks in which Mr. Keir Hardie and Mr. Tom Mann indulged I have no complaint to make. As each Congress came round, Mr. Hardie assailed me on questions which were before the Congress and gave him a perfect right to criticise my actions; and although his attacks sometimes exceeded the limits prescribed by strict fairness, they were at any rate face to face and left no rancour in our hearts. Besides, they afforded the other delegates a pleasurable change from the rigorous monotony of business procedure. Mr. Mann was not at that time a delegate to the Congress, but I have met him since and always on terms of friendliness, if not friendship. Both in him and in Mr. Keir Hardie I have ever recognised men of exceptional abilities and earnestness of purpose; I have always admired their devotion to the principles they have espoused.

But I cannot say the same of others who pursued me with a malevolence and subtlety not easy to baffle. Not satisfied with the articles and paragraphs in *The Labour Elector*, they scattered leaflets and pamphlets broadcast through the country, and in one case I received information that a hundred thousand copies of an address purporting to emanate from the workmen of London, and savagely assailing me, had been despatched to selected workmen in the provinces. Occasionally some of my colleagues came in for a share of this abuse, though generally in a milder form than that with which I was favoured. We were stigmatised as a gang of place-hunters scheming to obtain Factory Inspectorships and other appointments under Government.

At the Dundee Congress the hostility came to a head; every accusation printed in these pamphlets and leading articles was hurled at me by men who were merely repeating, parrot-like, the words put into their mouths by my bitter enemies, few of whom were entitled to be present as delegates, though some of them occupied seats in the gallery as spectators of the fray. The grand assault began early on the second day of the Congress, Mr. Keir Hardie and a representative of the London Society of Compositors being the protagonists. The gist of the charges formulated against me by these speakers was that I had supported the candidature of two employers of labour, in spite of the fact, as it was alleged, that these gentlemen conducted their businesses in a manner inimical to the interests of Labour.

How false and malicious these allegations were I

had little difficulty in proving. In 1887 I had assisted Mr. Brunner in his candidature. Soon after the election he revised some of the conditions of labour in connection with his vast works, and among the alterations was the establishment of an eight hours' shift, with certain financial adjustments which would ultimately work out at about the same wages for the shorter hours as for the longer ones. A great mass meeting of the workers was held to consider this proposal, and one of the Directors was invited to accept the post of chairman. I was asked by the workmen to be there to speak, and I strongly recommended them to accept the eight hours' shift, on the ground that they and their families would be permanent gainers by the physical economy consequent on the shorter working hours and the moral advantages that would follow the increase of their leisure. These suggestions were adopted, and I have reason to believe they proved beneficial not only to the workers and all dependent upon them, but in a great measure to the substantial and lasting advantage of the firm itself. A system of annual holidays without deduction of wages, subject, of course, to certain regulations, educational provision for the children, compensation for accidents to the workers, whether the firm was legally responsible or not, and other mutual arrangements were established, which altogether have placed the firm of Brunner, Mond, & Co. in the front rank of model employers in this kingdom. It will thus be seen that I have no cause to regret my association now with Sir John Brunner in the political arena. As a politician and as a social reformer, scarcely a vote he has given or a speech he has made in the House of Commons during his membership can be successfully criticised from the workers' point of view. Giving my own opinion of him, both as an employer and as a popular representative in Parliament, I can only say that if all were like him, our country would be happier, more prosperous, and freer than it is to-day.

Until four o'clock in the afternoon of that day I sat quiet, while the enemy pounded my position with all the artillery of argument, abuse, and calumny they could bring to bear. Then came my turn : a letter containing a practical vote of confidence in me which had reached me that morning from the Chairman of the London Society of Compositors enabled me to take my less formidable opponent on the flank, greatly to his discomfiture. I occupied some fifty minutes in my speech of vindication ; and when a resolution of confidence was put to the Congress, my opponents secured only eleven votes, while my supporters numbered one hundred and seventy-seven.

The scene that ensued baffles description. The Gilfillan Hall, where the Congress met, was crowded with spectators and delegates, and when the votes were read out the greater part of the audience sprang to their feet and cheered wildly. Hats were thrown into the air, men sprang upon chairs and tables to vent their feelings of satisfaction more easily, and in some cases

MR. BROADHURST ADDRESSING THE HOUSE.

From *The Westminster Gazette.*]                    [By kind permission of Mr. F. C. Gould.

strong men were utterly unable to control their emotion. I am far from narrating these facts as merely significant of my popularity. The satisfaction manifested at the utter rout of my traducers went much farther than that. My supporters recognised that my triumph meant the vindication of the solidarity of the organised trades against the continuous and savage onslaughts directed against trades-unionism and its leaders by a mixed band of free lances.

I need hardly say that this ordeal left me completely exhausted, and I was glad to be rescued from my enthusiastic supporters, who crowded on to the platform to congratulate me. A few hours of entire seclusion and an afternoon spent on the Carnoustie golf-links sufficed to put me on my feet again. I was enabled to carry out my duties for the rest of the Congress, as well as to fulfil several engagements at public meetings.

I had previously accepted an invitation to visit Sir Leonard Lyell, Bart., at his place in Forfarshire, which, by the way, lies close to Kirriemuir, the "Thrums" of Mr. Barrie's books. Sir John Leng happened to be going on a visit to the same house, and kindly took my niece and myself by road. The drive from Dundee to Kirriemuir, through the Vale of Ogilvie, about twenty miles in all, was a welcome refreshment after the long hours spent in the heated Congress Hall. Sir John had instructions to take us to lunch at Glammis Castle, which lies midway between Dundee and Kirriemuir, and where we received a hearty welcome from the Earl of Strathmore. I was delighted to have an opportunity of inspecting this ancient pile, indissolubly associated with the name of Macbeth. I was duly shown all its wonders, and they are many, and especially the haunted chambers, which called to mind the many legends associated with that historic place.

Few of the ancestral halls of Great Britain can boast so many ghostly associations as Glammis Castle. Here Duncan was foully slain by Macbeth, and many another deed of blood is associated with its history. Spectral carpenters hammer and plane invisible planks ; ghastly faces peer into windows ; and at times the courtyard rings with midnight shrieks, and a ghostly man in armour patrols the lonely corridors at dead of night. Beyond these weird occurrences there is a terrible family secret connected with a hidden chamber in the massive stone walls, and known only to three living persons—the Earl of Strathmore, the heir-apparent, and a third person. The place fascinated me vastly, and it was with uncommon regret I took my leave of a castle of so many imaginations.

This was not my first visit to the Lyells and their pleasant and interesting old house, situated in the midst of a well-wooded estate within easy distance of the Grampians, and so secluded that to me, long accustomed to the busy haunts of industrial man, its silence seemed almost awe-inspiring. On a former occasion, when spending a few days there, I had redeemed a promise, made some years before, to visit Airlie Castle, which stands half a dozen miles from Kinnordy in an even more remote and lonely situation. The Dowager Lady Airlie was at home, and I spent a very enjoyable and instructive half day in the midst of the treasures of that celebrated mansion. Its historical associations are so well known that I will not weary my readers with an account of them in this place. But the impression left upon my mind by visits to these "lordly pleasure-houses" is that they form invaluable retreats for the exhausted and weary brain, if one's temperament will permit one to rest contented in a solitude where the voice of man is silent, and the only sounds are the calls and cries of beast and bird and insect.

For some time I had seriously meditated resignation of the secretaryship of the Parliamentary Committee. This act I postponed in order to meet the promised attacks to be made at the Dundee Congress: it was not due to the brow-beating to which I was for years the victim, but to a far more serious reason. In the latter part of 1888 I was seized by a form of disease from which no patient ever obtains full release. It was an acute phase of this illness that I was suffering from when attacked by Mr. Bradlaugh in the House of Commons at the end of the session of 1888. A prolonged rest the following winter somewhat restored me, but later I had several relapses, and at times my suffering was severe. In 1890 my eyes became affected, and I was obliged to have recourse to Mr. Nettleship for treatment. At one stage many of my friends believed that I should not permanently recover—an apprehension which I myself shared. At last matters came to a head; I saw clearly that I must definitely choose between the resignation of the secretaryship of the

Parliamentary Committee and a complete breakdown. After careful consideration I took the former course and asked to be relieved of my responsibilities.

During the winter of 1890–1 I was so seriously ill that I was compelled to relinquish my purpose of moving a resolution in favour of a Fair Wages agreement being inserted in all Government contracts. The object of this resolution, which was drawn up at the suggestion of the London Building Trades Council, was to put an end to the vicious system of subcontracting of Government work, and to make it possible for the higher class firms to gain the contracts. The motion was eventually accepted without a division, though in a considerably modified form. At my suggestion the charge of the resolution was handed over to Mr. Sydney Buxton, who discharged the task with credit to himself and advantage to the cause of Labour. As the constant dripping of water wears away granite stone, so ceaseless attacks of a band of men acting in concert, aided by a subsidised paper, may undermine the strongest constitution, especially in the case of sensitive natures.

At this time the disease from which I was suffering assumed an intermittent form, and for four years I was subject to severe attacks at intervals. But relief from my secretarial responsibilities and, again, a long rest in the early part of 1891 worked a beneficial change, and in the spring of that year I was able to resume to some extent my political work both in Parliament and in the country. My first action was in relation to the lamentable state of the poor in our great industrial centres. I introduced a motion calling attention to the frightful state of overcrowding in the large towns, and advocating the adoption of the Glasgow system of cheap municipal lodging-houses. I also invited consideration of a project for giving the poorest class of children attending the elementary schools one good meal a day. These proposals were looked upon with suspicion, and I was regarded as a visionary Socialist. However, I have since had the satisfaction of seeing some at least of my suggestions carried to success.

The only work of a strictly political character I attempted in the House that session was a notice of motion in favour of all polling at a General Election taking place on one and the same day. I was unfortunate in the ballot, and did not obtain a place for my motion. But in the Registration Bill introduced by Mr. John Morley in 1892 a provision to the same effect found a place ; and at the time it was erroneously stated that this was the first occasion on which the matter had been before the House.

Outside the House I was almost continuously working in the constituencies until the close of the General Election of 1892. For instance, I spent nearly a fortnight of August, 1891, assisting Sir Donald Macfarlane in his candidature for Argyllshire—an extraordinarily difficult constituency. There were some hundreds of miles of coast line to be visited, and the only effective means of reaching the scattered fishing-hamlets was by water. Sir Donald is an enthusiastic yachtsman, and had at his disposal a handsome craft of five hundred tons called the *Hiawatha*. She possessed splendid sea-going qualities, and was well equipped in every way. By her aid we touched at nearly every waterside village between Campbelltown and Inverary, and many varied experiences fell to our lot.

I well remember the close of our tour. Being driven into the Holy Loch by stress of weather, we held two successful evening meetings in the neighbourhood of Dunoon. Returning from one of these gatherings we had some difficulty in finding the landing-stage, at which a boat was in waiting to take us aboard the yacht, for a strong westerly breeze drove the heavy rain in our faces, making the blackness of night almost impenetrable. At length we gained the object of our search, but to my horror I found that, as it was low water, in order to reach the boat I must descend a steep flight of steps, wet and slimy, and totally innocent of any handrail to assist the descent of the nervous lands-man. The prospect of a slip in the dark and a plunge into the black waters amongst the timber of the staging completely unmanned me; and had there been any possibility of obtaining quarters for the night near at hand, no power on earth would have induced me to go on board the *Hiawatha*. But at last my fears were abated, and with the assistance of two sturdy mariners the perilous descent was safely negotiated.

After a fortnight's cruising I began to pine for more space to move about in than the limits of a cabin and deck parade allowed, and I was not sorry when the end of this marine campaign was reached. I spent my evenings on board alternately in the saloon and the forecastle, where I struck up a great friendship with the crew, who were all intelligent men, fond of a good smoke and a long yarn; and I am quite certain that the feeling of regret at my departure from their midst was mutual.

My old chief, Mr. Childers, who was member for South Edinburgh, had been obliged to go abroad by a severe attack of rheumatism, and as he was under promise to address his constituency, he asked me to undertake this duty in his stead. This I readily consented to do, and in consequence spent some pleasant days in and about Edinburgh and on the golf-links at Dunbar. Having fulfilled this commission, I made my way north to Inverness-shire to attend the annual meeting of the Highland Land Reform Association at Dingwall.

One memorable day I spent in the Black Isle visiting croft after croft, seeing with my own eyes and hearing from the crofters' lips the kind of life they led, its hardships and its advantages. It was a splendid autumn day, and I greatly enjoyed my experience. At one of the crofts I was hospitably entertained in the traditional Highland manner by the housewife, whose "gude man" was from home, and plied with unlimited meal bread and butter, with capital milk to wash it down. The roof of the croft sheltered cows, pigs, and poultry, as well as human beings, though not all in the same apartment.

Small as the building was, it contained a parlour, in which I was entertained.

Bit by bit I extracted the life story of my hostess as I enjoyed my repast; while through the open door appeared the shock head of an urchin of six or seven years, extracting unlimited amusement from my southern accent, and trying to induce a fine collie dog to mimic my strange speech. Straitened as were the resources of the household, they had yet, by dint of self-sacrificing frugality, succeeded in saving enough money to give the eldest son a university education at Edinburgh. Unfortunately, the lad's tastes did not run in the direction of theology, and forsaking his studies, he had enlisted. At the time when I visited his parents' croft, this young Scotsman, by his own exertions and bravery, had won rapid promotion from the ranks, and was serving as a commissioned officer in the Egyptian Army. Very proudly did his toil-worn mother draw from its tin case and display to me the parchment containing his commission.

Another incident which stands out in my memory concerning that day was my meeting with a stone-breaker on the high road. He was an elderly man, of aristocratic mien, and displaying in every word and movement that natural refinement that seems to be a perquisite of the rugged sons of the North. I found he possessed a wonderful knowledge of public affairs, and we had a long and interesting conversation on current politics. My guide on this journey, Mr. McLeod, of Inverness, still occasionally informs me that the old stone-breaker inquires after me; and through the agency of Mr. McLeod I have on several occasions forwarded to him Parliamentary papers affecting questions in which he took an interest.

The demonstration of the Highland Land Reformers which I attended at Dingwall on the following day was of a character not easily to be forgotten. People had gathered from all parts of the Highlands as well as the Shetlands to take part in the proceedings. To commence with, I was treated to a serenade of bag-pipes at an early hour in the morning under the windows of my rooms. When the hour of meeting approached, I had to head a procession, followed immediately by the pipers skirling away with all the abandon of true "cocks of the North." Thus we promenaded the chief thoroughfares of the town of Dingwall, finally arriving at the platform, which had been erected in a field where Mr. Gladstone had spent many happy hours in his childhood while visiting a relative.

During this visit I received many invitations to extend my tour to the more northern towns, and none was more hearty than that from the people of Skye. To make the offer more tempting, they promised me my choice of the best dog in the island if I would go and choose it for myself. I have always been an enthusiastic lover of dogs, and collie dogs in particular have an intense fascination for me. I do not mean the breed so fashionable at dog-shows in the present day, with narrow jaws, tapering foreheads, and eyes within an inch of each other. To obtain these results the brain accommodation is so compressed that the animal becomes of little service, fit only for ornamental purposes. Give me the animal in his natural state, with big, broad, open countenance, wide forehead, and space enough between the eyes to accommodate a brain full of intelligence, receptivity, and memory, the whole dominated and completed by a warm and loyal heart excelling almost all hearts in affection and friendship.

After my return from Dingwall I spent the remainder of the time that elapsed before the General Election in various parts of England. It was during this period that I spoke for the last time on behalf of my dear and valued friend Mr. Arthur Winterbotham. My friendship with him dated from the early " Eighties," when I met him on the platform of a great Liberal gathering at Hereford. Our acquaintance quickly ripened into friendship, and notwithstanding the divergence of our views on the Home Rule question, upon which Mr. Winterbotham sided with the Liberal Unionists, our friendship remained firm through that stormy period, when many ties were rudely broken and old comrades parted in anger. But I always felt confident that he would return to the Liberal fold, and my expectation did not long remain unfulfilled. Naturally, the fact of his return to the Liberal camp had to be announced to his constituents, and naturally also the selection of the time and place for this reversion to renewed faith in his old leader cost him much anxiety. His constituency was the Cirencester division of Gloucestershire, and Stow-in-the-Wold was eventually selected as the place of assembly. To his request that I should accompany him I readily agreed, and an intensely interesting occasion it proved to be.

Stow-in-the-Wold is a quaint old country town, built mainly of limestone, with picturesque roofs of thick stone slating, and remote from the great trunk lines. The meeting was held in the Town Hall, an antiquated building dating back several hundred years, and reached by a very old but firm staircase. The interior of the hall was entirely in keeping with the outward aspect, and bore many a trace of mediæval workmanship. The place was packed to its utmost capacity. The refinements of town audiences were quite unknown to these honest and simple folk ; unhidden shirt-sleeves formed the evening dress of the majority. But the absence of fashionable garments was amply compensated for by the wild enthusiasm manifested throughout Mr. Winterbotham's address, as he sought to justify the course he had taken. When he sat down, I was called upon to extend to the returned wanderer a hearty welcome in the name of Liberalism. A big fellow in the audience had made himself conspicuous by his hearty demonstrations of delight at the proceedings, interjecting exclamations of approval in the dialect of the country-side, which had been familiar to me from my boyhood. I had never visited the town before, and every person in the hall, except Mr. Winterbotham, was a total stranger. However, I could not resist the temptation to congratulate this Gloucester giant on his enthusiasm for the cause, saying that he, at least, had killed the fatted calf in celebration of the prodigal's return. Much to my surprise, this personal reference was received with an uncontrollable outbursts of delight; I had evidently made a happy hit in the dark. The mystery was solved by the chairman whispering in my ear that my friend in the audience was the local butcher.

Never shall I forget the happy hours spent in the peaceful atmosphere of Mr. Winterbotham's home. The jovial freedom of his manner and the heartiness of his welcome reflected truly his attitude towards the other members of his establishment; every inmate, down to the horses and dogs, loved the master of the house. I particularly remember an enjoyable day spent on the Minchinhampton Common golf-links under the guidance of one of his sons, a fine young athlete and an accomplished golfer. By Mr. Winterbotham's desire the local professional lent me his clubs for this occasion, and I developed quite a passion for the cleek, which seemed to me the handiest club I had ever gripped. With its aid I made a very fine tee shot across the mouth of a gaping quarry, landing close to the hole. At the end of the round my young friend would not hear of my relinquishing the club with which I had made this fortunate shot, and then and there paid the professional a handsome price for it, and it became my property.

Mr. Winterbotham did not at all like my prospects of re-election at West Nottingham, and coupled with this he was most anxious to win the seat at Stroud from the Tory Party. He felt absolutely confident that if I would contest it I should win by a good majority. He pressed this view most strongly upon the central Liberal authority in London, and went so far as to offer to pay the whole of my expenses if I was allowed to stand for Stroud ; but this was refused. Mr. Winterbotham took a special interest in the representation of Stroud, it being near to his home. Such was his extravagant kindness to me that he always said I could in a fair fight win any place for which I put up.

At the last meeting which I attended in the company of Mr. Winterbotham I experienced that strange sensation of foreboding which the Scotch call " being fey." I had finished a series of political engagements in the southern counties, and on my way to Yorkshire I passed through Wiltshire and Gloucestershire. The meeting was at a small town some distance from Cheltenham. Mr. Winterbotham, his cousin, and I journeyed together to the meeting, which proved a most successful one. But try as I would I could not succeed in throwing off this feeling of depression, and I fear that my speech assumed a somewhat maudlin character, as I dwelt upon the noble qualities of my old friend. Even on the return journey my usual buoyancy refused to come to my aid, and silence, unusual in that company, reigned supreme.

Next morning Mr. Winterbotham saw me off, and in a few months' time I heard that death had robbed me of one of the best and most loyal of friends. One of his last requests was that I should succeed him as Liberal member for Cirencester. As I had just lost my seat at West Nottingham, I would gladly have acceded to his desire and contested the division. But Fate willed otherwise ; the fracture of a muscle in one of my legs compelled me for a season to forsake politics and lie by with my wounded limb in splints.

But I have not yet told my readers how it came to pass that I was in want of a seat. For some time I had felt very doubtful concerning my chances of remaining the representative of Nottingham, and had felt strongly tempted to accept several offers to stand as candidate elsewhere. For example, in 1892 I was informed that I should be an acceptable candidate for the city of Norwich. Every influence that could be exercised was brought into play to induce the Liberal managers to allow me to stand for the old city, where it was thought, for various reasons, I had a better prospect of winning than any other available Liberal candidate, always excepting Mr. Colman. Sore and deep was the disappointment among those chiefly responsible for the Liberal interests in that city when it finally became known that I was not to be permitted to accept their offer. It was declared again and again by those entitled to speak that had I been the second candidate in conjunction with Mr. Colman, both of us would certainly have been returned. I felt myself that my old associations with the city and the constant connection I had maintained with the political and other affairs of the county would have been a material help towards success, but it was not to be. Personally, I much regretted it, and nothing would have given me greater pleasure than to have represented Norwich in Parliament.

It is a city rich in historic associations and remarkable for its industrial past. At one time it was almost the chief home of the silk trade in England, and its shawls were world-renowned for their texture, design, and beauty of finish. During the long years of my association with the Trades Congress I have of necessity been brought into contact, and in some cases almost familiarity, with many trades and callings. In years past I have been in frequent communication with both the employers and the workpeople engaged in the silk industries, and have been much interested in the revival of this trade in Great Britain, largely the result of the labours of Sir Thomas Wardle, of Leek, whose efforts were so ably seconded by her Royal Highness the Duchess of Teck, and the Duchess of Sutherland. In some personal interviews on the question of the silk trade with the Duchess of Sutherland I was surprised and greatly pleased to find what a grasp she had of the question, and how clearly and thoroughly she realised and set forth the only means by which prosperity could be revived in the silk trade. In the winter of 1895-6, through the kindness of the editor of *The Eastern Daily*

*Press*, I endeavoured to arouse some interest in the city of Norwich on the silk trade question, both by communications to that paper and by interviews with the Trades Council. I saw both shopkeepers and manufacturers, and my proposal was that samples of the textile goods still made in the eastern counties should be collected and submitted to view under the patronage and in the presence of these ladies and others to whom I have already referred. My advances were courteously received and my good intentions kindly acknowledged by those chiefly interested in the trade, but they unanimously rejected them. In my opinion there are goods now being made in the eastern counties, not only by motive power but by hand-looms, that, if brought conspicuously before the public, would command a wide and increasing sale, and would bring proportionate benefit to the employers, the workpeople, and to the county.

After aiding in the campaign in different parts of the country, I found that the time had arrived for looking after my own political fortunes. Hurrying back to Nottingham, I found myself confronted with a struggle which threatened disaster to my chances of re-election. For some years anterior to this Election the question of an eight hours' day for miners had assumed great prominence in the country. West Nottingham contained a good percentage of voters who earned their livelihood underground. I had already been sounded as to my position with regard to the proposed reform. Personally, I have never

regarded legislation of this character with any degree
of favour, but I did not hesitate to assure my constituents that if an Eight Hours Bill should pass
the second reading stage in the House of Commons
I would, if re-elected, loyally accept the decision, and
do my utmost in Committee to see that the full intention of the promoters of the measure was realised.

During the interval which had elapsed since his
defeat in 1886, Colonel Seely had been assiduously
nursing the constituency, giving freely to the various
philanthropic causes in the neighbourhood. He owned
most of the mines in the division, and took an early
opportunity of announcing his intention, if elected,
to support an Eight Hours Bill. As proprietor of
many mines, there was nothing to hinder his adoption
of an eight hours' day for the miners in his employ
without the necessity of formal legislation ; but he
contented himself with securing the support of the
miners by his promises and his vivid pictures of the
terrible risks incurred by the men whose bread was
earned underground. In spite of all this, I have never
been convinced that the Eight Hours question was
to any appreciable extent the cause of my defeat at
the polls.

I have already alluded to my opponent's far-reaching
influence as an employer and his vast wealth. He
possessed the means of satisfying the social ambitions
of many persons who were inferior in social status,
but whose adherence at an election was by no means
to be despised. All this he could do without laying

himself open in the slightest degree to the charge of exercising undue influence. Such powers will always be the possession of men of wealth and position, and so long as social influence exerts a sway over human nature, and that will be as long as human nature lasts, so long will such men be able to attract to their side the support of large numbers of their neighbours.

As the contest proceeded I missed from my meetings a number of influential persons who had supported me in 1886. I found also that the organisation at my back was greatly inferior to that which I had experienced in my previous campaign. Want of cohesion and lack of energy were painfully conspicuous. Little attention had been given to the work of registration in the past six years, and many voters having qualifications in either division had transferred their vote from the western to the eastern division. As time wore on I found a daily increasing band of well-dressed and energetic canvassers attacking all quarters of the wide division in the interests of my opponent; while I had no counterbalancing support, with the exception of a few faithful friends whom no influence could detach from me, but whose circumstances left them little or no time for work, except in the evening.

The election took place on the first Monday in July. On the Saturday a great open-air demonstration was held at short notice in the Forest grounds. No speakers from the outside world were there to assist me, but I received great aid, as I had done at all

16

my meetings, from the able and devoted Labour
leaders in Nottingham, representing every branch of
industry in the town except miners. This gathering
proved an enormous success; it was estimated that
6,000 or 8,000 persons were present. I was put
into a carriage and drawn by hand through great
crowds of people lining the Forest Road and all the
streets through which I passed to my lodgings, and
was only released after further speechmaking in the
street. On the previous day I had received a letter
from Mr. Gladstone expressing his hope that I
should win my contest, and saying many good things
about me, but it was too late to be of service. The
demonstration on Saturday afternoon somewhat revived
my drooping spirits and raised faint hopes of my prospects. On Monday, as I went from district to district,
I felt that my doom was sealed. In the afternoon I
made arrangements to leave Nottingham at an hour's
notice, and when the result reached my lodgings,
through the kindness of a newspaper reporter, everything was ready for the journey home, and I reached
London before 4 o'clock next morning.

Colonel Seely won the seat, but the miners who
supported him gained little by his presence in the
House. When the Eight Hours Bill was introduced,
the new Member for West Nottingham voted, I
believe, in support of a motion which, by rendering
the measure optional, robbed it of all practical value
in the opinion of its supporters. In my opinion no
Government is likely to make any serious effort to

bring about this change in the industrial life of the nation for many years to come.

Although I attributed my defeat to the social prestige of my opponent rather than to any considerable alienation of the mining vote, I must confess to a feeling of keen disappointment at what I am justified in calling the ingratitude of the miners. When I contested Nottingham in 1886 no miners' organisation worthy of the name existed. Everything was practically in a state of chaos when Mr. Bailey, the newly appointed miners' agent, arrived on the scene. I gave this gentleman every assistance in my power, introduced him to many of my political friends in the locality, and requested all my supporters to aid him as far as was in their power in his task of organising the miners. On several occasions I made special journeys from London to attend his meetings. Yet when the contest came Mr. Bailey openly espoused the cause of Colonel Seely and exerted every effort to secure my defeat. Notwithstanding all this I have always said, and am convinced of its truth, that in 1892 I received as many miners' votes as I did in 1886.

My position as a defeated candidate was the more unpalatable from the fact that, after six years in the wilderness, the Liberal Party had reached the Promised Land of power once more. Still, I had no intention of following Achilles' example and retiring to sulk in my tent. I presented myself at headquarters to offer my services during the remainder of the Election, and I took part in several contests, returning to my own division in Norfolk to vote for and support to the utmost of my ability the Liberal candidate. But my cup of misfortune was not yet full, for, in the early part of September, in taking a long jump over a bank I landed with one heel in a rat's hole and broke one of the muscles of my leg. This crippled me entirely for six weeks, and several months elapsed before I regained the full use of the limb.

In the latter part of 1892 a Royal Commission was appointed to inquire into the condition of the aged poor. The late Lord Aberdare acted as chairman, and the Prince of Wales was a member of the Commission. An invitation to join it was gladly accepted by me, securing as it did a continuity of association with Parliamentary affairs. We sat from the end of 1892 to the early months of 1895, and even after this prolonged investigation the opinions of the members were so divergent that it was impossible to get anything like a unanimous report. I think it may be fairly claimed that all the members of the Commission applied themselves faithfully and steadily to the discharge of their task; but the work was extremely exacting, and before its completion the hand of death deprived us of our chairman, the remaining business being conducted under the presidency of Lord Playfair.

From the beginning the Prince of Wales was a fairly regular attendant, and took the liveliest interest in the proceedings, frequently examining witnesses for himself, and displaying considerable skill in the work. But the sympathy with which his Royal Highness regarded the subject of the inquiry was more accurately gauged in private conversation than in the public proceedings of the Commission. Unfortunately, the conclusions arrived at by different sections of the Commission were so diverse as to make it practically impossible for the Prince to give public expression to his opinions without displaying the divergence of his views from those of one or other of these sections.

For my own part I have always entertained strong opinions on the treatment of the aged poor, and have again and again protested in vigorous terms against the degradation and injustice inseparable from the present administration of the Poor Law. I have always regarded the aged poor as members of a great national family who have not reaped their fair share of reward for their labours on behalf of national prosperity. On these grounds I hold that they are entitled, not to a pauper dole, but to a moderate and honourable pension carrying with it no more stigma or reproach than the pension of the civil servant and the soldier. To ensure this result I maintained that these rewards of a strenuous and hardworking life must be paid from the Imperial purse through independent channels as opposed to the system of local taxation and relief. This proposal, associated with proper safeguards and accompanied by some suggested reforms in the administration of the Poor

Law, I embodied in a memorandum to which I obtained no other signature than my own.

In a moment of weakness during the sitting of this Commission I consented to contest the vacant seat at Grimsby. Grimsby was one of the few towns in England I had never visited, although I had received many invitations to do so some dozen years previously, when I introduced the Leasehold Enfranchisement Bill. I arrived in Grimsby on the Saturday, and my Address to the constituents was due on the following Monday. On the way to my first public meeting the tram-car in which I was riding ran off the line at a bend of the street and nearly broke into a shop front. I am of a highly superstitious nature, keenly sensitive to my environment, and I immediately accepted this accident as an evil omen, though I took care not to reveal my forebodings to my supporters. As time passed, my anticipations of defeat grew clearer, and in less than twenty-four hours after my arrival I wrote to the Chief Whip of the Liberal Party that I had not the least chance of success, and that had not the writ been moved I would certainly have retired from the contest. Notwithstanding these private misgivings, I put as good a face on the position as possible, and found after two or three days that I had made considerable progress. Then a change came over the scene ; from all parts of the country flocked helpers and agents for the Conservative candidate, Mr. Heneage. It was the old gang who had dogged my steps before and whose tactics I have already described. With might and main they strove to discredit me with the workers of Grimsby by spreading the old libels, and it was because my opponent seemed tacitly to approve of these underhand tactics by refraining from disowning them that I felt compelled, when the result of the poll was announced, to refuse to take his proffered hand. To add to my difficulties Sir William Harcourt introduced the Local Veto Bill two or three nights before the polling day, and this attack on their interests rallied the licence-holders and brewers to a degree I had never before witnessed to the Tory side. The case at once became hopeless, and I felt no surprise when I found myself at the bottom of the poll.

In the following year (1894) my friend Mr. Picton retired from the representation of Leicester, and I received a most unexpected and unanimous invitation from the Liberals of the town to succeed him. The terms of the invitation were such that I gladly acceded to this request, which had been endorsed by a large public meeting. By a curious coincidence Sir James Whitehead, the other member for Leicester, was seized with a serious illness which necessitated a long absence from the House of Commons. The Government's majority was too narrow to lose even one vote; so Sir James also sent in his resignation, and thus a double election was brought about in August.

In conjunction with Mr. Walter Hazell I was fortunate enough to secure a sufficient number of votes to place me once again within the sacred precincts of St. Stephen's. But I had short time to enjoy the fruits of victory; within twelve months Government was defeated and Parliament dissolved, and I was again in the throes of an electoral contest. Thus in three years I was engaged in four contested elections, in two of which I met defeat and in two victory.

This was not my first connection with Leicester Liberalism. Eleven years before the 1894 election a number of my friends came from Leicester to London to press me to become their candidate if I should receive an invitation from the Liberal Association of their town. This I was unable to promise; I had no desire to make any change at the moment, and so I declined their request, never dreaming that on a future occasion Leicester would be the constituency to rescue me from the political wilderness. So far as I was concerned the contest was one of the pleasantest I had ever experienced. The struggle was fierce, but personalities were avoided and we fought on broad party lines. The Independent Labour Party forced the fighting with indomitable and untiring energy; their candidate, Mr. Burgess, was a worthy champion of their cause; but throughout this contest and the succeeding one in 1895 he never made use of any but the fairest and most above-board weapons against me.

# CHAPTER XIII

## *A SOJOURN IN THE DESERT*

AS session succeeds session the opportunities for
initiating legislation open to private Members
grow less and less. Except in the case of absolutely
non-contentious measures, the private Member has not
the remotest chance of success. Even then the risks
are greater than anyone outside Parliament would
imagine. By a series of fortunate circumstances a Bill
may slip through the various stages to the third reading,
and then an incident as trivial as the proverbial straw
may wreck its chances of becoming law, unless, indeed,
the Government should extend to it a gracious blessing
—a favour which is rarely granted to a political
opponent. It is astonishingly easy for Ministerial eyes
to discover in the proposals of an opponent possible
dangers, which are rapidly transformed into desirable
reforms if the measure be the pet lamb of a political
supporter. The same principles are applied to the
answering of questions. Simple outsiders might
suppose that Ministers, being public servants, are bound
to assist Members on both sides of the House when
they make inquiries in the interests of their constituents.
Yet if a Member of the Opposition puts a question

whose purport is as plain as a pikestaff, but which is not framed in a minutely exact and technical manner, the Minister to whom it is addressed may blandly ignore its meaning and merely reply to its literal wording. To rise immediately, explain your meaning, and press for another answer, require an intellectual agility which few men possess.

I am strongly of opinion that we are drifting towards a Parliamentary despotism which, if unchecked, will relegate to the limbo of the past the freedom of action of private Members. Government majorities numbered by hundreds instead of tens may be a very present help in time of trouble to a jobbing and reckless Ministry, but they may also prove a serious menace to the liberties of the people. During the national fit of delirium which preceded and accompanied the early stages of the war in South Africa attention was drawn in the House of Commons to cases of serious rioting at public meetings and even in private gatherings. In some cases the police were alleged to have failed in their duty of protecting public and private rights. The flippant and unworthy apologies offered by responsible Ministers from the Treasury Bench were cheered to the echo by the apparently unanimous ranks sitting on the Government side of the House. Yet among these Conservatives there must have been some who possessed an elementary knowledge of the law by which citizens are entitled to the protection of the authorities in the exercise of their undoubted rights of free speech. Yet none dared to court the chastisement inflicted upon men like Sir Edward Clarke, who was driven from Parliamentary life because he dared to criticise the diplomatic blundering and chicanery which characterised the Government's policy towards the South African Republic, or like the Member for Westminster, upon whose devoted head the Leader of the House poured out the vials of his wrath because he dared to denounce the incapacity and mismanagement which marked the treament of our wounded and fever-stricken soldiers. If you have an overwhelming majority you can afford to apply the lash to restive units. One vote more or less does not matter, and the punishment is a warning to the rest. Thus a big majority and its effects may strike at the very heart of representative government. Who can wonder that, amidst such surroundings and influences, few Members of the Opposition find an opportunity of exercising their skill as legislators? Their main chance of distinguishing themselves lies in guerilla warfare and "sniping"; but the prospect of promoting a full-dress combat on orthodox lines is practically non-existent.

During the Parliament of 1895–1900 the Party with whose fortunes I am identified was mainly engaged in protecting the public purse against the raids of class interests, in defending elementary education, and in endeavouring to maintain the Protestant character of the State Church. Two Bills directly affecting the interests of workers were introduced in its course. The most important measure was the Compensation Act of 1897. This measure contains elements which, if carried to their logical issue by future legislation, will prove a great Charter of Rights to the men and women of coming years. But to realise this aim will be a vast and difficult task, for there is one large class for whom as yet no provision has been made. The seafaring population possesses no articulate voice in Parliament, though ship-owners are influentially represented, and the man before the mast is therefore a negligible quantity.

The second measure was the Factory and Workshop Amendment Bill, introduced by the Home Secretary. I regard this as the most reactionary and insidious attempt to put back the clock of progress in modern legislation. It even went the length of proposing to permit a return to Sunday labour, thereby striking a blow at the fundamental principle of the protection of the labouring class. It would have made a rent in the shorter hours of labour movement at one stroke which might have destroyed the whole network of the laws restricting the working time of old and young, male and female alike. What amazed me was the absence of anything like a united national protest from the workers. A few conferences were held here and there, but nothing of the character of an impressive demonstration. The enormities of the Bill and its far-reaching and evil consequences were pointed out in an admirable tract issued by the Fabian Society. This statement of the case against the proposed measure was the clearest, most convincing, and most complete I have ever seen in matters relating to the Labour cause. I believe it did more to destroy the Bill than anything else. In the House Mr. Tennant put down a motion which would have forced a debate on the defects of the Bill; and after consultation with Sir Charles Dilke I gave notice of a motion that the Bill

MR. BROADHURST OBJECTS TO CLERICAL DOLES.

From *The Westminster Gazette*.]      [By kind permission of Mr. F. C. Gould

be read "this day three months," thus giving a direct challenge to the Government. From time to time I addressed questions to the Treasury Bench as to the date when the second reading would be moved, and a large number of trades-unions sent me letters and resolutions approving of my attitude. Week followed week, but no second reading came, and finally the Bill was abandoned. Its author is no longer found in the Lower Chamber; he has gone to that " other place " whence no traveller returns to the House of Commons. So we may suppose that his Bill will never be resuscitated.

One other reactionary proposal highly dangerous in my eyes I was successful in opposing during these years. A measure was introduced called " the Savings Bank Bill," which proposed to repeal the existing law fixing the interest paid on deposits in the Post Office Savings Bank at $2\frac{1}{2}$ per cent, and to give the Treasury power to determine at the end of each year what rate of interest should be given to investors. Under this arrangement no one would know what their deposits had earned till the end of the year, the one thing certain being that it would not be $2\frac{1}{2}$ per cent. I strenuously opposed this tampering with the principle on which the great national incentive to thrift is based. At the present time it is the only safe refuge for the savings of wage-earners. They know where their money is to be found at any time, and they know they will receive once a year sixpence for every pound saved. They have no anxiety about its security, and they have not to calculate in decimals the amount due. But once the arrangement is disturbed, a disastrous blow might probably be dealt at the national thrift. The habit of thrift is a shy bird, and once seriously alarmed, it would be a long and hard task to get it to roost again. What is a small deficit at the Treasury compared with a danger such as I have mentioned? The advantages derived from the State by the poor are meagre compared with those gained by the rich. I believe all well-wishers of thrift will agree that the State should exert all reasonable efforts to encourage the saving habits of the poor, even if such a course involves a slight annual loss.

With the outbreak of war all prospects of further social legislation vanished, and to all appearances the nation was very well content that this should be. Parliament was dissolved at a time when the fewest possible votes could be recorded, and the date of polling was so arranged that it could not fall on a Saturday, the day most suitable for workers. The suddenness of the dissolution took many people by surprise, but at Leicester the powder was dry, the train laid, and the fuses prepared. It only needed the application of the match to precipitate the explosion. The addresses of both Mr. Walter Hazell and myself were in type, and election literature of every description had been printed and waited distribution. Committee-rooms had been bespoken, though not formally occupied and a splendid body of workers had been warned to hold themselves in readiness. So when the call came every man was at his post, and with the irresistible ease with which a well-launched vessel slides off the slips into her native element, the Leicester Liberals, under the command of our agent, Mr. Smith, entered the fray.

Under such favourable circumstances the candidate's part in the battle is of secondary importance. I held myself in readiness night and day to obey the orders issued by the Committee and the election agents. Every morning at ten o'clock the day's plan of campaign was issued. In my list of meetings a side-note opposite each meeting informed me of the probable character of the audience and the class of subjects most likely to interest them. A loyal though critical supporter went through the newspapers, and at five o'clock each evening brought me helpful extracts with introductory notes for use at my meetings; this service proved of the greatest value. The spare hours of the daytime I occupied in dictating letters and telegrams in support of fellow-candidates in different parts of the country. Then I had constantly to explain by wire why I could not be in several places at the same time, say, in Edinburgh and Cornwall on succeeding nights, or in Essex and Cheshire on the same date. I owed much at this time to my shorthand writer, whose accuracy and faithfulness, coupled with an excellent knowledge of affairs, never failed.

What a fight it was! The keenest political observer could not forecast the issue with a population of more than two hundred thousand. My chief danger lay in the war in South Africa. Some of my best friends disapproved of my uncompromising attitude on that question, and six months before the election I had been called upon to explain my position to the Liberal

Council. True, I received a unanimous vote on that occasion ; but the Council numbered only a thousand, and in the background was a vast inarticulate mass of twenty-four thousand voters. Which of the names would they favour with the sign of the cross before it entered the ballot-box ? I tried to comfort myself with the sight of influential men joining the ranks of my workers and signing my nomination paper ; but the uncomfortable question would keep cropping up, "Where are the others?" Until the result of the counting was whispered in my ear, I had no rest from my anxiety.

When polling-day came I was provided with a "one-hoss shay" hired from a jobbing yard. A glance at the animal between the shafts revealed obvious defects of age and infirmity in the fore-legs. We had not gone far on our tour of the polling-stations and committee-rooms when the poor old steed gave us a taste of his quality by subsiding in the road just opposite a Conservative stronghold. Luckily, only the near knee was damaged, and (where I had been sitting when the accident occurred) I took care to sit on the off-side for the rest of the day. But the incident served to arouse my superstitious fore-bodings. I saw in this incident an evil omen for the Liberal Party, though as the fall had not occurred on my side, I felt that the brunt of it would not be borne by me. My forebodings proved only too correct. The fortune of war went against my colleague, and never did colleague feel more keenly for a comrade's

17

disaster than I felt that night when the news of Mr. Hazell's defeat reached me.

Although my majority was diminished, I polled an increased number of votes, nearly one thousand more than in 1894, and about seven hundred more than in 1895. Thus allowing for the increase in the number of voters, I could not have lost many supporters on account of the war. In fact, many of my best friends and devoted supporters were found among those who disagreed with my views on this question, but gave me the credit for being actuated by worthy motives and by a real regard for the honour and integrity of the British Empire. To their magnanimity I owe a deep debt of gratitude. If this spirit had been shared by Liberals in other parts of the country, the Party of Progress would be in a far stronger position to-day.

My election took place on October 2nd, and I immediately proceeded to Market Harborough, and thence to the Loughborough division, addressing three meetings at each place. My engagements then took me to the Rushcliffe division of Nottinghamshire, the Northwich division of Cheshire (where I spoke at five meetings), the Crewe division, and the Chesterfield division of Derbyshire. After addressing eighteen meetings in a fortnight from my own polling-day, I reached home on October 15th, just a month and four days since my departure for Leicester.

In connection with the Rushcliffe and Crewe meetings two incidents of interest occurred. My first visit for political purposes to the former division had taken place sixteen years before, when Mr. John Ellis first contested the seat. Now I came on the same errand for the same candidate in the same hall, and this fact with the reminiscences it enabled me to recall was of great assistance at the public meetings. Mr. Ellis had served his constituents faithfully and well for sixteen years, but now he was assailed and " hard put to," as Bunyan would say, by the enemy. He was labelled a pro-Boer, and the letters he had written to persons in South Africa—absolutely innocent and even justifiable—were represented as an act of disloyalty. The gravest fears were entertained for his success ; but character must and will tell in the long run, and the people had time to brush away the closely woven webs of calumny. As I stood before the two great meetings preceeding the polling-day, looking straight into the eyes of the people, I thought I could detect a favourable sign in their expression. So it proved, and Mr. Ellis came through the ordeal with a firmer hold than ever on Ruschliffe.

At Crewe the same story was repeated. Mr. Tomkinson, the Liberal candidate, was nicknamed a pro-Boer, and every vote given to him was, of course, a vote for the Boers. I drove into Crewe from a meeting at Sandbach, only arriving at Mr. Tomkinson's meeting at 10 p.m. I was at once called upon for my speech, and went straight for the enemy's position. My aim was to show that the most useful ally of the Boers had been the incapacity displayed by the Tory

Government, and to support my contention I read extracts from the letters written for *The Daily News* by the Australian war-correspondent, Mr. A. G. Hales. I have never seen an audience so quick to grasp the situation or so full of enthusiasm. Mr. Tomkinson's long and faithful service on behalf of the Liberal cause, in the course of which he had been defeated in more than one keen fight, was rewarded by a notable success, and he was returned by a great majority. With this gleam of success my labours ended, and the story of my life is told.

Writing on the threshold of the New Century, I confess the future looks dark and cheerless. The Nineteenth Century is closing amid wars and rumours of wars. In South Africa the largest army ever enrolled beneath the Union Jack has been decimated by disease and the rifles of the enemy to minister to the Mammon-worship of greedy capitalists. At home the image of the Golden Calf stands upon almost every altar. The clock of moral and social progress has been put back a quarter of a century, while militarism and clericalism walk hand in hand to and fro in the country. How many years must elapse before the ebbing waves become the flowing tide, I cannot tell; but I fear they must be many. England, once the champion of oppressed peoples, has been incited to openly rob two tiny Republics of their cherished independence, and her name has become a by-word among the nations for this violence and oppression. Yet at home all but a small minority are drunk with the war-fever. The clergy are dumb or openly espouse the cause of the Jingoes. Where are thy prophets, O Israel? is our cry; but there are none to answer. And so the Nineteenth Century sets blood-red amid dark and threatening clouds.

# CHAPTER XIV

## ELECTIONS AND ELECTIONEERING

FEW men have had a wider experience of elections than has fallen to my lot. I have traversed the length and breadth of the land, at one time or another, to take part in some party contest, and there is scarcely a town of any importance in Great Britain where I have not appeared on a political platform. In his time his Honour Judge Waddy possessed a great reputation as the hardest traveller in the Liberal camp, and his mobility was envied by many younger men. But I doubt whether even Judge Waddy's record would leave mine far behind. In this chapter I have collected some of the odds and ends of my political career, curious incidents which have given colour to a strenuous life; and at the outset I will instance a few of the political engagements I have successfully fulfilled, with no slight strain upon my physical strength.

In the days of my Leasehold Enfranchisement Bill I paid a round of visits to the principal towns of Devonshire and Cornwall to expound the principles of the measure. Leaving town in the morning, I attended a great meeting at Devonport, and then proceeded to Camborne, where I addressed a huge gathering of men from all parts of the mining division. A reception for social intercourse followed, which kept me up till the small hours of the morning ; but before daylight I had resumed my journey, and travelled, by way of Bristol, Gloucester, and Cheltenham, to Birmingham. Here I addressed a large audience at eight in the evening on my Bill, finally reaching my host's house after a trudge through melting snow at 10.30 p.m., thus completing an eighteen hours' day full of excitement and the strain of travel in severe weather.

On one occasion I left London, after a hard week of late sittings in the House, at 10 o'clock on Saturday morning, addressed a large meeting at Bishop's Auckland, in the county of Durham, and regained my London home in time for breakfast on Sunday morning. Another time I left Brixton at an early hour of the morning for Tredegar, in the hills of South Wales. On my arrival I marched at the head of a trades-union procession round the town, addressed a meeting in the public hall, and after a slight interval for refreshments was in the train for London, reaching my home about midnight. While on a political mission in the West of England I travelled from Plymouth to London, caught the night train to Glasgow, and kept an important appointment in Lanarkshire early next morning. Perhaps my hardest bit of work was the occasion on which, after addressing a public meeting in Manchester at night,

I left early next morning, and spoke at a gathering of several thousands of people in Greenock the same night ; it was only after the meeting was over, when I had reached Pollokshields, a suburb of Glasgow, that I found time to take my first meal since breakfast. Even an iron constitution could not stand the strain of such journeys without some creaking of the over-taxed machinery, and I have since had reason bitterly to regret some of the prolonged fasts.

In my numerous railway journeys I have frequently met fellow-passengers whose agreeable conversation has pleasantly whiled away an hour of travel. But I have also had impressed on me the unwisdom of speaking unreservedly to strangers. In one instance I recollect, the matter had a pleasant sequel which makes it worth repeating. I was travelling from London to my home in Cromer, and had for a travelling companion a most interesting and well-informed lady, who talked well on most subjects, had travelled far and wide, and possessed a keen and instructed eye for the beauties of nature. During the journey she remarked the fine church of Worstead, and, struck with the elegance of its architecture unusual in so far-away a village, she inquired whether I thought it would be well attended. When I replied that most likely the congregation would seldom be large, she went on to say that she believed I was probably right, for it was a dreadful habit of the poorer classes to associate themselves with Nonconformist bodies. On that point I expressed no opinion, but assured her that, at any rate, she would find a fine church to worship in at Cromer. "Yes, so I have heard," said the lady; adding, "I presume you attend its services." Her consternation was almost pitiable when I replied that I was one of "the poorer classes" and associated with a Nonconformist body—*viz.* the Wesleyan chapel, whose services I attended on Sunday. But her penitence did not end with the profuse apologies at once proffered. On the following Sunday morning she presented herself at the Wesleyan Chapel, placed a a handsome contribution in the plate, and when the service was over expressed her pleasure and profit she had derived there. Addressing me by my name, which she had learned since the preceding day, she frankly expressed her indebtedness for the rebuke so gently administered in the railway-carriage; and so the incident closed to our mutual satisfaction.

Poverty, runs the proverb, gives one strange bed-fellows; and certainly political pilgrimages make one acquainted with every kind of accommodation, from the lordly mansion to the two-roomed cottage. I remember in one county bye-election having to address a meeting in a straggling village through which, in days gone by, many of the mail-coaches travelled. The only remaining evidence of those prosperous times was what had once been a well-equipped hostelry, which had fallen on evil days. Upon my arrival, the doors of this hotel were closed to me on the ground that all the available sleeping accommodation was engaged—a statement which I had strong reasons to doubt—indeed, it was obviously untrue. As I could not stay in the street all night, I sought and obtained accommodation in a labourer's cottage, where every exertion was made to supply my wants, and it was not the fault of my friends that their efforts were not entirely successful. I paid my bill in the morning, and as the poor woman did not know what to charge me, I made it out myself, receipted it for her, and handed her the money. She was scarcely able to find words to express her gratitude, for it probably amounted to more than a week's wages of the farm labourer in the neighbourhood. I took care to publish abroad in the remaining portions of the division my experience of this particular place; and a gentleman who had taken an active part in the contest on the opposite side declared, after the election, that they lost the battle mainly through the stupidity of refusing me sleeping accommodation in the village hotel.

On another occasion I was selected to deliver the annual address to some political institute or other in a large northern village. I had been informed by letter that one of their chief men would entertain me for the night if I would accept his hospitality, to which, of course, I readily agreed. It was a cold, damp night in early December when I arrived at my destination, and my host and others were in attendance to receive me. I was conducted with considerable pomp and ceremony to his house, which I found to be a general provision shop. The entrance to the residential part of the establishment was through the shop, under the flap of the counter, and then across a large storage shed, which seemed to contain principally paraffin oil casks and other highly inflammable material— at any rate, so it appeared to me. I was amply entertained before the meeting, though to an epicure the viands provided might have seemed to be lacking in quality. A huge teapot filled with the blackest and strongest brew of that herb which "cheers but not inebriates" was set before me, and I was compelled to declare that it was entirely contrary to my habit to drink tea so late in the afternoon on account of its effect in preventing sleep. This did not raise me in the estimation of my host, who declared it was the strongest drink he ever allowed on his premises. If any beverage ever deserved the name of "strong drink," that terrible decoction certainly did. Besides being a total abstainer of the most violent description, my host proved to be an anti-tobacconist, a vegetarian, and an anti-vaccinator, having recently testified to his conscientious convictions by undergoing imprisonment for his anti-vaccine principles.

My sleeping accomodation was about as narrow as my host himself. After scaling with difficulty a corkscrew staircase, I was ushered into a chamber wherein there was no danger of losing oneself. I experienced the greatest difficulty in finding space for myself, except in a recumbent position on the bed. A lean-to roof and a suspiciously closed fireplace did not add to my comfort, for I have always been one of the most fidgety and nervous of people respecting my sleeping accommodation. However, I found some consolation in the fact that my whiskey-flask was quite full. I was glad enough to finish my repast and get away to the place of meeting, for I badly wanted a smoke as well as opportunity of hearing the political news of the district. I was in no hurry to begin the meeting, for as soon as it was over I must return to my dubious quarters. So far as I can recollect this is the only occasion on which I have longed for a meeting to last all night.

However, all things have their end, and spin it out as I would the meeting terminated at last, and I returned to the general provision shop. Once again I was conducted through the shop, under the flap of the counter, and through the oil warehouse to the living-rooms. My apprehensions of a fire returned with extraordinary strength. I remember that I resorted to every expedient I could summon to my assistance to engage my host in conversation, and thus while away the hours of night. Politics, vaccination, temperance, anti-tobacco, woman suffrage, the opium question—all these matters were questions upon which my friend had strong opinions. Every one proved as successful as I anticipated, and so the time went merrily on, until I had exhausted every subject I could think of. In despair I turned to my host's business affairs, suggesting that they must be extensive and hoping that they were profitable. But I had selected my topic in an unlucky moment, and my host's reply proved entirely destructive of any prospect of sleep that I might have entertained.

It occurred in this way. He began by explaining the difficulties encountered and the watchfulness necessary in connection with shop-assistants, and he went on to expatiate upon the sins of mankind in general and the carelessness of apprentice boys in particular. This was not disturbing to my nervous system, but when he added that he had been lately suffering from an invasion of rats and mice, my hair nearly stood on end, for no woman in creation was ever more ready to scream or faint at the appearance of these creatures in a bedroom than I. But even this was not the worst. He went on to describe their destructive habits in this particular establishment, where cases of lucifer matches were housed in the same shed with the paraffin oil, and he told me how only a few nights before one of these inquisitive vermin had gnawed through a case containing many dozens of boxes of the old-fashioned red brimstone matches, which were guaranteed to light anywhere with the least possible amount of friction. Then, with great pathos and indignation with the rat race, he described how one of them had just worked through a packing-case and was immediately upon the matches themselves when it had evidently been disturbed. Had a few more minutes elapsed before the interruption, the contact of its teeth with these explosive goods would undoubtedly have set the case on fire. The dozen or so oil barrels would most certainly have joined in the fun, and that establishment with others would inevitably have been destroyed. He proceeded to assure me that when you lived under these conditions there was always the fear of an outbreak of fire at any moment. Then, as if to cap the whole situation, he explained that my bedroom was immediately over the oil warehouse, and warned me that if I heard any noises in the night I was not to be alarmed. Then with a hearty good-night the worthy man took his leave.

Wellington's petition for " night or Blucher " was not more hearty than mine for daylight or sleep. Very early in the morning I descended from my unkindly couch, and with the excuse that the country habits of my youth were sometimes not to be denied, I escaped the offer of breakfast, and caught the first train of the day, thankful that I had escaped the fate of untimely cremation.

On another occasion a somewhat similar experience befel me. I was speaking at a public gathering in the West of England. My host for the night was a man of humble position, but, like all West-country folk, exceedingly hospitable. Before proceeding to the meeting I was invited to partake of a repast, for which, after my long journey from London, I was quite ready. My hostess had evidently made most elaborate and plentiful provision for my needs, but the assortment of dishes was scarcely inviting. They consisted of a plate of mussels, another of winkles, with cold bacon and plum cake as side-dishes. My heart—or some other portion of my anatomy—quailed before the sight, and I

hastily assured my hospitable friends that my tastes
were exceedingly simple, that bread-and-butter formed
my staple food, and that my doctor absolutely forbade
my touching shell fish.   I felt no small compunction at
the disappointment clearly felt by my refusal to partake
freely of the dainties, which had evidently been most
carefully prepared in the strongest of vinegar and the
hottest black pepper.

Nothing is easier for a public speaker than through
ignorance of local feeling to make a serious blunder
when addressing a meeting in a strange locality.   On
the other hand, luck may turn this very ignorance to
unexpected account sometimes, as it occasionally has
done for me.   On one occasion I was addressing a
meeting in support of Mr. Cozens Hardy at Melton
Constable, and as we were on the borders of Mr.
Joseph Arch's constituency, I did not forget him in my
speech.   Wishing to get home that night, I hurried
through my address in order to catch my train, and was
just about to leave when a man in the audience rose
and begged leave to put a question.   About this time
the Tory Party, through the medium of the Primrose
League, were endeavouring to poison the minds of the
agricultural labourers against Mr. Arch on account of
the large measure of failure then attending the operation
of the Agricultural Labourers' Union.   My questioner
wanted to know if I could give any information about
the balance-sheet of Mr. Arch's Union.   I replied that
it was a matter with which I was not personally
connected and into which I had no right to inquire.

I added that I knew nothing more of the Union's balance-sheet than I knew of the balance-sheet of my questioner, and with that I left the platform. As I hurried to the station I caught the sound of repeated roars of laughter which rather mystified me. Later on the mystery was explained. It appeared that the gentleman who had displayed so much anxiety about the solvency of Mr. Arch's Union had himself been recently in financial straits, from which he had only been relieved by the process which is known as " passing through the Courts."

Another instance of the same good luck occurred at a large meeting in Worcestershire. The main burden of my speech was the advocacy of Home Rule for Ireland. A well-dressed man sitting a dozen rows from the platform kept interjecting remarks that would have been very confusing to many speakers. While I was pressing home one of the chief points in my argument he suddenly exclaimed, " You had better give them whiskey than Home Rule." I turned to the interrupter and assured him that although his sole aim in life might begin and end in the consumption of strong drink, the Irish people had objects far loftier than the gratification of such a desire. At this the meeting broke out into a mighty cheer and rose in a body to jeer the interrupter, who promptly made his escape. I heard afterwards that he was one of the hardest drinkers in the district.

A curious incident of mistaken identity, in which a newspaper reporter was taken for me, occurred at a great meeting I addressed in Crewe. The reporter in question was good enough to send me an account of the incident, and I cannot do better than let him tell his tale in his own graphic manner.

## MR. HENRY BROADHURST'S GREATEST TRIUMPH

### A MEMORABLE NIGHT

#### PART I

IF twenty-four hours were allotted me in which to arrive at a decision on the question whether I would prefer death to a repetition of the worst ordeal I ever suffered in my life, I think the time would be spent in earnest prayer for the withdrawal of Mr. Henry Broadhurst from the political sphere. It would afford me the only means of escape. But by the cleverest design or arrangement it would be utterly impossible to place me in such a predicament that I should again be lionised by an enormous crowd of persons in mistake for the great electioneering champion of the Liberal Party, whose eloquence had aroused them into a state of wild delight. The effect of that eloquence upon myself is lifelong. Since they called me " Mr. Broadhurst " and paused for one of *his* speeches from *me*, I have most carefully avoided situations in which it would be possible for me to perform the smallest part of a public speaker.

I am stating here a few simple facts, and in order to make them quite clearly understood I would ask for the difference to be specially noted between an orator with a marvellous influence over his audience and a nervous man who would fall speechless if called upon for a sentence. These two persons—namely, Mr. Broadhurst and myself—happened to meet one night in November, 1885. It was the time when the whole world was interested in the question of alleged intimidation of the artisans of Crewe by their foremen in the service of the London & North-Western Railway Company. I only refer to it now in trying to convey an idea of the vast importance of the contest in which the local political parties were then engaged, and to emphasise the special reason why the Liberals sought the help of their most influential leaders who were likely to give it. After a secret conclave the local Liberal leaders agreed unanimously to invite Mr. Henry Broadhurst, as their chief speaker, to a demonstration. The fact that the municipal elections, fought on political lines, had gone overwhelmingly against the Liberals 'greatly increased their anxiety and accentuated their fears. For it was taken as a positive indication that the workmen, who on former occasions had given abundant proof of their Radicalism, were really afraid to vote against the railway company's officials, who were the Conservative candidates.

When it was announced that Mr. Broadhurst would address a meeting in the Corn Exchange on behalf of the Liberal candidate for Parliamentary representation, not a great many were expected to constitute his audience. Yet so attractive was the personality in that specimen of a working man whose life was an example to self-helpers, that hundreds of men who lingered outside the Corn Exchange ventured inside when he rose to speak. The place became crowded, and crowds remained in the main street immediately outside who were stronger in common curiosity than in political feeling. For a while the meeting was passive merely, and I, a reporter, had already made notes about insipidity, coldness, despondency, and so forth, A change, a marvellous change, occurred within an hour. As a Pressman of considerable experience I have attended hundreds of political meetings—meetings which were addressed by Cabinet Ministers and by Ireland's most eloquent representatives (modern Mark Antonys, some of them)—and it is with perfect sincerity and truthfulness that I commit myself in writing thus: the most enthusiastic of all was Mr. Broadhurst's meeting at Crewe, with only the solitary exception of the " record " meeting in Bingley Hall, Birmingham, where an audience of 20,000 people addressed by Mr. Gladstone on Home Rule cheered him continuously for ten minutes.

The hearts of the Crewe artisans were touched.  There was a fellow-feeling between the speaker and themselves. Mr. Broadhurst secured their close attention and then their deepest sympathies by a most entertaining and touching account of his experiences and hardships in early life—of the " insolence of office and the spurns that patient merit of the unworthy takes."   All that gloom, that ennui which characterised the early part of the proceedings was dispelled, and an appeal (I can liken it to nothing I ever heard elsewhere) to the chivalry of free men completed the transformation perfectly.  I write of it, possessing a memory on which that occasion will ever remain indelibly impressed, as about the most sensational fact of electioneering history, that in an hour Mr. Broadhurst, single-handed, crushed the great monster of intimidation which had become such a terror, and captured Crewe, then one of the new divisions, for the Liberal Party.  I am not sure that the misadventure that occurred to me after the meeting did not save Henry Broadhurst's life.  The men might have killed him by a demonstration of personal attachment.   With this " possibility " in view, prudence was exercised in devising a means whereby the hero might escape the crowd, which in increasing proportions waited without.

[*Exit* BROADHURST ; *enter* YOUR HUMBLE SERVANT.

## PART II

REALISING how inconvenient it would be to push through the dense crowd at the main entrance, I waited inside the building for a porter who had promised to lead the way to an exit into a quiet side-street. Fifteen minutes previously—just before the meeting ended—a gentleman had entered this way. He said he had been in a neighbouring hotel, and I readily believed him. He was not able to express himself very clearly in giving me to understand, as he did, that a cab was waiting in the side-street to take him home, a few miles in the country ; and as I was going in the same direction homewards, I was delighted when he said, " Come along with me." We reached the door, and it was suddenly flung open just as I was asking him what all the hubbub outside was about. The meaning of it—there was not time to realise it before striding across a narrow footpath to the cab-door—was plain enough after we were seated in the conveyance. The impatient crowd, suspecting the subterfuge to avoid an open-air demonstration—the strategy to get Mr. Broadhurst away— had rushed round from the main entrance to this side-street, being perfectly right in supposing it was intended to convey him off in this very cab. Someone had seen it and guessed the secret. It was Mr. Broadhurst's cab. What right had I in it ? The thought brought on a great dread of all kinds of punishment.

The night was dark, very dark, and there was little or no light—a fact which had been considered over the plan of escape. When, therefore, we two persons emerged from the doorway it was impossible to discern what we were like in general form. I heard afterwards how Mr. Broadhurst got away. It was simple enough. Finding the main entrance clear, when the crowd rushed round to the cab, he slipped off unobserved. I, even I, the most nervous being alive, was that Mr. Broadhurst, the invisible object of the admiration of the wrestling, yelling, delighted multitude, for a space which, though an eternity in the imagination, was limited in actual time to some five minutes. A strange metamorphosis, indeed! The proceedings in that period, commencing with three thundering cheers that " made the welkin ring " as the people crushed us into the cab, it is impossible for me to adequately describe.

The cabman waited. Of course I had no authority to order him on. He told me later that his orders were to wait for Mr. Broadhurst and three other gentlemen who were to accompany him in the drive to his hotel, and he was waiting when we entered for " the other two." The clamour of the crowd for a speech developed into a sort of madness, and as the cab remained motionless, feelings of hope and wonder must have become strangely mixed. Some wondered¡ " what was up," and some said " he was only thinking of what he had to say."

My friend expressed his firm conviction to me that everybody was mad drunk, and it was a pity, he observed, that he was the only man who could take a glass and keep sober. My life, I felt, was at stake, and so I durst not curse him. Louder and wilder became the demand for a speech, and the pressure around the vehicle increased as the throng itself increased with " outsiders," attracted by the " scene." Amid all the fearful tumult my companion coolly dropped the window on his side and, thrusting his head out, tried to make himself heard. Some little time was spent in noisily calling for silence. Then, commanding attention by shouting " Ladies and gentlemen," he succeeded in convincing them of his inability, through circumstances over which he certainly ought to have had control, to make a speech. No one knew what he was trying to communicate or what more there was in his mind than some confused ideas about closing-time, Broadhurst's good health, his own pugilistic abilities, and admiration for himself and the Grand Old Man. In a maudlin manner he called for three cheers for—presumably for me. The crowd, doubtful hitherto which of us two was Mr. Broadhurst, knew positively now, and after my friend had withdrawn everybody made for my side. Efforts were made to open the door. I held the handle inside with all my strength, and I suppose they concluded that the door was locked. Everybody joined in renewed clamour for a speech. I was dumb enough already. They paused for a response. Shouts followed: "Let him take time," "Give him a chance," "He's done up," "We'll *make* him say something." One man insisted that if I was too exhausted to speak, I should at least condescend to lower the window and shake hands with my admirers. A further pause, then more clamour. I heard another voice imploring, "Now, Harry, lad, just one word," and yet another, as if coaxing me to sing, "Just a little more encouragement." It surprised them that I still remained mute. It alarmed them. Said one suspiciously, "Why the devil won't he speak? There's something up with him."

The darkness of the night was so far my best protection, but I had now practically given up all hope of escape. Every moment I was expecting the appearance of Mr. Broadhurst and his friends, and wondering how many there were, and what the torture would be when he had indignantly cast me out upon this mob, incensed as they must be by my deception. Mutilation and inquests came across my mind. I mention this seriously, truthfully. I believe my heart sank to the very lowest depths of despair when someone exclaimed, "Broadhurst must be ill. Let us break the window and get at him. Who has got some matches?" Matches were produced and struck. The wind came to my aid while I ducked down and tried vainly to crouch under the seat. I was sure they would presently discover me, drag me out, and pitilessly lynch me. My friend, who had hitherto seemed little concerned, now began to manifest some uneasiness. He tried to tell the cabman to drive on. The cabman understood; and himself much alarmed, accepted the order and cracked his whip. By the horror of the situation I was bereft of sc much of my wits that I could not think of the possibility of being driven off deliberately in Mr. Broadhurst's cab. Before the driver could find an opening in the crowd, though he desperately sought one, it was proposed by one madman and readily decided by a host of others to unharness the horse and draw their hero themselves triumphantly to the Liberal Club. The endeavour occasioned greater excitement, alarming confusion, provoked the cabman into hostilities—he slashed his whip right and left, and startled the horse, which had already been prancing about impatiently. Its rearing and plunging caused a stampede, the driver laid on mightily with his whip, and the animal dashed off wildly. The mob who followed were soon outpaced, and only three persons knew where we halted.

Before that night the Conservatives boasted of promises being made to them of votes which, after reasonable allowances, would give them a majority of about 2,000. The result was, the return of the Liberal candidate by a majority of over 800. It was Broadhurst's greatest triumph, and *I* know it.

In an earlier chapter I have alluded to a vein of superstition which runs in my blood. This may be the result of heredity or of the rural environment of my early years; but whatever its source, I have never been able to get rid of it. I remember as a lad of sixteen working in a village six or seven miles from my home, and my way to and from work lay across fields and a large common, where I seldom met any human being. I used to leave home on Monday morning at half-past three, in order to be at work by six, returning on Saturday night at six o'clock. One dark winter's night I was taking my homeward way at a brisk rate along a footpath bordered on one side by a thick hedge. Suddenly I thought I heard someone on the other side of the hedge calling in distinct tones, "Harry! Harry!" I recognised the voice instantly as that of the wife of one of my brothers, and so strong was the impression made upon me that I stopped short and listened intently. But no other sound was to be heard, and I continued my journey. The first news that greeted me on my arrival home was the announcement of the sudden death of the person whose voice I had heard calling me by name.

After an interval of many years I was the recipient of another intimation of death, though hardly of so striking a character. It was in the autumn of 1886 that, at the earnest solicitation of a friend, I spent a month's holiday in Scotland. The spot selected was Gullane, a quiet, sandy village lying between North Berwick and Aberlaidy. Readers of the works of Robert Louis Stevenson will remember that he makes Gullane the scene of Allan Breck's escape and David Balfour's capture in "Catriona." It was here that I first saw golf played, and, needless to say, in a few days caught a very severe attack of the golf-fever. Unfortunately, urgent business called me back to London before I had been at Gullane a week; but the affair did not take long to settle, and I was able to return to Scotland by the following night mail. For some inexplicable reason I have always experienced some timidity in crossing the long bridge which spans the Tweed at Tweedmouth and Berwick, and my imagination would· persist in picturing the vibration sustained by the masonry from the weight of the heavy locomotives and railway-coaches. On more than on one occasion, when crossing the bridge, I have drawn a mental picture of a fearful disaster caused by a collision or by the giving way of some portion of the structure.

On this particular journey I had slept well till we reached Newcastle. As soon as we had left that noisy station behind I dropped off to sleep again. But my slumbers were disturbed, and presently I was dreaming that the train was in the middle of the stone bridge over the Tweed when one of the arches gave way, and the train was precipitated into the river. Dragged down beneath the surface of the water, I experienced a terrible feeling of suffocation and realised the pangs of death. In my dream I fancied my old friend Alfred Bailey, of Preston, was with me, and in the midst of my death struggle I wondered if he were sharing the same ghastly sensations.

I awoke from this horribly vivid nightmare in a perfect frenzy, the perspiration standing in great drops upon me. Rushing to the window, I found the train whirling through the Berwick station just as daylight was breaking. Needless to say, I had no more sleep, and was glad to reach Edinburgh, where a refreshing bath and a substantial breakfast at the Club in Prince's Street speedily restored my composure. I caught an early local train to Longniddry station, and drove thence to my lodgings in Gullane. As I entered the garden-gate a messenger ran up with a telegram addressed to me. Tearing it open, I found it contained the announcement of the sudden death of Mr. Bailey at Preston. He certainly had been ill for some weeks, but no one expected a fatal termination to this illness. These two events—the dream and Mr. Bailey's death—made a strong impression on my mind; and a week later, meeting the chairman of the East Coast Railway, I related my vision of the night. I believe as a consequence the bridge was thoroughly examined by the company's engineer, and, I need scarcely add, it was found to be as stable as a rock and as firm and solid as the day it was first opened for traffic.

In the foregoing stories I am afraid I have dwelt too much on my own success at repartee. To convince the reader that self-complacency is not the principal ingredient in my character, I will tell one or two incidents where the laugh was certainly against me. A few years ago I went one morning to call on Lord Rosebery at Berkeley Square. Near the Liberal leader's residence extensive repairs were being carried on, and this so changed the appearance of the place that I could not determine whether the house under repair or the next was his. Unfortunately, I had forgotten the number, and I was at a complete loss to know at which house to knock. As I stood uncertain a butcher's boy came along laden with a tray of meat. Of him I inquired which was Lord Rosebery's house, and pointing to the one I had just decided to try, he answered, " That's it." I thanked him, and was just about to ring the bell when I heard a shout. Turning round, I found the lad gesticulating furiously ; pointing to the area gate, he was calling out in loud tones, " That's the way for you ! There's the area gate ! You mustn't go to the front door, I tell you ! "

Another experience of the same kind befel me when Mr. Somers Somerset, the son of the Lady Henry Somerset, made his first bow before the electors of the division of South Herefordshire. I was deputed with Mr. Ellis Griffith, the Member for Anglesey, to attend the demonstration which was to be held on August Bank Holiday. I was to stay at Eastnor Castle, but I had not been informed of the place of meeting. My train was late in arriving ; I was tired and hungry after a long journey, and I felt I must get some refreshment before facing the audience. Coming out of the station I found a pair-horse carriage awaiting me, with a smart coachman on the box and a dapper little fellow in top-boots and cockade with his hand on the door. When we had got clear of the town I asked the coachman where he was going to take me. " Oh ! to the front door, sir," he replied. I thanked him and ventured no further inquiries. Of course, I intended to find out whether I was being conveyed direct to the meeting before going to the Castle.

An amusing instance of mistaken identity occurred during the prolonged sittings in the early part of 1880. On this particular occasion I had remained in the House till seven o'clock in the morning, when I gave notice to the Whips that I must go home. They urged me to remain another hour or so, but I refused, alleging that my house was entirely un-protected except for my dog, and he would want his breakfast by the time I reached home. This statement, duly embroidered, was repeated with much success by one of the legal advisers of the Government, gaining a wide circulation, and at each stage receiving many interesting additions. A few days later, when, thanks to the exertions of the Irish Party, all-night sittings were of almost unbroken continuity, Mr. Grant Duff happened to meet Mr. Thomas Burt on the terrace, and of course the obstructionist policy of the Irishmen was the burden of the conversation. Now, Mr. Grant Duff had heard the dog story, but somehow confused the hero and ascribed its origin to Mr. Burt. Being a noted dog-fancier and breeder of dogs himself, he naturally alluded to the incident, and remarked, " Yes, Mr. Burt, it is a killing time ; but I agree with you that the dogs should not suffer, and I am glad to hear that you insisted upon going home the other morning in order that your bull-dog might have his breakfast at his regular hour." Only those who know the grave and staid Member for

Morpeth can realise the look of horror which over-spread his countenance at the idea of his owning a bull-dog. "I don't know to what you refer, Mr. Duff," he exclaimed. "I never owned a dog in my life, and certainly not a bull-dog." Mr. Grant Duff hurriedly withdrew, with profuse apologies. But the story did not end there. At a later hour in the evening another Member was discussing with Mr. Burt the all-absorbing topic of the exhaustion of Members and its effect on their health, when Mr. Burt exclaimed, "Yes, and on their minds too, for Mr. Grant Duff has actually been asking me what time in the morning I retire from Parliament to feed my bull-dogs!"

# CHAPTER XV

## *LABOUR MEMBERS IN PARLIAMENT*

I HAVE often been asked what I think of Labour representatives in Parliament, and this seems a favourable opportunity of jotting down some impressions on this large question. In the early days of trades-unionism the idea of Labour Members of Parliament was opposed by nearly all classes, and received even by the great mass of workmen with indifference. In fact, working men have never been enthusiastic about having representatives of their own class in the legislative assembly. If it were otherwise we should have at least fifty Labour Members in the present House of Commons, in spite of financial obstacles. In most of the great centres of industry the working class population possess an overwhelming preponderance of votes, and if they were determined to be represented by one of themselves they could sweep away all opposition. They could relieve him of the expense involved in the hiring of large halls for public meetings; the considerable cost of postage might be avoided by mapping out the division into streets and half-streets, and the necessary literature distributed by men appointed to visit each section; and the heavy outlay on bill-posting could be dispensed with by the use of the windows of voters' houses. In such ways the cost of a contested election might be reduced to reasonable limits. Of course there would still remain the official or returning officer's charges. These frequently amount to two or three hundred pounds for each candidate, and the sum must be paid down before the returning officer will accept the nomination papers. It is a monstrous shame that in a country boasting of a free Parliament this golden bar to freedom of selection and election of a Parliamentary representative should be maintained. So long as it continues there can be no free representation. I have on more than one occasion made efforts in Parliament to relieve candidates from this imposition and transfer the burden to other shoulders, as is now the case in all local government elections. With fifty Labour representatives in Parliament instead of the present number, less than a dozen, now returned, the reform I have outlined might easily be obtained from the most reluctant of Governments. Other reforms would quickly follow, such as the payment of Members, including a rearrangement of the hours during which the House of Commons sits, securing the adjournment of debates at ten o'clock in place of midnight, which would enable Members to reach even suburban homes without trouble. This is an extremely important matter for Labour Members, because accommodation can be obtained at a distance of miles from Charing Cross at one-fourth the cost of that in central London.

These points will readily suggest others to thoughtful politicians. Speaking from my own experience, I have found Parliamentary life for a man of circumscribed means to be a life of drudgery and of great personal sacrifice. Then why not retire? the reader will naturally ask. My reply may seem paradoxical, but it is true that in some cases it is easier to get into Parliament than to withdraw from it. For example, Party exigencies often compel a man against his will to remain a Member, and when one is committed to a contest no Britisher cares to lose the game. Again, if you have spent a half or even a third of your life at Westminster the fascination of the place gets hold of you. The excitement of the opening of each session rouses even the most jaded Member. There are always many interesting men to be met at St. Stephen's whom one could not encounter elsewhere, at least, not under the same favourable social conditions. There are the distinguished visitors of all colours and nationalities. And to descend from great things to small, there are the strawberry teas on the terrace in summer. Although the characteristics of this function have greatly changed during the last few years, but sometimes even now you may find there men of world-wide fame in different walks of life. To these charms you must add the pleasure of showing your friends and constituents the historic features of the buildings and its contents. If your visitors happen to be uninteresting your knowledge of the place becomes very limited. If they are of the opposite character, and especially if they happen to be young and attractive members of the predominant sex, the cunning legislator enlarges on his theme, and when knowledge ends is not above improvising. These are a few of the elements which an analysis of the fascinations of the House of Commons reveals. Every August when the House rises the weary and washed-out legislator vows never again to enter those dreary portals; but the early days of February find him among the first-comers to place his hat upon the sacred cushions, his loins girded and his sword buckled on, fresh as any young blood for the fray.

Many good folk of unimpeachable Liberal sympathies look upon the idea of the payment of Members with grave suspicion. They believe it would degrade the dignity of the British legislation. But why? Lord Salisbury and the Duke of Devonshire are millionaires, and the pay attached to their respective offices must be a matter of utter indifference to them. Yet they take their ministerial salaries as regularly as the humblest messenger in their departments. The receipt of a stipend does not offend their sense of dignity. Take the case of Mr. Chamberlain. No one supposes he cares two straws for his five thousand a year as Colonial Secretary. This emolument does not influence his work; he could do equally well without it, and never be compelled to take one cigar or one hansom less than he does now. Then why should the Labour Members lose dignity by receiving from the State a stipend which would enable them to obtain the necessaries of life in the discharge of a national duty without those irksome and galling necessities at present inseparable from their existence? The British Parliament stands almost alone in refusing to remunerate its Members. It is difficult for the outsider to realise the constant calls on one's pretty cash account. Cabs are out of the question, except in pressing emergencies, and to meet the exceptional outlay retrenchment in other directions must follow. You must eat and drink, and the most frugal meal will cost you twice the amount of a meal taken at home. You cannot tell a visitor, especially a constituent, that to give him a cup of tea will put an inconvenient strain on your resources. Your dress must be decent. Postage is one of the most constant and serious burdens to a poor man; the most moderate estimate on this head is sixteen-pence a day, and woe betide the luckless victim who has charge of a motion or a Bill which attracts even partial interest in the country! Equally to be deplored is your fate if a considerable body of your constituents take a deep interest in a Bill promoted by another Member and express by letter their desire that you should support the measure. You may reply by postcard, certainly; but a couple of hundred postcards cost a good deal of money. All Ministers have their letters franked, and they possess secretaries to deal with their correspondence. Rich Members can find similar relief from the drudgery of letter-writing; but to the Labour Member this correspondence forms a continuous physical and financial tax which he ought not to bear.

The belief that Members are paid for committee work is not confined to the working classes. I remember twenty years ago being advised by a solicitor of mature age, who had acted on several occasions as election agent to a prominent politician, to take care to get my share of committee work ; the pay would be a great assistance to me. Many people who are too polite to refer directly to the matter share the belief of my lawyer friend. This foolish but widespread error is, I believe, a considerable hindrance to a poor Member's receiving the consideration his pecuniary position entitles him to. Yet it is not confined to the outside public. Only a year or two ago I received a note from a Member of Parliament of more than twelve years' standing in the House of Commons, asking in confidence whether any payment attached to service on a Royal Commission? To be credited with receiving handsome payment when you are getting nothing aggravates your comparative poverty.

Other opponents of the payment of Members object that it would encourage professional politicians and adventurers. It is the greatest delusion in the world that the present condition of affairs keeps them out ; but of course I cannot enlarge upon this point without involving myself in unpleasant personalities. I firmly believe that the reduction of election expenses in the direction suggested above, together with the payment of Members, would introduce to political life many men of great ability who are prevented now from offering their services by reason of insufficient incomes.

I think it may fairly be claimed for those of my order who have been or are now in Parliament that, amidst all the display and glitter of wealth by which their lives in the precincts of the House are surrounded, they have not lost their heads, but have retained the simple habits of life in which they were reared. In fact, I have no hesitation in affirming that their frugal and homely habits have exercised a restraining influence upon some of their wealthy colleagues. Most of them have their homes in the provinces, and this involves a separation from family life for the greater part of the year. The result is an additional cost beyond the ordinary one of maintenance.

Two great interests lack Parliamentary representatives on the Labour side—*viz.* agriculture and shipping. It is most desirable that intelligent representatives of these vast industries should be found in the House of Commons. Their needs were formerly voiced by Mr. Joseph Arch and Mr. J. Havelock Wilson, but neither are now Members. The capitalists and owners in both interests are largely represented ; but it cannot be for the highest good of the State that these two interests, which are the basis of national prosperity, should possess only a one-sided representation in the National Assembly.

I believe a good case for the success of Labour Members of Parliament can be made out from the records of the past thirty years. When one thinks of the mistakes which might have been made but have been avoided by the small band of working men who have found their way into Parliament, one is bound to express admiration at their good sense and self-restraint. To realise the full meaning of this statement the reader must carry his mind back to their original condition of life. Some were born before the days of board schools and compulsory education; all were the children of poor parents. Some began to earn their living at an age when the majority of their fellow-members had not escaped the charge of the nursery governess. Their future appeared to be hedged about by the necessity of physical toil for a weekly wage; Parliament and politics were meaningless terms to some. Even now their situation amazes them; they have been thrust from position to position without design or forethought. They find themselves in a whirl of excitement, surrounded by the possessors of vast wealth, the bearers of noble and ancient names, the learned professor, the profound philosopher, the intrepid world-traveller. Yet in this vast human maze they hold their own with credit. Here and there may be found eccentricities, but no boorishness, little if any vulgarity, and no disordered minds. They have earned a reputation for their class of solid and abiding worth to the commonwealth.

# CHAPTER XVI

## *MEN I HAVE KNOWN*

MR. JOHN BRIGHT was always regarded with some suspicion from the trades-union point of view. This was probably inevitable from the nature of his opinions in all matters affecting trade. He was essentially for absolute freedom of action in this and kindred matters; but the trades-unionists thought that he carried this practice to extremes in connection with Labour matters, and on the question of Labour representation he was not thought, from the workmen's point of view, to be orthodox. He had spoken against class representation, and so had the workers; but their position was better defined, as being opposed to class exclusion, which was the case until the period commenced in 1874 and 1880 and further developed in 1885 and 1892.

As Secretary of the Labour Representative League I had had some correspondence with Mr. Bright with regard to some speeches he had made on the proposed sending of workmen to Parliament, and none of his replies were considered to be quite satisfactory. As a general politician, apart from Labour questions, he was, of course, universally idolised by the workers, and no part of the community more highly appreciated his great statesmanship and magnificent oratory.

When I was returned for Stoke in 1880, these little divergencies of opinion did not prevent his giving me a warm welcome to the House of Commons, and during the remaining years of his life he was always exceedingly friendly, perhaps I ought to say exceedingly kind and generous, in his bearing towards me, always ready with a jocular remark, never patronising, and many and many an hour have I spent in his company in the smoke-room listening to his talk on subjects weighty as well as witty ; no man's company and conversation afforded me greater delight, instruction, and entertainment.

The meerschaum pipe presented to me by the Glasgow Trades in 1881 was a formidable-looking object, and required considerable care in handling for fear of breakage. I am not a lover of meerschaum pipes, nor indeed of any pipe except the good old clay ; but having received this as a token of goodwill, I thought it my duty to colour it in order to testify to my Scotch friends my appreciation of their kindness. I used to charge this pipe with great care and exactitude, that the colouring process might be carried out systematically, and with some regard to finish and effect in that line of art. Mr. Bright, in a jocular manner, would persist in taking the deepest interest in the progress of that undertaking ; he would frequently examine the result of my labours, and inquire as to the time occupied and the cost incurred, and what period of time I thought would be necessary successfully to accomplish my task. His inimitable humour when pursuing these inquiries can only be appreciated by those who were privileged to know him in his arm-chair moods. I became greatly attached to him, an attachment which almost amounted to affection, and this apart altogether from his public life and great position in the nation.

I have heard some of his great speeches, and I shall never forget the St. James's Hall speech in the 'Sixties during the Reform agitation. His peroration was magnificent, and its effect electrical. It seemed to exalt the very soul of the audience, and left an impression which few of his hearers can have forgotten.

Another speech which deeply impressed itself upon my mind was made during the debate on the Burial Bill in the Parliament of 1880, when Mr. Bright was pleading for greater freedom for Nonconformist interments in churchyards. During this speech he described the devotion of an old worker with whom he had been acquainted, who for many years had walked fifteen miles each Sunday to visit the grave of his dead wife, buried in unconsecrated ground, and with tremendous effect he asked the House to say whether devotion of this kind would desecrate the consecrated ground of the Church. The passage was almost sublime. He spoke from the Treasury Bench, his long white locks shining in the rays of light streaming through the western windows of the House; the combination of colour and the age of the orator, his deep pathos and his great earnestness, produced an indescribable effect upon the House, and did much to soften the tone of debate and to promote a freer passage for the measure through Parliament.

It will be an everlasting regret that no worthy likeness in statue form is left to the nation of the Great Tribune. His was a face, like many others, that cannot be reproduced in marble after death ; the only effective likeness I can conceive to have been possible of him would have been one modelled from life in clay by a supremely sympathetic artist. The great characteristics of sympathy, love, and devotion written deep on some faces are, in my opinion, utterly impossible to reproduce in marble, and the attempts made and the failures experienced should not be too severely visited upon the heads of the unhappy sculptors who take up a task almost humanly impossible.

Another man for whom I had an exceptionally deep personal regard was the Rev. C. H. Spurgeon. I looked upon him as one of the strongest men of our age, the simplest and kindliest of men. A two minutes' chat with Mr. Spurgeon was like a week's sea-breezes to the weary metropolitan worker. I met him only on rare occasions, but I count it one of the good fortunes of my life to have known him even thus slightly.

One event in my life in connection with the American people I shall always remember with pleasure and pride. I think it was in 1877 that General Grant visited London. I was charged with the duty of preparing an address and organising a deputation of Labour representatives to present it to the distinguished soldier-statesman. He was not a man easy of access, and it was with difficulty that we were enabled to arrange an interview with him. But when the preliminary obstacles were overcome he received the address and the deputation with marked favour, and it was said by one who knew him that his speech in reply, short as it was, was marked with exceptional warmth of feeling and pleasure. A man less like a great soldier and the defender of a great nation in outward appearance could not be conceived, and it was only in the indescribable atmosphere of his presence that one could at all realise his greatness and strength of character.

The only other American of distinction it has been my good fortune to have personal acquaintance with was Mr. Russell Lowell. I first met him at a breakfast party at Mr. Gladstone's house. I had read his poems, with many of which I had been greatly fascinated, and some of which I liked better than any I had ever read. Of course this led me to regard him with more than usual interest. I liked him in person as much as I did in his works. I met him again at a public dinner a few years after, and was surprised at his approaching and speaking to me in a familiar manner, as if we had been in the habit of frequently seeing each other. He was a capital speaker, so far as I heard him, and his conversation was most enjoyable.

Cardinal Manning was another man for whom I had a great regard. I first met him when serving on the Royal Commission on the Housing of the Poor. I do not regard him as a great statesman, or as one having what might be described as the grip of things; but undoubtedly his soul was overflowing with the milk of human kindness, great forbearance towards the weaknesses of humanity, and deep sympathy with its trials and sufferings. At his request I met him on several occasions at his private house. Our common bond of sympathy was the bettering of the condition of the workpeople. My speech against the opening of museums and picture-galleries on Sunday enlisted his hearty sympathy and support, and on one occasion, when discussing this question in his house, he asked whether the great fact had ever occurred to me that London, the centre of the world for civilising and Christian influence, in addition to being the greatest centre of commerce that the world has ever seen or known, almost voluntarily agreed to forgo the delivery of letters on Sunday, and apparently suffered no inconvenience in its competition with the world from this fact. He spoke most strongly against the growing habit of Society of turning Sunday into a day of pleasure, frivolity, and social gatherings, assuring me that he made it a rule never to dine out on Sundays, and that he had endeavoured to use his influence with his friends to cause as little labour as possible either in their own domestic circle or outside it on the sacred day of rest. Then he descanted with that beauty of language and refinement of feeling peculiar to him on what life might have been without the day of rest, and the danger to Labour of tampering with its sacred observance. A discussion and a homily from him on such a subject as this had a similar effect upon one's emotional feelings to that produced by a magnificent sunset on a summer's evening.

In these occasional interviews and chatty half-hours he only once raised a subject upon which I could not agree with him, and that arose in connection with the education question. Knowing that I was a worshipper with the Wesleyan Methodist Church and that I had all my life been associated with that body, he approached me on the question of religious teaching in the schools, and seemed to be under the impression that the overwhelming majority of Wesleyan Methodists held similar views to his own. Although having no authority to speak for them, I could and did unhesitatingly speak for myself, and expressed strong views against increased grants for sectarian teaching in elementary schools, and I ventured to express my gravest doubts as to the information which had been given him regarding the position of the majority of Methodists in relation to this subject. He was visibly disappointed —I might almost say that his face betrayed evidence of some pain at the views I stated. With some expressions of regret the subject was dismissed, and it was never again referred to, but I do not think it in any way lessened his friendly feeling towards me.

In many respects two of the most remarkable dinners I have attended were both held at Greenwich. One was given by Lord Rosebery as a compliment to the Labour Party early in 1886. Among the guests were Mr. Gladstone, Mr. John Morley, and a few other prominent members of the Liberal Party. Lord Rosebery was at the head of the table, and I was on Mr. Gladstone's right. The dinner was the most jovial I ever remember ; politics were abandoned, and the feature of the evening was the telling of good stories by our host, Mr. Gladstone, and Mr. Morley. Needless to say, the Prime Minister easily took first place. Some of his House of Commons reminiscences of the time of Peel, Palmerston, and others would have been worth preserving had I been in the habit of keeping a diary. Possibly some of the others present may have done so.

One anecdote, however, I remember quite well. I think it was Palmerston who, Mr. Gladstone told us, had a wonderful habit of sleeping in his place on the Front Bench, and his head would move backwards and forwards to such an extraordinary degree that it frequently attracted the Speaker's attention, and even alarmed him. At the close of the session the Speaker privately gave orders for the backs of the two front benches to be heightened, so that those occupying them might, with very little inconvenience, rest the head on the top of it, to the delight and comfort of dozing Front Bench Members in the next session. This explained—what I never understood before—why these benches are more comfortable for a lounge than those in the other part of the House.

Mr. Gladstone also reminded us that in those days the tea-room in the House was arranged very much after the fashion of a London coffee-house—that is, having rows of settles, with a narrow table between—where it was the habit for Members to get their chops, accompanied by a fragrant drink made from Chinese tea. On one occasion when Palmerston was enjoying his evening repast at one of these tables, Hume went over to Mr. Gladstone, who was sitting in the same room, and remarked that he thought Palmerston had something in him and might possibly prove a useful and active Member of the House in course of time !

The second political dinner, curiously enough, took place in the same year, and also at Greenwich, in the month of August. At the first one we were a great and powerful Party, and to many there appeared to be a brilliant future in store for us. But the disasters which followed upon the introduction and rejection of the Home Rule Bill in the June of that year had by August left us a scattered and disjointed remnant of the all-powerful Government of a few months before. On this occasion our host was Sir Henry (now Lord) James. The company numbered about a dozen. Amongst them were Sir William Harcourt, Mr. Chamberlain, Mr. Jesse Collings, Mr. Asquith, and some others, including myself.

We went down in the orthodox style by boat from Westminster. It was the first occasion on which I had noticed Mr. Asquith. On the way down I kept wondering who he could be, but before going in to dinner Sir Henry James introduced me to him. I failed to catch his name, and I took the first opportunity of asking Sir Henry to tell me who he was. I said : " I did not catch the name of the young man to whom you introduced me just now. He is an interesting looking chap, and I should like to know more about him." Sir Henry's reply was : " You will very soon know about him ; he is one of the ablest and most brilliant among the new Members elected to Parliament of late years." He certainly made some impression upon me, but in what direction I could not well say. He appeared to contain great strength of will : a rather strongly hewn Yorkshire face showing unmistakable pugnacity of character ; bluntness,—principally in manner only. On the whole, I took him to be a man with whom it would not be wise to have an unnecessary quarrel. How far Sir Henry's estimate of his future has been fulfilled all the world now knows. Certainly Mr. Asquith's outward appearance has undergone a remarkable change, for at the present time he is one of the best dressed and most presentable men among the Liberal leaders.

The dinner was one of the most elaborate I ever sat down to, with regard to the number of courses, the quality of the food, and the variety of wine and fruit. It was a curious gathering, and for the first half-hour or so the conversation seemed to hang fire and there did not appear any prospect of its becoming a cordial meeting. Our resourceful host exerted all his marvellous powers of ingenuity to infuse life into the company, and presently addressed an inquiry to me across the table as to the state of health of my bull-terrier, asking whether I had lately brought him to the House of Commons. I replied that he had not recently visited that place with me, but I thought the time was coming when it would be necessary to bring him in order to clear out the rats. The tone, the occasion, and the manner prevented the remark from being considered offensive, and no one joined more heartily in the laughter which greeted my hint than Mr. Chamberlain and his friend Mr. Jesse Collings. The meeting at once became more genial, and a very pleasant evening was the ultimate outcome. I have always thought that the real object of that dinner was to prevent, if possible, the unhappy differences which had so lately culminated in placing the Conservatives in power from becoming chronic. I firmly believe that some at least of the Unionists at that time were quite unaware that the cleavage was so wide and reunion so remote as it has proved to be, and that the gathering was intended to be a golden bridge by which the two sections of the Liberal Party might be reunited. Events have proved how great was the disappointment of those who hoped for this result.

During the years in which I was frequently in personal contact with Mr. Gladstone I always received at his hands the deepest consideration. Nothing could exceed his forbearance and civility to me. During my residence at Brixton Hill I cultivated pretty successfully a fine bed of carnations and some very lovely pinks, the roots of the latter being given to me by the late Baron Ferdinand de Rothschild. Of the carnations I was particularly proud, and on several occasions I sent small boxes of them to Mr. Gladstone, who wore some of the blooms in the House of Commons. During the progress of my illness from 1888 it was thought that the only chance I had of living for any considerable time was to leave London and to reside permanently in the country. For this purpose I built myself a cottage at Cromer, to which I removed in May, 1890. Before I left London Mr. Gladstone came to my house at Brixton and took tea with me, a neighbouring doctor who attended my family, my wife, my niece, and a lady friend of theirs being the only persons present. He spent something like an hour and a half with us, recounting some most interesting personal reminiscences, and talking pleasantly of the events of the earlier part of the century. Then he plunged into the story of the Free Trade conflict, telling us of the price of sugar, tea, coffee, bread, and other necessaries of life. It was one continuous, gossipy conversation from the time he entered to the time he left. I remember his noticing a large photograph of my famous bull-terrier, for whose warlike and determined appearance he expressed admiration, and suggested that one or two of that breed would prove valuable defenders to the public purse, if they could be placed at the entrance of the Treasury Department. Then he drove back to the House, and from that time I had but few opportunities of personal intercourse with him.

Mr. Gladstone's civilities to me were not merely personal, but intended, as I always felt, to show that he recognised the claims of the labouring people to consideration. Probably no statesman uttered words so helpful to Labour representation as he did. Speaking at Birmingham in 1888, on the occasion of receiving an address of the workmen of that town, in the conclusion of one of his speeches, the like of which no other man could make, and speaking of the difficulties of selecting the right representatives, he used these striking words, which I may perhaps be pardoned for quoting :—

"I can assure you that I never submitted a recommendation to Her Majesty for the filling of a political office with greater satisfaction than when I submitted the name of Mr. Henry Broadhurst. I did so, not only because I knew that he was the representative of the working men, chosen by the working men, but I had had the opportunity of seeing his character and his qualities tested, in circumstances of difficulty, and I knew that there was not a more competent and capable, and more creditable and honourable representative of the working classes than Mr. Henry Broadhurst. I will add this, that if by any unhappy accident Mr. Henry Broadhurst had been taken out of our view, and had been found in any circumstances not in a position to take office at that time, there would have been no difficulty in selecting from his colleagues another representative of Labour, a man who would have done honour to the same office if he had been appointed. We all wish, we all sincerely and cordially wish that the number of working men in Parliament should be increased. We are very glad to have those who are already there, but undoubtedly the number ought to be increased."

On my way to the Aberdeen Trades Congress in 1884 I found it necessary for the discharge of some official duties to break my journey at Edinburgh, and subsequently learned that that particular night had been suddenly fixed upon for a great reception to Mr. Gladstone in the Waverley Market. The Edinburgh Trades Council had been invited to nominate a speaker to represent the Labour Party of the city, and they unanimously selected me for that purpose. On receiving this great compliment I saw at once that such an arrangement would not be satisfactory, nor would it fulfil the object in view, and I pointed out that the speaker must be an Edinburgh man. This view of the case they reluctantly acquiesced in ; but I received a platform ticket to witness this great sight. It was stated that there were 16,000 persons in and about the covered market that night. As Mr. and Mrs. Gladstone entered the building the combined bands struck up and the vast mass of people joined in their national song, "Scots wha hae for Wallace bled." The effect was tremendous. I did not after all escape a part in the meeting. There were loud calls for me from several parts of the hall, and I had to respond. Up to this time Mr. and Mrs. Gladstone had no knowledge of my presence, and when I left my seat for the rostrum, they both rose and gave me a hearty greeting, which event appeared to excite great enthusiasm amongst the audience.

The next morning I resumed my journey to Aberdeen, and found just outside Edinburgh that a saloon car sent on from Dalmeny had been attached to our train. Thus I became a fellow-traveller, as far as Aberdeen, of the great leader. It was the first occasion on which I made a journey in the same train as Mr. Gladstone, although not the last one. From Edinburgh to Aberdeen was one continuous and brilliant march of triumph. The fact that the idol of the masses was to travel in that train was known throughout the districts abutting upon the railway for the whole length of the journey. Every station was lined with people ; at some of them presentations were made. Constant delays of the train occurred, and the utmost exertions of the railway officials, supported by bodies of police, were needed at the stations to prevent accidents to the people, who clambered up steps and on the roofs of the coaches to get a glimpse of their hero. At Perth most elaborate preparations to prevent rushing and crushing had been made, and the regulations were strictly observed by the people until the train pulled up. Then with one united plunge forward, locks, bolts, and bars were rent asunder, police and station officials were overwhelmed, and the whole building was flooded with a seething mass of human beings. In a lesser degree this state of things continued till we reached Aberdeen. Here my journey finished. If I remember rightly, Mr. Gladstone went on to Haddo, Lord Aberdeen's house near by, and the following week to Braemar, from which place he sent me a cordial invitation to spend a day with him at that Highland holiday resort, but I found it impossible to do so, on account of my official work at the Trades Congress.

The most interesting occasion outside the House of Commons at which I was present in connection with Mr. Gladstone was in July, 1888, when those who served under him in his late Government and some few others of his close and most faithful political supporters presented him with his portrait on his Golden Wedding day. We assembled in one of the large reception-rooms at the house of Lord Spencer. A space backed by folding doors opening into an adjoining room was roped off, and within this were seated a few intimate friends. Presently the folding doors opened, and Lord Granville entered with Mrs. Gladstone on his arm, he carrying a bridal bouquet, and she wearing a long veil, said to be the one she wore on her marriage day fifty years before. They were immediately followed by Mr. Gladstone in semi-

wedding dress, who took his place beside his wife.
When all was ready Earl Granville approached the
aged pair, with that refinement of manner for which
he was so justly celebrated, and in a voice full of
feeling and in tones bordering upon reverence he
read a short address of congratulation, and, if my
memory serves me truly, he mentioned the fact that
he had met Mrs. Gladstone before she knew Mr.
Gladstone.   Then, in a kneeling position, he kissed
her hand, bowed, and took his stand behind them.
Mrs. Gladstone's few words of acknowledgment were
almost inaudible by reason of her emotion.   Mr.
Gladstone then spoke, shortly referring to his long
friendship with Lord Granville, and with some references of a touching nature in harmony with the event.
Then the proceedings closed, and we all dispersed.

I have in my time seen many notable events.   I
was in St. Paul's at the Thanksgiving Service on
the recovery of the Prince of Wales ; I have seen
nearly every great demonstration held in London
since 1866, and have taken part in most of them ;
I was at the opening of the Imperial Institute in
May, 1893 ; I was present at the laying of the
foundation stone some six years before ; I had a
good position in Westminster Abbey on the occasion
of the Jubilee Service in 1887 ; I have seen ship-
wrecks and gallant rescues.   But I have never witnessed a scene so rich, so full of pathos, so suggestive
of the higher life, the ideal co-existence attainable by
poor human nature, as that shown on this occasion

by the aged couple whose life was so lofty and noble. Its effect upon one was that of a wedding of two pure and spotless souls, rather than that of the fiftieth anniversary of the marriage ceremony. Few in the room there were who could have articulated clearly at that moment, had they been called upon to speak ; a silence as of the grave prevailed among the forty or fifty privileged persons. Speaking for myself, I felt the whole scene so intensely that I seemed incapable of speech or thought of anything except the feeling engendered by the scene just witnessed. If some master hand had been present to have described it in adequate language or painted it with a living brush, the scene in Lord Spencer's house that day would have lived long in the history of the country.

Of the world-wide day of mourning when we committed the ashes of our dead leader to the grave in Westminster Abbey I shall not attempt to say much. It was the culminating hour of weeks of anguish. We do not know, we cannot tell whether the spirits of the departed ever know of the streams of pure love which gush out from the souls of those who are left behind when a dearly loved one is committed to the earth. If they do, how must the soul of William Ewart Gladstone have been uplifted on the surge of tears shed by those he knew, and by countless numbers whose faces he had never seen, but whose lives had been ennobled by his hallowed life !

My place in the procession was a little in advance of the coffin. We had waited lingeringly round the mortal remains of him we loved, as a broken-hearted mother clings to her dead first-born. But the order came, the sections filed past, and we emerged from the great doors of Westminster Hall into a keen and wintry air. My eye involuntarily sought the clock-tower, on whose tall flanks I had worked, chilled to the bone, nearly thirty years before; and memory recalled one bitter cold, wet day in the winter of 1858-9 when, almost barefoot, I had crossed the Palace Yard on my way to the club-house of my union. The contrast was almost overwhelming : then unknown and penniless; to-day in a place of honour, the sorrowing colleague of the greatest Englishman of the century. So we passed on between the solid walls of humanity, standing with bared heads in absolute silence.

Within the Abbey my place was on the north side of the grave. On my immediate right was the late Lord Chief Justice, and on my left Lord Justice Rigby. Behind sat the Lord Chancellor, and as the Duke of York retired from his post of pall-bearer he brushed against me. Then the Prince of Wales, to-day the King of the mightiest Empire the world has known, advanced in reverence to Mrs. Gladstone, and before us all kissed the trembling hands of the widow of the greatest commoner of our land. Thus did the first gentleman of the nation acknowledge the equality of all humanity in the presence of the King of kings.

# INDEX

www.ingramcontent.com/pod-product-compliance
Ingram Content Group UK Ltd.
Pitfield, Milton Keynes, MK11 3LW, UK
UKHW030825281224
452734UK00010B/110

9 781535 805346

# Under the Tuscan Blunder

*By Richard Lucchesi*

*This book is dedicated to my father*
*Dick Lucchesi.*

*He was a wonderful man who exemplified the*
*American values of someone who grew up in the 1950's.*
*I aspire to be the kind of father and human that you were.*

# Table of Contents

*"In the middle of the journey of my life, I found myself within a dark woods where the straight way was lost."*

**— Dante Alighieri, Inferno**

# Chapter 1 - House Hunting in Tuscany

The train ride from Pisa to Bagni di Lucca was comfortable, but more importantly direct, and took almost exactly an hour from departure to arrival. The mountains outside my window grew in size the deeper north we traveled. Once inside Annabella's car, I was whisked away down long, winding roads nestled in between the Apennine and Apuan Alps. Large, moss covered trees lined both sides of the road leading towards Ponte a Serraglio, the little hamlet where she was taking me first. I had never seen anything like it.

Annabella was waiting in front of the station inside her tiny late model Fiat Panda when I turned the corner towards the parking lot from platform one. With long greying, well-maintained hair, she wore a mask and spoke natively in English. I loved that, and I should have known better that nobody is perfect, especially in Italy. But I was in Tuscany on my way house shopping, and finally living la dolce vita after a year of lockdown. I wanted to enjoy this moment. What could go wrong? Throughout the day, there was no indication that things would quickly go sideways with Annabella.

While possibly well intentioned, what seemed like friendly help and advice at first wasn't just that at all. I wasn't *just* a one time client in her eyes buying a home, but rather a more permanent one who 'needed' lots of help in the transition phase of moving here. For instance, she'd recommend a plumber when we needed one. Then, she'd set the appointment on my behalf, broker the fee once the job was completed, and I'd pay *her* directly. All this instead of just giving me the man's number, and letting me deal with it like I had for decades with my own properties in America.

She'd remain in my life 'helping me out', and then charging me every time for said help until I'd put a stop to it. I no longer contact Annabella, but still see her around town occasionally and cordially say hello in passing. My wife and I appreciated her efforts initially, but some of the biggest frustrations experienced once living in

Italy were a result of Annabella 'helping' my family transition. But *nobody* is a dick when you represent a possible commission check plus residuals.

## You Can Renovate!

It had been *extremely* difficult scheduling a real estate agent to show me Italian houses. Anyone who's serious about purchasing property in Italy, and doesn't understand the system here has experienced this. In Italy, you don't even need a pre-approval letter to view homes for sale. You need nothing but someone to unlock the door. What's more, Annabella wasn't even my initial contact person. I had originally reached out to a British gentleman who runs a Lucca property website. That man put me in contact with Annabella, and she showed me everything he had available. Because of the immense friction and difficulty arranging showings *in any part of Italy*, by the time I arrived here, I'd look at *any* houses a realtor would take me to regardless of price or location.

Annabella chatted my ear off. She insisted on telling me about the history of the region, but I blocked out the chatter. I hadn't asked about it, and this wasn't my first rodeo purchasing property. I was much more focused on what the area looked like, how far we were traveling from the train station, and anything that stood out. I sensed she would keep talking whether I wasn't listening closely or not.

The first property was up a steep road with switchbacks. We parked alongside a stone wall with no room to park just outside the original natural thermal spa that made Bagni di Lucca super famous with Napoleon's sister. Located inside a cave, that thermal spa is now permanently closed. As we approached the building, the last one before the entrance to the old spa resort, I looked up and saw a man on a small terrace directly above. I smiled and waved, but he didn't smile back. He just stared judgmentally and shook out a towel to hang. Would that be my neighbor if I bought this place?

The front door to the apartment was about two meters from the building's shared entrance. We entered into a small living room, with a window to the right and the hallway to the rest of the apartment on the left. The apartment was all hallway with doors on the right straight down to the bathroom. First was a small kitchen with semi-upgraded cabinets. If I had to guess, it hadn't been used in years. Then, a bedroom, then a second much larger double bedroom, and the bathroom was at the end of the hall. The small bathroom had been severely neglected, with a mildewy shower curtain dangling from a broken, plastic shower surround. It was the worst room in the apartment.

"You can renovate and redo the bathroom however you like," Annabella assured me.

*Renovate* the bathroom? I could barely fit in there! I was not reassured. But other than the awful bathroom, it was a good first showing.

The second house showing was back down the hill, and very close to Ponte a Serraglio's piazza. A lively place called 'Bar Italia' was in the center of the piazza. We parked just up the road, and made our way along the narrow sidewalk towards the apartment. We were met by two grandiose solid wood front doors with large fixed, hand made wrought iron door handles. They were one-off art pieces that I did not know were put there by the current owners. Standing outside the apartment while fiddling with keys, Annabella said something surprising.

"The nice thing about this apartment is that there are three units in total if you purchase it," Annabella stated.

I was enticed. I took a few steps back to the side, and snapped two photos of the front with a street view.

"Are we going to get to see all three units today?" I asked.

"If I can find the keys," she answered.

**Good Vibes**

"Another nice thing about this apartment is the private entrance. The owners do not share this entrance with anyone," Annabella said, right before inserting the key into the lock.

I didn't think much of it. I understood what she meant, but did not digest the gravity of her statement. However, after living in Italy for two years, having a private entrance into your home is a *huge* deal if you live in a shared building. *Not* sharing is heavenly.

She opened the oversized door, and we entered into a very spacious, double groin vaulted living room. The walls were painted faint yellow, and the enormous ceilings above were white washed. There was a large table in front of the door, and a few pieces of furniture to the side covered with white sheets. It was an impressive space with lots of potential. A magnificent square brick pillar sat at the center of the apartment. The kitchen's backsplash was painted orange, and the background wall had a pleasing texture. The cabinets and countertop were white, and to the one side were open shelves where pots and pans sat. Colorful artwork adorned the kitchen walls.

The back wall of the kitchen had a tall double door with windows. Annabella unlocked the door which led to the elevated, substantial terrace overlooking a beautiful, emerald green river. I could hear the river from inside the kitchen, but once outside, I could see bits of it through the trees and shrubs. From the terrace, a cast iron stairway to the left led down to a very nice, grassy garden below that was shared with a few other neighbors. The entrance from the street into the front door was at ground level, but out the back door was raised up high above the garden. It was a homey, satisfying scene, and I was taken by how nice and natural it all was.

On the right side of the terrace was a small laundry room with a washer and a few shelves for storage. It used to be this apartment's bathroom, which means inhabitants had to go outside every time

4

they needed to wee. Annabella failed to tell me that, but she knew. Of course she did. She'd spent the last thirty-five years in this small town, and knew everyone's business. It wouldn't be the last time she'd omit important, valuable information. Once we purchased this place, I'd later find out from another realtor that the main apartment we were viewing used to be the town pharmacy, but Annabella never mentioned it. I'd also find out that the new pharmacy, which sits besides Bar Italia in the piazza a hundred meters down the road, is owned by a man who lives on the top floor. He used to own the entire building, and over the years had been slowly dividing it up and selling it off. I wonder what else Annabella would 'forget' to tell me.

Back inside the kitchen, there was an arched entryway to the bedroom, but no door. It was another very large room with a huge ceiling. The bathroom off the bedroom wasn't humongous, but was oodles better than the previous apartment. The shower appeared to be custom built with small, square, cream colored tiles. The custom made, cast iron door to the bathroom had pixelated glass, and no latch or lock.

Annabella was still in the kitchen fixated on her phone. She was always on her phone. I paused for a moment in the bedroom, admiring my new surroundings. Could this be the one? It was hard to say, especially since Annabella had more viewings planned that day. I wasn't really interested in a one bedroom home either, but this apartment had class. I was digging this space the more I stood there, and could sense that Stephanie might too. It had a vibe. I pulled out my phone and started recording video.

"Shall we go downstairs and look at the second apartment?" Annabella suggested.

# Chapter 2 - The Butcher, The Baker.. & The Pharmacy?

I followed Annabella outside onto the terracotta tiled terrace, and then down the stairs to the garden. I had to admit, the environment was beautiful. The river was a deep color of green, looked pristine, and flowed gently over visible, underwater rocks. How soothing. A waist high rock wall with ivy growing every which way ran the length of the garden parallel to the river. I approached to get a closer look. Over the other side was a steep drop down to river level. Even though we descended a large set of stairs, we were still up high above the water. The garden was green, *very* overgrown, and serene.

I was encouraged, but I hadn't come to Europe for a one bedroom. Other than upstairs *being* a one bedroom, I hadn't yet spotted any major flaws, not yet anyway. Everything around me was like a dream.

We approached a double-hung finished wood door at garden level that unlocked with a skeleton key. Cobwebs were strewn like Halloween decorations. An oversized window carved out of the foundation was to the right side. The door and window were underneath the terrace from the first apartment. Two chairs and a small table sat nestled in front of a very nice, covered patio. Square cement pillars held up the roof of the patio and terrace above, and were crumbling a bit at the base.

"This is a cantina," Annabella said.

Inside was an industrial space being used as an art studio.

"There's electricity, heat and running water," Annabella indicated.

I was met with another groin domed ceiling just like upstairs, but made entirely of brick. It was covered in black soot and *still* gorgeous.

Like the first apartment, the space was impressive. Someone cared for it. A large, rectangular porcelain stationary tub sat against the wall in the front. It was clean, and the water pressure was normal. The oversized sink was set on treated lumber possibly constructed by the current owners. An old cabinet sat to the left, and the unstained wood from the sink extended to the right as a sort of countertop. A simple hot and cold faucet was fastened to the cement wall.

Cast iron rings about the size of a giant's fist were bolted to the cement walls in a few different spots around the spacious room. A rusted pulley hung from above in the center, and three or four metal shafts stuck out of the walls near the base of the ceiling like daggers. The bars and rings were all painted over, but not the pulley. I couldn't make sense of what I was seeing.

Six industrial double fluorescent light fixtures hung above in perfect fashion. Three were in the front, and three in back. They were externally wired with plastic tubing in a way I had never seen before. Light grey tubes, some bendable and others straight, stiff and made of hard plastic ran all over connecting the lights. Sloppy white paint covered the walls except for a grey cobblestone wall dividing one half of the space. There were several drafting desks, and other items neatly placed around. In the back corner behind a temporary wall was a toilet, bidet and sink built onto a raised plywood platform. It was nothing impressive to look at, but I was grateful to see plumbing and a working toilet. This makes things *so much easier* if you ever wish to renovate, which I did once this place was purchased.

Another door inside this apartment, probably original, opened to a spooky stairwell that led up to the street. It was considerably big, very old, rotten, and did not shut properly. It didn't have a key, either; it was tied shut. Annabella untied the wire, and opened it.

"These stairs go up to street level next to where we originally entered. I'm not going to open that door to the street," Annabella informed me.

Standing behind her, I stepped up two stairs into an unattended stairwell. More spider webs, dust, and rubble. Asymmetrical stairs led up to street access. It was dark and smelled awfully musty.

7

Clearly, nobody wanted to be down here. There were several other locked doors, and a light switch that didn't work.

Unfamiliarity was hitting me all at once. There had already been a lot of adventure today, and it wasn't even lunchtime. In less than two years time, I'd invite a carpenter into this 'Cantina' to do an estimate to replace this hefty, decaying door. He'd ghost me, but not before telling me something incredible. As a child, he'd been down here before. His parents used to shop here he told me. This cantina used to be the local butcher shop.

Annabella never said a word about it.

## Barred and Crumbling

Leaves crunched beneath our shoes as we crossed the overgrown garden. It was unclear where I was being led. Up ahead was another patio *filled* with junk and trash. The vibe felt different. Would this trash be cleared out before I bought these places? I couldn't think that far ahead.

A very badly broken double hung glass door was the entrance into the third apartment. One side opened with a key. The other side was stuck and partially shattered. It was a real mess. Glass shards lay on the floor where we took our first steps in.

This second garden apartment, already the third I was viewing at this property, was nothing like the first two. The glass door entrance led into a vaulted vestibule with two terracotta steps up, and a second door at the other end entered the apartment. Inside were three rooms unevenly divided, two more debilitated doors, and four windows all covered with rusty bars. It was striking how different the third space looked and felt. One door opened to the outside going up some stairs to the main street. Another door, also ancient and wired shut, opened to the inside of the building where the rest of the tenants lived and shared the main entrance. Literally all the doors for the second and third apartments would need replacing.

This third space also had high ceilings, but wasn't domed or vaulted. The timber ceiling had seen better days. Gigantic logs sat crossways holding up the floor above, and had been cheaply painted over. The paint was peeling, in some places badly, and cobwebs hung in every crevice. Years later, I'd study the beams carefully. Three different types of beams were there, indicating repairs probably took place many times over the course of decades.

The apartment was chuck full of ceramic statues, artworks, shelves, tables, plastic coverings and materials for making art. It was unorganized and only used for storage. Four carbon copy fluorescent lighting fixtures hung from the ceiling, and another porcelain sink identical to the other cantina was in one of the rooms. The apartment had a small Italian fuse box, but I didn't know where the electric was coming from. Annabella either never mentioned, or didn't know a commercial electrical cord had been run the length of the building from the cantina to electrify the apartment. Water wasn't running, either. The sink was dry with stuff piled into the basin. Water pipes into the apartment came in from a corner of the ceiling, and were capped. The water line below the caps had been cut. Space 3 was in rough shape.

What if this place were mine? I tiptoed around the three rooms trying to figure out anything I could think of. It was too much to contemplate.

"€75,000 for all three," Annabella said, staring at her phone.

I looked over at her, but didn't respond. She had been on her phone for maybe 90% of the showing.

"No wait. €70,000. The total price for all three apartments is €70,000," she said, correcting herself.

"€70,000. Are you *sure*? All three units for €70,000?" I asked.

"Yes. That's correct. €70,000," Annabella clarified.

9

# Can I Make It A Residence?

All three apartments were classified as a 'C' property. In Italy, a 'C' property classification means 'commercial'. If I purchased and wished to move in permanently, this signified major implications to declare residency. I wouldn't be able to until the property was *reclassified*. Most people buying homes in Italy do not have this problem. Welcome to my world.

I was assured by the realtor in charge, *not* Annabella, that the main apartment could *easily* be reclassified if I wanted to purchase it, and then declare it as my primary residence. But let's back up a little.

If I wanted to become a resident in Italy, and live *here*, I'd need to hire a 'geometra' first. This person would then need to do an assessment of the property and *then* petition the town to get the classification changed. And this could only be completed by me *after* the purchase was finalized. It seemed somewhat insurmountable considering how quickly things move in Italy, which is exactly what I told the realtor in charge.

"It's not impossible. In fact, it could probably be completed in only a few months," he said.

Deliberation with the real estate agent in charge regarding the purchase *and* reclassification eventually convinced me it was an easy, but costly process.

"It'll most likely cost between six and eight thousand euros for reclassification," he informed me over WhatsApp video chat once I was back in Florida.

I had the money set aside. Three apartments for seventy thousand euro wasn't expensive, either. In comparison to American properties, it was *very* cheap. I had nothing to complain about. So, I chalked it up as the cost of doing business, and informed him I'd make an offer. He still needed to find a geometra (surveyor) that was up for the challenge.

"We need to find someone who gets things done," he said one morning on a video conference.

## Keep it in the Family

Months later when the sale was finalized, and the geometra's work was completed and paid for, I was provided a deed, an official updated Italian property document about seven pages long. I'd use this document often for Permesso di Soggiorno, Italian Public Health Insurance, and residency. At the top was my name, and next to the address was the letter 'A' for residential property. This document had the entire history of property ownership, too. Ironically, the original owner was a man named Lucchesi. By then, we had found out that my wife was pregnant. Thus, the property was going to be home to a new generation of Lucchesi. It seemed like it was meant to be.

Thus began our journey as Italian homeowners. Throughout updates and renovations, I would inadvertently learn that, in addition to the first and second apartments, the third property used to be the town bakery. Coincidence? I'm not sure. Either way, I had purchased the old town pharmacy, butcher shop, and bakery. The entire town's people had been inside my properties before.

# Chapter 3 - Visa Adventures: Can We Even Stay Here?

The Italian consulate in New York City is a four story brick building located in Manhattan on the corner of Park Avenue and 69th Street. The Italian and European Union flags hang proudly over the center facade on Park Avenue. Other than the flags and a small oval plaque over the door that says 'Consolato Generale d'Italia' in all capital letters, the building is indistinguishable from any of the others around it.

We woke up bright and early on the day of our visa appointments. Mine was scheduled at 11am for an Italian study visa. Stephanie's was *also* right at eleven in the morning for an Elective Residency Visa, or ERV. It was extremely difficult setting visa appointments, and unprecedented ours were at the same time. Prior to driving the six hours to the city for our appointments, every document was meticulously prepped according to the guideline on the Consulate's website. Our money orders to pay for the visa applications were ready, too. Everything was filed into a single full sized envelop and labeled.

We arrived to the Italian Consulate ten minutes after ten in the morning. Once the taxi dropped us off, I spotted a few people waiting for appointments on the sidewalk of 69th Street, so we joined them. This was the first indication we had a problem.

**Sprinting Across NYC**

Scotch taped to the black side door of the Italian Consulate building was a US Priority Mail envelope, and three paper signs with information below it. One of the signs gave updated information for study visa applicants. It was all haphazardly posted, and very worrisome. Before seeing this, I was confident my pregnant wife and I were ready. But now this?

'Every visa appointment must bring a standard size, pre-paid United States Priority Mail envelope. Any appointment without this will automatically be turned away' read the sign taped to one of the doors of the Italian consulate. The website never mentioned this, so of course we didn't have it. Good thing we arrived early.

"There's a post office less than three blocks away, on 72nd Street. I'll be right back," I told Steph, glancing at the map on my phone.

I sprinted. At the post office, there were only two people in line, one of which was there for the *exact same reason*. Why didn't the Italian Consulate add this requirement to the website? Seemed disorganized. At the window, I purchased two Priority Mail pre-paid envelopes with tracking.

Back outside the consulate, more applicants had gathered on the sidewalk. When it was our turn, we entered and handed our cell phones to the security guard. We walked into another room with some scattered plastic chairs. Several consulate employees were working behind a full size, thick plexiglass wall. I pulled a chair over for myself, and took a seat next to Stephanie. Then a lady called us up.

"Buongiorno," I said, politely trying not to act nervous.

"Buongiorno. Please, give me everything you have," the lady said in Italian.

I wasn't expecting Italian language. Good thing I had been practicing. If I hadn't made Italian friends to practice speaking on those language exchange apps, I would have been lost.

I handed both application files to her through the opening in the plexiglass. She unclipped mine first, and skimmed each document in the pile.

**Where is your Italian Language Diploma?**

"You are applying for the study visa?" she asked in Italian.

"That's correct," I responded.

"And you already paid for the classes?"

"Yes. The documents from the school are there," I explained.

She studied my paperwork more prudently, wrote something on a post it note, and stuck it to the school's receipt document.

"And, where is your Italian language diploma or certificate?" she asked, shuffling my documents.

This was going to be a problem. The Italian government had recently implemented a new requirement for Italian language study visas. As of one month prior, Consulates were now requesting that *all* study visa applicants show proof of an Italian language degree from university, or some sort of certification from an approved Italian language school in Italy. This information was not posted online by the New York Consulate, but had popped up in recent Google searches. I noticed people asking about this in online forums just weeks before our appointment. It just hadn't been added as a requirement to the Consulate's website. Not yet, anyway.

"I never studied Italian language in university," I said.

"But you must have a certification in Italian language to qualify for the study visa. Do you have it?" she wanted to know.

"I've been studying Italian for the past two years online, making Italian friends to practice speaking. I speak Italian, and hope to improve it once in Italy. That's why I paid for a full year in advance at this Italian language school in Lucca," I responded in Italian.

Suddenly, I felt sick to my stomach. Here I was communicating in a foreign language I had never formally studied *and* learned as an adult with the lady who had ultimate decision capability over my future. However, the news she was sharing with me was not encouraging.

"I understand. But, you *don't* have an Italian language certification?" she asked again, shaking her head.

"I do not have it, no. I want to study Italian language more. I even bought a house in Tuscany. And, we are moving to Italy so I can apply for my Italian citizenship," I responded.

"There is no correlation between owning a house in Italy, and living in Italy. You understand that, right?" she asked.

"I understand. But we hope to live in Italy, so I bought a house to live in permanently," I said.

Oddly, I was in awe of myself, communicating entirely in Italian at the Italian Consulate. Miraculously, the Italian language was coming out of nowhere! That surely had to account for something, right?

"But again, you do not have any diploma or certificate?" she asked one more time.

Why did she keep repeating herself?

"No. But, I didn't see this on the Consulate's list. It's not listed. It wasn't a requirement," I said in Italian.

I watched her take a deep breath, and nod slightly. She understood, and my answers made sense too. Did that mean I was okay? Clearly, my Italian language was decent. I felt proud, but still was very nervous. I tried not to fidget. Then she turned squarely towards my wife.

"And you….. *you* wish to move to Italy on a retirement visa?" she asked in English to Stephanie.

"Yes, that's right," Stephanie replied.

Stephanie was thirty-six years old. She was also pregnant but not quite showing. We weren't sure if that would help or hinder us, so we didn't mention it.

"And…. *why* are you two applying for different visas?" she asked, pointing at each of us.

She really wanted to know, and I didn't blame her. From the outside, it may have seemed odd, because I doubt applicants usually do it this way.

"As you probably know, making an appointment at this Consulate here in NY is very difficult. We live in Rochester, six hours away by car. It's far, very far away. We mainly did it this way so we could come for our Consulate appointments on the same day and at the same time," I said in English to add emphasis.

15

It was the truth. To move to Italy, each adult needs their *own* consulate appointment. Study visa and retirement visa appointments were listed in separate categories on the website. I had my own appointment for June that I cancelled because I couldn't get a second appointment for Stephanie. This time when I scheduled, each category had an eleven in the morning slot available *on the same day*, so I rapidly took them so we could go together.

"Okay. Just a moment," she said in English.

She got up from her seat, and returned moments later. She started to deliberately assemble our two applications, then paused and looked up.

"Are you *sure* you want to apply for these visas?" she asked slowly.

"Yes," I responded.

Maybe I should have said no. What else *could* I say?

"Okay. We will be in touch," she responded with a smile.

Her smile saved me. She seemed sincere. We both thanked her, walked out, and collected our phones outside the door from the guard. Would our applications be enough to approve our visas? I had hope, but it seemed like a long shot.

We left the consulate that day very, very nervous. We had staked our future on a lady in the NY City Italian Consulate that we barely knew. She held our fate in the palm of her hand.

## Do Not Email Me!

A month had passed, and nothing. I was anxious and jittery everyday. I had been checking the tracking numbers on the pre-paid envelopes with no sign of anything delivered. Stephanie was now seven months pregnant, and there had been no communication from the Consulate since our interviews on August 11.

For residency visa approval, Italian consulates require proof of a registered rental contract *or* proof that you own a home to live in once in Italy. Consulates *also* require that you pre-book flights and submit the itinerary as part of your visa application. We had done all that. We were flying with our two cats, and our flights were scheduled for the morning of September 26, exactly two weeks away. To say I was concerned was an understatement.

I woke up early to compose an email to the Consulate. In it, I politely explained that my wife was seven months pregnant, and that our flights to Italy were exactly two weeks away. I fired it off shortly after eight in the morning, closed my laptop, and laid back down in bed.

At twenty-five minutes after four in the afternoon on the same day, my phone rang while napping on the sofa in the basement. I looked, and the caller ID said New York, NY. Was the Italian Consulate calling? I fumbled my phone when I reached for it almost dropping the call.

"Hello?" I said.

"Hello. Is this Richard Lucchesi?" a lady with an accent in English asked.

"Hello! Yes, this is Richard," I answered upbeat.

"This the Marta calling from the Italian Consulate in NY. I received your email message today," she said.

I took a deep breathe. "Hi Marta. That's great, thank you for calling."

"Can I ask you some questions?" she asked.

"Yes. Sure, ask anything you want," I said.

"You wife, she is seven months pregnant?" Marta asked.

"Yes, that's correct. She's seven months pregnant," I said.

"Richard, that's not good! Will the airline even allow her to fly?" she inquired.

"Yes. She is permitted to fly up to thirty-four weeks on Neos Air. She will be thirty weeks along when we fly," I responded.

"But isn't it *dangerous* to fly pregnant?" she asked.

"I will take very good care of her," I said as assuredly as I could.

"Seven months pregnant is not good Richard. Flying pregnant is very risky," she said.

"I promise I will take extra special care of her. She will be fine."

"And the airline is okay she is pregnant?" she asked.

"We contacted the airline. It's no problem," I responded.

It was a very appropriate line of questioning. Some airlines do not permit pregnant women to fly past thirty weeks of pregnancy, or even twenty eight weeks.

"That makes me very nervous, Richard. And what about your passive income?" she asked.

"I submitted twelve months worth of bank statements with my application for my income," I said.

"I know, but what about *passive* income? Do you have it?" she asked.

I had a feeling she was going to ask about this, too.

"No, but *did you see* the balance in my bank account?" I was sure to say.

"I see it. But no passive income is very bad, Richard. What about investments? Do you have investments?" Marta inquired further.

"Yes, I have investments," I said.

"I don't know about this," Marta said.

She paused. I could hear papers shuffling. I sat up and leaned forward. I was nervous.

"And what about your Italian language. Do you have a diploma or certification?" she asked.

"No, I do not have that. I explained about this during the interview already. It wasn't listed as a requirement on the website," I said.

"Not good. Do you know this is a requirement for study visas?" she asked.

"When I applied I didn't know. It was a new requirement. If I knew, I would not have applied for a study visa," I said.

18

"And your wife, she will not work in Italy?" she asked.

"No. We are having a baby, and she will stay at home after the baby is born," I answered.

"I don't know about this, Richard," Marta repeated.

There was another pause.

"Alright Richard, I need to think about this," Marta stated.

"Please Marta. Stephanie and I have been planning to move to Italy for years. This is our dream, that's why I bought a house there. My great-grandfather.. he was born in Tuscany. I have collected all the documents, and am applying for my Italian citizenship once I arrive, too. We are serious, very serious. My wife and I hope to have a baby in Italy and stay long-term to raise our son," I pleaded as slowly and clearly as I could in English.

"Yes Richard, I understand," she said.

"Wonderful. Thank you for your consideration Marta," I said warmly.

"And Richard, do not email me!" Marta said, and hung up the telephone.

Why did she hang up like that? Had all this effort been for nothing? I slithered back down into the sofa cushions feeling like a failure.

Two days later, I pulled up the U.S. post office website, and typed in one of our tracking numbers. The next screen confirmed that one of our pre-paid envelopes had been mailed from the consulate! Two days later, on Friday September 16, ten days before our flights, our passports arrived with Italian visas stamped inside. Just in the nick of time. All of a sudden, there was a lot to do again, and not much time left to do it.

We were moving to Italy.

# Chapter 4 - Applying for Residency: A Comedy of Errors

Moving to Italy? How exciting! With a residency visa stamped in your passport from your home country's Italian consulate, new residents to Italy have eight business days from the day you arrive to register your residency, called Permesso di Soggiorno. Once your Permesso di Soggiorno is granted by the local questura (police station) where you live, you have officially succeeded. Welcome to la dolce vita!

The first step is successfully submitting your Permesso di Soggiorno application, called a KIT, at your local post office. The KIT *is* the Permesso di Soggiorno residency application. It comes in a large white envelope with a bright yellow stripe along one of the edges. There are several thick packets of bubble sheets inside that each person applying for residency must fill out correctly. Even one minor mistake may cause you to have to rewrite the entire application. They are super strict with forms here. Are you excited for la dolce vita yet?

Every person moving to Italy needs to do this without exception, except maybe diplomats, but don't quote me on that. Most importantly to note: the meter is running to get this done from the moment you touch down at the airport.

But good news: Entire blogs and YouTube videos have been created and dedicated solely to filling out the forms. Because the KIT is altered slightly every year or so, even the most up-to-date websites with examples don't necessarily match the new forms.

In our area, there are three post offices. The closest to us is in Ponte a Serraglio, and we go there all the time. It is only open in the mornings on Wednesdays, Thursdays, and Saturdays, but at least they are open *sometimes*. The other nearby post office branches in Bagni di Lucca and Fornoli are larger, and open weekdays from half past eight until about half past one. Keep in mind, posted hours are somewhat subjective. I once walked down to our post office at eleven-thirty on a morning they were open only to find a hand-written note taped to the door saying they'd be back in thirty minutes. No starting time was included.

**Welcome to La Dolce Vita (aka Italian Bureaucracy)**

We arrived to Malpensa, Milan's airport, early on a Tuesday morning after 30 hours of travel. We didn't reach our new home in Tuscany that same day until after dark. Stephanie and I were so utterly exhausted we *both* slept that night for a full eighteen hours straight! Time stamps from photos the following day at Bar Italia show us experiencing our very first cappuccino and croissants precisely at 4:20 in the afternoon. Post offices had long been closed that day. Then it rained heavily on Thursday. Not having a car, we didn't leave the house. So Friday it was! Stephanie and I ventured out into our new neighborhood with all the dreams and aspirations in the world. But we couldn't dream *too* much. The dreaming could begin once we secured two Permesso di Soggiorno KITs, but that alone would prove to be an adventure.

On Friday morning, we walked all the way to Fornoli seven months pregnant. Locals *never* make this walk if they have a car. There is no sidewalk between Ponte a Serraglio and Fornoli; it's a perilous tree-lined road, and European drivers whiz by like they're driving Formula 1. In retrospect, I cannot believe I encouraged my pregnant wife to make that walk.

In Fornoli, *nobody* was in line at the post office. I think that's the only time that's ever happened. I entered but didn't see any workers. Minutes later, someone came out, so I asked for two Permesso di Soggiorno KITs, in Italian of course. I was *so* happy to be practicing Italian. She cocked her head, retreated back into the room and emerged moments later with a large envelope.

"We only have one. You'll need to go to Bagni di Lucca for another one," she said.

La dolce vita was closer than ever! Truthfully, I remember feeling frustrated. Was I already experiencing Italian bureaucracy after one day in Italy?

Spare me.

Remember: eight business days folks, the clock was ticking. My pregnant wife and I only had *eight business days* to complete everything, and submit the KIT for residency. I had five days left to hunt down another KIT, fill both out and submit all of the paperwork.

We walked over to the main road through Fornoli, entered a local bar, ordered cappuccinos and croissants, and took a deep breath.

"How are you feeling?" I finally asked Stephanie.

"Winded. I've been better," she said.

I'd been better too.

While sipping coffee, we checked our phones. It was nearly four kilometers from Fornoli to Bagni di Lucca straight through Ponte a Serraglio. We'd have to take a bus to get there before the post office closed, and I *needed* to get there today. The way to la dolce vita was through the post office. There was no other way to get there.

I peeked inside the KIT. There were *at least* twelve to fourteen pages of bubble sheets. There were other forms in there too. But good news: it was still only eleven in the morning, and the next bus towards Bagni di Lucca arrived in forty-five minutes. We finished our breakfast, paid, walked over to the bus stop, and waited for the E10 to arrive.

Little did I know that I'd encounter even *more* friction in the Bagni di Lucca post office.

## May I Have Another Italian Bureaucracy Please?

We caught the bus in Fornoli, and got off a few stops later in Ponte a Serraglio where we lived. I walked Stephanie home, dropped off the one KIT, grabbed my backpack, and walked back out the door. On foot, I arrived to the center of Bagni di Lucca about twelve minutes later, making a beeline straight to the post office on the far side of town. The post office was in Piazza Adamo Lucchesi.

There were three people in line, which gave me a short stint to case the joint. Two clerks were helping customers behind a full sized, thick plexiglass window. One, a young man with a brown beard, and the other was an older woman. Everything in Italy was so new, so I watched without trying to stare. After two and a half seconds, I discerned I'd much rather be assisted by the young guy. When it was my turn, that's who helped me out.

"Buongiorno. Two Permesso di Soggiorno KITs please," I asked in Italian.

I ordered an extra KIT in case of mistakes. Surely that was the right choice.

He turned his head back towards the shelves behind him without even moving his chair. I watched him squint his eyes, then get up, walk over to a shelf with a few boxes, and shuffle some items around. I don't know why, but the way he was digging made me nervous. I'd soon learn that much of the way Italians do things can make you nervous if you watch too closely. Best approach to this country is with horse blinders. Trust me.

He returned with a KIT.

"This is the only KIT for Permesso di Soggiorno we have in the building. If you need another KIT, you may want to go to Fornoli's post office," he informed me.

"The post office in Fornoli?" I asked, pointing out the door.

"Yes, Fornoli. Do you know where it is?" he asked.

## It's All Wrong

Two days later, on Sunday, Stephanie and I cleared our evening schedule. We had one goal: attain la dolce vita through Permesso di Soggiorno. We laid out the forms on our new marble kitchen

23

table left by the former owners, and got started. After several meticulous hours, we had filled in every possible section we could, about ninety-five percent of everything. There were a few tiny sections we were not sure about, so we left those blank, confident the employee at the post office would be kind enough to help us with the final bits. Besides, bloggers online all had 'wonderful' post office employees who were so 'supportive' and even 'eager' to help. Literally, that's *all I read*. No bad experiences at all! La dolce vita here we come!

Wrong.

On Monday, we arrived to a busy post office in Bagni di Lucca. This time, it was solely staffed by the older lady from Friday. She was sitting in her same seat on the far left side. We waited patiently in line for about thirty minutes, and when it was our turn, she turned my very pregnant wife and I away in literally the blink of an eye. She didn't even pull all forms out of the KIT's envelope before rejecting us. It was baffling.

"No. Nope," it sounded like she said in Italian.

"What's the problem?" I asked.

"It's not filled out here. You're missing information there. It's not correct, you have to fix it," she stated loudly for everyone to hear.

She handed back everything in a huff. It *seemed* like she told us to take a seat, indicating with her left hand to go sit over there and wait for the line to finish. So we did, we sat down. I pulled out the forms, and looked everything over carefully once again. We *still* didn't know what to do. After more than an hour, everyone had been helped. It was our turn again, but that's when things went from bad to worse.

"No. It's all wrong. You have to go to the INAC to get it fixed," she said, rolling her eyes.

Wait a second… was I the one being a dick? Actually no. I wasn't being a dick, not at all, but she was treating me like one, and it did *not* feel good. We didn't deserve it, either. Thank God it

24

clicked in my brain that I didn't understand what 'INAC' meant, *and* that had the gumption to ask.

"INAC? What is INAC? This is Permesso di Soggiorno. It must be done at the post office. I don't understand," I finally said in Italian.

Let's be real. I speak Italian okay, but I don't understand *everything*. My eighth day in Italy, and the post office lady was barking at me like *this*?

"INAC. The INAC office. It's in Bagni di Lucca over here," she said, pointing back towards town.

"It's where? What is it? I don't understand what you're saying," I said.

Fire was permeating out of her nostrils. She was toxic.

I'd later find out the INAC was the local union office. They handle all sort of civil matters, including applications like Permesso di Soggiorno because they are often difficult and cumbersome for newcomers like my wife and I. If you need help with a government application, you set at appointment at the INAC, and they assist you free of charge. At the post office, I didn't know any of that! Can you imagine if neither my wife nor I spoke well enough in Italian? And how come I didn't read anything about the INAC online?

She was hostile, a true dick in every sense of the word if I ever saw one. But I'd never seen *anything* like this at a post office. Never in my life!

**No Avoiding the Post Office**

Two days later, every form, document and bubble sheet for our Permesso di Soggiorno KITs was triumphantly completed thanks an extremely supportive, insightful visit to the local INAC in Bagni di Lucca. Their staff were amazing, and the man in charge was wonderful. I cannot recommend them enough. We were in his office for nearly an hour, and at the end of our appointment, there was nothing to pay for.

Unfortunately, we were *not* out of the la dolce vita woods.

"I'm starting to dread post office interactions," Stephanie said, as we exited the INAC.

"You've been inside an Italian post office once. There's *no way* that happens again. Besides, the INAC guy set us up good. Our applications are straight now. We're not going to have any more problems," I assured her.

I could *not* have been more wrong! Upon seeing us walk in the doorway, the *same* lady tried to pull the *exact same stunt* a third time. Before I even pulled the KITs out of my backpack, she stopped me in my tracks, claiming we needed to 'come back tomorrow' because the post office was closing in fifteen minutes. My wife and I were the only customers standing inside *the open post office* when she said that, and my wife was about to pop! Couldn't she see my wife was pregnant?

The deadline to submit our Permesso di Soggiorno application was the next day. As a post office employee, how could she *not* know about the deadline? My chest felt so heavy I could barely breathe. Was this lady *the devil* of Bagni di Lucca?

I had had it. I couldn't hold back. I was so angry and frustrated at her lack of compassion for my obviously very pregnant wife that I started screaming in English. I sat down in the waiting room, questioning everything out loud in English. Tears began streaming down my face. We were inside the post office with a deadline to submit *and* pay for an Italian residency application *required by law,* and there were no other customers. I just *could not understand* what was happening. Every emotion from moving and transitioning to a new country hit me all at once. And then, a miracle happened.

She waved us over.

Was she doing us a favor? No. She was doing her job. All that for her to do what she was *supposed* to do all along. It was nonsense.

I stood up, walked over, and looked her in the eyes.

"Thank you very much," I said in Italian.

I'm not too proud to do the right thing. I am not a dick.

We stood by the plexiglass barrier while she ran some of our application documents through scanning machines, and punched information into a computer. When the dust settled, we paid the fees by credit card, and she handed us receipts for residency appointments at the Lucca Questura for December 27, two and a half months away. Outside, I hugged my wife tightly in the post office parking lot.

"It's over. La dolce vita here we come," I joked.

Through trial and error, maybe the greatest lesson I've learned in Italy is when speaking the local language, for some reason, *some* Italians might take advantage of you. Moreover, when these same people hear English in a certain tone, they change their tune so fast, and fall in line. It's *so* strange. By now, it's happened too many times for me not to notice. One would think that by trying to speak in the local language, things might go better. But no, at least not for me anyways. Speaking English in stressful situations has worked wonders; on the contrary, speaking Italian has screwed me over, made me feel worse, and made things far more complicated. It might be different for others, but this has been *my* experience.

You have to wonder, why *did* she finally decide to do her job when I was speaking in English, but not before when I was trying my hardest to be polite in Italian? Because that day in the post office, that's what happened. It would need to happen like that many more times before I'd observe a similar pattern occurring between Italian and English. But all that is for another chapter.

Filing for residency was the *worst* post office experience of my life. I've never been back to the Bagni di Lucca post office since.

# Chapter 5 - The Garden: Trash, Rice and Birds

Our garden in Italy is not huge. It runs the length of our building, is about ten meters deep towards the river, and is two tiered with a small upper part on the far side in front of Space 3. A waist high rock wall runs the length of the garden facing the river. Ivy grows up, over and through it. If there wasn't a wall at the edge of the cliff, the garden wouldn't be nearly as enjoyable.

The other side of the wall is a ten meter drop off straight down to the Lima river that runs by our home. Down there, I call it the swamp. It's muddy in some spots almost like quick sand, and bugs linger like bad perfume. It's so humid where we live that some roads never dry up, even after weeks without rain. But our little emerald green river looks *so* beautiful from above; that is, until you take a closer look. Trash around the river's edge is often left to rot, and there's no enforcement for people who litter.

One huge monster of a tree in front of the Cantina used to tower over everything else until one of the neighbors rallied everyone to cut it down. And good thing we removed it. It was ill as suspected, with a huge metal stake running up the center core of the tree trunk. The arborist almost ruined his chain saw attempting to chop up the stump.

My wife loves gardens. In order to cope with the stress of everything, it seemed like the perfect place for her to get some fresh air. Even if shared, it's nice to have easily accessible outdoor space. The wall makes the garden complete. It's quite a serene little space, but la dolce vita it is not.

Upon our first in person glimpse as a couple, we arrived to a very, very overgrown garden that nobody seemed to manage nor care about. It was massively overgrown, full of dead leaves, and seemed to be used for all the wrong reasons. Someone left *an entire kitchen cabinet set*, along with full length bathroom mirrors and doors on the patio in front of the Cantina window. Piles of trash had been left to die in front of Space 3. Apparently, nobody had lifted a finger in the garden for years.

## Trash is Complicated

Garbage must get Italians' blood pumping, because it's everywhere. Weekly in our little town, workers replace heavy duty black plastic bags in trash cans all over, but it's not enough. The collective community trashes the streets anyway. In parts of the south, trash piles up in public places so high with no where to go, and no end in sight. Some of it resembles a third world country.

Regular trash is picked up every Saturday morning in front of our home. If we want them to take it, and we do, we must use a special colored bag for Saturday's pickup. If it's not sorted properly, the collectors do not take it. Rejection materializes in the form of a large sticker stuck to your bag or bin notifying you of your mistakes. Even with regular trash pickup for everyone, the public bins down the street between our home and Bar Italia are constantly overflowing. There's trash all over the sidewalks and street, and that's just in front of our house. Everywhere you walk in Italy you see it.

Additionally, recycling in Tuscany is a six-day-a-week effort. Sundays and Wednesdays are for food waste. Mondays are for glass, Tuesday is plastic, and Thursday is paper and cardboard. Each household has a different colored bin for each day, so households easily store five bins apiece. Bins get messy, sticky, and smelly quickly. We store our bins in the outside laundry room, but most others who live in buildings are not so fortunate. And just like on Saturdays, if recycling is not correctly sorted, it's rejected, *and* they reject often. Personally, I've had every day rejected at least once. Luckily, everyone has Saturdays off!

Is your head spinning yet? Remember: you need hard core recycling skills if you want any chance at la dolce vita.

Truthfully, the trash system in Tuscany is one of the most complicated parts about living here. You and most others sort every day, and yet trash is all over the streets. It doesn't make sense. Occasionally, I miss America dearly when I'm in our laundry room sorting trash and recyclables several times throughout the day.

In the garden, it took lots of maneuvering, tons of trips to the recycling center outside town with carloads of trash, and many months of effort to reverse years of neglect. The majority of trash wasn't mine, either. In the process, I'd determine the cumbersome steps to schedule a bulk pick-up. A second electric weed-wacker would replace the first one that busted, and a battery-powered reciprocating saw would be purchased too. After all, we were the only ones cleaning up the garden, and trimming anything. Eventually, we'd tame the dragon collecting and growing out there, but would the endeavor be worth it? Would we discover la dolce vita at the end of the garden tunnel?

## The Rice Conundrum

My pregnant wife and I had been living in Italy for less than a week when we saw our first neighbor. We were hanging out in the garden stepping on crunchy leaves, and casually removing overgrowth when we looked up and saw a woman with her daughter. They were watching us from a window above our main apartment. The woman was maybe in her early thirties with long, dark hair. Her daughter was about five years old. They seemed nice. We smiled and waved. The woman waved back, and then must have told her daughter to wave too. We'd stop cordially waving to each other soon enough.

The following morning something strange happened. At the bottom of the outside stairs into the garden was a big pile of uncooked white rice. It was scattered everywhere. Grains of rice were on the concrete stoop where we walk, in the grass, in a garden bed, and even stuck in leaves of nearby bushes. The rice must had fallen from a window. Had the same neighbor accidentally dropped rice out of the window?

I looked straight up. A small bag of food waste hung from a hook right below the woman's window. There's an apartment above hers, the top floor, but I had yet to witness any activity. The green shutters from the top apartment hadn't moved once. Whether inadvertently or otherwise, the rice must have come from the young woman's apartment directly above us. All activity above seemed to come from there.

I let it be. It could have easily been swept up, but it wasn't mine. Whoever did this would take care of it I figured. Seemed logical.

Apparently, this is *not* how la dolce vita works in Italy.

Two days go by, and nobody cleaned the rice. Being *very* new to the environment, I didn't want to assume anything. I also try extra hard to be kind to neighbors, especially in the beginning. But after two days, the rice was bothering me.

On day three, while outside in the garden, I noticed activity in the window above. I looked up, and the young woman was opening a window. I waved, smiled, and she waved back. This was our second encounter.

"Excuse me. This white rice, is this yours?" I tried to ask politely in Italian, pointing at the concrete.

She either *didn't* understand, or *pretended* not to. A moment goes by, and nothing.

"White rice. Right here. Is this yours?" I reiterated.

"No," I heard her say, wagging her finger at me.

Her eyes widened like golf balls. The intonation on the word 'no' went up like a slide whistle. I'd never heard anyone say no like that before in Italian, and haven't heard it since. I looked back down at the rice, and the window slammed.

Had I just caught the neighbor in a lie? I took a deep breath, walked over to the shed, grabbed the broom and dustpan, and swept up the rice.

31

I wonder if she watched.

## Patricia the Bird Lady

Another day, I spot an older lady in the garden from the terrace. She was standing at the rock wall facing the river. There was a small bag to her right, a plastic tray to her left, and you wouldn't believe what she was doing!

In the months leading up to the birth of our son, I was so eager to practice Italian language. I moved to Italy hoping to make new friends, speak Italian everyday, and quickly become fluent. I was ultra motivated. My Italian language classes were helping, but I hoped to chat with local people organically too. It wasn't difficult to strike up conversations with locals down at the bar per se. The much bigger challenge was establishing genuine connections.

I moseyed down the stairs and over to the neighbor to politely say hello in Italian. Patricia, as it turns out, is from Sardinia. To her left sat a pile of small, dead black feathered birds in the tray. She was holding one of the birds, plucking its feathers, and dropping them over the wall. On the right were several featherless birds in a plastic bag. I looked down, and black feathers collected amongst the ivy vines.

"My brother raises these black birds on his farm. He gives me the extras this time of year," I think is what she said.

She continued to pluck. I watched her technique. She held the bird in her left hand while plucking with her right. With each pull, a few feathers came out. It was a tedious process. It was like watching a child discover a new task for the first time. If she had done this before, it certainly didn't seem like it.

Patricia was elderly, and spoke with a heavy lisp. Between the lisp and her Sardinian accent, I couldn't understand everything she said. Still, I smiled and nodded like everything I was seeing and hearing was normal.

"These taste great when baked in the oven. Do you want some? I have too many. Go ahead. Take these ones here," Patricia urged.

Before I could say anything, Patricia pulled out a second tray from below the first one, and started piling birds onto it. Two.. three... four.....

"Here, take one more," she said, and set another bird on top of the four.

Jesus! What the fuck is going on *here*?

"No, no, no," I said, waving my hand to object while holding a smile together.

My body language might have insinuated to Patricia that I welcomed taking the birds. She either misread my interest, didn't notice, or didn't care. She might have prepared birds like this for dinner often, but I hadn't. However, it was already too late. Patricia insisted, handing the tray of dead birds over like she was gifting me something valuable.

"Wow! Grazie mille," I said, looking down at the tray.

Patricia briefly explained how to prepare them, but I could no longer understand her. My ears had shut down. I didn't know whether to smile or barf.

I carried the tray up the stairs. Stephanie was resting on the couch.

"I just met one of our neighbors in the garden, and you'll *never guess* what she just gave me," I said sarcastically, hiding the tray behind my back.

33

# Chapter 6 - How *Not* to Buy a Car in Italy

Our capacity for delusion, it can serve us well. Admittedly, it helped me *immensely* when buying an Italian vehicle.

Are International Driving Permits required to rent a car in Italy? If visiting Italy, is one required to drive here? Whether or not an IDP is required to rent a car boils down to *who* is checking your credentials. I once rented a car in Sardinia in 2021 with nothing more than my driver's license from America. At the car rental counter in Alghero's airport, I showed the employee my NY State driver's license, my passport, filled out a bit a paperwork, signed it, and minutes later, I was inside my shiny new black 5-speed rental car in the parking lot. I peeled out of there fast, and was soon cruising the Sardinian streets. *That* was a hint of the la dolce vita I was looking for!

Driving in Sardinia felt freeing. The roads are wide, a bit curvy, and the scenery is mountainous and rocky. Covering more than 300 kilometers in just over a twenty-four hour period, Sardinia's open roads in the hilly mountains and along the coast were sensational, and didn't resemble mainland Italy. I spent the night in Castelsardo on the roof of my guesthouse admiring the coastline and drinking beer. The next day, I drove all the way to Santa Maria Galleria and barely found a parking space, which I found strange for a Tuesday. I walked to the beach and sat down for a pizza overlooking the water where we could see all the way to Corsica.

None of these experiences would have been possible if the rental car agent followed what some people consider 'the rules'.

## Car Buying Preparations

Right after moving here, I did *not* look carefully online about car purchasing requirements. Whether or not I could legally buy a car in Italy *didn't even cross my mind*. Of course I could buy a car in Italy, I thought. Why *wouldn't* I be able to buy a car in Italy if I had the money? Was I delusional to search for a new car after less than a month living here? Maybe. Regardless, I started hunting for something reliable right away.

By the end of the first week of online shopping, I'd browsed just about *every car* under twelve thousand euros in *every city in Italy* within two hundred kilometers of my home. There were *so many more* things to know about in Italy that are not required in America that I kept learning about the more I looked. Chiefly, cars were mainly for sale at dealerships, with a smaller number being offered by private sellers. Simply put, it's much more difficult for a private seller, and a private buyer to transact a car in Italy. The more I looked, the more I could see the private sellers' inexperience. Most probably hadn't ever *sold* a car before. Whether the private sellers had something good or not, they were mostly overpricing their vehicles, and just trying to get rid of something they either no longer liked, or no longer could afford. The safe bet seemed to be buying from a dealer, something I'd never done in my forty-six years on earth.

When it comes to buying a good used car, what somebody might see as ambition I call delusion. I want the *very* best car for the *very* best deal imaginable at all costs, and will stop at nothing to achieve that. With used car purchases, I do not care about convenience, nor will I settle. In the end, I landed an incredible car for a much lower price than I expected. But how did I do it?

For context on how I pulled off an incredible car purchase in just over a month's time living in Italy, let's backtrack.

## Thank You Salvatore

My Italian grandfather was a very hard worker, but he was no saint. Throughout my childhood, he was mostly in a bad mood due to poor health in his senior years. Due to this, and also partly to my own stubbornness, I never got to know the man well. Then, on a random day in January, he dropped dead in a Boston Market while standing in line on his lunch break from work at seventy-nine when I was twenty-one years old. He was literally still working on the day he passed away.

He was a hobby mechanic like so many in his generation. Back in the fifties and sixties, he owned his own business and made enough money to purchase a brand new car every two years. That was the environment in which my father grew up. He was still doing this by the time I came around, housing two cars, one new and one used, in his garage at all times.

He and my grandmother shared the used car. It was their daily driver for short trips around town, and anything else. On the day he purchased a new car, he'd drive it home and change the tires *that same day*, setting the brand new ones aside in the garage. Meanwhile, he replaced the new tires with slightly worn, discarded used tires from any of the various mechanic shops he frequented, and drove around on those tires for two years. Many of the local mechanics knew my grandfather well, and let him take any used tires they no longer needed. Then, two years later when it was time to buy another new car, he'd put the brand new, unused tires back on, and drive on those to the dealership. Even into his seventies, grandpa was still mounting and replacing all his own tires on both cars in his garage. In his garage and out on the open highway was grandpa's version of la dolce vita in America.

"Best to keep the milcage as low as possible on the nice car for the trade-in value," he told me once.

Grandpa would travel for a good deal too, especially on a new car. He bestowed much of this knowledge onto my father, and indirectly onto me. My dad was a wonderful father, but during my teenage years, however unwittingly, my car buying instructor was Salvatore.

## Italian Car Requirements

Italy's car market is a different animal entirely. There are requirements that exist in Italy for new drivers that do not in most other countries, like South Korea. Principally, for the first three years, you are only allowed to drive a vehicle with an engine size that is 55 kW/t (kilowatts per ton) or less. A 55 kW/t motor is a little over 70 horsepower. Every time I've been stopped by officers, this has never come up. I don't think police care at all. But it's the law, so it makes the used car buying process challenging.

As a new *foreign* driver, you're permitted to drive on your home country's driver's license for up to a full year. After that, you're no longer legally able to operate a motor vehicle in Italy, and *must* take the Italian driver's test. No exceptions. And, for all the times I've ever been stopped and questioned by the Italian police, an International Driver's Permit has never come up or been mentioned.

For *all* drivers, every vehicle on the road has a Euro 1 to Euro 6 emission level rating, with Euro 1 being the lowest. These ratings were implemented in the 1990s with the goal of lowering emissions year by year. Drivers can still operate vehicles that have a Euro 1 rating, but theses days, are limited to when they can drive it, and where. Plenty of used cars for sale have a Euro 2, 3 or 4 rating, and these cars are priced lower. They seem like a very good deal until you understand the emissions rating system. Each year, emissions restrictions increase, and driving a Euro 2 car on the wrong street at the wrong time could be costly, causing you to receive tickets from a street camera, and fines. With stricter emissions ratings year over year, if you do not want *any* trouble, purchase a vehicle rated Euro 6. It may cost more money, but you won't have to worry about any road restrictions for awhile.

## The Hunt Was On!

While it is possible to purchase a used vehicle here for less than ten thousand euro, the mileage probably won't be low, and it most likely won't be a one owner. It's quite difficult to find something for under that price that's a one owner, has low mileage, hasn't been in an accident, and isn't all scratched up and dented.

I looked and looked and looked and looked. I knew I needed a car if I wanted to thrive in Italy, so I searched and searched. By the end of week one, I knew all the best websites that sold used cars in Italy. Each day, I called three or four dealers to ask about vehicles, in Italian of course. These dealerships were all over. I called dealers in Firenze, Pisa, La Spezia, Genoa and many places in between. I even looked in Rome and Milan to see what was available. It was daunting and exhausting.

I finally found a vehicle in La Spezia that seemed to fit the bill. It was a one owner 2013 Peugeot 207+ with 90,000 kilometers on it for under seven thousand euros. It had a 54 kW/t engine size, and was rated Euro 6, the highest rating that existed. This car had cruise control and air conditioning, which were must haves in my book. The plus sign in the 207 meant it ran on both unleaded fuel *and* natural gas (GPL in Italy, LPG in most other countries). The interior looked pristine, it had never been in an accident, and I didn't even see any chipped paint or scratches in the photos. This equivalent vehicle at the only dealership down the road from my house in Bagni di Lucca was listed for nearly eleven thousand euros! It wasn't a one owner, and had more kilometers too.

I wasn't exclusively looking for something that ran on natural gas, but I wasn't opposed to it either. I had owned a natural gas-only van in South Korea once before, and liked the idea of owning another. No other used car in Italy even came *close* to this price that fit all the requirements I was in search of. So, I called the guy, he answered, and I told him I was coming to see it. It was the first

38

car I looked at, and would end up being the one I purchased. You just won't believe the circumstances in which the deal got closed.

## An Unbelievable Transaction

In Italy, you do *not* receive the car registration for your new or used vehicle the day you drive it home. The dealership doesn't even provide you a temporary registration document. You literally leave the dealership without the car registration. Instead, it arrives in the mail to your house about a month after the purchase is finalized. I've always been baffled by this. What if you're stopped by police in that first month, and they ask for it? This, of course, happened to me.

The train ride to La Spezia from Bagni di Lucca is close to a three hour trip. The small used car dealership was located over a bridge on the other side of the city. On the day of the test drive, I downloaded a bike share app and rode a share bike to the car lot. Inside the dealership, it was uncomfortable from the start. I was met unceremoniously by one of the owner's employees, a young man on his phone that didn't even look up when I entered. After some minutes by myself, the owner appeared.

"I'll be right with you," he said in Italian.

This transaction, if completed, would be conducted entirely in Italian. The Italian language classes I'd been attending every morning since moving to Italy hadn't covered how to buy a car. Not yet, anyway, but I doubted they *ever* would. Even Salvatore, the king of car purchases, would have lost his mind.

Italy was exhausting me. It felt like half the time when I spoke Italian, people would roll their eyes. 'Here comes another foreigner trying to live la dolce vita' some of them probably thought. I'd been running around like a chicken with my head cut off with no end in sight! I'd already had three Permesso rejections at the post office, a few visits to the INAC, several more visits to the Agenzia delle Entrate building outside town for Italian public health insurance documents for my pregnant wife, plus doctor's appointments all over the place. And I had a son on the way!

I was taking four hour long Italian languages classes every morning in Lucca learning mostly about coffee culture in Italy with tourists who thought it would be fun to study Italian while on holiday for a week. Students in my classes changed at a dizzying pace, and it wasn't what I signed up for. I'm not sure *what* I signed up for, but it wasn't this. Every time I *needed* to speak Italian, I couldn't refer to anything I was learning in class. I'd only been in Italy a month, and la dolce vita was *kicking my ass.*

I couldn't complain though, it was all my own doing. Salvatore would have come to La Spezia for the best deal on a car, right?

When the owner was finally free, he approached and shook my hand.

"Richard Lucchesi?" he projected in Italian.

"Yes."

"Nice to meet you. And, you are here for the black Peugeot?" he asked.

"That's right," I said.

"Shall we go look at it?" he asked, already knowing the answer.

He went behind his desk, opened the top drawer, shifted some papers, and found the key. We walked outside, up a small hill, and he manually opened a gate securing absolutely nothing. We passed through, and were met with three cars. A light blue Smart Car was parked on one side of the car I was there to see, and the other side was wide open. Did he only have three cars for sale?

I did a once around, and the car looked immaculate for a nine year old vehicle. Someone had taken good care of it. I bent down on my hands and knees to look underneath. There was no rust, but cobwebs were connected from the asphalt to the bottom of the car. Had nobody driven this car lately?

He opened the car door, and started it. It fired right up. He stepped back. I leaned in, reached for the front hood latch, pulled the plastic lever, and saw the hood pop. I walked to the front, found the lever underneath, lifted the hood and propped it with the crooked small metal bar. Engine looked clean and sounded quiet. I let the car run for several minutes, waiting to see if any oil leaked underneath, but nothing. The asphalt below was dry as a bone.

The dealer ushered me into the car for a test drive, and we were off. His dealership was behind a set of front row buildings. We squeezed our way past some loading docks to the front, and turned left onto the main road which ran parallel to the harbor. He drove me through a pair of traffic circles, and into a dead end where he instructed me to perform a three point turn. He had a set route for test drives, indicating every which way to go.

Once I determined that the AC blew cold air, and the cruise control functioned normally, we returned to the office.

Back at the dealership, I couldn't negotiate in Italian language to save my life. Salvatore would have cringed. What little Italian I could use certainly wasn't persuasive. In the end, he reduced the price by one hundred euros from the original listing, and offered to have brand new tires put on the vehicle at my expense, adding an additional three hundred thirty euros to the total cost. The new tires and labor were worth it, so I told him to do it.

"Total cost for the car *before* tires, taxes and fees is €6360. Is this okay for you?" he asked.

Truth be told, it was an excellent deal. After a deep dive on the web for a week's time, I'd discovered it was *nearly impossible* to get a one owner Euro 6 emission certified vehicle with an under 55 kW/t engine and low mileage for under ten thousand euros. Plus, this car had cruise control and air conditioning. If I wanted the best deal on a good car, I'd found it. Salvatore may not have approved of my negotiation tactics, but who cares.

"First, what is the total cost with everything included? Also, please explain the documentation I need," I requested.

He rattled off the information as if he'd delivered it a thousand times before. My head spun like a top.

"I'm sorry. Did you say the registration is sent to my house?" I asked politely in Italian.

"Yes. I cannot give you the registration next time you come back. There is no temporary registration, either. You drive home without it, and it comes later in the mail. That's how it works in Italy," he explained.

"Okay. Also, I moved to Italy one month ago. This is my *receipt* for Permesso di Soggiorno," I said, pulling out my passport and Permesso receipt from my pocket.

He stuck out his hand, and I handed over the Permesso receipt. He studied the receipt for a moment but said nothing.

"I do not have my residency card yet. This is all I have," I continued, pointing at the receipt.

"No problem. Passport please," he said, standing up and reaching out his hand.

I handed over my passport. He walked over to the copy machine, made copies of everything, and returned quickly handing me back my passport and Permesso receipt. Was I *really* buying a car like this so quickly?

"Please fill out this application," he said, handing me over a simple one page document.

I looked it over with hazy eyes. There were just a few lines to fill out.

"Name here. Address here. You came from Lucca, right? Lucca?" he repeated, pointing directly at the address line.

I wrote out my name, filled in my correct street address, and wrote 'Lucca' in the city slot. Major mistake.

I lived in Bagni di Lucca, and this minor brain fart turned into a grave error. The new car registration, once finalized a month later, was sent to an address that didn't exist in Lucca. It took three months just for it to be returned to the dealer before he could change the address, adding about five months until the car registration finally arrived to my home. Meanwhile, I was stopped *twice* by police without it, but that's another story entirely.

42

"Okay, very good," the owner said once the short application document was completed.

He took the application and placed another document in front of me.

"This is the total amount for the car, the tires and the registration. This is the amount you must send by bank transfer, and this is the remainder you must pay in cash when you come back. Also, when you come back to pick up the car, you must bring valid insurance," he pointed out.

"I understand," I said.

**My Italian Failed Me**

I shopped for car insurance the following day after Italian language classes, ultimately deciding on the company with the very best rate for minimum coverage. However, something very strange happened to me when I paid for the car insurance online with my credit card. I watched the transaction process on my computer screen, and finalize once completed with a confirmation screen appearing in Italian. What I thought was a policy number at the top of the screen wasn't an insurance policy number at all. It was a reference number indicating my policy information request had been saved, but the transaction never went through.

Anyway, not realizing *any of this* at the time, I printed a copy of what I *thought* was the new car insurance policy with all the coverage to give to the dealer.

Long after the transaction was finalized, I'd learn another important thing. Non-Italians weren't allowed to legally purchase vehicles in Italy until they had an Italian identity card. And, you cannot get an identity card in Italy as a non-citizen until your Permesso di Soggiorno is finalized, *and* your Permesso card is issued. The *only* way to get a Carta d'Identità (identity card) in Italy as a non-citizen is the bring your Permesso card to the comune (town hall) where you reside. Comunes do not issue identity cards to non-citizens without them. I had purchased a car in Italy and drove it home *without* an Italian Identity Card, without *any car insurance*, and, my new car was registered to the wrong house address.

I'd gotten away with murder. Unfortunately, I wouldn't be so lucky once the police found out.

# Chapter 7 - How I Became A Dad

No matter *how many challenges and difficulties* I've had in Italy, I cannot express how grateful I was that our son was born here. All day long, my wife was in pain on the day our son was born. She started laboring at four in the morning, and gave birth about seventeen hours later. We messaged all day until half past three when she summoned me to the hospital as instructed by her doctor.

"Hey sweetheart," I answered on the phone.

"Hey. You can come to the hospital now," Stephanie said straight away.

"Okay. I'll leave shortly. How are you feeling?" I inquired.

"I'm in pain, a lot of pain. I just got back from speaking with the doctor. My water broke. I'm officially in labor. It really hurts," Stephanie said.

"Holy shit, your water broke!" I exclaimed.

"I'm only 2cm dilated. It needs to be closer to 10," Stephanie explained.

"Got it. 10cm and then I'm a daddy," I joked. "Alright, I'm on my way!"

**A Gorgeous Day to be Born**

The drive into Lucca at dusk was *one* of the most sensational of my life. The sunset over the Ponte del Diavolo (Devil's Bridge) as I approached Borgo a Mozzano took my breath away. I thought fondly about my wife and future son as I admired the opulent reds, oranges and yellows peering out over the mountains in the distance. I wasn't ready to be a father, but is anyone ever? I knew in my heart it would turn out to be a glorious day, one my wife and I would never forget.

The sunset was still visible when I arrived at the hospital. I parked in the same lot I'd been parking in for weeks, snapped a few photos of the sky, and quickly walked towards the building. I slipped on my mask outside the front door. The staff were at the Covid desk, and I had my American vaccine card ready. But by then, every employee knew I wasn't in the system, and just let me pass.

Stephanie's situation at the hospital was unusual on a number of levels. It wasn't that she was the *only American* giving birth in San Luca Hospital's maternity ward. She had also just spent nine days there the previous week! The morning of the tenth day, she was discharged. It was American Thanksgiving. By then, *all* the staff nurses and doctors in the maternity ward were aware of who she was and her situation. She'd been admitted with a headache, which we discovered was due to gestational diabetes. What were considered normal levels in the United States were dangerously high here. Doctors put her on a strict diet and insulin regimen. In retrospect, she and I agree it was one of the *greatest* things to happen during her pregnancy for the health of our future son. But while it was happening, it was, without a doubt, very hard on Stephanie.

Yesterday, when she checked into the hospital to be induced, she was admitted and placed in the *same room* she had been staying in during the previous nine nights. The entire hallway and section of the hospital was already a strangely familiar place. Once in the maternity ward, I entered Stephanie's room but she wasn't there. I was a bit frantic, so I popped back into the hallway where I encountered one of the many nurses I'd seen working before.

"Calm down. Don't worry. She's fine and hasn't given birth yet," she said, holding back a bit of laughter.

She wasn't simply trying to calm me down. It was *in her Italian nature* to take it slow. Unless it was an emergency, she wasn't in a rush. I had already spent enough time in San Luca Hospital during lunch and dinner visitations to understand that, the more I looked around, the more unfamiliar it looked. That's saying something because my mother was a nurse, and I practically *grew up* in hospitals.

The nurse casually escorted me down the hallway, and into another section of the hospital I'd never visited.

"She's in there," she said, pointing to an ajar door from the hallway.

**Hey Sweetheart**

I walked through a small room into a much larger one where Stephanie lay on a hospital bed all by herself. It looked so lonely in there! I really felt for her.

"Hey sweetheart," I said, greeting Steph.

"Hey," she replied.

"How are you?" I asked, caressing her shoulder and arms.

"I've been better. It hurts. I'm in pain but I'll survive. They have me in here all by myself. I guess I should be grateful for the privacy," she tried to joke.

I reached over, held her hand and squeezed.

"It's going to be okay. I'm here now and I'm not going anywhere. I'll be right here by your side," I reassured her as best I could.

Neither of us knew what would happen, but soon the room would be buzzing. I had arrived at the hospital ten minutes before five o'clock. By six, Stephanie's midwife was there on deck.

"Four centimeters," she said in Italian.

"It hurts," Stephanie moaned.

"You're a rock star," I said, encouraging her.

She shimmied in her bed, uncomfortable in her own skin. I could see it in her face, and it was startling to witness. My wife was the strongest emotional being I knew, often hiding her discomfort no matter the circumstance. I had seen her walk on a broken foot, and pass a 9mm kidney stone over our many years together. However, this was maybe the *only* moment in her life that she couldn't hide from. She was facing down her demons, and I was so proud of her for it. I wanted so badly to take the pain away,

47

but there was so little I could do besides hold her hand and reassure her. I stood by her bed, and held her left hand tightly with mine. Inside, I wept. I felt awful she had to go through this. I wasn't pulling my weight, and I'd never know what it was like. I'd always been grateful I was born a man, but right then I felt the guilt.

"You can see the baby's head. He has hair," the midwife said in Italian, and pointing.

I looked and could see the head, but it was difficult to make it out the hair. I was skittish to even look. Once I did, I wouldn't have known what I was seeing unless she spoke up.

Right at eight o'clock, the Italian midwives changed shifts. Despair hit me when I realized this. The new girl was younger and clearly less experienced.

Shortly after eight, the rhythm of my wife's breathing fell into a pattern that matched what her body was going through.

"Keep breathing, but don't push. Not yet," the new midwife said.

The breathing was getting heavier. I hadn't let go of Stephanie's hand in an hour. By eight twenty-five, it was time to push hard.

**Like A Rocket**

"Eight centimeters. Okay, on the next interval, give me a big push," the new midwife said.

"One.. two… three," I cried out.

Stephanie pushed hard. When the pushing subsided, I turned around. At least eight hospital staff, all women, were now standing behind me. They were arranged like bowling pins, stoically staring at the scene unfolding. It was mind-bending that I didn't notice any of them enter.

"10 centimeters. Five more big pushes, and the baby is delivered," she instructed.

"Okay. One.. two… three," I said again.

48

"The baby is coming. Give me another big push," the midwife said, while touching the heart monitor.

"One... two..... three!"

Stephanie pushed even harder, and my son shot out like a rocket into the world, landing nearly a meter away from her body! I watched with all the awe and wonder of every man that's ever become a father.

But there was a problem, a big one. Our son was blue and wasn't breathing. A whirlwind of action hit the room. One nurse cut the umbilical cord as fast as she could, and my son was whisked away instantly. Three nurses carried him behind me to a small table with warm red lights directly above. I turned to see, but did not realize the problem. I was clueless.

"Is he breathing?" Stephanie screamed, her voice cracking and weak from childbirth.

That was the first instance I ascertained something was wrong. At the same time, a woman in a black surgical gown, possibly the oldest in the room, slid up in front of Stephanie on a round hospital chair with wheels. Alongside her were two more women in blue gowns. The first lady immediately began to sew, working her hands as fast as she could.

I did not realize what was happening with Stephanie *or my baby*. I had been fine up until that point. But now, other than standing there and continuing to hold Stephanie's hand, I was utterly useless. A thin blanket was hanging over Stephanie's knees, so I couldn't see either.

"Scusa Stephanie," the lady doing the stitching blurted out. Then her hands moved forward towards my wife's body, and inserted a needle to form a stitch.

I didn't know *what* was happening. I turned around, eyes wide as billiard balls. The three nurses were desperately administering CPR and pumping my son's chest. One of them appeared to stick something down his throat. I really began to panic. What the fuck was happening?!? Was he going to make it?

"Scusa Stephanie," she projected, again inserting another stitch.

I turned back towards my wife, my eyes even wider. My stomach tightened as I tried to comprehend the gravity of the situation.

I turned back around, watching with horror as the three women attended to my one minute old son. But then, he let out a screech! He was breathing! I watched him take a breath, and start to cry. Our son was alive! He was okay! He started breathing normally, and I started breathing easier too. It was an absolute miracle.

"He's breathing. He's okay, he's okay, he's okay," I said to Stephanie, who was still somewhat delirious.

She was laying back and couldn't see what I could.

"Scusa Stephanie," I heard the lady say again.

Meanwhile, the three nurses cleaned up our little man in unison, wrapped him in a white blanket, and brought him over to the new mama, placing him gently in her arms.

It was the most beautiful moment of my life. I pulled out my camera, and took a photo of my new son, the first ever.

"What time? What time was he born?" Stephanie asked in English.

I looked up at the round public school-like clock on the wall. It was not even quarter to nine yet.

"Eight-thirty. Eight-thirty in the evening," the lady in the black gown stated without missing a beat.

Charlie Lucchesi was born in San Luca hospital in Lucca, Italy in the end of November, 2022 at 8:30.

**That's My Boy**

The greatest moment of my life happened in a hospital in Italy. I could have never predicted that when I was younger.

Once our son was born, he never left our sight. There was a point where staff needed to administer some medicine. A nurse picked him up from his new mother and brought him over to the counter in the room. As she carried out her task, he started crying badly. He was still wailing when she brought him back, and handed him to me. But then something incredible happened. The moment he was in my arms, he stopped screaming instantly. It was the first time I'd ever held my son. I'll never forget it.

"Hi Charlie. Daddy's here, how are you little guy? It's so nice to finally meet you! We've been waiting for you to come. I'm so happy you're here now," I whispered softly.

He looked right at me, his eyes dazzled by the light in the room. He was calm now, no longer crying. I couldn't believe it! Such a transition from a moment earlier. Did he realize who I was?

"You're okay now. You're with us. You're safe with us. I'll always be here for you, I promise," I continued.

I held him for a bit while Steph rested. Then, very cautiously, I handed him back to Steph. A nurse was there assisting Stephanie with breastfeeding, but the hospital gave us space. It was such a wonderful moment that we had for ourselves.

Around midnight, we were instructed to move back to Stephanie's designated hospital room. A nurse picked up little Charlie out of Stephanie's arms, and placed him in a small hospital baby bed with wheels.

"You will push him to the room, and I will push your wife" she instructed.

The boy was half awake when we started moving. I delicately guided us out into the dark hallway, waiting for the nurse to come out with Stephanie and go first. We exited the hospital wing, and proceeded towards the maternity section.

As we moved, I glanced down at my boy. He was already taking in his environment. I pushed a bit more quickly, and then *bang*! The wheels on his bed cart hit a fixture protruding from the floor. Had I screwed up badly already? I looked down at Charlie apologetically, but he was fine. He almost smiled.

"That's my boy, that's my boy!" I whispered enthusiastically.

51

# Chapter 8 - The Birth Certificate Saga, Part I

I wish I could forget my first visit to the Comune in Bagni di Lucca.

We all make mistakes. Mine wasn't terrible, but regrettable. Walking out, I was terrified I'd foiled my future plans. Would my actions that afternoon in any way affect my chances with Italian citizenship recognition?

My first son had just been born in Lucca days earlier, and Italian bureaucracy had already taken its toll. Our baby was doing great, but we hadn't yet successfully created his birth certificate in the hospital like *all the other parents*. I was told we'd easily be able to do it, and I had all the documentation ready. But when it was my turn, the man checked, and my name wasn't in the system. I'd been living in Italy over two months already, and he couldn't find me in his computer? That was a scary moment.

Regarding my son's birth certificate, Italy offers new parents two options. I had either three days after he was born to create it at the hospital, or ten days to do it at the Comume where we established residency. Since the first attempt failed at the hospital, this meant I had to go with option two: Creating my son's birth certificate in the Bagni di Lucca Comune. This was the *only other option*.

In theory, the process seemed simple enough. Just go to the comune and do it, the perfect la dolce vita scenario. But I'd already burned three days at the hospital with the futile attempt, and then there was the weekend. Monday on day five, we transferred our son home. Day six we had a doctor's appointment outside town. Day eight was a national holiday, the Feast of the Immaculate Conception, and day ten was a Saturday. I was stressed, nervous, and wasn't familiar with the Italian system at all. The pressure felt like a two-ton barbell chained to my neck.

Stephanie's important doctor's appointment in Lucca, a childbirth check-up at Campo di Marte hospital, was on the morning of the sixth day after Charlie was born, a Tuesday. I had four days left to create his birth certificate in Italy, but who's counting? For doctor's appointments, I acted as my wife's Italian language translator, which is *not* a good idea. This was draining, as I'm certainly no expert in Italian medical terminology. We drove our car into Lucca, found parking on the street, and made our way inside.

## You're Not in the System

Bagni di Lucca's Comune opens every weekday at half past eight in the morning, and closes for lunch at one. On Tuesdays and Thursdays, it also has afternoon hours starting at three-thirty. After the doctor's appointment, we pushed little man in the stroller to Lucca Centro to have lunch. We decided on sandwiches to go at Pan di Strada, choosing to sit on a bench in front of the fountain near the Porta San Pietro and eat under the warm November sunshine.

We arrived back in Bagni di Lucca in the afternoon, parking in front of the Circolo dei Forestieri restaurant when it was still a parking lot. We slung baby Charlie along in his brand new carrier all bundled up, walking the one hundred meters or so into the heart of the village where the Comune is located.

The Comune's administrative office is on the ground floor through a narrow door in the far left corner of the lobby. Inside the office, the front desk is high with plexiglass sitting on top. It's a typical administrative room that the town keeps warm in the winter. The room behind the main office was a second private office where the lady worked who would ultimately decide the fate of my Italian citizenship. I had no idea of this at the time.

Sofia, the administrator at the front desk, is a *very* kind woman with long, dark hair in her late forties that speaks fluent English. Over the months and years as a resident, this woman has single handedly assisted with every administrative task I've ever needed to accomplish. She's available in person, by phone or email, and her office is efficient in a way not so familiar in Italy. Frankly, she's overqualified. She and I both know it, and that woman deserves a raise.

But that day I knew none of this. I entered carrying little baby Charlie in my left hand. Stephanie was behind me, and stepped to my left once we were both inside. After that, she took control of the carrier. Before I could say anything, Sofia peeked over the desk at our son, and smiled. I was enamored at her reaction. Sofia's smile could launch a thousand ships.

"Good evening. We live in Bagni di Lucca, and we are here to create our son's birth certificate," I said as politely as I could in Italian.

"Okay, let's take a look. Do you have your ID cards?" She asked, taking a seat in front of her computer.

We did not. Non-residents are not permitted to create them until residency has been granted, and we hadn't even had our residency appointments yet. I handed over our US passports, and the residency receipts we received when we submitted our Permesso di Soggiorno KITs at the post office. On the receipts were confirmation numbers Sofia could use to pull up our information. But because the Lucca Questura, the police department in charge of granting residency applications, had not yet processed ours, Sofia couldn't find us in the computer either.

"I don't see your name in the system. I'm terribly sorry," she said.

Strike two.

I didn't react, but inside I was a wreck. Meanwhile, Stephanie kept checking on our kiddo.

Sofia stood up and walked to the doorway to the private office in the back. I heard the two ladies converse in Italian, and moments later the second lady emerged from the office. She came over to the side where Stephanie was standing with Charlie, and congratulated us all. Then, she explained that, if we wanted to create the birth certificate for our son, we'd have to go *back* to Lucca, and visit the Comune there to do it. That was our *only* option.

Why wasn't this explained at the hospital? Had nobody else ever been in this situation before?

"Could you possibly *call* the Lucca Comune to double check this is the correct process please?" I asked the woman.

I tried to be as polite as possible, but I seriously doubted my request came out the way I intended it. Nevertheless, the woman retreated into her back office. Seconds later, I watched her pick up the phone, dial, wait, hang up, and try again several more times. During the third of fourth attempt, without looking up, I could hear her say in Italian that nobody in the Lucca Comune was answering the phone.

It was an awful moment. I felt frantic. I wasn't just out of my element; I had been catapulted into another universe. Italy's bureaucracy is infamous, and right now, it was slapping me so hard my face was numb. Was *this* la dolce vita?

Little did I know that my trip to Lucca the following day would have consequences, and wreak havoc on my little family.

# Chapter 9 - The Birth Certificate Saga, Part II

The following morning, I woke up at 7am, and was irritable. I did not sleep well, and my head hurt badly. Our son had been home two days, and was restless most of the night. It was typical newborn behavior as any parent knows, but that didn't mean I had to like it. Terrible head pain had plagued me the last two years from symptoms related to a severely degenerated C4-C5 disc in my neck. It occurred from an old football injury when I was about twelve years old.

I had *no choice* but to persevere. My seven day old son *needed* me to create his birth certificate, and the deadline was fast approaching. It was Wednesday, so I only had today or Friday to do it. Per the visit to the Bagni di Lucca Comune yesterday, it needed to be done at the Comune in Lucca. Today would be another action-packed day full of adventure and new experiences. I didn't know as I prepared to leave the house that I'd be bring back more than just official copies of Charlie's new birth certificate. I'd be carrying with me something much more sinister.

I rode my new pedal-assist electric bike to the train station, locked it to a nearby telephone pole, and boarded a train heading south to Lucca minutes later. I realized as soon as I sat down that I forgot to bring a mask. This would prove to be my mortal sin of the day, but there was nothing I could do about it now.

Once in Lucca, I walked directly to the comune. As I entered, an intimidating female security guard was standing in the lobby. This was already nothing like the Comune in Bagni di Lucca. I told her why I was there. She glanced at her clipboard, and then led me to a room on the same floor. She knocked, and a woman came to the door. The woman smiled, and extended her hand to indicate I could enter the room. I overheard her tell the security guard that they were expecting me. The boss in the Bagni di Lucca Comune must have called this morning before my arrival.

The lady instructed me to sit. She was well aware why I was there, and told me she used to work in the Comune in Bagni di Lucca six years ago. She handed me an application to fill out. Once completed, I handed it back to her. She read it over carefully, then looked up at me.

"Are you *sure* you want to name your child by this name?" she asked slowly in Italian.

"Yes, I'm sure," I replied.

"But it's strange," she said, looking at me.

The lady took another look at the application, took a deep breath, had me sign it, made a copy, and stood up. She told me she'd be back in a moment, and then left the room.

"Do you live in Italy?" I heard a voice ask in English.

I turned, and a younger gentleman was there. I saw him when I entered, but due to the nature of the appointment, I wasn't paying close attention to my environment.

"Yes. My wife and I just had a son. That's why I'm here today," I said slowly in English.

"Congratulations. Your surname is 'Lucchesi'?" he asked.

"Yes, it is," I responded and nodded.

"Did you know that 'Lucchesi' is the most common surname in this area?" he asked, swirling his pointer finger downward in a circle.

"I don't know that much about Italy to be honest," I said, smiling and shaking my head.

Since moving into our new home, I've seen my last name constantly. Most restaurants seem to have a Lucchesi dish named after it. The biggest car dealership near Bagni di Lucca shares my surname. And, unlike in America where most people still cannot even pronounce my name correctly when they read it out loud, everyone pronounces it correctly here. I'm quite possibly the *only* Lucchesi in all of 'Lucchesia' that doesn't speak Italian natively.

"Did you know that the original Lucchesi families are not actually from Lucca, but from the area surrounding all of Lucca?" he asked.

"I did not know that. That's interesting," I said honestly.

"So, you have moved here to claim Italian citizenship?" he wondered.

"Yes, how did you know?"

"If I were you, I would not submit your paperwork for citizenship here to the Lucca Comune," he said.

"Really?" I asked.

I wasn't planning on doing that anyways. In fact, I'm not allowed to unless I live in Lucca. People applying for Italian citizenship in Italy can only do so through the community where they've established residency. For me, that's Bagni di Lucca. But this guy didn't know that.

"The process here is very slow. It will take years I'm sure. And, maybe there are too many people involved. I recommend you find a smaller town to do your application," he stated.

I nodded affectionately. I could see he was sincere.

"That's a great idea. Thank you very much for the advice," I said.

The lady walked back into the office with more paperwork for me to look over, confirm it was correct, and sign. She handed me three copies of my son's new birth certificate 'Estratto' signed and stamped by her office. I was all set. I kind of couldn't believe it.

I graciously said thank you and goodbye several times to both she and the young man before I left. Outside in the hallway, I thanked the security guard too. She smiled warmly. Little did I know that I'd be back in the Lucca Comune before I knew it. After all, she tried to warn me that my son had a strange name. I had no idea just strange it would turn out to be.

# Chapter 10 - Navigating Italian Healthcare: A Crash Course

If you haven't experienced much Italian bureaucracy, you're incredibly lucky. In some ways, Italy's bureaucracy is indescribable. Travelers unintentionally stumble into the weeds of Italian bureaucracy, and it only gets worse if you live here. That's why it was nothing short of a small miracle the day we were approved for the National Italian Health Insurance.

I'd love to sit here and say that the Italian system sucks. Or, that Italians are so kind and helpful at every turn. Neither is accurate, for the truth lies somewhere deep, deep deep deep *deeeeeeeeeep* in between. In all honesty, although often slow, the Italian system works. I've seen it work with my own eyes, and have been proven wrong time and again. The vast majority of people here want a system that works, too. Why wouldn't they?

There's *no place* in Italy that la dolce vita can be experienced more genuinely than at the local post office. I remember once standing there patiently waiting my turn to pay a few bills before I had an Italian bank account. A young woman worked the counter by herself, and every transaction took as much as ten minutes or more for some customers. But I didn't care; I was so grateful to interact with this kind soul after the horrible experiences in the larger Bagni di Lucca branch.

When it was finally my turn, we greeted each other warmly, but I didn't have the forms filled out correctly, so she offered to help correct the mistakes.

"It's complicated for foreigners here," I said graciously while she assisted.

"It's complicated for *everyone* here," she responded.

She dropped a truth bomb. In Italy, it often takes more energy from everyone to accomplish the same tasks. Take the post office customers that day. They come and go from the post office, secretly taking note of who came in first. Sure, there's a ticket dispenser at the counter, but nobody is using it. Instead, everyone knows who is next by mere observation. People are standing, sitting, inside, outside, and no line had formed. That day, I was probably number twelve in line when I entered. Once inside, I began taking note of everyone who came behind me. I didn't realize *everyone else* was doing it, too.

Instinctually, as a child I did this, but I had no idea it was in my DNA! Nowhere else on earth have I witnessed the observation skills that most Italians possess. For a keen observer like me, it's incredible to behold.

### No, No No No.....Yes

Thank God for my wife. Without her, I doubt I would have discovered that Italian public health insurance was available for everyone in Tuscany with only a residency application receipt. Tuscany has a robust health care system, and it's organized. It's something to consider if you're thinking about moving to Italy.

Just days after submitting our first residency application, we had temporary public health insurance cards. In order to get them, first stop was at the Agenzia delle Entrate located a twenty-five euro taxi ride south of Lucca. You can also walk or take a bus, but it's a terrible location honestly without a car for how many people rely on this place. I needed this agency to fork over two official, original blue-stamped Codice Fiscale documents, one for my wife and another for me, that I would then bring with me to apply for Italian healthcare. I already had these documents, but unknowingly, only had copies.

Once inside the Agenzia, there's an employee at the front desk helping patrons with a touch screen ticket system that does not rely on pure Italian observation. Too many visitors apparently. In reality, people are there for all sorts of reasons, and the large number of employees who work there specialize in specific solutions.

"You need this, you don't have that," the lady clamored once my number was called.

I couldn't understand a word. She was *insisting* I didn't have the correct documents. I knew I was entitled to health insurance, so I stayed calm. Sitting at her desk felt like utter failure, and I badly needed this lady to cooperate if I wanted Italian health insurance for Stephanie, so I'd do whatever she said whether I liked it or not. Living in Italy is often stressful, no doubt about it. With this woman in particular, it was 'No, no, no, no, no…' and then fifteen minutes later it was 'Okay, yes', and nothing changed except her mind. So strange.

In the end, I left with the blue stamped Codice Fiscale document I needed, but not Stephanie's. She instructed me to return the next day with Stephanie's signature on something, so early the following morning I walked about an hour from Lucca station. This time around, there was no sign of the woman from the previous day. Instead, I was helped by a very mild-mannered gentleman who gave me no trouble at all. He even wished me well as I left.

**Drowning in Paperwork**

Campo di Marte hospital is an older facility located not far outside the ancient walls of Lucca, and fully walled in. I found a public school and playground attached to the hospital, but could *not* find the entrance. I walked the entire perimeter before sneaking through a parking garage to enter. The waiting room was upstairs, and a TV calling out ticket numbers was above the entrance door. It reminded me of OTB.

When my number was called, I entered a small office with four desks all with plexiglass shields. Two desks were empty. One employee was helping a customer, so I approached the free desk. Although I smiled and greeted the worker warmly, she saw me coming a mile away. She's seen guys like me before,

61

unaccustomed to Italy. It's almost as if the smiling on my part makes things worse. She named several forms in Italian that I had never heard of, so I wrote the names down, but I still walked out confused. I needed *real* help, and knew just where to go.

"Buongiorno," I said, entering the front office of my Italian language school.

"Richard! Buongiorno," Anita said.

Anita, the school secretary, was a sweetheart. As a mother herself, she was so excited my wife was pregnant. The school was lucky to have her, especially since two of the three teachers were mediocre at best, with the third being downright awful.

"I'm applying for the Servizio Sanitario Nazionale, and I'm drowning in paperwork. I could really use some help," I said.

"How can I help you?" she asked in English.

I pulled out the folder from my backpack. One by one, I gently laid documents onto her desk so she could see. Watching her reaction closely, unlike me, I noticed she was quite familiar with it all.

"I see. You need the health insurance?" she asked.

"That's right, and I don't know what I'm doing," I replied.

The majority of students at this language school attended for a week while in Italy on holiday, and then vanished. I was the rare student enrolled for an entire year. As a travel language school, new students were shuffled into my class every Monday like it was normal. Even if I made friends, they left after Friday's class. It seemed most students just wanted to learn how to order a coffee. If you're seriously learning Italian, attend elsewhere. But I was grateful for Anita.

"Because you're a student, you have a fixed annual fee for health insurance. It's one hundred-seventy euro. This fee covers you for the rest of the year. However, the fee is the same whether you apply for insurance on January 1st, or December 31st. Next year in January, if you want insurance, you will have to go through this process again," she explained.

"I see. What about for my wife?" I asked.

"Because she is here on a retirement visa, her fee varies according to her income from the previous year. How much money did she earn last year?" she asked.

I wrote down a number on a sticky note, and she started calculating. Anita filled in the rest of the application for me, and set her pen down.

"Okay, here's how you calculate the insurance fee. This is what you need," she said, shuffling documents in my direction.

"Wonderful! You're the best, Anita," I said.

"It's complicated, but they should accept this," she said.

"You're a lifesaver," I said, packing up my bag.

## Progress...?

The Medico di Base office in Campo di Marte hospital reopened after lunch at three o'clock. This time around, the employee at the *other* desk was available. Her name was Justina. Unlike the other employee, Justina was empathetic, and demonstrated she understood how difficult it can be for people in my position. Although she sent me away unsuccessfully for not making the proper calculations for my wife's insurance payment, she told me I could email her the remaining documents.

I left her office with my head held high. The post office on the other side of the city was open until seven in the evening, so I walked over there to pay the remaining balance. That evening at dinner, I emailed everything Justina requested, thanking her for her kindness, and for allowing me to send everything digitally. The next morning, we were approved, and she emailed temporary insurance cards for my wife and I that we could print. Her email *also* included our new primary care physician's name, office address and telephone number. Our *actual* Italian public health insurance cards arrived several weeks later in the mail.

It felt like things were finally falling into place.

What a difference one human can make! A few months later in January, I'd dig up her email again for insurance coverage in 2023. Within a few exchanges, we were once again approved. In September that year, I contacted her again when my son and I became Italian.

"You're Italian now, so you'll *never* have to go through this process again," she wrote.

La dolce vita at last. But in 2024, when my wife's health insurance ran out before her Carta di Soggiorno was approved, I contacted Justina like always by email. Instantly, I received an automated email response indicating that the Medico di Base was no longer accepting digital communications for insurance requests, and that everything now had to be done in person.

# Chapter 11 - Learning *Everything* the Hard Way

In my lifelong quest to be a kinder, gentler version of myself, and *not* be a dick in my old age, the realtor signing me up for European utilities, and utility companies themselves would prove a formidable opponent.

"You're all set. I've signed you up for water, electric, and gas. Everything will be on and working when you arrive," Annabella said.

"That was very nice of you. What do I have to do on my end?" I asked.

"Nothing besides pay the bills when they arrive. I will pay the first few months on your behalf since your wife is pregnant, and you can pay me back," Annabella elaborated.

I was on my mother's back porch in New York drinking coffee. Was she *really* going to pay for my utilities? Why would someone do that?

"That's so wonderful! Very kind and helpful," I WhatsApp texted Annabella, not overthinking it.

But in December, after three months living in Italy, when I found out those monthly gas, electric and water bills all arrived to her address, *not* mine, *and* that her email address was listed on *all my accounts*, I'd want to scream at her. Good thing for her about the 'don't be a dick' mantra I'd instituted. Otherwise, I would have.

**Why I Avoid Local Taxis**

The taxi Annabella arranged for us was here at the station, just as scheduled. I saw the taxi man, smiled and raised my hand.

"Richard Lucchesi?" the taxi driver asked like he didn't *already* see me acknowledge him.

"Yes," I said, already feeling twangs of disappointment.

Straight away, something seemed a little off with him.

The man's taxi was a small minivan. We had four suitcases, two back packs, two cat carriers, and a bun in the oven. He opened the back trunk door, and I started carefully loading our suitcases in. Each time I let go of a suitcase, he'd touch it. Not move it, just touch it. I was sure he was touching and not moving. What the hell was he doing? We'd been in Italy for less than twenty-four hours. Was *this* la dolce vita?

With everything in, and the cats in the back seat with Stephanie, I stood back from the open trunk door waiting. He stepped up to the trunk, touched everything *again*, and didn't shuffle or move a thing. It was senseless. I knew what I was seeing was unintelligent, but being new to Italy, who *knows* what was actually happening. He dropped us off at our new home, I quickly unloaded everything without his help, and I paid him ten euro cash.

I'd harken back to this *exact moment* over a year later when I called him for a ride once more in a pinch. On the telephone, I queried if he could meet me for a ride home from the train station.

"Tomorrow, seven o'clock in the evening from Bagni di Lucca station?" he asked.

"Yes. I'll need a ride from Bagni di Lucca train station to Ponte a Serraglio. How much will it cost?" I wanted to confirm.

The previous trip had cost us ten euros. Instead of answering me, he blabbered on and on about God knows what for minutes. I listened carefully, thinking he'd eventually say a number. I politely asked several more times, always remembering to avoid being a dick. He was talking in circles.

The following evening at the station, I had one backpack with me. After carefully laying it in his trunk, I let go. He touched it without moving it. Infuriating. At piazza Ponte a Serraglio, I asked how much.

"Whatever you want," he said.

"Is ten okay?" I asked, holding a ten euro bill in my hand.

"It's expensive these days, blah blah blah," he jabbered, pointing at some license document paper-clipped to the visor above my head.

"So ten, it's enough?" I prodded.

"If you want. But it's so costly to operate a taxi in Italy," he whined.

I reached in my wallet and grabbed another five. I didn't want any issues, not that I would have any. I handed him fifteen. Instead of saying thank you, he said okay. I opened the car door gritting my teeth. I was upset, but at least I wasn't a dick.

## Unfortunate Utilities Surprise

Arriving in late September, the first moments in our new home were somewhat straightforward for being in a new country on a new continent. Other than the musty smell smacking us in the face, Stephanie seemed pleased. We'd air the place out and clear the funky smell soon enough. The important thing was we were here, and we were safe.

"Welcome home," I told her sincerely as we hugged.

I held Stephanie tightly, her baby bump brushing against my belly. I let the cats out of the carriers to explore, preparing their litter box in the almost empty living room, and checked the thermostat. 21 degrees. Annabella must have set that for us when she dropped off the small bag of groceries to hold us over.

I never thought to ask Annabella about the thermostat after that. Why should I? I knew how to use them. But this was Italy, a place where utilities like natural gas are notoriously *far* more expensive than in the United States. Instead of acting like I knew everything, I should have *grilled* Annabella with questions, like at what temperature she sets *her* thermostat in September. I'd soon learn November is the month most people in this area begin to light pellet stove fires to keep warm. They do this to avoid high energy and utility costs, a totally different world in Tuscany. Nobody in our neighborhood turns on the thermostat in September, and most certainly not as high as twenty-one degrees. It wasn't even cold outside! Why would Annabella do something to us in our home that no-one else does, *and* not say anything about it?

Our apartment's super high, arched ceilings in all the rooms may look beautiful, but are absolutely awful for keeping a place warm. As it got colder outside, no matter what the thermostat's temperature setting, Stephanie was only warm with sweaters under blankets. Furthermore, our son's birth in the end of November meant utility costs were an afterthought in those first crucial months.

Already opened envelopes started appearing in our mailbox in January. They were addressed to me, but had Annabella's real estate office address written on them. These opened envelopes were the first time I'd laid eyes on any utility bills. When Annabella slipped December's gas bill into our mailbox in early January, it was €496. This amount was for a single twenty-eight day cycle of natural gas usage. During roughly the same period, the single month electric bill from a different provider was over €350. Was I being overcharged? Was another neighbor *also* on my meter by accident? It didn't make sense.

These were astronomical figures, and sadly, Stephanie was *still* cold in our home. I made a video explaining about my utility prices on social media that received hundreds of comments. Most people couldn't believe it, either. Many were asking if the bill was bi-monthly, something some Italian utility companies do. Others wrote that I was flat out lying. The level of absurdity all around was incomprehensible.

"Everyone has the same experience in their first year in Italy," Alfie said.

He was Annabella's partner, the man who *actually* brokered my Italian home purchase.

"If everyone here is aware of this and I'm new, why didn't someone warn me?" I asked.

A bit of communication would have gone a long way. As a property owner four times over in America, paying my own property taxes, and setting up utilities was second nature. I'd even installed rooftop solar *twice* in multiple states. Once I laid eyes on my *Italian* utility bills and logged onto my online accounts, I couldn't believe what I was seeing. Digital communications, including monthly bills, were being sent to Annabella's email address, *not* mine. Even after I began paying my own bills, monthly bills were *still* emailed to Annabella, *and* my bills continued to be physically mailed to her agency. She'd continue to open my mail, and slip already opened envelopes into my mailbox many months after I began paying my own utilities.

Annabella could see how much I was paying for gas, electric and water long after she stopped paying for my utilities. When I finally contacted the three utility companies to change everything, it was challenging to remove all her information. One company never removed her email address even after multiple requests. Eventually, I'd switch gas and electric companies, but not before finding out something despicable.

## Why Didn't She Explain?

"When are you going to pay me for the utilities?" Annabella wrote in a message on WhatsApp in early January.

I sighed. "I can pay anytime. Can you provide copies of the bills first please?"

"Would you like me to drop them off, or would you prefer scanned copies by email?" she asked.

"Scans in an email message would be great," I said.

A message to my inbox with attachments and a spreadsheet arrived weeks later. I opened the spreadsheet first. Incredibly, I owed Annabella two thousand seven hundred euros. It had to be wrong, I thought.

I was fuming. My mind raced around like a roadrunner. When it finally slowed down, I landed on the thermostat setting from the evening we moved in. The last time she visited my home before we arrived to Italy, she set the thermostat at 70F, twenty-one degrees in Celsius in September. In *September.* Like a fool, I thought that was normal for Tuscany.

It wasn't just the thermostat. Utility companies do something sneaky in Italy. They offer better gas and electric rates to Italian citizens than they do to non-citizens residing in Italy. They also offer more favorable rates to residents than they do to non-residents. Therefore, vacation homeowners that do not reside in Italy tend to have the highest gas and electric rates. Annabella used my name to sign me up for gas, electric and water *months* before we arrived to Italy when I hadn't yet become a resident. Why didn't she explain about any of this?

A level of sadness fell over me not felt before. Eight hundred fifty euros for a month to heat and light a one bedroom home, and we were *still* cold. I just had never experienced anything like this.

Another opened electric bill arrived days later in the mailbox, this one for €388. Lamentably, the two thousand seven hundred euros I owed Annabella didn't include the over twelve hundred euros from these three most recent utility bills. It was obscene in aggregate. At the post office, I quietly watched the clerk process the bills one by one, taking acute note of her face when she noticed the prices. For her, it was impossible not to react in at least mild astonishment.

I felt like the dick.

# Chapter 12 - Why I Love Italian Grocery Shopping

I love grocery shopping in Italy. No matter how frustrated I get by Italian bureaucracy, I can always find la dolce vita at the grocery store. Normally when I grocery shop, I'll snag my backpack and walk to Conad in Bagni di Lucca. I love it there! They are friendly, and it's eleven minutes door to door on foot. Sometimes, I'll also go to Coop in Fornoli by bike. A third supermarket, Carrefour, opened up near us last year too. I've been there maybe three times total. My first visit was on opening day. The cashier didn't greet me when it was my turn, and no thank you or have a nice day when I left.

Yesterday, I needed groceries. I left the house around quarter to three in the afternoon, hopped in my car, and drove to Esselunga in Marlia, a suburb of Lucca. It was the perfect time to go. This sentiment was cemented when I arrived at Esselunga. The first spot next to the main entrance was open, so I parked there. And good thing, because I was about to break the record for number of trips into an Italian supermarket.

## Big Supermarket Haul

Esselunga near Lucca is a legit supermarket, much larger than anything around here. A fun element to Esselunga is a pricing feature called 'prezzo bloccato', or price blocked. I love prezzo bloccato as much as I love la dolce vita. American supermarkets should adopt this. I think it means the price for an item is locked in for eternity. Price blocked items are usually Esselunga branded goods priced way lower than equivalent name brand products, catching your attention. For instance, price blocked Esselunga eggs are €1,69 for a pack of ten eggs. All the other eggs are priced around three euros or more for ten or a dozen. Price block exists for many staple items that people use regularly in the kitchen, like eggs and butter.

Price blocking is different from products on sale, because those prices are for a limited time. Like I said, price block is forever.

For my first trip inside, I head straight for the toilet paper aisle. The Esselunga brand toilet paper is price blocked at €2,19 for a four pack of two ply rolls. Each roll lasts way longer than it should, so I always buy these. I grab five packs, use the self-checkout, pay cash, and my total including two plastic bags is €11,11 which, as everyone knows, is a lucky number. I'm in and out in about five minutes.

My second trip is for paper towels. They are opposite all the cleaning supplies, and *not* in the same aisle as toilet paper. I guess this makes sense. Paper towels in Italian are called 'carta casa', or house paper, which I find amusing. I buy the Esselunga brand again, but paper towels are not price blocked. At €3,29 for a four pack, I grab five packs, all I can handle without a cart, head to self-checkout, and the total comes to €16,45. I pay cash, and I'm back at my car in a flash loading up the trunk.

I parked right next to the shopping cart return, and grab a shopping cart on the third trip. Shopping carts are locked, and only available if you have a one or two euro coin. Just slide the coin into the shopping cart lock, and it unlocks from the next cart. When you return it, you get your coin back. One time, I needed a large shopping cart at Conad, but didn't have any change. A worker saw me fiddling with the carts, walked outside, pulled a one euro coin from her pocket and just handed it to me, saying nothing. Of course I went looking for her when I finished shopping, but I don't think she expected the money back.

I pushed the shopping cart past all the other shoppers, snaking through the produce and making a beeline straight for the frizzy water section next to the hard alcohol. Bottled water at Esselunga has its own room, and there's a digital price board listing everything for sale, too. A six pack of one and a half liter bottles of my favorite sparkling water is €2,82 per pack. That comes out to €0.47 per 1.5 liter bottle. I grab six packs. It's so much water that it hardly fits in the cart! I stack it up, and lug the shopping cart to the beer selection one aisle away. Italian beer is on sale for €3,49 per six pack with the Fidaty card, Esselunga's membership, so I grab six of those as well. I also pick out a few German brews for Stephanie, two IPA three packs, a large Belgium blonde bottle, and now have a very heavy shopping cart.

I carefully nudge the overstuffed cart to checkout aisle number thirteen. An older employee is sitting down scanning groceries. All checkout workers are seated, and don't often help bag groceries. I'm next, so I set one pack of water, one six pack of beer, and the rest of the beer onto the conveyor belt.

"Buonasera," I say first.

"Buonasera," she says.

We exchange smiles. She's a heavy set woman about sixty years old. I point to the water pack first.

"Six of these, and six of these also," I say in Italian, pointing to the various items.

She leans over the scanner slightly to check out my cart, barely leaving her seat. All the beer is behind five big packs of water and she can't see it. She grabs the pack of sparkling water first.

"How many?" she asked.

"Six in total," I responded.

She scanned it, moved it along, and grabbed the six pack of Moretti.

"Five of these?" she asked.

"Six," I said.

She scanned the rest of the beer. There was zero judgment on her part.

"I'm really thirsty," I said, handing her my Fidaty card.

She chuckled, scanned my card, and the price reduced nearly fourteen euro to €50,62. I didn't have enough change in my pocket to cover the sixty-two cents, and I *knew* she would ask. I handed her a fifty and a five.

"Do you have the sixty-two?" she asked.

73

I grimaced, reached in my pocket, pulled out the forty-five cents I had, and held my palm out flat as I could so she could see for herself. She nodded.

"It's in there," I joked, pointing directly at the cart lock with my one euro coin in it.

I got her to laugh more loudly that time.

"Thank you so much. Have a nice evening," I said as she handed me my change.

"Arrivederci," she replied kindly.

I loaded the trunk with packs of sparkling water, filling it to capacity. The beer went onto the floor behind the driver's seat. I returned the shopping cart, retrieving my one euro coin, and opened the driver's side door. I took a seat, and checked the center console. There was about five euro worth of change in there from our most recent road trip to Germany.

"I knew it!" I thought. "The cashier would have really appreciated that."

**How Many Trips Does it Take? 1, 2, 3, 4...**

Before heading back in, I glanced at my final shopping list:

Lemons
Limes
Oranges
Mozzarella
Salami
Bread
Butter
Eggs
Pizza

I entered, chose a plastic pull cart, and picked up bananas, lettuce, a slice of pumpkin, a big bag of green apples, a pack of sweet Tuscan peppers, a huge box of clementines, and portobello mushrooms on sale, forgetting to grab the first two items on my list. I escape the produce section unharmed, and grabbed some Milano pre-sliced salami packs, discovering a four pack of mozzarella balls on sale as well. I selected the price blocked eggs and butter, and six packs of penne, ziti, and ditalini for soup, all on sale. Right away, I have almost everything on my list in the cart.

I meander to the meat aisle, and come upon a roast along with two packs of Tuscan sausage that look good. I browse the chicken, but nothing jumps out at me. I scored a nice loaf of fresh Tuscan bread, and in frozen foods, picked up two La Numero Uno frozen pepperoni pizzas, a four pack of Esselunga brand Margarita pizzas, and two 30 piece boxes of chicken nuggets.

There's a new lady at self-checkout this time handing out plastic bags. She greets me with a huge grin, hands me two bags and says 'prego' even before I say anything. That *never* happens.

At self-checkout, I take my time, scanning and bagging everything the way I like it. One time at Esselunga's self-checkout, I pressed the wrong button on the screen, and a random alert was activated. An employee rushed over to rescan every item I had *already* packed up neatly in bags, negating all my efforts. The woman kept repeating that it was a random check, but that's all she ever said. Afterwards, two eggs were broken.

I needed three more bags, so I turned around. The new lady stood there arm extended with plastic bags, saying 'prego' every time she'd hand a bag over. It was delightful.

My total came to €88,76. I paid with a credit card, delicately picking up my five heavy bags. I acknowledged the friendly employee one last time with a 'thank you, have a nice evening' before scanning my receipt to open the self-checkout gates. I walked briskly past customer service, the bar, and bathrooms out the door because of the weight on my fingers. As I'm loading up the back seat, I text Stephanie to see if she has any last minute requests.

'Definitely milk' she texts.

I load everything else, lock the car, and reenter Esselunga a fifth time. While in the milk aisle, I notice there are stacks of the brand of shelf-stable milk we usually buy. Six packs of one liter plastic bottles are all neatly wrapped up. It's expensive at €1,59 per bottle, but it's the only brand that has Vitamin D written on the label. I grab two six packs, and before I can grab a third, an employee stocking shelves replaces the open space I just made with more milk. I grab those, he replaces those two again, and I grab one last six pack. There was no more room in the plastic pull cart. I wheel the plastic cart about ten feet, stop, take a photo and send it to Steph.

'That's only milk. Maybe I should get more?' I wrote.

'I think we should invest in a cow,' she wrote.

# Chapter 13 - Four Doctors in Two Years

While applying for temporary health insurance, I was instructed to choose a primary care doctor. Justina patiently walked me through the steps and said I could choose anyone from the list on her computer. It was quite an extensive list! I browsed, noting the locations of each doctor, and ended up choosing one of the only female doctors in our area. Once approved, my very pregnant wife could finally get the ball rolling with her new Italian doctor.

Stephanie was nervous, and I didn't blame her. We had a lot riding on this move, but the pregnancy superseded everything. When I lived in Spain, I never visited the doctor once. In Korea, we only went to the doctor when we were ill, and *never* had a primary care physician. Instead, hundreds of doctors were everywhere, and under Korean universal healthcare, doctor visits cost pennies. What would Italy be like? Had I chosen the correct doctor randomly? And, would she be helpful, or more like that witch at the post office?

Early on, I was *very* anxious about it all. I didn't feel relief when our Italian health insurance was approved either, because we still needed to *actually* go to the doctor together, and probably a bunch of times.

Justina informed me to call the doctor's number for an appointment. I'd just left Italian language classes in Lucca when I did, and nobody answered. About twenty minutes later, while standing in the sun on the train platform, my phone rang.

"Pronto?" I said, answering the phone.

"Is this Mr. Lucchesi?" a female voice said in Italian.

"Yes, I'm Mr. Lucchesi," I replied in my best Italian.

Was my new doctor calling me directly *from her own phone*?

"Buongiorno Mr. Lucchesi. This is Doctor Salvini. I missed your call just now, I am so sorry. I've been working all morning long, and it has been a hell of a day. How can I help you?" Dr. Salvini said in Italian.

She sounded so cheerful! Doctor Salvini had a level of confidence I wasn't expecting. Had I chosen wisely?

"So, we just arrived to Italy, and my wife is pregnant. We need to see a doctor and make an appointment," I explained in my best Italian possible.

"Do you prefer if I speak in English?" Dr. Salvini asked, switching to English.

I paused.

"English would be great, thank you," I said.

"Okay, so your wife is pregnant. How many months pregnant?"

"She is seven months pregnant."

"You came with your wife to Italy seven months pregnant? You are *very* brave," Dr. Salvini said confidently, with a laugh.

"We are a little crazy," I admitted.

"A little brave, a little crazy. It's okay! We should make an appointment for her right away. Let me take a look," she said in English.

I waited. I could hear her walking, and a car door shut. It was authentically nice to speak in English with the doctor. I already appreciated her so much.

"Can your wife come this Friday at one o'clock in the afternoon?" she asked.

"Yes, yes she can. That would be great," I replied.

"Okay. I will see you on Friday. And you know the address?" Dr. Salvini asked.

"Yes. Fornoli, correct?" I asked.

"Yes. Okay then. We will see you soon," the doctor said.

"Thank you for calling back so quickly," I replied sincerely.

I hung up and immediately texted Stephanie the good news. La dolce vita was looking up!

## The Best Doctor

We arrived early to Fornoli on Friday for Stephanie's first doctor's appointment in Italy, and took a seat in the small waiting room. Were we sitting in the basement of a house?

"Hello! Hello," Dr. Salvini said, appearing from the back hallway.

"Hello doctor," I said.

She leaned up against the door frame. She was my height, slim, appeared to be Stephanie's age, and blonde.

"How are you?" she said, looking directly at Stephanie.

"Overall, I'm okay, but I'm tired," Stephanie said, with a chuckle.

"You are a very brave woman," Dr. Salvini said.

"I'm proud of her," I said, with a solid grin.

"Me too. Please, follow me," she instructed.

There was an office at either end of the short hallway behind her. We entered her office and sat down in front of her desk where, unbeknownst to us, we would remain the entire time. Stephanie had all her American medical documents, and handed everything to the doctor. Dr. Salvini opened the folder and carefully looked at each document before flipping to the next one, asking questions when she didn't understand something. We stayed seated. After looking at everything, she looked up.

"I'm going to schedule you for an ultrasound. You will go to the clinic in Barga. I also recommend you visit San Luca hospital in Lucca to open your file. That's where you will give birth," she said all at once.

This lady didn't mess around. By the time we left, Stephanie had her ultrasound referral, and I had my own doctor's appointment with her the following week. Dr. Salvini was the best thing to happen to my wife and I during our early days in Italy. Too bad her tenure as our doctor was short-lived.

## Rotating Cast of Italian Doctors

While waiting for *my* doctor's appointment, I sat in the waiting room with several others. I was, by far, the youngest person in there, and we all were wearing masks. Once inside her office, I learned Dr. Salvini would be transferring out of our area soon.

"It's not final yet. Please, do not tell *anyone*," she said in a whisper, like she trusted me.

I instantly picked up on what was happening. She was moving to a larger, more affluent and desirable area, possibly a city. Our area, which is not really *that* far outside Lucca, apparently is not sought after in the medical profession, and Bagni di Lucca is more of an area where new doctors start out.

"But *we* just got here," I joked.

"I know, but.. the new place, it's a good opportunity for me and my family," Salvini whispered, even more quietly than before.

"Good for you. I'm very happy for you, seriously. That probably makes you very happy, too," I said earnestly.

"It's not finalized, maybe not until January, so shhh," she smiled, placing her pointer finger over her lips.

I *was* happy for her too. But personally, la dolce vita was shattered. We really *had* just arrived. Even with no other primary care doctor experience in Italy with which to compare her, we *knew* she was exceptional. Once, while eight months pregnant, my wife fell down two stairs injuring her ankle badly. Luckily, nothing was broken and the baby was fine. Dr. Salvini called us back right away, clearing her schedule to make a same day appointment. She inspected my wife's injury carefully, making the diagnosis in English, and even called personally days later to check up on her.

Sadly, she was our doctor for only four months, after which we were automatically assigned a new one. The second doctor was elderly, and wore two separate face masks over one another to cover his mouth. Sure enough, old double mask retired shortly thereafter.

Our third doctor was a young red-headed male who was probably fresh out of medical school. His last name was Irish, but was Italian nonetheless, and was *very* attentive to calls and messages. Unlike the first two doctors, he took up residence in the brand new medical facility in Fornoli.

One time, due to severe skin irritation on my behind, I needed to see a doctor urgently, so I scheduled with Dr. Patrick on WhatsApp. The new facility had a set of double doors, a lobby to the right, and doctors' offices to the back left. The chairs in the seating area were bolted to the floor. There was a bathroom off the lobby, but I believe it was locked. Because the lobby and hallway were a bit disjointed, doctor's either had to leave their offices and walk down the hall to call patients in, or shout from their doorways.

I showed up for my appointment early. When I arrived, about half a dozen other patients, *all* older women, were already there. A few were in the waiting room, and others stood down the hall in front of the doctor's door. I found out *none of them* had appointments like I did; they were there hoping to see the new doctor during his assigned office hours. He had to explain *one by one* that patients with appointments took precedence. To at least one woman who wouldn't leave, it was like he was speaking a foreign language.

Once inside his office, he took a quick look at my butt, and retreated behind his desk. I pulled up my pants and took a seat in front of him.

"Those ladies in the waiting room, they really like you," I said, trying to joke with the doctor in Italian.

He was busy writing out my prescription. Without missing a beat, he responded.

"They.. they are a *huge* headache for me," he said in English, rolling his eyes and shaking his head.

But like the rest, he didn't stick around. We were notified by a group WhatsApp message from his account that he was leaving to become a surgeon. I'm sure the old ladies were devastated. I know I was.

Our fourth doctor made a poor first impression when I reached out to her about a painful infection in my finger. She didn't answer the phone, never called back, and took several days to respond to messages after multiple attempts. When she finally did, she provided basic instructions without offering to see me, information I'd already found on the internet.

A few months later, my wife and I *needed* to see her together. She set an appointment for both of us to see her the following day. When we arrived at five minutes to three in the afternoon, she was standing in the hallway outside her office door.

"Hello. Are you Dr. Gabriele?" I asked.

"Yes," the woman answered.

"Nice to meet you. My name is Richard Lucchesi. My wife and I have an appointment scheduled with you for three o'clock today," I said.

"Ah! You have an appointment?" she asked.

"Yes. You scheduled us yesterday for an appointment today," I explained, showing her the message she wrote to me yesterday.

Had she *really* forgot we were coming? I wonder if she'll be transferring soon.

# Chapter 14 - Sleepless Nights and Pediatric Fights

Our beautiful baby boy was born two months after we moved into our new home in Italy, but residency application interviews for Stephanie and I at the Lucca police station were set for a month later. This meant mine and my wife's names were not listed in our comune's database of residents. Our non-resident status caused enormous consequences beyond our control for our newborn son.

Luckily we were in Italy, a land it seems where newborns have more rights than everybody else. I write that in jest, but soon enough we'd learn that no doctor or nurse would *ever* turn our son away for medical treatment regardless of whether or not we were insured, or whether we were official Italian residents.

"Here are pediatric documents for you. You will have three follow up appointments here at the hospital. After that, Dottoressa Donato will be your son's new pediatrician," a doctor at the hospital informed us.

I was standing beside my wife. She was laying in her hospital bed holding our son. They nurse handed my wife the documents including the new pediatrician's contact phone number.

"You can call the pediatrician once you return home to set up his first check-up appointment," she told us both in Italian.

"Thank you very much," I said warmly to the doctor at the hospital in Italian.

## I Can't Help You

Our son's first doctor's appointment outside the hospital was shortly after the two month mark. The pediatrician's office was in Fornoli, right next to the main pharmacy in the center of town. Anyone who lives close by and has a baby has probably been to this office before.

"Prego," we heard a woman's voice say from the far end of the hallway.

83

It was Dottoressa Donato. We entered her office and closed the door behind us.

"Do you have your son's pediatric book?" Dr. Donato asked in Italian.

"Yes," Stephanie said, handing it over.

Unlike Dr. Salvini, Dr. Donato only spoke to us in Italian. She looked the book over, and turned to her computer. She typed a little bit, but seemed confused.

"I cannot find you here. You are Lucchesi?" she asked.

"Richard Lucchesi, yes. We had our residency appointments at the Lucca Questura, but have not received our residency cards yet. Our situation is complicated," I tried to briefly explain.

She didn't seem to care *at all* what I was saying. We were either in her system, or we weren't.

"Okay, let's check your son. Please take off his clothes and bring him over to the examination table," she stated, motioning to the table.

Dr. Donato went through a series of checks, then measured and weighed him.

"Your son is due for his first vaccinations. Normally I do this task, but I cannot administer them right now," Dr. Donato informed us in Italian.

She it made it seem like this was a big problem. Instantly, my nervous system spiked.

"What do we do then?" I asked.

"You have to take him to the medical clinic for his vaccines," she stated.

"Are you referring to the building across the street?"

"Yes, the main medical building in Fornoli," she said.

"Okay. So, we just take him in there and they'll do it?" I asked.

"I don't know. I suggest you walk over right after this appointment and ask," Dr. Donato said.

"And what vaccines does he need?" I asked.

"The doctor will know," she elaborated, looking away as if trying to end the conversation.

"Will it cost money?"

"Again, I do not know. You will have to ask."

She had everything in a drawer to administer the first round of vaccines, but refused to do it because of protocol. She wasn't being a dick, *and* I didn't blame her either, but her advice still stung. Dr. Donato also made it seem like walking over and requesting vaccines would be easy, but I knew better. I didn't even know which vaccines he needed, and she couldn't print anything official out on our behalf, either.

**Confusing the Medical Staff**

Our appointment with Dr. Donato finished just after twelve noon, and nearly everywhere except restaurants close down at one o'clock. Thankfully, staff were still behind the counter when we arrived at the medical facility.

"Buongiorno," I said gracefully, coming through the front door.

"Buongiorno," the young man replied.

"Our son's doctor told us to come here. He needs his first vaccinations, but we do not have residency in Italy yet. Our names are not in the system," I started off.

I could see extreme confusion wash over his face like a tidal wave. I knew this was going to be hard.

"If you need a vaccine for your son, you go to your son's pediatrician," he explained in Italian.

"Yes, I know. But she cannot do it. We have health insurance, but he doesn't have health insurance yet," I said.

He was perplexed, because everyone in Italy has health insurance. *Everyone.* The idea of 'not having health insurance' is an American construct, but I could not think of any other way to explain our issue in Italian.

"Do you have your health insurance card?" he asked.

"Yes, just a moment," I said.

He took my card, punched my information in, and studied his computer screen for some seconds.

"What is your son's name?" he asked.

"Charlie Lucchesi," I said.

"How old is he?"

"Two months old."

"Okay. And he needs vaccinations?" he asked.

"That's correct," I said.

"Has he had any vaccinations before?" he asked.

"No. He needs his first vaccinations," I said.

It felt like we were finally getting somewhere. In Italy, I'm usually met with initial confusion followed by execution. It's a repetitive cycle. I was so grateful this guy finally understood our situation, and was helping our family.

"Okay. Right now, there is no doctor on call. Come in at ten in the morning tomorrow. The doctor on call will administer the vaccinations at that time," he informed us, handing my health insurance card back.

"Wonderful. Thank you so much," I said kindly.

So helpful, and not a dick at all!

## Sticky Note System

Fornoli's brand new, state of the art medical facility had a busy waiting room the next morning. Stephanie and Charlie took a seat while I stood in line. I glanced back. We were the only parents there with a child. When it was my turn at the window, I said my name, and the staff checked the computer. When she couldn't find us, she turned and asked for help from someone behind her. Then she looked down and saw a bright green sticky note with my name on it.

"Ah! Here it is. It'll be just a moment. Please have a seat," she said, kindly guiding me with her hand to the waiting area.

My name was on a sticky note. The system was working!

"Lucchesi," a nurse said appearing about ten minutes later.

She led us into the first room down the hall where another nurse was waiting for us, and an older doctor was sitting behind the desk.

"Buongiorno," I said upon entering.

"Buongiorno," the man said cordially.

He took the baby book from me, opened it, and said something brief to the nurse on call. I glanced down, and vaccines vials were already sitting in front of him on his desk.

"Italian or English?" he asked in Italian.

"Maybe if you speak English it's better," I answered.

"Today is three vaccines. We will put them in the leg," he explained in English.

"Okay, great," I said, looking the doctor in the eye.

We maneuvered Charlie to Stephanie's lap, pulled down his pants, and held him firmly. The nurse performed the injections while the doctor stayed seated. She worked quickly, covering up each spot with a cotton ball, and taping it to his leg as soon as the vaccines were completed. The first went smoothly, but he screamed after the second one. The doctor wrote the date under the vaccination type, taped a small sticker from the vaccine bottle to the booklet, stamped it with his name and registration number, and initialed the stamp.

"I wrote the vaccine information in the book. When his name is finally in the system, we add the information to the computer. Until then, this book has his medical information," he expounded.

"Okay, I understand. No problem," I confirmed.

"You can return here in six weeks for the next vaccine schedule if you need to, and we will administer it," he said.

"Six weeks. That's terrific, thank you," I said sincerely.

"You're welcome," he replied.

"Also, do we make the payment today?" I asked.

His eyes shuffled. He turned his head, saying something softly to the nurse, who promptly left the room. Surely, some sort of payment associated with today's appointment was required, right?

"Let us check," he said.

She returned, stood in the doorway and wagged her finger.

"There is no payment today," the doctor said, smirking.

He almost let out a chuckle too.

# Chapter 15 - Random Police Encounters

Autovelox is a large, often orange box on the side of roads that has speed cameras inside. These are quite common in Italy. Usually, the speed cameras shoot radar in both directions. It's the ultimate speed trap. When driving, you'll see a sign for an Autovelox up ahead, but usually, no where in sight do you see the posted speed limit of the road. The lack of speed limit signs around the area where police might be shooting radar would drive responsible American drivers up the wall. More often than not in America, when you're pulled over for speeding, the officer will point to the speed limit sign as *extra proof* that you should have known better than to speed where he or she caught you speeding.

In 2024, two brand new, shiny orange Autovelox camera boxes were installed along the only road between Ponte a Seraglio and Bagni di Lucca. You can't miss them. It caused a stir on Facebook amongst the local population the day they appeared, with most people against them. Locals claimed they are a waste of money, and suck money out of the population. I tend to agree.

One afternoon, a man representing the post office with an envelope knocked the door. I needed to sign digitally before he handed over the delivery. It was a formal police letter indicating I was caught for speeding in Borgo a Mozzano, a town in between Bagni di Lucca and Lucca. I was caught driving 61 kilometers per hour in a 50 zone. I read and reread the letter carefully, but nowhere on it did it state the *exact* location of the infraction. Just Borgo a Mozzano. The date of the ticket was three months previous, and no photo of my vehicle was included.

In Italy, you have five days to pay a speeding fine from the moment you receive a ticket, regardless of how long ago it happened. If you fail to pay on time, the amount increases quickly. In my case, it was one hundred thirty-seven euro. I walked over to the post office, filled out the payment slip, and promptly paid my fine the following morning.

Seven months later, another knock. Same thing as before, but this time, I couldn't make out what was written. I read it over several times, calmly used my translator, but it still didn't make sense. So, I took a photo of the document and sent it to my trusted friend Fabiano.

"Ah! Did you receive a speeding ticket? If so, you didn't send the form to the police telling them who was driving," Fabiano expeditiously replied.

What form?

This new infraction for not sending the form was over two hundred euros. This time, I needed to pay the fine *and* send the form to the police station by registered mail with a *registered return receipt* of delivery within five days. If I didn't do it this way, it wouldn't be valid he told me.

## The Hated Little Sign

Although cameras are everywhere, the number one way of receiving a traffic citation in Italy *has* to be the random police checks. Italian police stand on the side of the road with a little sign, and wave in advance for you to stop. If this happens, you must pull over. People who live and drive here will say that if you have all your documents in order, you have nothing to worry about. While in theory this may be true, police officers along the sides of roads needlessly instill fear that otherwise wouldn't be there if they didn't do this. In our area of Tuscany, at least *three* separate police units conduct these random stops. I see police constantly on the streets, and I don't even drive much.

In America we have random stops too, but Americans would *freak the fuck out* if we had them as often as Italians. Non-Europeans who come over here for vacation, and rent a car are not prepared for these in the way they should be. Random police checks are a way of life for Italians.

90

My first random police stop was by Carabinieri in front of a car dealership showroom in Chifenti. I'd owned my car less than three weeks, and had barely driven it. Steph was admitted to the hospital the previous evening for gestational diabetes during her ninth month of pregnancy, and I was on my way to visit her during lunch.

The posted speed limit where I was stopped is fifty. Once you pass the dealership heading south, it increases to seventy. I was *definitely* going over fifty kilometers per hour when the officer stopped me. I pulled over, and a young officer approached. A second, older officer was standing behind the police car. The officer requested my driver's license, and my libretto, which is the car's registration. I didn't have my libretto because it comes in the mail one to two months after you car's purchase.

I handed over my NY State driver's license, explained about the libretto, and told him I was on the way to visit my pregnant wife in San Luca Hospital. He retreated back to the police car. I peered through my rearview mirror to see what the officers were doing, and could see my surname in bold black letters on the cement building behind them.

When the officer returned, he handed me back my license.

"Due cose," he said. Two things.

He spoke clearly and slowly in Italian to accommodate me. I nodded.

"First, what is your address?" he asked.

"Via Vittorio Emanuele 89. Bagni di Lucca," I said.

"Okay. And your insurance please. Do you have it?" he asked.

I had purchased car insurance online as a pre-requisite to buying the vehicle, but had given my *only* copy to the dealer. I did not have a print out of it, but this was not a problem. I pulled out my phone, and started frantically scrolling through my emails. When I found the email from the insurance company, I held out my phone so he could look at my screen. He glanced at it for a moment, and stepped back from the car.

"Okay. Grazie. Buona giornata, e auguri," he said cordially.

Did he just *congratulate* me?

"Grazie mille. Buona giornata," I responded, and smiled.

And with that, he let me go on my way without an Italian driver's license, without a libretto for the car, *and I would learn later*, without a car insurance policy.

I wouldn't be so lucky next time.

### A Simple Trip to the Store?

"Could you drop by the bathroom supply store, and pick up the parts for the toilet?" the plumber asked.

It was mid-morning. The plumber was connecting the new toilet in the Cantina, and the internal parts hadn't arrived along with the toilet. I preferred not to go anywhere, but I also needed a working toilet because my mother was set to arrive to Italy in less than two weeks from NY, and wanted this renovation completed before her arrival.

"Sure, no problem," I told the plumber.

I left around quarter to twelve with plenty of time to pick up the parts before the supply company closed at one o'clock for lunch. I drove through Fornoli and crossed the bridge over the river to Chifenti. Right after the bridge, I saw local police on the side of the road. I wasn't speeding, and drove right by.

As I passed by the same dealership where I was stopped the first time, I could see the police were following me. It was probably a coincidence I thought. As I approached Devil's bridge, one police officer was waving the sign out her window at me, so I pulled into the Devil's bridge parking area along the river, and they followed behind me. It was Borgo a Mozzano Municipal Police. Both officers were female. Because of a mixup in my address, I still hadn't received my libretto. But this was not the issue.

"Insurance please," one of the officers said.

Luckily, I printed my car insurance policy last week. I reached in the glove compartment, and pulled out the printed copy of my insurance all written in Italian. However, the printed copy was of the *estimate* to my insurance, and not the actual policy. After some back and forth, the officers finally made me realize this.

They held me for over an hour, and issued me a thirty-five euro ticket for failure to have my insurance policy present during a traffic stop. The officers also gave me very detailed instructions to visit the police station the following afternoon at two o'clock, and to bring my valid insurance policy with me. Once I did this, they'd throw out the thirty-five euro ticket.

During the stop, my phone was blowing up. The plumber was messaging me, and so was the bathroom supply sales representative. The officers finally let me go, and I arrived to pick up the toilet parts well after one o'clock. When the sales representative handed me the parts, he asked why I was late.

"I was stopped by police in Borgo a Mozzano," I told him.

He didn't seemed surprised, and showed no sympathy whatsoever.

## An Honest to Goodness Mistake

That afternoon when I returned home with the toilet parts, I opened up my computer, but found no evidence of a purchased car insurance policy. Had the auto dealer let me drive my new car off the dealership lot *without car insurance*? And if so, how was I *just realizing this*?

After some contemplation, I realized *exactly* what had happened. In Italy, my American credit cards have always worked fine for retail purchases. But for some reason, American cards don't always align properly with European *online* systems. They might work at first, but if you try to use your card often online in Europe, it'll eventually stop working. In other words, there's a big difference between paying with an American credit card in person, and online shopping while in Europe. After about a month living in Italy, unbeknownst to me, all my online transactions ceased functioning except Amazon purchases, and this was right at the time I tried to buy new car insurance. Truthfully, it was nothing more than an honest mistake, and bad timing.

That afternoon, I bought and paid for a *new car insurance policy*, this time using my PayPal account to pay for the entire year in full.

### Costly Car Insurance Mishap

Borgo a Mozzano, it turns out, is *not* a good place to get caught by the cops.

The following day, I arrived on time to the police station, and brought my new car insurance policy with me. Once there, I explained to the same two ladies in the best Italian language I could that my American credit card stopped working online right around the time I purchased the car insurance, and this was all an honest mistake. Nevertheless, it made absolutely no difference how honest I was, or even if I spoke in Italian. Once I was done pleading my case, one officer retreated down the hallway to speak with her boss in the back. When she returned, the two officers hit me with the highest possible fine they could, a more than six hundred euro ticket that needed to be paid within five days.

I walked out of the police station with my tail tucked between my legs. At the post office, when I handed the worker the slip to pay the fine in full, she gasped.

"What is *this* for?" she wondered.

"Exactly. What *is* it for?" I responded.

# Chapter 16 - Playdates and Parenting in Italy

Bagni di Lucca, deep in the mountains of Tuscany, is a little village nestled in a valley along a river between high slopes. It is a place with its own train station two towns away. Although from an outsider's perspective it may seem like the town has seen better days, the local government might beg to differ. They just constructed a brand new piazza in the middle of town, complete with a living fountain pond with lily pads and water plants in the center, taps for potable water scattered about, and another tap emitting warm, non-potable natural spring water from the mountains high above from a statue's mouth.

The main park in Bagni di Lucca is a wide rectangle one block over from main street with a nice playground for children on the side. The park itself is set on a gentle slope, and workers keep the grass manicured in the summer months. A circular marble fountain with a statue of a woman sits near the middle. Recently, the largest pine tree right by the playground was chopped down, closing down the play area for several weeks.

The first time Charlie and I stopped at the playground in Bagni di Lucca was on a beautiful Friday afternoon in early September. The place was packed with kids and parents. Charlie could stand but couldn't quite walk yet, so we found a spot in the grassy field above the playground to watch kids run and play. One girl, about four years old, was the only one with a pedal-less bike. She'd run with it up to the top of the slope past where we sat, and coast down the hill towards the playground with several of her friends in tow on foot. Once at the bottom, she'd turn her bike around and strut right back up the hill. Charlie was glued.

He and I had arrived to the park by bike. We'd purchased an Italian-made child seat that fastens onto the front handlebars. I have an electric pedal assist mountain bike, a miracle for these mountain roads. Shoulders on roads are scarce in Italy, and non-existent where we live, so I'm careful and cautious when we ride. But he loves it out there, and so do I.

## Bike Riding Routines

The main road directly through Ponte a Serraglio in front of our home is also the main road through Bagni di Lucca's village. Where we live, it's 'Via Vittorio Emanuele'. In Bagni di Lucca, it's 'Via Roma'. But it's the same road.

The sidewalk in front of our house is narrow. Some cars fly through our stretch of houses, so simply getting out the front door and onto the bike is possibly more dangerous than riding. Once out there though, I feel confident most drivers see us and provide a bit of space as they pass. European drivers might have more experience sharing the roads with bicyclers than Americans.

On every bike ride, we stop somewhere. There are playgrounds in Fornoli and Bagni di Lucca, but those aren't the only places we stop. If I'm feeling up to it, we'll venture along the mountain road south towards Borgo a Mozzano to Ponte del Diavolo, and stop to walk up the thousand year old bridge. I'm positive I'm the only parent riding with a child along the serpentine cliff road coming from Chifenti. It's a deadly route even in a car. Regardless of what it looks like externally, I take extra good care of my son when we bicycle together, and safety is our number one priority even if it doesn't appear that way to others.

In Bagni di Lucca, we sometimes stop in the new piazza in front of the 'Circolo' restaurant, and wander down to the pedestrian suspension bridge that crosses the river behind it. There, we dart across the foot bridge, pick up pebbles and toss them into the water below. Italians love a good baby, and we often greet passersby.

After the bridge, it has become tradition to walk back up to the road, hold hands, cross the street, and enter the Gelateria for a snack. Nothing in Italy reminds me more of my childhood spending time with my dad in a donut shop than this place. It doesn't *smell* like a typical NY donut shop, but it has that underdog, gritty feel. It's not the most popular place in town, but Charlie doesn't care. Now that I'm a father, I'll quietly shed a tear from the joy of watching my son munch potato chips in there.

## Meet the Grandparents?

Once my son could walk, Bagni di Lucca's playground became the hotspot. And, as anticipated, I'd meet parents at the playground from time to time too. One time, after more than half an hour at the playground, Charlie and a little girl began to play with each other. So naturally, the parents and I began to chat.

"Ciao," I said, taking a few steps closer to the parents sitting on a bench.

"Ciao," they both replied.

"How old is the girl?" I asked in Italian.

"Four," the man said.

"My son is twenty-three months," I said.

The man's eyes were kind. He sensed my heavy Italian language accent. Everyone does.

"Where are you from?" the man asked.

"New York. But we live here now. My son was born here, in San Luca Hospital," I said.

"New York to Italy. That's interesting. So you live here in Bagni di Lucca?" he asked.

"Down the street in Ponte a Serraglio, near Bar Italia," I said.

"Ponte a Serraglio, okay," the man said.

"He lives right here on the main street, Via Roma," his wife said.

"We are the *grandparents*," the man stated, pointing at his granddaughter.

"Really? No," I said surprised.

The man laughed. He was older than me, so it should have been obvious. Then, Charlie ran towards the swings, so I followed.

Later, as the grandparents and little girl were leaving, the man approached again.

"Nice to meet you, I'm Angelo," the man said, extending his hand.

"Richard. Richard Lucchesi. Pleasure," I responded.

"Lucchesi. That surname is from around here. Do you have relatives in the area?" he asked.

"Probably, but I don't know them. My great-grandfather was born in Viareggio," I said.

"I'm from a small town near Napoli. You know Napoli, where they have the authentic Buffalo mozzarella?" he asked.

"The Buffalo in Napoli is better than here?" I half joked.

"The best," he said, making a strong hand gesture like I was crazy to suggest otherwise.

"Wow," I said, impressed.

"I don't have many friends in the area because I'm not from around here. Would you like to meet for coffee sometime?" he asked.

"I would like that. I don't have many friends here, either," I said.

I was touched. It was the first time an Italian ever invited me for coffee.

## Playground Brawl?

I'll never forget my very *first* encounter with a parent at the playground. It was summertime around dusk, and the playground was mostly empty. There was a boy around Charlie's age accompanied by what appeared to be his mother.

"Hello," the woman said in English, after our boys had interacted by the slide.

"Hi. You speak English?" I asked cheerfully.

"Yes. I was born in America and grew up in England. We are visiting from France," she said, speaking natively in English with a very strange accent.

"That's cool. I'm American too, but we live here. How do you like it here?" I asked.

"It's our first night in town. We came from southern Tuscany earlier today. From what I've seen so far, it's lovely," the woman said.

"It's beautiful around here. We live in paradise," I said proudly.

It was true. That evening, the sunset over the mountain range was extraordinary, like out of a painting. The woman arrived on the perfect night.

"How old is your son?" I asked.

"He just turned two. What about yours?" she asked.

"Twenty months."

Charlie sprinted over the crushed stone towards the big marble fountain, her boy closely following behind. As we trailed the boys, we exchanged stories about living in Europe. She seemed nice, and I like that her boy was practically the same age as Charlie.

"Do you happen to know a good swimming hole around here?" she asked.

"I sure do. The best one close by is literally outside the back of our garden," I said.

I wasn't lying. We have an excellent swimming spot that locals flock to on hot summer days. It's deep enough to jump off the rocks on the other side. I even dove in once from the upper rocks. The emerald green water is clean, and almost too good to be true. The river by our home is a real gem.

"Really? That's amazing. Where do you live?" she asked, her face perking up.

"Right down the road, in that direction," I said, pointing my arm towards Ponte a Serraglio.

"That's so cool. If the weather is hot tomorrow we'd love to check it out," she said.

"I swim there with this little guy. He loves it. These days, locals swim there, too," I said.

"Could we exchange numbers in case I want to go there tomorrow?" she asked.

"Sure. What's your name?" I asked.

"Anna."

"I'm Richard, pleased to meet you."

"Nice to see you too," Anna said.

"What's your number? I'll call you so you can have mine," I said.

By then, the boys had surrounded us. She gave me her number, and I typed it in as Charlie clutched my right leg with his left arm. Her boy was in front of her legs facing Charlie. It was a nice moment, one that was about to end because it was getting dark. Suddenly, out of nowhere, her boy wound up and punched Charlie right in the face!

What the fuck? Like, what the *actual fuck* just happened?

"We don't punch," she said to her son, kneeling down quickly.

I was absolutely stunned. I was angry too, but tried not to show it. Charlie took a step back confused, raising his hands to his mouth and scrunching his face. It affected him and probably hurt. Immediately, I crouched down to check on my son, not reacting other than to show him care. What I really wanted to do was punt her son across the park.

"Are you okay?" I asked, looking right at Charlie.

"That's not nice. We don't punch other boys," Anna said.

Twenty month old Charlie was fine, but definitely dazed and shaken. I instantly felt guilty for even engaging with Anna. Friendly conversation had turned into a fiasco. What was wrong with her kid?

"You're okay. You're tough, aren't you? You're a tough kid," I said, rubbing his arms up and down, and reassuring him.

"We don't hit other people," she said again.

Anna was repeating a version of this over and over. She was kind, but her boy was already a monster. Poor thing, too. Does he live in a household where he's seeing somebody hit someone else? I rubbed Charlie's arms even more, already realizing tomorrow's tentative swimming hole plans were off.

"Alright, it's getting dark. Time to go," I said encouragingly to Charlie.

"I'll send you a message later on WhatsApp about swimming tomorrow," Anna said.

"Sounds great," I lied as I picked up my boy.

"Have a nice evening. It was lovely meeting you Richard. Bye Charlie," Anna said.

"Have a great trip, Anna. Take care," I said, waving to her son but not calling him by his name.

"Bye," she said, as we walked off towards my mountain bike.

I waved too, but I never saw Anna again.

# Chapter 17 - At Bar Italia, You're Family

"Excited for your first cappuccino and croissant at your local bar in Italy?" I asked.

It was a rhetorical question. Of course Stephanie was excited.

"Umm, yeeeees. I've been waiting for this moment. Isn't this the dream?" Stephanie asked.

It was. We had created a dream scenario, but this time around, it didn't feel like it. It felt a bit more like work.

The following morning, we were back again at Bar Italia. This time, we ordered two cappuccinos each, and three pastries to share. Two days in Italy, and we had to try *all* the new goodies. When it came time to pay, I had sticker shock.

"Four cappuccinos and three sweet pastries comes to €8,50," the bartender said from behind the counter.

In what universe do seven gourmet items cost that little?

Eat your heart out suburban America. We were at Bar Italia, our new local joint one hundred meters from our new Italian home.

**Not Every Bar is Equal**

I had *no idea* Bar Italia would develop into what it is today: the closest thing I've *ever* felt to family in Italy. It shocks me even to write this, but it's true even if the employees see us no different than other patrons. Early on, it was just another place to eat and drink, but somewhere along the way, it turned into more. People talk about food establishments being family all the time, but I'd never had this happen before.

One time, on a short walk back into town from one of our only visits to the Bagni di Lucca post office, Stephanie and I were dying for coffee. We were still new to Italy, and stopped in the first bar we saw. *Big* mistake.

"Buongiorno," I said, pushing the glass door inward and holding it for Stephanie to enter first.

"Buongiorno," I thought I heard the lady behind the counter say half-heartedly.

We were the only ones inside. We ordered cappuccinos and croissants, but noticed the pastry selection was bleak. Was that normal? When the coffees were ready, the lady placed them on the counter, and shuffled towards the back where she sat down and hunched over her phone. I transferred the coffees to our table.

"Is it me, or do these cappuccinos taste like instant coffee?" I asked Stephanie.

We paid, left, and my heart sank immediately. Another fifty meters further down the road into town was another bar *filled* with people. It looked so good! I wanted to go there for coffee so bad. *Why* had we ducked into the first place we saw?

Never again, I vowed. Never again.

## Spotting Good Italian Bars

Just like *anything* else in life, selecting a good bar for morning coffee in Italy takes practice. But it ain't that hard, folks. Maps and review sites online help, but if you have any common sense at all, a map isn't necessary.

I've been to many bars in Lucca, but always gravitate back to my favorite. While visiting Arezzo, we walked down the main boulevard quite a ways, passing several bars before choosing a place to sit down. The bartender where we ended up, a man in his mid-thirties working the bar alone, brought the cappuccinos to our seats outside from around back of the bar. *Expect that* at good places in Italy. The afternoon we arrived to Montepulciano by bus, I designated the place we'd consider going the following morning. Sure enough, that's where we enjoyed coffee before catching the bus. The lady inside was considerate, and had a decent selection of pastries. While visiting Reggio Calabria, we ventured over to Bar Veneto 1976 after strolling through the main shopping thoroughfare. Excellent choice!

"Two cappuccinos, one pistachio croissant, and a chocolate one please," I told the young lady behind the counter.

She handed me the croissants on small saucers, and we sat down. When she arrived moments later with our coffee, she brought three cups! Stephanie's had 'Love' written in cursive on top in chocolate syrup, and mine had 'Amore'. She *also* brought a baby cappuccino comprised of steamed milk only for Charlie. You never saw a toddler gobble a drink up so fast! They never charged us for the baby-cino either. Talk about treating strangers like family.

In Torino, we drank 'bicerin', a typical drink made of espresso and chocolate, after a patron recommended we try it. Delicious. In Lecce in 2021, the bar providing breakfast per my guesthouse turned out to be the most popular in town. It smelled like heaven in there. I'd sit in the small seating area secretly observing the bartenders, bakers and patrons. The baristas were probably all lifers, banging portafilters on the coffee machines like a hammer, and producing new drinks seemingly every minute. Dozens of tables outside during mornings were full. Locals and tourists crowded the place. On my last day, the Carabinieri parked around the side, came in for a coffee, and were gone within minutes. Do Italians *actually* drink their coffee in one sip?

You learn as you go. In my Italian experience, women usually service bars better, but men overall make better drinks. When the pastry selection looks appetizing, that's a great sign. The better the selection of pastries, the better the coffee will most likely taste. But, after eleven in the morning, the pastry selection may disappear even in outstanding bars. Once during mid-afternoon, I entered a bar for a coffee in Genoa simply to use the bathroom. There were no pastries in sight, both baristas were seniors, and the coffee nonetheless was exceptional.

Fornoli, one town over from our home, has several local bars in the center. We always stop for coffee after doctor's appointments, and frequent the same place. The coffee is great, and the workers have always been very friendly with us. Recently, we entered for breakfast, and the smell was *so* familiar.

"Fresh croissants just came out of the oven," the man behind the counter said, signaling to the croissants still on the rack.

I glanced over. They looked divine.

"Two please," I said.

He brought everything over and set it on the table. The croissants were *covered* in glaze, which is not unusual in Italy. What *was* unusual was the consistency of the fresh baked dough.

"You know what? This tastes like Krispy Kreme," I said to Stephanie, after I swallowed the first bite.

Stephanie gasped. "Really?"

She hadn't tasted hers yet.

I nodded. "I *knew* the aroma smelled familiar when we walked in!"

This croissant sure tasted like a Krispy Kreme glazed donut. There was no other way to describe it. I've eaten plenty of warm croissants in Italy, but *nothing* super soft, fluffy and chewy like this. Had the owner done something most Italian bar owners *wouldn't dare*?

Weeks later, another strange thing happened at the same place. Stephanie and Charlie were in Fornoli one afternoon without me, and stopped in the same bar for a snack.

"What did you have at the bar in Fornoli?" I asked Stephanie later that evening.

"I had a glass of wine, and Charlie had a colorful cookie. The cookie selection was slim, though. Nothing like Bar Italia," she said.

"Really? How much was it?" I asked.

"€2,50 for the wine, and.. *€1,90* for the cookie," she said, reaching in her back pocket.

"Really?"

She handed the receipt to me.

"Yup. €3,90. That's expensive for a cookie around here," I said.

Cookies at Bar Italia are forty cents apiece.

## He Loves Her

Having our son in Italy has been one of the biggest blessings of our lives. But besides my wife and son, I don't have family here. Some days, I don't know *what* I'm doing in Italy. Luckily for us, our local bar has been steadfast. Other than Sofia at the comune, it's the *only* place I go where people sometimes ask how I'm doing. It's a little sad, not having family close by when you have a young child if I'm being honest.

In Bar Italia, it's always the same five or six ladies working, and has been since we moved here. During my very first visit, Stella was the first person to wait on me. Until recently, I didn't even *know* who the owner was.

"Ho ho ho. Is Santa coming to town soon?" Stella said to Charlie in Italian on a recent visit from behind the counter without missing a beat.

Charlie smiled and laughed. He *loves* her. Stella is his favorite because of how much love she shows him. She acknowledges him like he's one of her own, as if it's written in her job description.

Admittedly, at two years old, he may very well understand Italian better than English. Our bi-lingual strategy of cartoons *only* in Italian, and English spoken at home *only* seems to be working. Lately, he's been demonstrating that he definitely understands Italian without effort. As American parents, we are blown away, and I'm ever so slightly jealous if I'm being honest.

So now when we go into Bar Italia, we see it. My son recognizes the language every worker and Italian patron uses with him. You can see it in his eyes, and in his reaction to them. Whenever *anyone* acknowledges him *in Italian*, he's right there with them even more than I am. And Bar Italia is a very, *very* Italian place. When someone speaks to Charlie in English, he gets confused.

He and I were sharing a snack one summer afternoon when a couple from out of town entered. They were asking about restaurants in the area in English. Stella couldn't understand them, but it didn't matter. She pulled out the menu because she understood what they wanted: food. Instead of suggesting the restaurant next door, she showed them what's available in Bar Italia's kitchen.

"Lasagna. Tordelli Lucchesi. Pizza Margarita. Pizza Pepperoni," she explained, handing them the menu.

There were more than four items on the menu, but those were the only items available.

The man sighed. "Thank you. Do we order here, or will you take our order outside?" he asked in English.

"Okay," Stella said, smiling and fully extending her arm towards the doors outside.

I snickered as they retreated onto the front patio with the menu. Charlie and I were still binging on snacks when the couple re-entered about five minutes later.

"We would like one order of risotto, and," they began.

Stella cut them off.

"No. Lasagna. Tordelli Lucchesi. Pizza Margarita. Pizza Pepperoni," she said again, patiently pointing at the menu.

It was the identical statement as before. This time they understood. It was pretty funny to watch.

Around here, and in many parts of Italy outside the cities, choice is sometimes constrained. There's actually a restaurant next to Bar Italia, but we've never been, and it's often empty. We thought about going when we first arrived, but now I'm glad we didn't. The only place we *ever* patronize close by is Bar Italia. And there's never not people in Bar Italia, either. Locals convene whether travelers are there or not. Bar Italia's grip on this immediate area is strong.

One of the last times we were in there, Stella snuck up behind Charlie and gave him little kisses on his neck. He shrieked with joy, jumped out of his seat, and chased after her.

## Bar Italia *Is* Family

"You Amazon deliveries will be dropped off at Bar Italia," Annabella wrote in a WhatsApp message the day before we moved to Italy.

I'd seen Bar Italia on Google Maps, so I knew it was close to our new home. Annabella had just returned from speaking with a Bar Italia employee, and they agreed to accept delivery on our first Amazon packages. In Italy, Amazon deliveries *require* someone to be home, or they will not leave it. Amazon Italia doesn't leave packages outside *anyone's* door, or anyplace someone could steal it.

Fortuitously, Bar Italia came through in the clutch. Then once, during Christmastime in 2023 when my friend Giuseppe gifted Charlie a rideable electric toy Vespa, it arrived while we were in Berlin. So naturally, the large box was left at Bar Italia, but Giuseppe never told me what he sent.

"Buonasera. I'm here for a delivery," I said to the woman behind the counter, after returning from Berlin.

It was the owner, but I didn't know. She smiled and turned around, glancing behind her at a package that wasn't mine.

"Is this it?" she asked, handing it over to me.

The name wasn't mine.

"No, not mine," I said.

"Hmmmm," she said, taking the package back and opening the closet door.

"A Vespa? There's a Vespa here. Did you order a Vespa?" she asked.

I kept hearing her say the word 'Vespa' but it wasn't registering. Did Giuseppe buy *a Vespa?*

"There's a Vespa in a box here, look," the woman blurted out.

She crouched down, reached in the closest, and pulled out a big box that was sitting on the floor. The full scale decal on the side was of a child riding a cream colored toy Vespa. Jesus Christ Giuseppe! You bought Charlie a Vespa?

"Is this yours?" she asked, picking it up.

The woman set the large box on the high counter. I couldn't believe my eyes. It *actually* was a toy Vespa brand new in the box. Giuseppe had outdone himself.

I slide the box around to find the Amazon address sticker, and sure enough, Richard Lucchesi was written on it.

"It's mine. It's for me," I said stunned.

"You got a Vespa and didn't even know it," the owner cracked.

She was right. I slid it into my hands, thanked her twice, and walked out of the bar in disbelief, carrying a box I hadn't ordered. Once home, I set the box down, took a photo of it, and messaged Giuseppe.

'Holy shit dude! A Vespa?' I wrote on WhatsApp in utter disbelief before thanking him profusely.

I wonder how many Vespas had ever been delivered to Bar Italia?

## It Was Meant To Be

About a year later, when the Vespa's charging cord frayed, we ordered a new generic one on Amazon.

"I'm sorry. We are at the Christmas festival. Could you leave it at Bar Italia?" Stephanie asked the deliveryman over the telephone.

That evening when we returned, and Charlie went down for a nap, I popped over to Bar Italia to fetch it.

"Good evening. I think there's a delivery for me," I said to the owner.

I was speaking with the *same woman* who handed me the Vespa a year earlier.

"Good evening. What's the name?" the owner asked.

"Lucchesi," I said.

The owner gasped. "Lucchesi? I'm also Lucchesi!"

She wasn't the only one in shock. You mean, all this time I've been coming here, and *the owner is a Lucchesi too*?

Before I could say anything..

"Sandra! He's a Lucchesi! she shouted deliberately across the bar, and pointing at me.

Sandra looked bewildered. She didn't care. I was just the American guy with the cute baby.

"His surname, it's Lucchesi," she continued.

"I had no idea we're brothers," I said to the owner in Italian.

"Yep," she said.

She handed over the package, and I ordered a beer. When I went up to pay, it happened again.

"He's a Lucchesi," the owner said to Sandra *again* like she was discovering gold.

I *had* found my family in Italy. They'd been at Bar Italia *all along*.

## Chapter 18 - Ode to a Carpenter

I'll admit, my first impressions of Marco weren't great.

A carpentry door specialist suggested by Annabella, his very first trip to our home was simply to see what needed done. During that first visit, I requested him to replace a broken door handle, replace the lock to the garden gate that I didn't have a key to, and to add new fixed door handles to the front doors of our main apartment after the former owners had removed theirs.

"Everything will be finished next time I come back," he insisted.

But after the second visit concluded, none of the three tasks had been completed to my satisfaction.

Eventually, I'd come to love knowing Marco was on the job. He was polite, friendly, curious, and always asked how I was doing. His work ethic on site was always rock solid. And, I could call on him for anything. But initially, he didn't present himself as qualified. I simply had no idea how complicated carpentry in Italy could be.

I had a lot of learning to do.

**Carpentry Renovations Galore**

Shortly after moving to Italy, I moved quickly to make repairs around the house. Principally, there were door issues with every apartment I now owned. Doors were old, withered, rotten, and didn't shut right nor lock. Most needed to be replaced. I also had badly broken glass on my hands, cracked glass, doors that didn't latch, and broken door handles. So with Marco, I decided to start small.

After Marco's second visit, the new Cantina door handle still wasn't working. The new garden gate lock which Marco installed wasn't lined up, and didn't shut correctly after the first time I used it. So, until he came to fix it on his third visit, the garden was unlocked. Also, he installed brass fixed door handles on the front doors we didn't choose. At first I hated them, but they grew on me. Luckily, during his first visit, I remembered to ask him for his number before he left. My realtor, who tried to control the situation, was now out of the picture.

Since he needed to return a third time, I contacted him directly. The following is the *actual* WhatsApp transcript, translated from Italian, of our first message exchange:

3:10 PM - Richard: Hi Marco. I'm Richard the American from Ponte a Serraglio. How are you doing? When can you come and finish the work on our doors? Thanks
3:11 PM - Marco: Hi if you're there I'll come on Monday after 5 p.m.
3:15 PM - Richard: I hope you can fix this on Monday. At the moment it does not shut properly.
3:15 PM - Marco: I'll get it working on Monday.
3:16 PM - Richard: Great. Also, the front door handles are fine. No need to replace them. Just the gate and the basement door handle.
3:17 PM - Richard: See you on Monday. Thank you.
3:17 PM - Marco: Ok perfect...see you on Monday

But four days later, Monday came and went with no sign of Marco. I was disappointed, but chalked it up to an oversight and figured he'd contact me soon. Three more days went by, and nothing. So on Thursday, I reached out to Marco.

2:23 PM - Richard: Good morning Marco. We missed you Monday after 5 pm. When will you come to fix our locks and finish the job? Thank you.

He never replied. I messaged him again the next day to follow up.

8:16 PM - Richard: Hi. Did you get my message yesterday?
8:19 PM - Marco: Hi yes sorry I didn't get back to you...if it's ok with you I can come by Wednesday morning at 11

But this time, I never replied, and Marco never showed up on Wednesday either. However, this time it was *my* fault, because he was asking if 'Wednesday morning at 11' was okay. He was expecting a confirmation. But at the time I didn't know that, so when Wednesday came, I was incensed.

3:49 PM - Richard: Marco! Where have you been today? I took a day off today and stayed home for our appointment.

But Marco never replied.

## My Neighbors Love Marco

Weeks went by, with neither of us messaging the other. The garden was still unlocked, and that was unacceptable. I'd decided that I needed a different carpenter, but who? And furthermore, I hadn't paid Marco for *anything* yet, including the brand new fixed brass front door handles he *already* installed. He hadn't even contacted me about paying him for those, either.

As Christmas approached, I contacted my realtor once more to explain the situation, and to request she help me recruit a new carpenter. She responded that she'd find me a new door repair man.

"That sounds wonderful," I replied.

Then, during the early afternoon hours of New Years Eve, I received a message from my realtor.

"The man is coming later this afternoon to work on your doors," she wrote.

The man? What man? The new guy was coming? She didn't say, and I didn't ask. I thanked her, satisfied that someone, *anyone* was coming.

Around five in the afternoon, we received a knock at the door. I answered, and a man holding some tools said he was here to fix the doors. I breathed a sigh of relief. I let him in, and he got to work.

He fixed the Cantina door handle quickly, and while carrying his tool bag across the garden to the gate, I stopped him.

"I'm sorry. What's your name?" I asked.

"Marco," he replied with a grin.

"Ah! Okay, thank you," I said, feeling slightly embarrassed.

The first time Marco came to the house over two months ago, was a quick visit during the evening. Marco's second visit when he *actually* worked on the doors occurred when I wasn't home. Stephanie had let him in. Besides, I really thought my realtor was sending someone else, because *she said she would*.

At the gate, Marco pulled out an angle grinder from his tool bag, and started grinding the deadbolt that was too large for the latch. Sparks flew, and I took a step back. It was loud.

He'd grind, then stop, take a look, and grind some more. In between grinding the deadbolt, the neighbor above started screaming out her window. Her shouting was louder than the grinding. Although I couldn't understand her, Marco and I could *both* hear her. He and I locked eyes, he paused, and neither of us moved a muscle. It felt surreal. I didn't say a word, but once she quieted down, I smiled, pointed at the latch, and nodded my head, so he kept working.

He finished the gate, and it worked! We could finally lock the garden again.

I didn't know it at the time, but he and I were at the very beginning of a mutual partnership that would bring Marco back to my property for carpentry work dozens of times. I thanked him, paid him in full, and we wished each other Happy New Year.

114

Here's something shocking you may not know: When you buy a home in Italy, if it's anywhere outside a city, don't *ever* expect to turn around and resell it. You may be able to sell it quickly, but don't count on it. My neighbor's very nice three bedroom home right next door to our house has been for sale since we moved in. It's a fine home, I've been in there, so why is it not selling? You tell me. I see homes like this all over Italy.

Take the simple case of my Italian friend Fabiano. I've known Fabiano since 2002. Last summer, Fabiano brought his family to stay with us for a few days. We explored his old stomping grounds here in Tuscany during the daytime, and drank red wine during quiet evenings in the garden.

"What about your mom's house in Garfagnana. Did you sell it?" I asked, while sipping my wine.

"It will be for sale forever," Fabiano joked back.

"That sucks. I'm so sorry," I replied sincerely.

"In Italy, these things take time. It was originally for sale for €149,000. After some years, we lowered the price to €129,000. We waited and waited, and nothing. Then, we lowered the price again to €99,000. Then again to €89,000. It's been over ten years. I think we must lower the price again if we wish to sell it," he said despondently.

Then, a few months ago, Fabiano contacted me with good news. They had sold the house!

"It only took fourteen years!" Fabio quipped over text.

## 4.5 Month Renovation

In my Cantina, we installed a brand new kitchen where none existed before. I also hired a company to sandblast the arched brick ceiling, the dirtiest job ever. A new custom wood door was hung that connected the Cantina to an external stairwell, and a second custom door connecting the stairwell to the street was also installed replacing an old door with a skeleton key about a foot long. And, all new electricity was run through a nearly meter thick wall to install lighting into the basement stairwell with a timer switch in between the two new doors.

The Cantina walls and floor were completely painted, and a beautiful mural of the Tuscan countryside adorns two of the walls thanks to my wife. All new lights were purchased and connected replacing the old industrial lighting, and new furniture was purchased. Plus, we fully renovated a bathroom with new tile, toilet, bidet, shower, vanity, and washing machine. For each of these jobs, I had to hire masons, plumbers, electricians and carpenters all separately. Astonishingly, all of it was completed in about four and half months, a true miracle in Italy.

## The Cantina Kitchen

The evening *before* Stephanie was admitted to the hospital to be induced to give birth, she and I spent several hours in IKEA Pisa with a specialist deciphering all the details of the new kitchen we wanted in the Cantina. What a trooper!

Many options for a new Italian kitchen exist, but my thinking was simple. I was new to Italy, and I didn't know *anything*. I wanted something done quickly, and didn't wish to spend a ton of money. If I overspent and wasn't satisfied, I'd be sick about it. Also, this new kitchen was for my second apartment, so top of the line wasn't the main priority. We already had a nice kitchen in the apartment that we lived in. Although there was running water, plumbing and electric, we were not replacing an old kitchen.

That evening at IKEA, we purchased cabinets and handles, a countertop, countertop molding, open-air shelves and brackets for wall mounting, a large, stainless steal sink, a basic faucet, a small refrigerator, a skinny dishwasher, an oven, an oven vent, and an induction stovetop. Every single item except the dishwasher was the *least expensive item* in its class. The dishwasher was the second least expensive. An employee designed it all while we chose the items, and we paid for everything upfront including delivery. Total price was just over three thousand euros, and I paid the total cost with my American credit card. I did not opt for IKEA's installation at the time, but later changed my mind.

On delivery day in December, two men began unloading everything, requesting to leave large boxes for the new kitchen inside my main apartment upstairs.

"The new kitchen will be installed downstairs. Can you please bring these big boxes downstairs?" I asked the main delivery man in Italian.

"No! Ground floor," he snorted.

He pulled the delivery invoice out of his pocket to show me.

"Downstairs *is* the ground floor," I explained.

Except I was wrong. Our Cantina opens to the garden on the ground, but cantinas are considered 'minus one' in Italy. Our main apartment upstairs opens to the street and *that's* the ground floor. While with the IKEA salesmen, when he asked, I thought they were both the ground floor. I had never heard the term minus one before the day IKEA delivered.

"Right here, it says *ground* floor," he shouted, pointing at the invoice.

Why was he shouting?

"Downstairs please. You cannot leave these here," I instructed.

"You fucking fuck off," the delivery man blurted out in English.

The two men began picking up boxes, and vacated my home as fast at they could. Not a good experience at all.

Later that day, I spoke with a very kind and informative IKEA representative in Milan who spoke English. I was able to get all my questions answered in detail, including what happened with the rude delivery men. It was during this call that I *also* opted for full installation, paying an extra three hundred-fifty euro over the phone by credit card. In the end, different delivery men arrived three days after Christmas with everything. They told me they were from Romania. With the exception of connecting the electric and plumbing, they set up everything in a matter of hours. When finished, the new kitchen looked divine.

## Trying To Find a Plumber

There's a general plumbing store in the main piazza of the neighboring town of Chifenti. I asked the owner if he knew any plumbers. He didn't understand what I was asking for at first, but once he did, seemed intrigued. He pulled out a sheet of paper, ripped it in half down the middle, and wrote down the names and contact numbers of two men. Once I was home, I called both numbers. The first guy said he wasn't available, and the second didn't answer. It was a challenge doing it all in Italian.

Unresolved, days later, I returned to the plumbing center to ask for more help. The owner called the second guy while I stood there, and in just a few minutes the man showed up.

"I'm retired," he said.

He must have been living that la dolce vita. Good for him.

Turns out even though he's retired, he's still working too. After a few more phone calls *and* speaking with his wife, he agreed to visit the following week. I met him at Bar Italia, we walked over to the house, and I took him downstairs to the Cantina.

"The idea here is the ancient mixed with the modern," I told him in Italian, using my hands and standing in front of the old toilet.

His smile said everything. He liked it a lot, I could tell.

"Call me after you install the kitchen, and I will connect the plumbing," he said.

That's when I realized I was *way* ahead of myself. He told me I'd need a separate plumber, electrician and carpenter to install the kitchen, because that's how things worked in Italy. I never hired him, choosing instead to go with the plumber my realtor knew. But when the realtor's plumber connected the brand new drain pipe below the sink in the new kitchen, it leaked. Water dripped into the new cabinet for weeks, and took two additional visits before he fixed it properly.

## Ghosted by Door Guys

"There's a man just outside of town that build customs doors," Annabella said.

"Sounds great, thank you," I said.

I drove to his store twice during business hours. The first time nobody was there. The second time, I spoke with a worker who I didn't know was the owner. He took down my number and said he'd call.

A week went by without a call. The following week, I called, and then texted him. Weeks later, on a Tuesday around one in the afternoon, he called back.

"I can be there in thirty minutes for the estimate. Will you be home?" he asked me.

"Yes."

I dropped everything. I wanted new doors desperately, and had no other leads. He arrived, and we walked through my second and third apartments together. While standing in the Cantina, he caught me by surprise.

"You know, I was in here before when I was a child," he said in Italian.

"Really?" I asked.

"Yes. See those rings attached to the walls, and that old pulley on the ceiling? This used to be the town butcher shop," he stated.

That's funny. Did my realtor know that too?

"That's interesting, I didn't know that," I said, trying not to seem shocked.

"I have a friend who could sandblast this ceiling for you," he said, pointing up.

I hadn't even *thought* about sandblasting the ceiling before. But after that, I couldn't *stop* thinking about it.

"Could I have his number please?" I asked, reaching for my phone.

He gave it to me on the spot, and we continued to Space 3. He took notes, writing meticulously on a note pad.

"I will send you an estimate on Thursday," he assured me after a thorough walk through.

Thursday came and went, and nothing. I called him on Friday, and again he promised to send it. On Monday, I texted him politely about the estimate one more time, but he never responded.

I sat down one evening, and reached out to seven local door installation companies. A total of one of them responded to me, and even *they* stopped responding after the second message. So, over the course of the following two years, I'd hire Marco to custom build and install everything out of wood. First, it was two brand new wood doors for the Cantina, and later three more doors for Space 3. Every single doorway was a custom size, so *everything* was built from scratch. He'd design the door, frame the door, cut custom molding, and seal everything after the door was hung. He'd remove and dispose of all the old, heavy doors too. Everything was included in the price, including my choice of door handles and hinges. He was a one stop shop.

He also designed and installed several brand new windows, *and* a total of seven beautiful window screens of varying sizes. I even hired him to design and custom build an entire screened-in patio, which is so nice in warm weather! The nice thing about having Marco as my local carpenter in Tuscany is that he'll drop by if something isn't working on his way to or from other jobs. Routine maintenance is part of what I've hired him to do. He and I have a handshake agreement. There's never a contract.

## A New Bathroom in Two Months?

With a fully functioning kitchen, and Marco on the door jobs, I set my sights on renovating the Cantina's bathroom.

One afternoon, I reached out to five companies in the bathroom tile and equipment business. Incredibly, within two days, all five companies responded! There was only one problem: none of the bathroom supply companies provided professional bathroom installation.

On the day of my appointment with Enrico, a bathroom supply salesman, he gave me good news: he knew a guy named Giacomo who installed bathrooms. He told me that Giacomo didn't work for his company. I'd have to hire him separately, and pay him separately. But since he was being recommended by his company, Enrico *assured* me I'd have no problems at all. I should have known better.

"The project *has* to be completed by early April," I said.

"We have two months. No problem at all," Enrico said.

I sighed. "Okay. How can I contact Giacomo?"

"He will call you," Enrico assured me.

Thankfully, Giacomo called a few days later. When I met him in front of Bar Italia, he emerged from a large white van to shake my hand.

"Giacomo, piacere," he said.

His hand had a very rough texture, and the clothes he wore were dirty. He shook my hand like a man who meant business, a trait I always appreciate. He then drove up the street to find proper parking, and I met him outside the Cantina's street entrance.

Once inside the Cantina, I walked him right over to the bathroom area.

"New shower here. Toilet, bidet and new washing machine all along *that* wall," I told him clearly, pointing at the cobblestone wall.

He nodded, and seemed to like what I was saying.

"No problem, no problem at all," he said in Italian.

It *did* turn out to be problem though.

## The Arched Brick Ceiling

Before starting the bathroom, Giacomo also provided an estimate for sandblasting the dirty brick ceiling. Before telling Giacomo yes to the sandblast job, I contacted the man that the door guy gave me. The new man was overly considerate. When we met in the piazza in front of Bar Italia, he was accompanied by a young woman.

"I am his English translator," the heavy set girl said in American English.

"Wow, your English is really good," I said.

"My mother is from Arizona," she said.

They followed me down into the Cantina. The contractor grew up in Albania, and was soft spoken. He carefully assessed the ceiling, and the two of them discussed in Italian.

"Approximately how much to do it?" I asked.

"Twenty eight hundred euro," he said, after a long pause.

"How long will it take?" I wanted to know.

"Three days," he said in Italian to the translator.

When he confirmed his team could start the Wednesday of the last week of February, the week *before* Giacomo was starting the bathroom renovation, I hired him on the spot.

It was cold and raining the day sandblasting started. Four workers showed up all wearing dark blue jumpsuit uniforms with Lucca Construction written on the back. Within the first minutes of seeing them, I felt *so* satisfied they were doing the sandblasting. They were professional and courteous throughout, covering and taping up every bit of the new kitchen with plastic. Every item inside was brought outside, placed under the patio, and covered. Doors and windows were removed too, but not far enough away from the doorway. The soot from the ceiling debris poured out of the Cantina's openings and covered the wood, leaving a dull, dark permanent stain. My doors and windows would need to be heavily sanded to retain their luster.

After three days of intense labor, Lucca Construction was finished. The brick ceiling above had transformed from dark grey and black in color, to shades of bright orange. It was a spectacular sight. A final worker who lived across the street helped sweep up most of the heavy excess, but the cement flooring would require more attention before the remaining dust on the floor was cleared out.

## Starting From Square One

Three days later on Monday morning, Giacomo arrived early with two workers. He noticed the new ceiling, but didn't say a word.

"Where do you want the wall constructed?" Giacomo asked, standing in front of the old bathroom.

"About right here," I said with my hand.

I had the design printout from Enrico in my other hand. Giacomo's men were building three new walls, two of which were to be put up directly in front of existing concrete walls. We had already discussed that and everything else during Giacomo's first visit when he confirmed the design I wanted. Unfortunately, Giacomo had forgotten everything we discussed.

"You cannot put a toilet and a bidet that close together next to the washer," Giacomo insisted.

"But Giacomo, we *already* discussed it," I said, showing him the architectural design printout.

He looked at the printout briefly, then walked over and pretended to sit down on an invisible toilet, demonstrating limited leg room.

"You see? It's impossible. Too close together," he said, while his workers quietly looked on.

In the end, I never did get the design I wanted all along for the Cantina's new bathroom. It didn't matter that Enrico had drawn up the *exact same design* Giacomo and I agreed to with precise dimensions. Also, this was out of Enrico's hands. I'd soon learn that, although he'd make a preliminary design, Enrico *only* sold supplies.

"I'm sure it'll *still* be a very nice bathroom when completed," Enrico texted me after I told him what Giacomo was doing.

## Not What I Asked For

Giacomo was a hard worker. He was, however, not without his faults. Once, he tossed a huge piece of bathroom tile clear across the room when his cut didn't exactly fit the uneven wall. Also, unlike my experience with Lucca Construction, Giacomo conducted more than ninety percent of his communication with me via voice messages on WhatsApp. At first I didn't mind. But because his native language was Romanian, I couldn't always understand his Italian.

As the bathroom took shape, it was turning out quite nice. Stephanie had picked out a dark colored tile that looked lovely against the bare cobblestone wall we were leaving exposed. A month earlier, while standing in front of a pure porcelain sink in the bathroom supply store showroom, I was *sure* to ask Enrico the exact material of the vanity's counter.

"Will the bathroom vanity's counter be made of Porcelain?" I asked, tapping a porcelain sink basin.

"Yes. Porcelain," Enrico said.

Except my new vanity *wasn't* porcelain. It was a solid surface countertop most likely made of vinyl. Enrico ordered the wrong internal toilet parts to be delivered too, and that pushed the timeline to finish the bathroom back an additional two weeks.

Giacomo brought his electrician in one day to run wires for switches and lights, and another day invited a plumber. In both cases, these guys were freelance workers. When the plumber, a man from Morocco, set up the shower kit, he did it with such precision I was floored. I asked for the new plumber's number, and have hired him for various small jobs ever since.

Unfortunately, Giacomo was less trustworthy. He found light fixtures on the floor by the front door for the stairwell outside, and *automatically assumed* they were for the bathroom. These were heavy, industrial outdoor fixtures. If I wasn't stopping in regularly to check progress, those would have been fastened to the new bathroom walls in whatever spot Giacomo saw fit.

Often, far too much assumption happens in Italy. Once, I drove to Lucca to purchase high quality paint for the Cantina's floor after deciding not to tile it due to cost. This paint store was massive, the largest outside the ancient Lucca walls. Several workers were helping customers, but one employee in particular really wanted to take care of me. This older gentleman was *sure* he knew what I wanted before asking, too.

"What's the paint for? he asked.

"My Cantina floor. It's made of cement," I said.

"What color are you thinking?" the employee asked.

"This one," I said, pointing to a brown swatch after sending a photo of it to Steph.

Other than that, he asked nothing, spending the next twenty minutes banging away on the computer keyboard while I stood there quietly. He returned from the printer, and came back with a sheet of paper.

I was stunned. "€1400?!! What is *all this* for?"

"This €350 is for two coats of primer before applying the paint. This other charge is for sealing the paint after it dries," he explained.

"But I never asked for primer or sealer." I said.

He crumpled up the paper as if *I had done something wrong*. I walked out of that store with less than €200 of paint, and that was enough to complete the floor.

Giacomo adopted this *exact same approach*, making choices about light switches, molding and light fixtures without consulting me first. Being overly nice in the beginning meant not getting the design he and I agreed to. In the final days of bathroom renovations, I had to watch him like a hawk, and couldn't wait for him to get out of my house.

When it came time for Giacomo to hang the sliding door I purchased from Enrico to the new bathroom, he refused.

"It's not in the contract," he said.

But door installation *was* in the contract. Plus, he had already built the wall for a slider, and *knew* I had a slider door. I contacted Enrico, who rectified the situation immediately, and Giacomo spent two days farting around with the slider. The door never worked right, and Marco helped fix it in less than thirty minutes.

## Finished?

The day before my mother's arrival to Italy to visit her new grandson, the correct internal toilet parts were delivered. If I hadn't pushed the plumber that evening to come at eight in the morning the following day for installation, the toilet would not have functioned for my mother. The bathroom renovation concluded only hours before mom touched down in Firenze's airport.

When we have visitors, they are always impressed with the Cantina's brand new bathroom. We've faced some issues too. Water is trapped somewhere causing mold. The vanity's top drawer scrapes the rubbery, non-porcelain countertop every time I open and shut it. The washer slides clear across the floor regardless of which spin cycle I use. There's a tiny leak in the bottom of the bidet I think. And, the toilet slowly drips from the tank into the bowl. I've asked my new plumber about the toilet. He says it's unfortunately normal, and that I should turn off the water to the toilet whenever we travel.

So I do.

# Chapter 20 - The Garden Chronicles

Everyone deserves to feel safe in their own home. Despite all of the problems I've had, any provocation was passive. That is, until I was bit by a dog in my own garden. It was a horrible experience.

The afternoon I was wounded, my family was preparing to leave at six in the morning for a road trip to Germany. I was cleaning the car for the trip, and came walking through the garden from the gate at the far end, crossing past three fairly large dogs that were out there with their owner. The man was speaking on the telephone.

I was in the Cantina for just a few minutes gathering paper towel and cleaner to bring back to the car on the street. I exited the Cantina with my supplies, started walking back towards the gate, and two of the dogs came sprinting at me. This is somewhat normal dog behavior when owners don't fully control their dogs, so to counter their action, I put my right hand out with my palm facing inward so the dogs could sniff it like I've done countless times before. Almost instantly, the white dog chomped down hard on my achilles, sinking all four pointed fangs into my flesh.

"Ahhhhhhhhh," I cried out.

All the neighbors must have heard me.

"Hey, hey, hey, come here," the man could be heard saying to his dogs in Italian.

But it was already too late. The dog got me good, right around the back of my ankle. I crumpled on the spot. I then hopped out of harm's way, and managed to shuffle to the side onto the cement path by the building.

"What the fuck dude! Your dog just bit me!" I screamed in English.

The man was still clutching his phone while he tried to corral his dogs back into the building. As he did so, he put the phone back up to his ear.

"C'mon, look at this! Dude.. dude... that's not okay. That's not okay!" I shouted.

I was bleeding, and the bite needed attention immediately. I stood up, and rushed up the stairs into our main house as quickly as I could. Stephanie, who heard everything, was waiting for me. She was frantic.

"Oh my God, what happened? Are you okay?" she asked.

We took a closer look together. Four spots were visible where the dog's canines had broken the skin. Two spots were deep enough to cause bleeding. Blood was on both sides of my ankle. The whole area was already swollen.

It was traumatic. Nobody ever expects something like this to happen, but in my *own garden*?

That evening during dinner in the Cantina, the man brought his dogs back into the garden. Our windows were almost fully closed, so we didn't see him. Normally he and his dogs are quiet while outside, but this time he must have somehow provoked his dog, because one dog barked loudly right outside our window. That never happens. It was uncalled for.

The following morning, we were on our way to Germany for Oktoberfest, hoping to leave the nightmare that was unfolding in our once peaceful garden in the past.

**New Neighbors?**

Around Christmas time the previous year, in 2023, a new neighbor showed up with two dogs. I had never seen him before. He and the dogs were in the garden everyday, several times a day starting around Christmas Eve. I wasn't sure if he was renting temporarily from someone, or if he had just bought the place.

Most importantly for me, was the new neighbor the type of guy that picked up the dog poop after his dogs?

He was not.

One morning I saw a woman with him. They were smoking cigarettes. She flicked her cigarette butt into the garden, and he let his dogs shit everywhere without picking it up.

By nature, humans are finicky creatures. In Italy, if you wish for someone to change their behavior, you must first speak with them in person. But sometimes, neighbors take it to a whole new level. Some people will do the exact opposite of whatever a neighbor hopes or wishes for simply to irritate them. It's sad, but it's true. This fact is universal.

I didn't wish to confront the dog owner about the dog shit mainly because I thought he'd be leaving soon. And I was right, he did leave, but not before committing a mistake he probably wished he hadn't. Little did I know that, after the dog attack, this man would double down, bringing the same three dogs, including the one that bit me, into the garden so much more than ever before.

**An Unexpected Birthday Present**

A few days after Christmas, while enjoying a quiet evening in for my birthday, a surprise notification popped up. Someone was in the garden. I open the app, and watched a man walk right onto the patio in front of the Cantina window. Then, he began peeing.

He had the classic male posture, jutting his pelvis forward to urinate, and arching his back. And then, he immediately left. What a wonderful birthday present.

Our shared garden is not large. It's also *not* a bathroom. I was boiling with rage. And I was having a such a nice, peaceful birthday too.

This needed to be dealt with right away if I didn't want it to happen again. I paused the video while he peed, and screen captured it. I pulled the printer down from the top shelf, and printed the screen capture in black and white. You couldn't see his face, so it wasn't incriminating. Then, I composed a short note in Italian, and hand wrote it onto the print out:

*Peeing in the garden is not permitted.*
*My son plays in this garden.*
*Please do not be rude and disrespectful to the neighbors.*

There are ten units total in our building, and I own three. All the units had permanent residents except for the dog owner's apartment, and two of ours. Out of the ten units, our main apartment is the only one with a private entrance from the street. The other nine units, including two of ours, all share the same entrance into the building. However, we don't use that entrance often because we can reach the Cantina and Space 3 from our back door into the garden. After living in Italy two years, I can't stress enough how nice the private entrance is.

Because I own two units that are accessed by the shared entrance, I have a key to that door. Later that evening, I walked over with my note and let myself in through the shared front door. I taped the note up high so it wouldn't be easily removable, shut the shared door behind me, and made sure it latched.

The next day, and for months after that, there was no sign of the culprit. But a bigger problem was just beginning.

## Chopping Down the Tree

In June 2024, after a few months during the spring in America, we arrived back to a fully overgrown garden. The grass was close to a meter high in some areas, and trash was all over too. Not a single neighbor had done anything back there. So, I purchased a high-quality weed whacker, and trimmed down the grass. Once finished, the garden was now usable to play and kick a soccer ball with my son.

In the fall, someone knocked the Cantina garden door. That was a first. Nobody has access to the Cantina from the garden except neighbors living in the building. It was Patricia.

"I want to have this big tree trimmed," she said. "It's dangerous."

She was right, it *was* dangerous. Stephanie and I also determined months ago that the tree was sick. But it was humungous, at least four stories high, and I wasn't about to rally the troops to remove it. So, I was pleased to chat with Patricia about this.

Patricia went on to explain that the heavy storm over the weekend caused the tree to sway dangerously, slamming into the building. The rain was so bad that the gutters on the roof overflowed, causing damage too. She was advocating for branches to be trimmed, which meant all the neighbors would have to agree to do it, *and* agree to pay for it.

"I spoke with the tree company. They've agree to chop off the big branches, and trim the top for five hundred euro. So, between you, me, and the other three residents, it would cost one hundred each. How does that sound to you?" Patricia asked.

"That's fine, but how much to cut the whole thing down?" I asked.

"I can ask him. This thing is dangerous," she reiterated.

She must have said it was dangerous more than ten times.

The following morning, Patricia knocked on the door again.

"Six hundred euro to cut the entire tree down," she said confidently.

I nodded with a smile.

"Each of us will only have to pay one hundred twenty euro," she continued.

"Perfetto," I responded.

"I'll let you know when he's coming," she said.

"Okay. Thank you very much, Patricia," I said.

## Stumps are Exciting?

We were overjoyed on the day the arborists came to chop down the tree. Stephanie went on a lunch date, so Charlie and I watched the operation from out the back door window. When the chopping concluded, a large mound of semi-rotten stumps sat in the middle of the garden up against the rock wall.

Little did I know the action in the garden was just heating up.

From the day the tree was down, things escalated quickly. Neighbors we hardly ever saw from outside our building started showing up on their back porches to get a glimpse. It was as if nobody had ever seen a tree cut down in the neighborhood before. And two days later, the dog owner showed up. This time, he had three dogs.

On the dog neighbor's very first day back, his three dogs took three big poops in three different places. It was utterly repulsive. But, unlike during the prior holidays when the grass was overgrown, this was no longer the case. I don't know what he was thinking, but clearly he wasn't. If he thought his visit to his apartment in Bagni di Lucca meant not cleaning up excrement after *all his animals* in the shared garden, he was sorely mistaken.

I couldn't have my child stepping in dog shit, and moved to correct the situation immediately. I grabbed three sections of paper towel, picked up three large chunks of poop, and set the paper towel clumps by the building's shared entrance to the garden. Then, I returned into the Cantina, and composed this message in Italian to be hung on the inside of the building's garden door:

*Pick up after your three dogs!!!*
*My son plays in the garden.*
*If your dog poops in the garden, clean it up immediately.*
*Poop left in the garden is rude. Don't be disrespectful to the*
*neighbors who share the garden.*

The next morning, I walked by the shared garden entrance, and the clumps of paper towel poop had disappeared.

## A One Sided Conversation

Once the tree was down, it was like a veil had been lifted. You could feel it in the air. The garden was so much more lighter and brighter than before! Our terrace dried off more quickly after rain storms, and portions of turf down below were experiencing sunshine for the first time in maybe decades. The garden had new life; it was a happier place than before.

On warm, dry mornings, we'd take Charlie down to play while we enjoyed our morning coffee. We'd sweep the concrete patio, pick up the small bits of trash thrown out the windows, and let Charlie 'help' us. He'd kick the soccer ball around and play with hand trowels. We'd smile and laugh together, experiencing short-lived bouts of joy.

For the briefest of moments, everything seemed right with the world. I should have known it would be brief.

A few days after posting the poop note, the three of us were in the garden when the dog owner joined us without his dogs. His stature was tall and imposing. I was in the bathroom when he appeared. I saw him out the window, and without preparing myself, I went out to say hello.

We exchanged hellos and spoke exclusively in Italian, putting me at a disadvantage. I was my kind, usual curious self, but I should have had my guard up. He told me that upstairs was his grandmother's apartment since 1973. He also said that he had a place near Lucca and Pisa with dogs, cats, a pony, and other animals. But once the small talk evaporated, he got serious.

"I don't like these cameras," he stated fervently.

He continued, and I listened.

"Nothing goes on back here. There is no need for this. I don't like it," he kept on saying, and pointing.

133

My Italian is not good enough to put up a fight and sound intelligent if I must verbally defend myself, so I don't even try.

He continued. "You need everyone's permission to have them. You don't have authorization."

It was a one-sided conversation

"You have to share the garden. This is not just yours. Everyone gets to share this garden. You do not have authorization for these cameras," he muttered.

I finally jumped in.

"Listen. I found broken glass, beer bottles and broken glass here and here" I said, pointing to the patio area in front of Space 3.

"Tell me in English," he said.

"I never wanted the cameras either. However, I kept finding broken glass in a plastic bag *right here*. Over and over and over I found it. After four times, I realized someone that lives here was probably doing it. So, I put up the cameras. And guess what? It stopped," I said in English, pointing to inside our building.

I could sense he *really* didn't care. Was he even listening?

"But you do not have authorization. You cannot just put up cameras. You *need* authorization," he repeated.

"I'm happy to have a meeting with everyone in person, and speak about this more. Until then, I'm not taking them down," I replied.

He was cordial, and ended the conversation repeating what he had already said. I nodded. Then, we said goodbye to each other, and he reentered the building.

The following day, his dog bit me.

**I Know You're In There..**

Once back from Germany, we didn't see the dog owner. He must have returned to his primary residence. But then, things got strange quickly.

Around ten-thirty at night on a random Wednesday about a week later, someone appeared *out of nowhere* in the dead of night right outside the Cantina window in the garden. My son was in his indoor swing suspended from our vaulted brick ceiling, and I was pushing him. The music was playing, and we were having a lovely family moment. Just as we were about to sit down for dinner, loud shouting could be heard right outside the window. Nobody is *ever* out there at ten-thirty at night. It scared my wife and I.

It was the dog owner. He had brought his dogs to his grandmother's house, and let them into the garden late. He had never done this before. His voice shrieked, and was intentionally intending to be intrusive. From the lights in our window, he could see we were preparing dinner. He could also tell that we didn't see him. If he didn't scream at his dogs, and his dogs don't bark, we would have never known he was out there.

After that, he commenced trying much harder to get my attention. One morning, he knocked on the Cantina window on two separate occasions. I didn't answer either time. About thirty minutes later, I went up to chat with Stephanie, but he must have been watching me go upstairs from his balcony. Not five minutes after arriving upstairs, there was a knock at our front door. It was him again. He was outside the door talking with someone. We didn't answer. He knocked a second time, and eventually went away.

The next day around lunchtime, he knocked again. I wasn't around but the Cantina window was left open. When he realized I wasn't home, he peered straight into the Cantina through the screen. He walked away towards the garden entrance, and four minutes later reappeared. He approached the Cantina, walked straight up to the door, and stared inside cupping his hand to the window over his brow without knocking. I only know this because of my security camera covering the Cantina entrance. Then the following Saturday, he brought his dogs into the garden, and knocked again.

"I know you're in there. I want to talk to you," I could hear him say loudly.

Forgive me, but it's *very* poor judgement to think I'd ever speak with him while his dogs that attacked me were at the foot of my door. I never did answer, and eventually he ceased trying. We still see him in the garden with his dogs on occasion, but the weather is colder now, and his primary residence was too far away to visit frequently. I guess the excitement from chopping the tree down had worn off.

# Chapter 21 - Dealing with the Bully Next Door

After about six months in Italy, in February, I noticed a wet plastic bag in the bushes while entering Space 3. It had been discarded. It was raining, and the bag was soaked. At first glance, it could have been a plastic grocery bag that blew in. I paid it no mind as I squeezed my way into Space 3's broken glass door that had yet to be replaced.

Next to Space 3's entrance is a shared cast iron gate with flat bars not more than three inches wide. The gate is old and stays locked. All the neighbors have a key. I haven't seen anyone use it but me.

On the other side of the gate is an old stone staircase leading up to the street, and down to the river. What should be a magical little path to the emerald green Lima river below instead collects trash like you wouldn't believe. Besides weeds, the flat-stoned stairs are covered in empty beer cans, polymer snack bags, discarded cigarette packs, and anything else people throw away. Among other things, I've found clothing, banana peels, whole lemons, grocery store advertisements, and wet stuffed animals. Bits of paper and broken glass are embedded in the cracks between the stone stairs. It's a disappointing sight, and dangerous to walk on. I've swept it a few times, but it's mostly effort wasted.

I exited Space 3 and walked over to the bag. It was underneath some branches. Inside were five beer bottles of different brands and sizes. One was broken. A shard tore the bag. How did *this* get here? Did someone chuck this through the gate?

Stale beer stench was unlocked as I tenderly lifted the bag from the mud. Liquid poured out. It was gross. There must have been beer left in bottles. I carried the bag upstairs, distributed the glass into our square green glass recycle bin, and separated the bag into the plastic recyclables.

## Who The Hell?

About every three months or so, I'd find another plastic bag in the garden in about the same spot. Each time, there was more than one size bottle and brand of beer. And, every time, at least one of the bottles was broken. La dolce vita must be a big fan of beer *and* smashing bottles. Who knew?

The second time it happened, I felt the muscles in my neck clench at the mere sight of it. The third time, other than doubled plastic bags, everything was the same. I was repulsed. Who the hell keeps ditching bottles of broken glass into the garden like this? I began to get suspicious that someone living in our building was doing this, but I had no proof.

In October, I flew to southern Poland. From there, I caught a train to the Ukraine border, and crossed into Ukraine by bus. I spent two weeks in Kyiv where I received stem cell injections from a specialist for a degenerated disc in my neck. The following two weeks were spent in Kharkiv volunteering at a place called Hell's Kitchen. Hell's was an industrial kitchen preparing food for injured soldiers and civilians in local hospitals.

When I returned to Italy in November, Charlie hadn't yet turned one year old, but was already walking. Winters in this area are mild, and once he could walk, as a family, we started hanging out in the garden more.

I wasn't even home more than a week when *another* wet plastic bag full of broken bottles was, again, abandoned in the garden bed bushes three meters from the gate. It was really too far to be flung from someone standing outside it. Four times?

My instincts were screaming. I had had enough.

That evening, I perused Amazon for security cameras with extra long power cords, and wireless connectivity. When they arrived, it took me a few days to install the first one. Space 3 didn't yet have internet, so I installed the first one above the patio in front of the Cantina. It faced out into the center of the garden. When I downloaded the app and took my first glimpse, I nearly squealed. The camera covered a lot of terrain. The view was perfect.

Once the first security camera was installed, beer bottles in plastic bags never appeared in the garden again.

## You Can't Just Sweep it Away

After the spilled white rice incident early on, nothing in the garden seemed out of the ordinary at first. However, you can bet your bottom dollar that la dolce vita in the garden went down hill fast.

Food waste and trash eventually started appearing often. At first, I just thought random bits of crumpled paper, and small items were blown into the garden by the wind or rain. I started finding rotting mushrooms, small pieces of wet bread, pistachio shells and other foodstuffs. For months, burned up incense sticks, bits of fabric, pieces of string, balled up paper, crinkled receipts, corners from snack packaging, and many other discarded items showed up. Everything I'd find had a certain weight to it that made it impossible to just be blown in. It wasn't long before I realized this stuff was tossed out a window. Trash accumulated on our terrace, our stairs, and the patio below. After awhile, someone was throwing out used contact lenses right in front of my Cantina door entrance. A single used contact lens appeared every three days for months, like clockwork. The same person was probably a woman too, because I started finding broken pink and red nails from a discarded manicure.

Had trash in the garden become a strategic bullying tactic?

In the fall that Charlie turned two, Stephanie and I went away to celebrate our wedding anniversary. When we arrived home, I went through my routine of opening windows and going downstairs to the Cantina to do the same. There was the normal accumulation of discarded incense sticks, wet pieces of bread, foil from yogurt tops, Italian twists ties from loaf bread, and crumpled paper bits on the stairs and patio from while we were gone. I swept up the big stuff, and picked up whatever I saw. Once completed, I returned upstairs to relax and hang out with family.

After several hours, I go back down to the Cantina. The neighbor must have purged her burned up incense assortment out the window, because three times the amount of burnt sticks were now on the stairs. Other trash had compiled as well. Does she *really* wait until I sweep up the terrace, stairs and patio just to throw more trash?

If I've learned anything, you can try to sweep your way to la dolce vita, but you may wear out the broom before you arrive.

## Throwing Objects at Babies

My walk home from the Carabinieri station was upbeat. Prior to that point, I'd been feeling utterly overwhelmed, questioning my very existence in Italy. Why did I move all the way over here just to be bullied by a loser neighbor's constant, daily trash?

My son had become a feeling of joy in this world I'd never known before; my wife loving and supportive. Still, being obviously bullied is a terrible distraction. Bullies get inside your head, and there's no escape. I sweep. They throw more trash. It's an awful experience, one I wouldn't wish on my worst enemy. I could no longer find peace in my *own home* with the thought of new trash steps outside the door.

Finally, I summoned the courage, and visited the Carabinieri the previous week to request they help put a stop to the daily trash. Unfortunately, they told me my issue was civil, not penal, informing me there was nothing they could do, and recommended I reach out to Italian lawyers, which I did. But after *yesterday's* atrocities, I returned *a second time* to the Carabinieri station in Bagni di Lucca today, this time coming home with good news. Would they help put a stop to the garbage in the garden once and for all? It seemed likely.

My anxiety was subsiding while I approached Ponte a Serraglio. Across the street, Patricia was parking her car in the garage. She and her elderly husband had the *only* garage in our neighborhood, a fact that made me green with envy. The rest of us parked on the sidewalk. Her husband was already walking towards the entrance to our building with a small bag while Patricia unloaded groceries from the trunk, so I crossed the street to see if she needed help.

"Buongiorno," I said enthusiastically, approaching the open garage.

"Buongiorno," she responded cheerfully.

"Would you like some help?" I asked in Italian, extending my left hand.

She was holding two bags, and almost couldn't believe her ears. She smiled, handing me a plastic bag with a stalk of celery hanging out. I had never been inside her garage before.

"Thank you," she said, as I grabbed it.

"It's nothing. How are you?" I asked.

"I'm good. Just finished the grocery shopping," she said.

"Wow, this is really nice in here," I said, glancing around.

As a stand alone building, her garage was spacious, swept and uncluttered. From the outside it was old, but not on the inside. There was almost enough room for two cars, with a loft in the front.

"Come look. There's a cantina too," she said, waving me towards the back.

She led me to a spiral staircase leading down behind her car with a black wrought iron railing. The circular hole cut clear through the cement. At the base of the stairs below was a large stationary tub. I couldn't see much else, but even down there looked well kept.

"It's an entire cantina down there. We used to store canned vegetables and other things, but don't go down there much anymore," she explained.

"Really nice," I exclaimed, nodding my head.

I turned around, peering through the open garage door to the street, and could see my parked black Peugeot on the asphalt sidewalk. I'd never viewed the road from this vantage point before. We stepped outside so she could manually shut the garage door. She set her bag down, reached up, and pulled the heavy door down to the pavement.

"It's so nice you have a garage. I really like it," I said.

She smiled. We stood in front of her garage for a moment, cars humming by behind us.

"Do you have a car?" she asked.

"I have the black one right over there," I said, lifting my thumb over my shoulder.

"That's nice. It's convenient for grocery shopping," she stated.

I nodded. "I used it often to clear all the garbage from the garden when we first arrived to Italy."

"You take the trash to the recycling center outside town in your car?"

"Yes, many times with a full car," I illustrated.

"So that *was* you who cleaned up the garden. There was *so much trash* on the patio below our house," she said.

"Nobody else was going to do it," I pointed out.

"I know. Years before you arrived, I used to take trash from the garden there, too. But it wasn't mine, and became too much. Your son.. he likes to run around in the garden, doesn't he?" she asked.

"Yes! He loves the garden," I said.

She took a step towards the building. I followed. I then turned slightly towards Patricia.

"I have a question. The man with the dogs, do you know his name?" I asked.

"Which man?" she asked, not realizing I was asking about someone in the building.

"The man who lives in the apartment below you. He has three dogs," I said.

142

"You mean Martin?" she asked.

"Ah, his name is Martin," I said.

"That's his grandmother's apartment. She passed some time ago. He comes by now and then. I don't see him often," she said.

"You know one of his dogs attacked me in the garden?" I asked.

"No! Seriously?" she asked, slowing her casual stride down even more.

"Yes. His dog bit me right around my achilles. Right here," I said, pointing at the back of my heel.

Patricia gasped. "Oh my! Are you okay?"

"It hurt really badly for several weeks. I have marks on my ankle from the dog's teeth. His white dog is the dangerous one," I explained.

"That's terrible," she said, expressing displeasure.

She took a step forward.

"One more thing Patricia. There's an issue with the girl who lives above me," I started.

"What girl? Giuseppina?" she asked.

"Yes. Giuseppina. Yesterday, she threw objects from her window at my baby while he played in the garden," I said clearly.

Patricia stopped dead in her tracks on the sidewalk. A delivery truck was parked directly across the street. Not the safest location because of passing cars, but Patricia hardly noticed.

"You're kidding," she said.

"No. Not kidding. It happened yesterday. She threw a lit incense stick out the window right where my son was playing," I detailed.

"The stick was on fire?" she asked.

"Yes. It landed in front of me, and twenty seconds later my boy ran over the same spot," I said.

Appalled, she shook her head in disgust. I sensed she *knew* I was telling the truth. Her empathy meant the world. She was like the long lost family member in Italy I've never had.

"It was very dangerous when it happened yesterday. Also, she throws trash out her window onto our terrace, stairs, and patio below everyday. Food waste, paper, all sorts of refuse," I continued.

She nodded affirmatively.

"I see your son playing in the garden sometimes. It's so nice, but this….. this is just awful," she said.

Instead of questioning whether or not I was telling the truth, she listened. She took another step forward, and I followed. At the building's doorway, I handed back her bag.

"You're very kind, Patricia," I said.

"But you carried my groceries! Thank you so much. Thank you," she said warmly.

"Have a nice day," I said, as she entered the open doorway.

"Ciao ciao," she said.

"Ciao," I replied.

# Chapter 22 - Incensed

I rang the buzzer from the sidewalk outside the entrance, and waited. Moments later, the two meter tall gate opened remotely. At the top of the stairs, an officer appeared outside the doorway. The following is the exact conversation that transpired with the officer I spoke with.

"Buongiorno," I said, stepping through the gate.

He was silent. I ascended the stairs, and he did not move. Once in front of him, I began pleading my case.

"I visited here yesterday after your office was closed. I spoke with a gentleman, and he told me to call 112 because something dangerous happened at my house. When I called yesterday, I spoke with Carabinieri in Garfagnana," I said in Italian.

"What happened?" the officer asked.

"The man on the phone was very kind with me. He told me to come here today," I prefaced.

"Okay," the officer acknowledged.

"The neighbor.. is throwing objects… from the window above at babies while they play in the garden," I said in Italian.

"Do you have video?" he asked.

"I have video, Yes, I have video. There is video," I answered.

"Ah, you have a security camera," he stated, pointing at my cell phone.

"Yes, it's on my computer on the table," I explained.

"I didn't understand," he said.

"It's at my house on the computer," I said.

"Your house computer, okay," he said.

I paused.

"What's happening is dangerous," I said.

"Is the garden yours, or is it shared?" he asked.

"It's shared. This happened in front of my door at the same time my son and I are playing together. It was a lit incense stick... that was thrown from the window above... while..... he is playing... I mean, at the same time," I elaborated.

There was a pause.

"This is *more* than what I explained happened the last time I visited here," I continued.

"This has happened another time?" the officer asked.

"Every.. Every day this happens. But this was the first time it happened while we are there. I saw it," I spelled out.

I gestured with my hands, making a sound effect demonstrating I saw the lit incense stick fall in real time.

"On the security camera video, I'm watching it fall in front of me," I said.

"Lit?" he asked.

"Yes!" I emphasized.

There was a long pause.

"Yes. I need help," I said solemnly.

"Where are you? Where is this happening?" he asked.

"Ponte a Serraglio," I said.

"Street?"

"Via Vittorio Emanuele. This, this street right here. In the center, close to Bar Italia," I said, pointing from the top stair.

"Number?" he asked.

"89," I said

"And the neighbor, it's a male neighbor? Female neighbor?" he questioned.

"A girl," I said.

"Okay."

"I don't know her well," I said.

"What's her name, you don't know?"

"Um.. her last name I don't know. Giuseppina? I don't know. I've spoken with her once in two years," I said.

"How old is this woman?" he asked.

"Thirty, thirty-two, thirty-four, I don't know," I said.

"Okay."

"With a daughter around six years old," I said.

"Little," the officer asked.

"My son is twenty-three months old," I said.

I paused.

"Twenty seconds after….. the incense stick fell, he ran over the same spot," I said.

There was another pause.

"Twenty seconds earlier, the incense stick hits him in the head," I said.

"It hit him? The incense stick hit your son?" he asked.

"No, but it could have. "Twenty seconds.." I said.

"Before?" he finished my sentence.

"Yes. It falls. Twenty seconds later, he runs to the same place, right here," I explained, pointing at the stone in front of my feet.

"Okay," he said.

"It's absurd. It's ridiculous and dangerous," I said.

"But you have residence here in Bagni di Lucca?" he asked.

"Yes."

"You have Italian citizenship?" he asked.

"Yes, my son and I. Dual citizenship," I said.

"You own the house? Or do you rent?" he asked.

"I own it. It's my house. That's right."

"Well.." he began in Italian.

"For this question, do you send the emergency to legal, a lawyer?" he asked in broken English.

It was the only sentence he spoke in English during the entire conversation.

"I spoke with a lawyer in an office in Rome. I also have an appointment this afternoon with a lawyer," I said in Italian.

"Send the video to the lawyer," he said.

"I will speak with a lawyer," I ensured him.

"He will open an emergency case," he said.

"Yes, but last week when I visited here, the officers explained it. Penal, civil, I understand the difference. This is not a civil

147

matter if the neighbor is throwing stuff at babies. At babies?" I asked sincerely.

There was a pause.

"This is dangerous. It's a dangerous thing what is happening," I explained politely in Italian, trying to plead my case.

"Do you want to make a 'denuncia'?" he asked.

"What is 'denuncia'? I do not understand the system here well," I said.

"The system here functions like this. If there is a criminal offense, a 'denuncia' is signed off by you, if you open a criminal investigation, we make an investigation. Then, if we see effectively that some sort of offense has been committed, we arrest the person. In Italy, it works like this," he explained.

"Okay," I said.

I understood what he said, but didn't fully grasp the process he was illustrating.

"Either way, you can hire a lawyer to defend you. If the arrested person did something wrong, they assist with the arrest," he continued.

"Is it possible to speak with her *before* I make a complaint?" I asked genuinely.

"You want that we speak with the person?" he reiterated.

"Yes, one time. Please," I begged.

"You want to do it together, you with her?" he asked.

"Whichever way is best," I said.

"Vittorio Emanuele.." he began.

"I would like to avoid making a 'denuncia' against her if possible," I said.

"You would like that the situation is resolved without filing a complaint?" he asked.

"Every day. Food... my son is still putting things in his mouth, things that he finds,"

"He puts things in his mouth that he finds?" he asked.

"Yes. This is a crazy situation in the garden for me," he said.

"I understand," he said.

"Look. I understand that the court system is very slow in Italy. I must wait three years for a lawyer to send the neighbor documents requesting that she stop for her to *finally* stop? And then, everyday, I still cannot use the garden because.."

"Because she is throwing things," he finished my thought.

"Yes," I said.

"You've made your point," he said.

"Okay."

"And, are you always home? Do you work?" he asked.

"I'm home," I said.

"You work at home? Smartworking?" he asked.

"Yes,"

"Okay."

"She's also at home all day I think," I said.

"Okay, good. One of these days, together during the morning or afternoon we will come by. We'll see if we can speak with you and the woman, and have a chat first. And, if we cannot solve this, you can go to a lawyer to file a complaint," he explained.

Sounded fantastic. Finally.

"I'm curious. *When* are you coming?" I wanted to know.

"We have to see. We could come in the morning, in the afternoon. We do not have a precise time," he explained.

"This week for sure?" I asked.

"Yes, of course," he assured me.

"Because, this really needs to be solved," I pleaded.

"Yes, yes, yes, I understand," he confided.

"Okay," I said,

"All good?" he asked.

I nodded.

"And you are mister…?" he inquired.

"Lucchesi. Richard Lucchesi," I said proudly.

"Perfect," he said.

I told him goodbye, turned, and walked down the stairs confident I'd taken an important step in the right direction.

## Life is Beautiful

Sadly, the trash continued. And the Carabinieri? They never did show up. After three visits to their office and a call, weeks went by, and nothing. Did the officer lie to my face? Or did he really plan to drop by, only for his plan to be nixed by a fellow coworker, or his superior?

Over the weekend, on a sunny Saturday autumn morning, Charlie and I played in the garden. He dug dirt with a trowel, picking up scoops and dropping it over the garden wall. He brought his toy cars outside, and we played with them on the pavers in front of the patio. He and I kicked the soccer ball around, too. Later, he pushed his little bike back and forth over the grass. They were beautiful moments filled with laughter, smiles and joy. Some of the best moments of my life. I'm truly fortunate to have such a healthy, fun-loving boy.

At one point, the neighbor above banged her window sills loudly. It was highly unusual behavior. Was she hoping to get my attention? I didn't look. I ignored her. When I turned around, a single orange incense stick lay harmlessly on the grey stone pavers at the base of the outside stairs to our apartment, less than a meter from where I was standing. Had she thrown it? I'm not sure, but one thing is for certain. I'll never forget that beautiful day with Charlie in the garden. The incense stick on the patio will help me remember it forever.

# Chapter 23 - Becoming Italian: My Citizenship Story

On September 19, 2023, I officially became an Italian citizen. I wasn't notified until the following day.

"You're Italian," the lady from the comune said in Italian over the phone.

Tears appeared instantly as vehicles whizzed by. I was riding my mountain bike home from the supermarket when I felt my phone vibrate. I stopped, looked, and noticed the number calling was a land line. My residency visa was set to expire in five days, and I'd been *waiting* for a call.

"Congratulations. When you have a chance, come into the comune for your new Carta d'Identità," she continued.

Barbara was a fast talker. The fastest. It's nothing short of extraordinary I made it through this *entire process* of Italian citizenship recognition in Italian language only.

The following day, when I went to apply for my new Carta d'Identità, I went flower shopping in Fornoli beforehand to show my appreciation. The administrative assistant Sofia greeted me. Barbara, the lady who worked my citizenship case, was on the phone in her office, so I left two flower arrangements with Sofia. Not two minutes after I arrived home, Barbara called to thank me profusely. I wish I had voice recorded the conversation. She couldn't express her gratitude enough. It was the least I could do.

I should have been thanking *her* profusely. After all, she single-handedly changed my life.

## How It All Began

It was a NY Times feature that started it all. The famed newspaper website was open on my MacBook Pro in my living room in Satellite Beach, Florida when I stumbled upon an article that would dramatically alter the course of my life. The article was titled 'The New American Status Symbol? A Second Passport'.

This piece, dated August 20, 2020, featured a forty-six year old woman named Juliana Calistri from Chicago. In the very first paragraph, it said her grandparents had grown up in Bagni di Lucca. How ironic that, more than two years later, at the age of forty-six, I would move to the *very same place*.

But that day, I missed the location within Italy entirely. I was *so much more* focused on second passports that, when I came to the hyperlink about Italian Citizenship Assistance, I clicked it and opened it in a new tab. Searching the contact information without more than glancing at the website, I dialed the telephone number in Los Angeles without thinking it through.

It was still morning in California. Miraculously, someone answered.

"Hello, good morning. My name is Richard Lucchesi. I was wondering if you could help me," I said in my professional voice.

"Buongiorno! This is Mario, how can I help you?" I heard a man say on the other end.

He wasn't a native English speaker. I didn't know I was speaking with the founder of the organization.

"I would like to find out if I qualify for Italian Citizenship," I said.

"You are an Italian American?" he asked.

"Yes, I was born in Rochester, NY," I said.

"And which person in your Italian line was born in Italy?" he inquired.

"My great-grandfather," I answered.

"Your great-grandfather, what was his name?" the man asked.

"Ferdinando. Ferdinando Lucchesi."

"When and where was he born?"

"He was born in Tuscany. I don't know the exact date of his birth, but can find it if you need it," I said.

"Okay, no problem. Was he married?"

"Yes."

He listened carefully. "So he had a baby in America. Was it your grandmother, or grandfather?"

"Grandfather."

"Okay, good. What is your grandfather's name?"

"Salvatore Lucchesi," I said.

"And when was your grandfather born?"

"November 15th, 1907."

"And yes, he was born in America?" he double-checked.

"Yes."

"And your *great-grandfather* Ferdinando, was he already living in America at the time?"

"Yes, they were living in Rochester, NY," I replied.

"And do you remember the year that your great-grandfather immigrated to America?"

"I believe 1904, or 1905."

"And your great-grandparents, they were already married when your grandfather was born?"

"I believe so, yes," I said.

Although Ferdinando died in 1940, my grandfather Salvatore died when I was twenty-one years old. Luckily, I knew most of the basic information this man was asking off the top of my head because I grew up with Salvatore in my life.

.  "Okay. Very good. So far, so good. Now, we must check the 1920 census in Rochester, NY to see if we can find Ferdinando's citizenship status," the man stated.

There was a long pause. I stared out at the palm trees gently swaying in my front yard as I listened to the man in California type and breathe.

"Okay….. let's see here.. Ferdinando Lucchesi," Mario's voice trailed off on the last syllable.

There was another pause. I hung onto my phone for dear life.

"Here he is. Yes, okay, I think I've found him. Is his wife Salvatrice?

"Yes, it is!" I blurted out excitedly.

"Okay good. I see Salvatore's name here too. I think I've found him," the man clarified.

"Oh wow, that's terrific." I said anxiously.

I was pacing the front of the living room now, listening intently and sweating.

"This must be him. Let's look," he continued.

There was *another* pause.

"There's an 'AL' next to his name. That means alien," the man said.

"Oh no. What does that mean?" I asked nervously.

"Well, if your grandfather was born in 1917, and your great-grandfather was still registered as an alien in the United States, it's good for your case," he explained.

"Really? That's a good thing?" I asked.

"Yes, that's a good sign. This signifies he wasn't a US citizen in 1920. If this information is accurate, it means he passed his Italian citizenship along to Salvatore, who then passed it to your father and you," Mario elaborated.

"Wonderful, that's wonderful!" I proclaimed.

"But you're not out of the woods. Not yet. We need to check the 1930 census. Your grandfather needs to naturalize in the United States. Let's go there now, and see if he's registered on the 1930 census," he said.

I felt the muscles around my eyeballs tighten. You could cut the tension with a knife. I still couldn't believe I was speaking with someone about Italian citizenship recognition. After what seemed like forever, he came back.

"Okay. I think I found Ferdinando again in the 1930 census. Ferdinando, Salvatrice, and your grandfather is Salvatore, right?" Mario asked.

"Yes. Salvatore, that's correct," I answered.

It felt like my life was hanging in the balance.

"Okay, let's see here…. Ferdinando Lucchesi.. 'NA' it says here next to his name. The 1930 census says 'NA'," he said.

"So what does *that* mean? What does 'NA' mean?" I asked desperately.

"Well, 'NA' means naturalized. By 1930, he was a naturalized citizen of the United States. Somewhere between 1920 and 1930, your great-grandfather became a naturalized US citizen. So, if your grandfather Salvatore was really born in 1917, that's good news for you," he said smiling through the phone.

"So, do I qualify for Italian citizenship?" I wondered.

"Well, so far it is looking good for you. Did anyone in your Italian ancestry line going back to Ferdinando ever renounce their Italian citizenship?" he asked.

"Never. Everyone in my family was very proud to be Italian," I said confidently.

I hadn't a clue. Everybody in my family hated paperwork and bureaucracy though, so why would they go and do that?

"There's always the question of whether anybody in your Italian bloodline renounced their Italian citizenship with the consular general of their home town. But it is not common. So, if nobody ever did, then, I'd say you qualify," the man said proudly.

"Oh my God!" I exclaimed.

My voice cracked, and I began crying. This was the shock of a lifetime, especially for a random Thursday stuck at home.

"I can't believe it. This is a dream come true. It's unbelievable. I *didn't even know* this was possible," I said into the phone receiver.

"Congratulations," Mario said.

"Thank you. Thank you so much. You've changed my life," I cried.

## The Journey Begins

After the phone call, I got cracking almost immediately.

My Italian great-grandfather Ferdinando Lucchesi was born on July 23, 1886 in Torre del Lago, a small coastal town just south of

Viareggio in Tuscany. However, I hadn't the foggiest idea of this in the beginning. Initially, I thought Ferdinando was born in Lucca. Luckily, his actual birth date had been passed down through the generations, and my Polish-American mother still had it filed away. Having his birth date made things *much* easier.

A quick internet search revealed an article about the process of Italian citizenship recognition written by a lawyer named Marco Mazzeschi in Italy. Turns out, he founded a law firm in Siena. I contacted them by email, and they offered an initial call for free. After the call, I hired their firm to do a consultation on my case for five hundred euro. As part of the consultation, they provided the full list of documents I would need to apply for Italian citizenship.

Once the consultation concluded, I learned that Ferdinando's birth certificate was in Viareggio, *not* Lucca. Mazzeschi also confirmed that I most likely qualified for Italian citizenship by descent. When I hired Mazzeschi again to procure my great-grandfather's birth certificate, something incredible happened. Ferdinando's Italian birth certificate from the comune of Viareggio, Italy arrived by international courier to my doorstep in Florida on the afternoon of June 17th, 2021, three years *to the day* of my father's passing.

Was it a sign from my father? Possibly. It seemed I was in *exactly the right place* at *exactly the right time* doing what I should be doing.

## Learning about Ferdinando

I needed birth, marriage and death certificates from Ferdinando, Salvatore, Richard Lee (my father), and myself. I also needed official naturalization documents from the United States Federal Government proving Ferdinando naturalized. Then, each document needed to be authenticated, and *then* Apostilled. And since I was applying in Italy, I needed every single document translated in

Italian. The Italian documents also needed to be officially certified, and then *also* Apostilled.

Oh, and I needed one more *very important document* as well, but I'll get to that in a moment.

But that was it. Once I had all of that, and once I was living in Italy, I could stroll down to my local comune, hand over everything, and pray, because someone in there makes the final decision.

Back in America, I already had *my* birth certificate, so one document down. I just need an Oath of Office on that document, and then I could have it Apostilled. After that, it was ready to be submitted. The rest of the documentation I'd have to apply for. Everything for me was in New York State except for Ferdinando's birth certificate, and his official naturalization papers.

Right away, I discovered that Ferdinando met his Italian wife, my great-grandmother Salvatrice, *after* arriving to America. They were married in 1906 in Rochester, but my first attempts to procure their marriage certificate failed. In fact, their marriage certificate was, by far, the hardest one for me to get without assistance.

When you apply for old documents, governments require proof you are related if the people's names on the forms are deceased. They want to know *why* you want the documents, too. This was the case with Ferdinando's marriage certificate and license. It took a bunch of back and forth messages with City Hall in Rochester before they accepted my application to procure Ferdinando's marriage license.

**Lawyers on Both Sides of the Pond**

In my experience, death certificates are the easiest to receive. Birth certificates are the hardest, especially for the deceased. In New York, if you want a deceased family member's birth certificate, you need a court order. Can individuals file court orders themselves? Yes. Did I? Hell no. I hired a law firm in NY state for that.

I first contacted the law firm I used in the fall of 2020 to procure my father and grandfather's birth certificates. During a nearly one hour consultation call after I hired them, they strongly advised that I also hire them to procure an official 'one and the same' document while petitioning the court for the birth certificates. A 'one and the same' document corrects all misspellings on every legal certificate you have, and provides official evidence from the courts that birth, marriage and death certificates with misspellings *are the same people*. The 'one and the same' forms are crucial proof that many in my situation need, because virtually all immigrants to America either had misspellings on important legal documents, or changed their names entirely. A named spelled differently between birth, marriage and death certificates can automatically disqualify you from receiving citizenship recognition, even if the misspelling was accidental.

The lawyers *insisted* I would probably need this document when applying for dual-citizenship, and they were right. So, in the end of 2020, I hired them for forty-five hundred dollars plus fees. In June 2022, the court order concluded. Salvatore and Richard Lee's birth certificates, along with the 'one and the same' order had been issued.

## I Will Call You

Everyone's path to Italian citizenship recognition by blood, called 'jure sanguinis' in Italian, is different. In the most honest way imaginable, between the moment I realized I qualified for Italian citizenship, to the actual moment I became Italian, more than three years had elapsed. It was such a long, tedious three years that, by the time I became Italian, I wasn't nearly as excited about it as that day on the phone with Mario. The process wore me down. And then, even after you become Italian, the fun the just beginning.

I had been living in Italy over six months when I finally had everything I needed for my Italian citizenship application in hand. I took proper photos of it all, and contacted an officially certified Italian translator. Translations cost me roughly four hundred euro. The translations were then handed off to another organization that certifies and Apostilles translations for Italian citizenship documents. The cost for certifications and Italian translation Apostilles was about three hundred euro. I received everything back, and the stack of documents had more or less doubled in weight. And then, in March of 2023, I walked down to the Bagni di Lucca comune with everything in hand to submit my Italian citizenship application.

I was nervous.

Because of having a baby, owning homes here, and applying for residency, I had become a regular inside the comune. Leading up to my citizenship application, every single time I was in there, I'd quietly gauge *if* and *when* I should ever mention that I would also be applying for Italian citizenship. Then finally one day when they weren't busy, I said something about it to Sofia, the front desk administrator. She couldn't give me specifics, but the seeds had been planted. Leading up to the day that I dropped my Italian citizenship documentation off, they were sort of already expecting me.

That afternoon, as I approached the comune, my forehead was dripping in sweat. I entered, told Sofia why I was there, and she directed me around the front desk to the back office. Sofia is fluent in English. Barbara, who was handling my citizenship case, spoke to me in Italian only. I handed everything to Barbara, and took a seat.

I watched carefully as she opened the folder.

"Oh good! Very nice, a Table of Contents. This will make things easier," she said in Italian.

She looked briefly at the documents towards the top. When she came upon the 'one and the same' packet, she stopped and studied it.

"Ah! So this.. is *this* the document that corrects all the misspellings of the relatives' names?" she asked deliberately.

"That's correct. Everything that had an error has been amended by the New York State court system. I hired a lawyer in New York for that document. Very expensive," I said smiling.

She nodded. "Perfect. This is *very* important."

She kept looking while holding the Italian translation of the 'one and the same' order in her hand.

"This. This is very helpful to your case," she reiterated, shaking the one and the same Italian translation packet.

She closed the folder, set it up by the corner of her desk, and asked for my phone number. It was written on the table of contents, so I showed her.

"Okay! Good, I will call you by July," she said.

"Bravissimo! Grazie mille," I responded.

I thanked her again, slowly backed out of her office, and said goodbye to Sofia. Then, I walked out the door, and burst out crying inside the comune lobby.

## The Call Never Came

Three nerve-wracking months later, and my phone never rang. I could hardly sit still anymore, and wanted an update badly. So on Tuesday July 18, I returned to the comune. I walked in, Sofia greeted me with a big smile, and directed me back to Barbara's office. Barbara greeted me too, and told me to take a seat. My folder was on her desk in the *same location* as it was three months ago. Had she even *opened it* in the last three months?

"I have your folder right here. Let's take a look," she said.

Whatever she was working on before I got there, she dropped it. We were officially investigating my Italian citizenship file, together.

She searched her computer. Once her screen was ready, she turned to my folder, pulled it closer to the center of her desk, and opened it. She carefully started looking through documents, investigating each stapled packet one at a time, keeping everything in order, and typing information about my Italian ancestors into her computer. She looked at everything, but seemed far more interested in the translations. I guess they were just easier for her to read.

When she came upon the translated packet of corrected misspellings, she picked it up and set it aside. That document seemed to legitimize everything else. The lawyers back in NY had been right all along.

After some time, she finished.

"I'm going to the printer. I'll be right back," she said as she stood up.

She walked out of her office, reappeared, and handed me a two page legal document. It was my official request to become an Italian citizen fully in Italian. It had Ferdinando's full name and information, Salvatore's, my father's and mine. It had Italian laws written on it, too.

"Double check all the names are spelled correctly. If everything is okay, I'll have you sign the second page," she informed me.

I looked it over carefully.

"This looks good. Everything's correct," I confirmed.

"Okay great! You'll need to purchase a sixteen euro marca da bollo before you can sign and submit this officially. Could you buy one now?" she asked.

"Of course!" I said energetically.

I left, came back to the office in no time, and handed over the stamp. Barbara affixed it at the top of the document, and stamped the comune's logo over it making it official. I signed the second page of the document, and Barbara took the documents to the copy machine.

"That's it. So now, I must submit everything. I think it'll be difficult to finish everything in August because of holidays. So hopefully, by September I will know something. Once everything is completed, I will call you," she said, handing over my copy.

"September?" I repeated.

"Yes, I think so," Barbara said.

"Wow, just wow. Okay, okay, thank you very much," I said, smiling.

I couldn't *stop* smiling. I left the office with a smile stuck to my face.

Then, on the morning of September 20, 2023, when I received a call from Barbara with the good news about my Italian citizenship recognition, I was overjoyed.

The following day at the comune, Sofia snatched my old Italian ID cards out of my hand so fast I couldn't believe it.

"These old cards.. they say USA on them right here," Sofia said, pointing. "They need to be destroyed. You and your son need new cards that say you're Italian now."

I welled up right there. Sofia *knew* how much this meant to me. It had been *such* a long process, and now it was over.

# Chapter 24 - Italian Passports and New Beginnings

After getting my citizenship, I wanted my Italian passport badly. If it wasn't for Sofia at the comune, I would *still* be trying to figure out how to set an appointment for my Italian passport.

"One of my colleagues has applied for her son's passport recently. You can apply for yours and Charlie's together at the same time by using your electronic identity," she wrote in an email.

But when I tried on my own, I couldn't. Either the system wasn't working, or I was doing something wrong. So I replied to Sofia's email to explain this.

"The website for Polizia di Stato says the office of Bagni di Lucca will be open this Thursday. The agenda begins at 9am tomorrow. So, try to go online between 8:45 and 9am. This way, you should be able to get appointments. I hope it works, let us know!" she wrote.

Appointments online open at 9am? What an angel. I would have *never* figured that out!

On Thursday morning, I woke up early and opened the website link at 8:30. Nothing. I refreshed at 8:40, and still nothing. But right at 9am, bam! A whole bunch of morning appointments to issue and renew Italian passports in Fornoli became available. I scheduled two appointments for me and my son for 10:00 and 10:15 successfully, screen captured the confirmation numbers, and closed the website. Two minutes later at 9:09, I opened the link again, and all the appointments had been scooped up.

## Submitting Passport Applications

I compiled the required documents and double-checked I had all the necessary identifications. We were ready for our passport appointments.

The police station in Fornoli is a few streets up the hill to the north from the center of town. We parked in the lot by the Coop, took a small breakfast, and made our way up the hill when we were finished. At the station, about eight people gathered outside in the sunshine holding folders and paperwork. We joined, and waited.

10:00 came and went. More than an hour went by. Slowly, people were let into the front door one by one when their name was called. As we sat waiting our turn, even more people showed up, many without appointments. I overheard those with appointments explaining to the walk-ups what Sofia explained to me. Even for Italians, the system can be confusing.

When my name was called, we entered the small lobby. I gave the young officer mine and my son's ID, and he put them neatly on a small desk. I used the bathroom in the back, and when I returned, we all sat as quietly as we could in the lobby for what seemed like another thirty minutes. A challenge with a little one! When the office door opened again, a man with a big smile ushered us in.

Davide, who appeared to be about my age, had our applications side by side on his desk. Unlike at the post office, he's there to make *sure* everything was filled in correctly. If you make it into *Davide's* office, you're golden. This man was a legend. I'd soon learn that Italians are often treated like royalty in comparison to non-Italians looking to reside here.

Charlie's application was more in depth, as he need parental approval to have his Italian passport issued. Once both applications were completed, Davide informed us that we could pick up the passports in two weeks time.

"Will I visit the Lucca Questura like I did for our residency for the new passports?" I asked.

"You're Italian now, so you don't need to go there anymore. You'll retrieve the new passports *inside* the Lucca walls," he said, and winked.

That took a moment to sink in. It's still sinking in.

## Retrieving The New Passports

The passport office inside the walls of Lucca was tucked away on a street I had not been to before. I entered the front door, and was immediately inside a courtyard. Across the courtyard, a single door sat open, so I walked in. Two people were seated in a sort of lobby area with documents in hand. A few other chairs sat empty. There was a doorway straight ahead, and another to the side. The side doorway had a table laying down blocking the entrance. I opted to stand.

A worker came walking through the lobby from the blocked doorway, and looked at the three of us. We recognized each other, but I did not immediately make the connection that it was Davide, the man from two months earlier.

"Buongiorno," Davide said, acknowledging he remembered me.

"Buongiorno," I said, returning the smile.

He asked the other two waiting something I did not understand, and then indicated to follow him. I realized immediately that the others probably had appointments.

Inside the back room was a long counter with plexiglass on top, and two chairs behind it. Davide was taking care of me that morning. He took my ID, set it down in front of him, and turned to a bunch of boxes behind him. They were filled to the brim with unissued Italian passports. I took a look around while he searched for mine, admiring how analog the whole office was. The place wasn't that big. Another older gentleman was helping someone else, and a third person, a woman, was working at the far side of the office on a computer.

He returned to his seat with two shiny, new passports. Each had a half sheet of paper inside. He pulled out the sheets, and handed over the passports just like that.

"Richard, please, check everything carefully. Make sure *everything* is written correctly. On yours, check the front page carefully. On Charlie's, because he is a minor, you and your wife's names are on the second page. So check both pages carefully. Make sure there are no misspellings. If anything is wrong, we can fix it quickly. Okay?" he asked slowly in Italian.

I had been caressing the outside cover of one of the passports with my thumb. It was like a foreign object. I understood 100% of what he said.

"Yes. Okay," I responded seriously, looking him in the eye.

I opened the top passport first. It was mine. The hair on my neck stood up and started tingling.

My last name was spelled correctly. My first and middle as well. Date of birth was correct. Expiration date was for 2033!

I closed mine, and opened Charlie's passport. I checked his even more slowly. First page correct. After a moment, second page seemed okay too.

I looked up at Davide. "Tutto bene."

Everything okay.

I handed back the passports, and he handed me the half sheets of paper to sign off. I signed, and handed the slips through the opening in the plexiglass. After a moment, he stood up, walked around to the front where I was standing, shook my hand, and handed me the passports.

"Here you go. You are Italian, so now, you have one of the *strongest* passports that exists. You can travel anywhere in the world," he stated proudly in front of the others.

"Beautiful! I can't believe it. Grazie mille, Davide," was all I could think of.

It *was* a dream come true. The moment overwhelmed me.

## My "F"-ing Mistake

I exited through the sun drenched courtyard into the street as quickly as I could, and immediately cried. These moments only happen once. I'd *never* go pick up my brand new Italian passport for the first time ever again. More than Italian citizenship itself, *this* was the moment I had been waiting for I realized.

I walked briskly over to my favorite coffee shop, ordered two cappuccinos, two pastries, and splurged. I could literally feel the weight lifted off my shoulders. I pulled the two passports out of my back pocket, and set them on the table upright like open books. I snapped a photo of my breakfast with the passports, and sent it to Steph.

"Just another normal breakfast in Italy," I wrote.

"Looks pretty normal to me," she replied.

I was giddy. I admired the table like a museum relic, and then reached for my passport. I looked it over sipping my coffee, and the almost spit it out. The sex on my passport was wrong. It said 'F' for female. The Italians thought I was a *woman*?

I was crestfallen. I fucked up. Davide warned me about mistakes, and yet I didn't catch this in the office.

I checked the time. 11:35am. The office closed at noon. I jumped up, gathered my items, paid, and sprinted out the door. I double-timed it back to the passport office, about a ten minute walk away. I arrived at ten minutes to twelve, walked in, and didn't even have to explain a thing.

"What is it?" the other gentleman inquired sternly.

He must have remembered me from earlier. He didn't seem mad, more disappointed. I could see Davide, but he was preoccupied.

"My new passport, it says that my sex is female," I said.

The whole office could hear me. Davide stopped what he was doing, and looked up. The man stuck out his hand for me to hand over the passport, so I handed it to him. He pulled out a hefty pair of scissors and started cutting. First he cut the top cover down the middle, and then the bottom. Then, full corners went missing. And he didn't stop; he just kept cutting and cutting. My heart was ripped out of my chest. I was horrified. It was possibly the ugliest sight I ever witnessed.

167

"That is why I tell you to *look everything over carefully* the first time," I heard Davide say in Italian.

He wasn't being mean or cruel. It was the truth.

"I know, I know. I'm an idiot. It's my fault, completely my fault" I said woefully.

The man nodded once. Davide walked to the other side of the room, and rummaged through a box on the floor. When he returned, he had my original passport application. When I saw it, it felt like failure. He ripped off the photo attached to the upper part of the old application, and handed it to the other guy who had just destroyed my old passport. They went over everything with me again, looked at a calendar together, and asked if next week worked to retrieve my new Italian passport.

"No problem. Absolutely no problem at all," I said.

# Epilogue

My first two years in Italy were a whirlwind of soaring highs and crushing lows—often so tangled together that it was hard to separate them. This book captures some of the most significant twists and turns from that rollercoaster ride. While I've changed *some* names and omitted *certain* details for clarity and privacy, what you've read is my painfully honest story, one that has indelibly transformed me. I like to think it's for the better—though I'm still not entirely convinced.

Is packing up and selling everything to move to a new continent the right choice for everyone? Probably not. Does *la dolce vita* truly exist? Honestly, I don't know. But every so often, I catch glimpses of it—especially when I stop to see the world reflected in the sparkling eyes of my son.

And as for whether I'm less of a dick than when I started? The jury's still out. But I'm trying. If for no other reason, I owe it to the next generation not to pass those habits along.

There are countless stories left untold—like the time Grandma visited Italy and *backpacked* across country with our little man in tow, or the unexpected adventures Charlie has already experienced in his short life. Those will have to wait for another book.

Even now, as I write this, the winds of change are blowing once again, carrying us back to the Far East. We're gathering documents, preparing visas, and bracing ourselves for new headaches and fresh lessons in bureaucracy. But this time, there's a difference. We came to Italy as two, with a baby on the way. And now, we leave as three, ready to face whatever new adventures lie ahead.

Stay tuned…..

169

# RICHARD LUCCHESI

# UNDER the TUSCAN
# BLUNDER
## GRANDMA BACKPACKS ITALY!

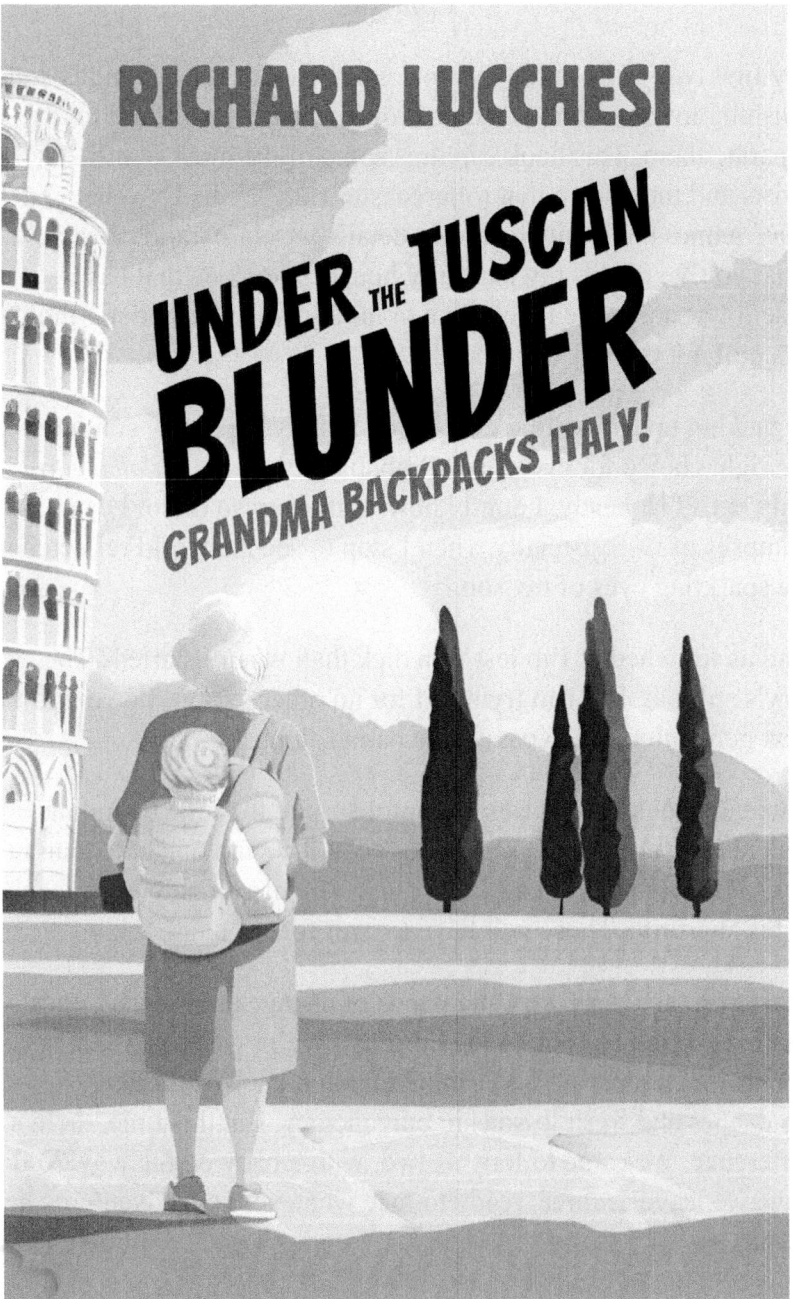

# Chapter 1 - Grandma's First Day in Italy

"Where is she?" I asked Steph.

Stephanie, Charlie, and I had just passed through the brand new electronic exit gates from the many platforms at Milano Centrale train station. The air is cool, and the station is not heated inside, but the atmosphere is full of energy. As we approach the center, the space opens into a soaring hall that commands attention. The building's bold mix of Art Deco, Art Nouveau and Fascist-era styles makes traveling through Milan by train feel more like stepping into a regal palace. We cut through the crowd towards the front stairs down to the front entrance as people move in every direction.

Our train ride from Pisa Centrale was slower than expected, and we were about an hour behind schedule. Grandma purchased 4G service for her trip days earlier, but once inside the airport, couldn't get it working. She was only able to communicate with me by connecting to free airport WiFi. No matter, I thought. She and I were old school, the type of people who grew up into adulthood without the internet, and *certainly* without functioning GPS navigation. Grandma had a decent sense of direction, too. I knew she'd be waiting for us somewhere logical inside or around the train station. But where?

After briefly checking outside the main front entrance where I *specifically instructed* her to meet us, and *not* seeing her anywhere, I began to worry. We *knew* she was already at the train station, so *where was she?*

Grandma had touched down several hours earlier in Malpensa, Milan's International airport. After a brief scare when her checked baggage didn't initially appear on the carousel, she found it on a different carousel entirely, and eventually made her way through the airport to the train platforms. There's a direct train line between Malpensa and Milano Centrale, so commuting into the center of town is a breeze. Little did we know that the action was just heating up!

Think Rick, think. Where would you wait for me if you were in *her* shoes?

"You wait here and watch our son. I'm going around the side of the building. Maybe she's waiting out there for us on the sidewalk," I told Steph.

Charlie was helping Mama push the stroller around the ground floor corridor to the train station entrance. I quickly walked outside to the west, and back towards the north to the train station's main side entrance. There, three men directly in front of the doors were fully decked out in military fatigues, but I didn't see Grandma anywhere. In Italy, when police and military are patrolling, it's best to not linger, so I kept moving. However, not immediately finding Grandma was making me more nervous by the minute.

I retreated back to the front corridor. Charlie, who had been practically good as gold for the train ride to Milano, was becoming restless. We'd been telling him repeatedly in the days leading up to today that grammy was coming to visit him in Italy. At nearly two years old, he understood. But when we arrived to the train station and didn't immediately come into contact with Grandma at the predetermined meeting point, he instantly lost faith. I didn't blame him.

Remarkably, although she lived on another continent, Grandma found a way to maintain presence in our lives. For nearly two years, she recorded herself reading children's stories on video, and posted them to YouTube. At first, she couldn't compete with the well compiled cartoons of the twenty-first century that Charlie had been watching. But Stephanie was diligent in creating a routine of waking up, and sticking Charlie in front of grandma once a day on a daily basis. Soon the routine caught on. It wasn't long before Charlie began recognizing grandma, and looking forward to watching those stories she read to him on video.

Turns out, Grandma on YouTube worked like a charm, and was the secret ingredient in successfully creating a bond with Charlie while in Italy.

## Great Minds Think Alike

Think Rick, think. Where could she be?

I couldn't help but be stressed. She was my mother after all, the grandmother of my son, and had flown all the way here to spend time with us. I was sure she was safe, but she could be anywhere, and Milano Centrale layout is humungous.

"Let's head back inside. Follow me," I said to Stephanie.

Charlie was in the stroller. I pushed with my wife close behind. Once inside, we turned left and headed towards in the direction where I had previously checked outside a moment earlier. Sure enough, Grandma was standing by the cafe just inside those very doors. I went running over to her.

"Hey Mom!" I said, running over and waving my arms.

"Hi Rick," she said with a huge smile.

She made her way over to us on the other side. Stephanie had already pulled Charlie out of the stroller, and he approached us before we made it to Stephanie.

"Who's that? Hey, it's Grammy!" I said excitedly to Charlie.

He looked up as he zig-zagged around me.

"Come here. Look at you, how handsome you are!" Grandma said in a high-pitched voice.

"Hey!" I exclaimed.

He kept running around us.

"You got so big! Come here," Grandma laughed, crouching down with her hands on her knees.

Charlie tripped, then got up quickly and darted over to Stephanie. His little pitter patter steps when he runs are literally the cutest thing ever.

"Oh, how are ya?" Grandma asked genuinely, as she hugged me warmly.

"We're good. I knew I'd find you," I said, happy to have safely found Grandma.

## Stepping Outside Your Comfort Zone

Grandma (my mother) was the angel in my life I don't deserve. With the birth of my son in late 2022, Grandma, at the age of seventy-two, was absolutely over the moon to become a grandmother again for the second time. However, because our son was born in Italy, Grandma couldn't be there in person. So, in late November, mom flew to Italy for the second time to spend several weeks with her two year old grandson. I could not ask for a more supportive mother.

On her *first* trip to Italy only four months after Charlie's birth, we took a once-in-a-lifetime expedition to Venice, Grandma's first ever visit in the enchanted city. But Venice isn't the only magical place in Italy, and I was hellbent on making her second journey here even more memorable than the first. This second trip was more last minute too, so we needed to plan accordingly.

"Just bring carry-on luggage when you come. You'll *never* forgive yourself if your checked luggage gets lost," I explained to Grandma.

Lost luggage is *always* a concern when traveling to Italy from overseas, especially with connecting flights. If you fly to Italy, and your suitcase goes to the wrong destination, it could take weeks to receive it. Even then, you'll probably have to go to the airport to pick it up. Just ask anyone who's traveled to Italy, and lost their luggage.

Nevertheless, when Grandma arrived at the airport, Delta made her reluctantly check her large carry-on bag. My plan was foiled, but thank goodness her luggage wasn't lost.

Apparently, once outside of her regular routine, Grandma had some trouble keeping track of her important belongings. At our guesthouse in Milan, Grandma soon discovered she had also lost a new sweater.

"It was brand new. I wore it once. I must have left it in JFK waiting for my flight because it didn't fit in my luggage," she confided.

Then, just like her luggage, she found the sweater. It was stuffed in one of the small outside pockets of her carry-on. Go figure.

## There's No Place Like Home

Shortly after checking into the guesthouse, we headed straight for Milan's Duomo. In the Metro station, Grandma and I shared the same credit card to enter through the turnstiles, and I showed her how to do it. Even so, it took Grandma several attempts to get through.

Once we exited the Metro station at Piazza Duomo, Grandma was in heaven. The Duomo's Gothic architecture almost seems otherworldly in its beauty and complexity. As we approach the immense structure, it's as if the entire building rises towards the heavens. The exterior is a symphony of pale pink and white marble. The countless spires and pinnacles reach skyward like delicate, carved lacework frozen in time.

"Wow, look at this," Grandma remarked, staring at the Duomo directly in front of her.

Steph was carrying Charlie so he had a better vantage point to see all around. Every branch of the tree was lit in blue lights to the max. The pavement was wet, but luckily it wasn't raining. Flocks of pigeons circled above. Grandma reached for her phone. The big smile on her face said it all.

"Oh, look at the Christmas tree!" Grandma said to Charlie, pointing across the piazza.

175

After a few moments, Charlie chased a legion of pigeons, so I followed close behind, leaving Stephanie with my mother to take photos. Not a minute later, I turned and witnessed Grandma with pigeons perched on her fully extended right arm. A random man was taking photos of my mom *with her phone*. He had offered her corn kernels to feed the pigeons, which she graciously accepted, and he was furiously snapping photos. I grabbed my son as fast as I could, sprinted over there, and I locked eyes with Stephanie who promptly snatched Grandma's phone out of the man's hands. As we quickly walked away, the man whipped corn kernels at the back of my head.

I scolded Grandma, reminding her that the man *expected* money, and might hold her phone hostage if she didn't pay him.

"You're not in Kansas anymore Mom," I said.

She was *totally* out of her element.

In the Galleria Vittorio Emanuele II, Grandma and I swung Bobby by his arms as we passed by designer Gucci and Prada stores. Stephanie took photos. As we headed back to the Metro, we enjoyed the Christmas tree and lights in front of the Piazza Duomo before entering the Metro. Once inside, we had another crisis on our hands.

"I dropped my credit card," Grandma said frantically, after descending the escalators towards the Metro.

"What do you mean you dropped the credit card?" I inquired.

"It's gone, Rick. I put it in my coat pocket, but it must have fallen out. I *never* normally do that. Whenever I pay with my card, I always put it back in my little change purse," she acknowledged.

"How could it be gone? We just entered the subway two minutes ago," I said.

"I'm out of sorts using it to enter the Metro," she confided.

"Hang on. Wait here. I'll go look for it," I instructed the three of them.

I retraced her footsteps, scurrying back up the escalator to the gate where we entered. Crowds of people continued to enter the underground as I carefully scanned the floor. I made my way back down the escalator we were just riding moments earlier, but her credit card was nowhere to be found.

Grandma had been in Italy less than twelve hours. Within that short time, she'd already misplaced a sweater, lost her credit card, and handed her smartphone over to a complete stranger. I'd soon discover that Grandma was a bit more forgetful than usual these days. The strong-minded, independent woman I'd known for most of my life was now just a lady doing her best to get through life, and enjoy it.

I started to wonder: Would Grandma survive the rest of the trip?

Only time would tell. But one thing was for certain: I was *so happy and grateful* Grandma was now with us in Italy.

# Map of Italy

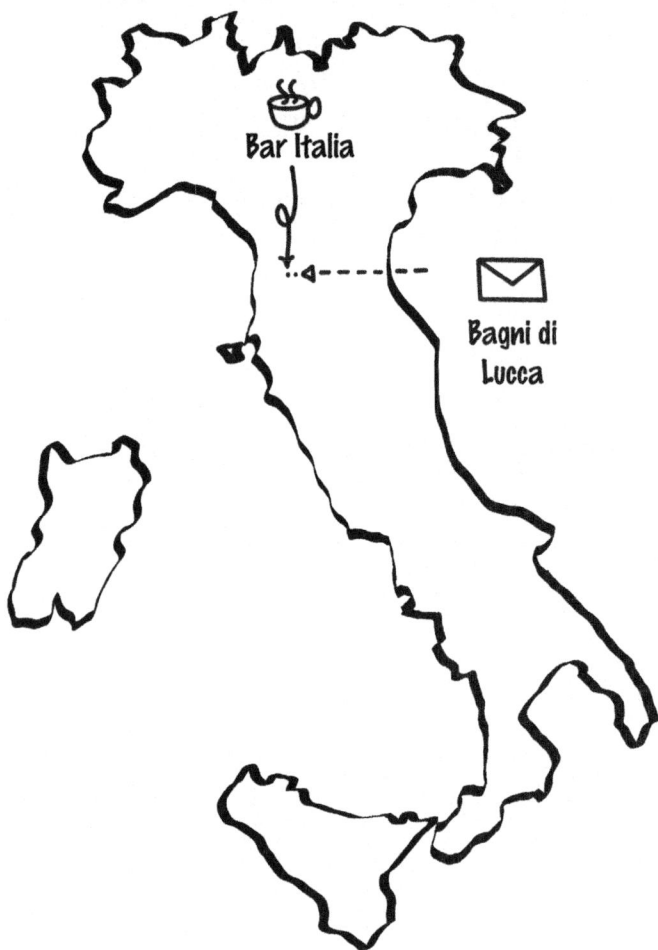

## A Note from Richard Lucchesi

Hi there, fellow adventurer!

If you made it this far, awesome! I hope you've enjoyed the journey through my chaotic, hilarious, and occasionally infuriating escapades in Italy. Writing this book has been a labor of love (and a few bottles of wine), so if it brought a smile to your face, a chuckle, or even a sympathetic groan, I'd love to hear about it!

Reviews are like gelato on a hot day—they make everything better. If you could spare a moment to leave a review on Amazon, Goodreads, or wherever you found this book, it would mean the world to me. Your thoughts not only help spread the word but also help other readers discover these stories.

Grazie mille for the time and support!
Richard

Printed in Great Britain
by Amazon